HOUSE OF LORDS

French Legal System

Visit the *French Legal System, second edition* Companion Website at **www.pearsoned.co.uk/elliottjeanpierre** to find valuable **student** learning material including:

- Regular updates on major developments in the French legal system
- Links to valuable resources on the web
- Glossary of key legal terms

Pearson Education

We work with leading authors to develop the
strongest educational materials in law,
bringing cutting-edge thinking and best learning
practice to a global market.

Under a range of well-known imprints, including
Longman, we craft high quality print and
electronic publications which help readers
to understand and apply their content,
whether studying or at work.

To find out more about the complete range of our
publishing, please visit us on the World Wide Web at:
www.pearsoned.co.uk

French Legal System

Second edition

Catherine Elliott
Catherine Vernon
Eric Jeanpierre

PEARSON

Longman

Harlow, England • London • New York • Boston • San Francisco • Toronto • Sydney • Singapore • Hong Kong
Tokyo • Seoul • Taipei • New Delhi • Cape Town • Madrid • Mexico City • Amsterdam • Munich • Paris • Milan

Pearson Education Limited
Edinburgh Gate
Harlow
Essex CM20 2JE
England

and Associated Companies throughout the world

Visit us on the World Wide Web at:
www.pearsoned.co.uk

First published 2000.
Second edition published 2006.

ISBN–13: 978–1–4058–1161–3
ISBN–10: 1–4058–1161–7

British Library Cataloguing-in-Publication Data
A catalogue record for this book is available from the British Library

Library of Congress Cataloging-in-Publication Data
      Library of Congress Cataloging-in-Publication Data

Elliott, Catherine, 1966–
      French legal systam / Catherine Elliott, Catherine Vernon, Eric Jeanpierre. -- 2nd ed.
        p. cm.
      Includes bibliographical references.
      ISBN-13: 978-1-4058-1161-3
      ISBN-10: 1-4058-1161-7
        1. Law--France. I.. Vernon, Catherine. II. Jeanpierre, Eric. III. Title.

      KJV233.E43 2006
      349.44--dc22

                                                                    2006047270

10 9 8 7 6 5 4 3 2 1
10 09 08 07 06

Typeset by 3 in 10.5/12pt Baskerville
Printed and bound by Henry Ling Ltd at the Dorset Press, Dorchester, Dorset

The publisher's policy is to use paper manufactured from sustainable forests.

Contents

Foreword

French law and the French legal system had an interest, perhaps a fascination, for English lawyers well before the British accession to the European Economic Community. Accession has made awareness of French substantive law (in relation to commerce), and court procedures (as reflected in the work of the European Court of Justice) more important and perhaps even more interesting. And yet we do not all have time, or perhaps command of French legal terminology, sufficient to read Dalloz or the Codes in depth, so that a relatively short book in clear English is welcome and valuable. In such a space this book does not deal, it could not have dealt, with the substantive law or rules of practice and procedure: it does, however, in detail, albeit concisely, admirably disclose the structure of, and concepts underlying, 'The French Legal System'.

The English reader will inevitably make comparisons, some favourable some unfavourable to each side, and some comparisons are expressly made by the authors. To this end it was helpful to begin with a brief historical description of what over the centuries has gone into the process of creating that which now exists. From the early array of local laws throughout France, tribal then regional, through Roman law and the King's law, applying first to the nobility and then more widely, on to the Revolution bringing in particular the still-extant *Déclaration des droits de l'homme et du citoyen*. Then most significant, and most significantly different from the common law, the Codes – the *Code Civil* produced with incredible speed by the draftsmen and the Parliamentary Assemblies under pressure from Napoleon, and others produced during Napoleon's reign, during the early nineteenth centuries and then vastly extended since 1945, not least by delegated legislation since 1999. Why and how did the Codes produce a very different role for the judge when 'applying' ('not creating') the law.

In the United Kingdom in recent years we have explored (and in part adopted) so many constitutional changes that a survey not just of the existing French Constitution, but also (even briefly) its development through the Third and Fourth constitutions to the Fifth Constitution of 1958 is very relevant to our own future constitutional development. Some of this may be strictly outside the French 'legal system' but it is crucial to an understanding of the French constitution (of which the legal system is a part) and it is an important aspect of the book. However their bicameral system is different from ours. Why is the executive seen as so far separated from the legislature? In what ways does the President of the Republic have primacy over the Prime Minister? Can cohabitation (two principals in different parties) ever really work? How far should the President be protected from prosecution once he is out of office? The cartoon is amusing (from the judges '*On reviendra quand vous serez moins occupé*'). Since the riposte to criticisms that we do not have a constitution is often that we do not have a written constitution as such, what is the implication of the 'constitutional block' which includes and is capable of being made to include instruments adopted before and after the 1958 Constitution?

This book is full of absorbing topics of immediate relevance and interest to lawyers from other jurisdictions. Such topics arise both at the constitutional and at the purely 'legal system' level – they include the referendum resulting in a 'statute' and the control by judicial bodies of the referendum. Having always thought that we had a dualist system and the French a monist system for giving effect to international treaties, one is surprised to read that in France some international treaties require parliamentary approval. How would the 'contaminated blood' case have been handled here?

In this country we have some familiarity with the role of the *Conseil d'État*, though perhaps misunderstanding its influence on the procedure of the European Court of Justice. My French colleagues in Luxembourg always insisted that the European Court Advocate General's role was quite different from any function exercised in the *Conseil d'État*. Perhaps we see less clearly the difference between the *Cour de Cassation* in France and the Court of Appeal and the Judicial Committee of the House of Lords in this country.

We have even less awareness, and perhaps some envy, of the role of the *Conseil Constitutionnel*. It seems important that we should look at this from time to time, to see what we can learn from it even though some of its functions may have no relevance to our constitutional arrangements here, such as those relating to the President and the different balance of functions between the executive and the legislature. The supervision of election procedures and the constitutionality of parliamentary legislation does not arise here in the same way as in France. Should there be a way of reviewing legislation proposed or enacted as to whether prescribed criteria have been adopted and whether prescribed limits have been respected? Have the French got prescribed limitations on the jurisdiction of the *Conseil d'État* right for us or right for them?

The description of the criminal courts and their jurisdictional procedures, the civil courts, Administrative Tribunals and Administrative Appeals Tribunals below the *Conseil d'État* and even their terminology is valuable and interesting not just as a comparative study but increasingly for those involved in creating an area of 'freedom, security and justice'. An awareness of the Courts of other Member States is important to a full use of the European Judicial area and for European Justice. As far as France is concerned they are in this book well described and explained.

In case it is not plain that I enjoyed reading this book, I state that fact expressly. It is in my opinion an important guide to the French system which we need to know about generally but in particular when deciding (for or against) our own constitutional and legal system changes. It is an eminently readable book and the authors are to be applauded (vigorously) for having included so much in a modest space. I strongly recommend this book to English-speaking lawyers. Those who wish to go further will find extensive bibliographies.

The authors must in any event keep it up to date. Publishers please take note!

Slynn of Hadley

Preface

The second edition of this book seeks to build on the success of the previous edition. It aims to provide a clear, accessible discussion of the French legal system in English. As many of the people who will read this book will be intending to carry out a period of study in a French university, it also includes practical material on university and vocational law studies in France in order to prepare the student for this experience.

English translations have been used wherever possible for French terms, to help the flow of the text, and the original French terminology has only been kept where this is not possible. The work has been inspired by, and works alongside, another book, *French Legal System and Legal Language: An Introduction in French* by Catherine Elliott, Carole Geirnaert and Florence Houssais. This seeks to provide a basic introduction to the French legal system while developing the reader's linguistic skills through the provision of legal terminology in context. It contains short texts in French, with translations of key legal vocabulary. Each section is followed by exercises to assist the learning process, with answers provided at the back of the book. Extracts of topical articles from French newspapers and periodicals, essay questions and further reading from French legal texts are included at the end of each chapter. Thus the earlier French text gives the student a basic introduction to the subject area while building their linguistic skills. The present book seeks to provide greater depth of knowledge and understanding of the subject area, which the reader would not generally be able to master in French. Thus the two books can be used separately or together depending on the skills and knowledge that they wish to develop.

The new edition benefits from a Companion Website which provides regular updates, English and French materials and useful weblinks to French sources.

Catherine Elliott
Catherine Vernon
Eric Jeanpierre
London 2006

Acknowledgements

We would like to take this opportunity to thank the Franco-British Lawyers Society for their generous support in the preparation of this new edition. Their academic award was made as part of their celebrations of the bicentenary of the Civil Code.

We would also like to thank Fabien Lafay and Maïté Roche of the University of Jean Moulin in Lyon for their thoughtful comments and assistance both in the preparation of this new edition and the accompanying website.

Publisher Acknowledgements

We are grateful to the following for permission to reproduce copyright material:

NF 2.2 from *Le Monde*, (Pessin, D. 2001), © D. Pessin
NF 2.2 Jacques Chirac's immunity and the judges, from *Le Monde*, 12th October 2001, © D. Pessin

In some instances we have been unable to trace the owners of copyright material, and we would appreciate any information that would enable us to do so.

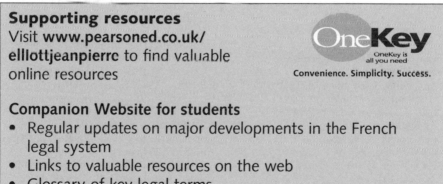

Supporting resources
Visit **www.pearsoned.co.uk/ elliottjeanpierre** to find valuable online resources

OneKey is all you need

Convenience. Simplicity. Success.

Companion Website for students
- Regular updates on major developments in the French legal system
- Links to valuable resources on the web
- Glossary of key legal terms

For more information please contact your local Pearson Education sales representative or visit **www.pearsoned.co.uk/elliottjeanpierre**

Table of cases

Table of statutes

Table of European and international legislation

Table of codes

1 Historical development of French law

PART I: PRE-REVOLUTIONARY, REVOLUTIONARY AND POST-REVOLUTIONARY LAW

The study of any legal system must include an understanding of the salient points in its development. In the French system we need to go as far back as Roman law, even though the Roman occupation ended over 1,500 years ago in 476. Roman law played a crucial part in the historical development of the French legal system. Some parts of modern French law, especially contract law, are indeed still based on it. Modern French law, in particular the Civil Code and the court structure, was developed following the 1789 Revolution in a remarkably short period of time.

▶ Pre-revolutionary law

Before the Revolution in 1789, there was no French legal system and no French law as such. Rather, there were many different laws and legal systems collectively referred to by legal historians as *l'ancien droit*. We will study some of these laws and indicate their origins, how they evolved over the centuries, their areas of application, and the interaction between the various laws.

The different types of law: their origins and evolution

From personal law to regional law
With the arrival of the Romans, the law that applied to each person depended on their origins. Roman law applied to the Romans but many local tribes applied their own laws. This is known as the system of personal laws and persisted for some time after the fall of the Roman Empire with Romans continuing to apply Roman law and each tribe its own law.

As society became organised in what is known as the feudal system, personal laws ceased to apply and each person was subject to the law of the relevant territory administered by the ruling feudal lord. France became divided into over 60 legal regions. Within each region there would usually be many more local laws applying only to particular localities within the region. The system of applying the law of the relevant region is described as territoriality.

The north/south divide

There was a great variety of regional laws but they can be roughly divided into two families. South of the river Loire, even after the departure of the Romans, Roman law remained important as a source for each region's written laws and it was also used to supplement gaps in those laws. Two written records were available for this purpose: first, a summary of Roman law had been prepared for the administration of Roman law for Romans. This was the Lex Romana Visigothorum, which was published early in 506. Then, from the twelfth century the Lex Romana Visigothorum was supplanted by the compilation known as the Corpus Juris which had been put together under the Byzantine emperor Justinian in the sixth century. This abstract is still used by modern students of Roman law but had been lost in the west, until the eleventh century when it was rediscovered by Italian scholars of Roman law. Law based on it was taught in universities in the south of France from the twelfth century.

North of the river Loire, the main source of the laws adopted by the feudal system was tribal custom, mostly from Germanic tribes. Law would be ascertained, as required, by the parties to the action. From the thirteenth century the method of proof was formalised by requiring the unanimous decision of a chosen group of inhabitants (usually ten). Gaps in the law would be filled by studying the law of adjoining regions and, as Paris grew in size, this often included the law of Paris. Roman law was increasingly influential, but the influence was resisted and the University of Paris was only allowed to teach it officially in May 1679. Nonetheless, from the twelfth century onwards it was used to fill gaps which were not covered by any customary law, particularly in contract law. From the outset some customary laws were recorded in writing. This became the usual practice. The law of Paris was first recorded in writing in 1510.

Some laws were not regional, but were applied across the whole kingdom, and even internationally. These included:

- *Canon law*: Until the sixteenth century, many matters relating to marriage were governed by canon law, that is to say the law of the Roman Catholic Church, not only in France but in most of Western Europe. It was not until 1787, two years before the revolution, that civil registration of births, marriages and deaths was introduced, thus enabling Protestants to be registered. Canon law also governed other areas more closely connected with the Church. It was taught in universities and had an indirect influence on other areas of law such as succession.

- *The King's law*: Much of the King's law in civil matters related to the nobility only. From the seventeenth century onwards, the areas of law emanating from the King, and applying to the whole of the kingdom, increased. These included civil and criminal procedure.

Interaction of the different laws

Interaction between different laws was complex and unwieldy. For example, a couple getting married would arrange a wedding in accordance with canon law, but their property ownership would be regulated by the law of the territory in which the marriage took place. To meet this situation the courts had to develop special conflict of law rules to decide which law would apply.

The court systems, themselves, reflected the diversity of laws. Each region had its own courts administering regional law. Ecclesiastical courts applied canon law. The King's law was administered by a court known as a *Parlement*, which was located initially in Paris. From the fourteenth century it also established branches in the provinces, so that by the time of the 1789 revolution there were 17 such courts. Though the *Parlements* were meant to administer the King's laws known as *ordonnances*, they often amended the legislation as it suited them.

General characteristics

Despite the diversity, it is possible to find underlying characteristics of the different laws applying in France before the Revolution. Some of the most notorious are:

Inequality
Individuals were divided into the nobility, the clergy and others described as the Third Estate. In each region, for instance, laws of succession for the nobility were different from those applying to others. Most laws of succession for the nobility required that one child (usually the eldest male child) inherit his father's land. Ordinary people were usually required to distribute property equally among heirs.

Authoritarianism
Work in the towns was organised in strongly hierarchical guilds with no power of personal contract. Within marriage all power was concentrated in the husband's hands, the wife having no independent power to contract and, in the North, usually having no power over property, which was jointly owned and controlled by the husband.

Feudal property rights
Various services were owed to landowners, similar to the situation in England at the time.

General legal principles of l'ancien droit

Lawyers were able to discern common underlying trends in the law of the various regions both north and south. They tried to extract general principles and order them in a logical manner. Two of the best known legal writers of pre-revolutionary law are Domat 1627–1697, author of *Civil Laws in Natural Order* (*Les lois civiles dans leur ordre naturel*) and Pothier 1695–1772, author of several treatises on civil law.

▶ Revolutionary and intermediate law

L'ancien droit was abolished by the revolution in 1789, though parts continued to be used during the revolutionary and post-revolutionary period until complete redrafting took place. The law developed during the ten years of the revolution (1789–99) and the five years afterwards is known by French legal historians as *le droit intermédiaire*, which can be translated as intermediate law. The revolutionary leaders, many of them with legal training, envisaged that a new system of law would be enacted which would apply to the whole of France. This was not achieved during the ten years of the revolution.

The first and best known legal achievement of the revolutionary period was the Declaration of Human and Civil Rights (*la Déclaration des droits de l'homme et du citoyen*), of 10 August 1789, which is still part of French law. The declaration incorporated the basic principles of equality, freedom of conscience, belief, association and expression, and the presumption of innocence, until convicted by due process of law.

Many other laws were passed during this time, but despite efforts to achieve a full-scale enactment of legislation to cover the whole field of civil law, this was not achieved. However, three main principles stand out:

Freedom

This was one of the basic principles of the Declaration and it was reinforced by legislation increasing:

- freedom within the family, with the age of majority and emancipation from paternal authority set at 21, freedom to divorce and remarry;
- freedom of contract and abolition of highly regulated work practices and corporations.

Equality

Feudal privileges and the privileges of the nobility and clergy were abolished. The elder son ceased to have special rights of succession.

Law emanates from the state only

All powers which rivalled the state (feudal powers and the powers of corporations) were abolished. Most importantly, the power of the Church, especially strong in the field of marriage law, was ended. Canon law and regional laws were repealed. The only law of the land was to be the law enacted by the state. The best known aspect of this principle is the separation of church and state.

Reform of the legal system

The regional courts were abolished. Various court systems were set up, but the present system of lower courts and regional appeal courts all administering the same law was not finally established until the early years of Napoleon's government. However, one lasting creation was of a central *tribunal de Cassation* in Paris to review the judgments of lower courts. This was to become the *Cour de Cassation*. All the courts ceased to have the power to make law.

• •

PART II: THE CIVIL CODE

In 1799 Napoleon Bonaparte came to power. He wanted the new order to be legitimised by the creation of a unified legal system. France, shortly before the Revolution, still had approximately 400 different local and regional customs. In the immediate post-revolutionary period Napoleon was instrumental in creating two pillars of the modern French legal system:

- the Civil Code, in 1804, which enacted civil law applying to the whole of the country for the first time;
- the *Conseil d'Etat*, created to control the legality of government work, a function which could not be carried out by the ordinary courts.

With these, the cornerstones were laid for a legal system based on legislation enacted entirely by the State.

The events that led to the Civil Code

Soon after the Revolution, an Act of 16–24 August 1790 brought into force a code of civil laws. The Code was simple, clear and applied to the whole country. The status of the Code of Civil Laws was reconfirmed by the Constitution of 1791. In 1792, a committee (the *Comité de Législation*), headed by Cambacérès, was set up with the mission of submitting to Parliament a draft Civil Code. A few months later, the first draft, composed of 719 articles, was rejected by Parliament as it was considered to be unnecessarily complicated. As well as legal principles it included also numerous philosophical ideals. Cambacérès submitted a more succinct version a year later, composed of merely 297 articles. This second draft was also rejected on the basis that it was too short, offering only a superficial outline of the law, rather than being a genuine code. The body of the Civil Code had been stripped to its bare bones. With its provisions drafted in such general terms it was feared that it might leave judges with excessive room for interpretation, and hence, with law-creating powers. A third draft prepared by Cambacérès never had time to be examined in Parliament as Napoleon's arrival to power stopped the proceedings.

On 12 August 1800, Napoleon revived the idea of codification by setting up a new commission that was again expected to prepare a draft Civil Code. This commission was composed of four practising lawyers, all politically moderate, and representatives of different regions and legal traditions in France. Two of them originated from regions with strong customary traditions (*pays de droit coutumier*). Tronchet (whose claim to fame was that he defended Louis XVI at his final trial) specialised mainly in the customary law from the Paris region. Bigot de Préameneu was an expert on the customs of Brittany. The two others were from the regions with strong Roman law influences (*pays de droit écrit*). Maleville came from the South West of France and Portalis from the Provence region. Portalis had been forced into exile in 1797 because of his support for the Monarchy and was a staunch advocate of Roman law and natural law.

The commission managed to produce a draft Civil Code within four months. It was first submitted to the higher courts (the *Tribunal de Cassation* and the *Tribunaux d'Appel*) for consultation and then to the *Conseil d'Etat*. There is no doubt that Napoleon played an essential role in the creation of the Code. He presided over more than half of the 107 sessions of the *Conseil d'Etat* (see Figure 1.1) while the remaining sessions were presided over by Cambacérès. During his exile on the Island of Saint Helena in the final years of his life, he apparently declared that: 'My true glory is not to have won forty battles; Waterloo will erase the memory of so many victories. What nothing can erase, what will live forever, is my Civil Code.' In December 1801, the two Parliamentary Assemblies (*Le Tribunat* and *Le Corps Législatif*) examined the draft Civil Code. It was initially rejected by the Assemblies. Napoleon reacted angrily by simply getting rid of the most serious opponents to the draft, and the entire project, composed of 36 laws, was adopted by the two Assemblies in 1804. The Civil Code was finally brought into force on 21 March 1804 and the previous Code of civil laws was repealed.

Fig. 1.1 Napoleon presiding over the *Conseil d'Etat*, discussion of the Civil Code. (Source: *Extrait de l'histoire du Consulat d'Adolphe Thiers*, Paris: L'heureux 1865, reprinted in Assemblee Nationale (2004), *200 ans du code civil, les lois qui nous rassemblent, Catalogue de l'Exposition,* Paris: Dalloz. © Ordre des avocats de Paris)

The content of the Code

The Code aimed originally to regulate a private individual's life from birth to death. One of the original drafters of the Code, Portalis, described civil matters as 'those that touch every private individual ... and which are present in the main events of his life and follow him everywhere.' Thus the Code was the main source for family, contract, tort and property law. To achieve a large acceptable consensus, it used the best ideas of past legislation and customs. In his inaugural speech for the Civil Code, Portalis mentioned how important it was 'to keep everything that does not deserve to be destroyed.'

The Code incorporated some of the main ideas of the Revolution and immediate post-revolutionary period but it also drew very heavily on *l'ancien droit*. Given the background of the authors of the Code, it made extensive use of the writings of Cujas, Domat and Pothier and provided a synthesis of certain aspects of *l'ancien droit*. The frequent use of these works ensured continuity in many areas of civil law.

❯ Incorporation of intermediate law

Important laws and ideas from intermediate law were incorporated into the Civil Code. Thus the freedoms enjoyed by the individual were reinforced. This can be seen first within the family with the secularisation of marriage and family law. The right to divorce was kept, but on much more limited grounds than in intermediate law and for a few years only, and was more limited for women than men. The need to support the patriarchal family was seen as paramount in the post-revolutionary period. This is an area where the Code has been much amended since its original drafting. Secondly, and most importantly, the Code developed the concept of freedom of contract, including the abolition of regulated work practices.

The value of individual equality was supported, so that feudal privileges, and the privileges of the nobility and clergy, did not form part of the new Code, and the succession rights of the elder son were not reinstated.

❯ Incorporation of *l'ancien droit*

Many ideas and rules from *l'ancien droit* were incorporated in the new law. Thus, contract law was derived from Roman law and from the interpretation of this law by Pothier. Family law was adapted from the customary laws of the North, particularly the law of the Paris region, and from some concepts derived from canon law. As mentioned above, subject to the introduction of divorce law, this is an area where intermediate law was abandoned. Apart from land law, which provided for ownership of land with no feudal rights, the detailed provisions for most other areas of law drew on *l'ancien droit*. In fact, without this inheritance, the Preliminary draft of the Civil Code could not have been completed in four months.

❯ The structure of the Civil Code

The Code is divided into three books. The first is concerned with citizenship, nationality and family law. The second covers the transfer of property. The third and largest deals with succession, contract and tort. It was inspired by Roman law and the Justinian Code and its division between persons, things and actions. There is a very brief introductory chapter with six articles. First drafts included a much larger treatment of the philosophical basis for the law in the Code, inspired by the natural law theory, current at the time. This theory has gone out of fashion (and others have come and gone). The Code was intended as a document for practitioners of law, drafted by practitioners, so the introductory chapter and its attempt to justify the law in accordance with fashionable theories was dropped. No doubt this has helped to ensure the durability of the Code. Nowadays, approximately half of the original 2281 articles have remained unchanged.

▶ Style of the Code

The Civil Code has a certain elegance in style which helped it become an integral part of French literature and France's national heritage. Indeed, the writer Paul Valéry called it 'the greatest work of French literature.'In a letter in 1840 to the famous author Balzac, Stendhal, another famous writer, recounted with a certain degree of affection how, during the writing of *The Charterhouse of Parma*, he used to read two to three pages of the Civil Code to impregnate himself with the Code's style. The former Minister of Justice, Jean Foyer, even describes the Civil Code as 'a monument of French culture just like Reims Cathedral or Versailles.'

A further factor which ensured durability was the practice, which can be traced to the original compilations of Roman law, of stating the general principles only, leaving it to the courts and detailed executory legislation to apply the principles to the facts. This gives great scope for interpretation and adaptation as circumstances change. The entire general rules on the law of tort, for instance, are contained in a mere five articles, of which several are limited to one or two paragraphs. The French style does not even include definitions of words used. Under the influence of Napoleon, who was a military man and not a lawyer, the Code avoids as far as possible legal vocabulary in order to remain simple and easily understandable.

Further flexibility was introduced by incorporating some laws which parties could choose not to follow, known as *lois supplétives*. These are most common in contract law, for instance the provision that payment is to be made at the domicile of the seller (article 1651) only applies if the parties have not made their own arrangements on the matter of place of payment. But the flexibility introduced into French law is limited: most laws are compulsory and cannot be amended. These are called *lois impératives*.

Since the Civil Code was drafted, it has been central to the French legal system.

▶ Further codification

A first wave of codification after the Civil Code took place during the Napoleonic period. Another four codes followed the Civil Code: The Civil Procedure Code (*Code de procédure civile*) in 1806, a Commercial Code (*Code de commerce*) in 1807, a Criminal Investigation Code (*Code d'instruction criminelle*) in 1808; and a Criminal Code (*Code pénal*) in 1810.

Generally legislation was the primary source for civil and criminal law but not for public law, which the *Conseil d'Etat*, formed by Napoleon to control government actions, was starting to develop. The Church in particular was stripped of any role in the law-making process or in the running of the State, as the roles of the Church and the State were completely separated.

A second wave of codification took place at the beginning of the twentieth century with five more Codes, among them the Employment Code (*Code du travail*) between 1910 and 1917.

After World War Two, the movement accelerated with approximately 50 codes being adopted. This included, for instance, the Customs Code (*Code des douanes*) in 1948, the General Tax Code (*Code général des impôts*) in 1950 and the Construction and Housing Code (*Code de la construction et de l'habitation*) in 1978.

The French Government has undertaken a major programme of codification in recent years. It created a Commission on Codification in 1989 to push forward this programme. This produced an initial set of Codes in 1993 including the Consumer Code (*Code de la consommation*). Thereafter, an Act of 16 December 1999 allowed the Government to adopt nine new codes by delegated legislation:

- the Education Code (*Code de l'éducation*);
- the Public Health Code (*Code de la santé publique*);
- the Monetary and Financial Code (*Code monétaire et financier*);
- the Code for the Environment (*Code de l'environnement*);
- the Countryside Code (*Code rural*);
- the Highway Code (*Code de la route*);
- the Social Action Code (*Code de l'action sociale*);
- the Code of Administrative Justice (*Code de justice administrative*); and
- the Commercial Code (*Code de commerce*).

We will focus here on the new Commercial Code. The Government felt that the original Commercial Code, drafted in 1806, needed to be updated as a mere 30 articles had remained in their original form. A first attempt at producing a new code was rejected by the National Assembly in 1994. The new version of the Commercial Code was eventually brought into force by an *ordonnance* of 18 September 2000.

The aim of the new Code was not to change the substantive law, but purely to make presentational changes in order to make the law more accessible and understandable. The Code attempts to bring together in a single document all the important existing legislation regarding commercial law. Some of the commercial legislation which had previously been left out of the old Commercial Code has been included in the new Code, such as the Act of 24 July 1966 which lays down the general rules that apply to commercial companies.

The legislator also tried to modernise the style of the Code, so that some of the provisions have been redrafted either by changing the tense, from future to present, or by using more up-to-date language. The structure and numbering of the Code was also changed. Whereas the Code previously began by focusing on the people to whom the Code applies (tradesmen, *les commerçants*), the present Code starts by defining commercial transactions (articles L 110-1 and L 110-2).

This new Commercial Code has been subject to numerous criticisms as French academic writers quickly identified a number of weaknesses. The effort at modernisation does seem to be incomplete, with a lot of old-fashioned language remaining in the Code. The new Code also failed to include the former article 631 which provided the general rules for the jurisdiction of commercial courts. An Act of 15 May 2001 was subsequently passed to add this provision to the *Code de l'organisation judiciaire* in a new article L 411-4. In addition, the headings used in the Code do not accurately reflect what is discussed in each section. For example, Title II of the First Book of the Code is named 'On commercial tradesmen' but it in fact also deals with the spouses of commercial tradesmen and with non-commercial professions. Finally, many important commercial rules continue to be found outside the Code. For instance, even though the current Commercial Code includes provisions on commercial companies, the definition of a company is still explained in the Civil Code (article 1832). Thus, the current Commercial Code, like the old Commercial Code, is not sufficient to provide a proper understanding of commercial law. It is therefore debatable whether the new Code achieved its aim of facilitating the use and understanding of commercial law.

▶ The future of the Civil Code

The Civil Code has outlasted all of its contemporary codes. The civil procedure code was replaced in 1975 by the new Civil Procedure Code, the Criminal Investigation Code was replaced by a Criminal Procedure Code in 1958, a new Criminal Code was passed in 1994 and, more recently, a new version of the Commercial Code was produced in 2000 (discussed above). Considered by many to be timeless, this does not mean that the Civil Code does not need amendments. During the bicentenary celebrations of the Code in 2004, the President of the Republic, Jacques Chirac, announced his intention to reform the entire law of obligations within five years. During the twentieth century, the Civil Code has been subject to efforts destined to put men and women on an equal footing in family law. This led Book One of the Code to be substantially revised between 1964 and 1972. In recent times, some further important revisions have taken place with, among others, the incorporation of laws on bioethics in 1994 and the introduction of civil partnerships (*Pacte civil de solidarité*) in 1999.

The efforts by the European Parliament since 1989 to create a European Civil Code (Eurocode) have raised many doubts as to the future of the Civil Code. Codification is viewed as the best way to achieve European unification in private law. The first initial drafts of such a Eurocode very much copy the more basic and logical structure of the German Civil Code. There is no doubt that the lack of influence of the French Civil Code on the European scale is closely linked with the decline of the French language internationally. English has become the *lingua franca* in Europe which, unfortunately, very few French academics speak. This has meant that French academics have been conspicuous by their absence abroad and in their influence over the framing of the potentially influential Eurocode.

• •

BIBLIOGRAPHY FOR CHAPTER 1

Arrighi de Casanova, C. and Douvreleur, O. (2001), 'La codification par ordonnances', *JCP* 2001, 61

Béguin, J. (2004), 'Entretien avec M. Jean Foyer – "Le Code civil est vivant. Il doit le demeurer!" ', *JCP* 2004, 543

Le bicentenaire du Code civil, Numéro spécial (2004), Paris: Recueil Dalloz

Bureau, D. and Molfessi, N. (2001), 'Le nouveau code de commerce? Une mystification', *D.* 2001, 361

Code civil (2005), Paris: Dalloz

Le Code civil 1804–2004 – Livre du Bicentenaire (2004), Paris: Dalloz and Lexis/Nexis Litec

Cornu, G. (2002), 'Un Code civil n'est pas un instrument communautaire', *D.* 2002, 351

David, R. (1972), *French Law: Its Structure, Sources and Methodology*, Baton Rouge: Louisiana State University Press

David, R. and Brierley, J. (1985) *Major Legal Systems in the World Today*, London: Stevens

Dekeuwer-Défossez, F. (2004), *Droit commercial*, Paris: Montchrestien

Lequette, Y. (2002), 'Quelques remarques à propos du projet de code civil européen de M. von Bar', *D.* 2002, 2202

Martin, R. (2004), 'Les cheminements des pouvoirs judiciaires depuis 1789', *RTD civ.* 2004, 251

Moreteau, O. (1995), 'Codes as Strait-Jackets, Safeguards, and Alibis: The Experience of the French Civil Code', *North Carolina Journal of International Law and Commercial Regulation*, 1995, 273

Reigné, P. and Delorme, T. (2001), 'Une codification à droit trop constant'. *JCP* 2001, 1

West, A. (1998), *The French Legal System: An Introduction*, London: Butterworths

Zweigert, K. and Kötz, H. (1998), *Introduction to Comparative Law*, London: Clarendon Press

Web Resources

Website: http://www.napoleon-series.org/research/government/c_code. html: French Civil Code in English.

Website: http://faculty.cua.edu/fischer/ComparativeLaw2002/ comp02rl.htm: French law materials provided by the Columbus School of Law.

2 The institutional framework under the Constitution

In this chapter we will look at the body of rules regulating the organs of the state, enacted in the Constitution of the Fifth Republic of 1958. The written Constitution interacts with other sources of law, which we will study in Chapter 3. We will also look in some detail, in Chapter 7, at one of the institutions regulated by the Constitution, the *Conseil constitutionnel*, whose role is to check that the Constitution is enforced. All articles referred to in this chapter are a reference to the Constitution, unless stated otherwise.

PART I: THE CREATION OF THE FIFTH REPUBLIC

▶ France as a constitutional laboratory

Since the first written Constitution of 3 September 1791, the French legal system has endeavoured to draft the ideal Constitution, and has produced 15 in all to date. Some of these Constitutions have proved to be very short-lived, with nine being passed between 1791 and 1848. Due to this history of constitutional innovation and experimentation, France is sometimes referred to as a constitutional laboratory. Table 2.1 shows the dates of the five French Republics. After the revolution of 1848, the monarchists were defeated, the Second Republic was created, and the republican system was briefly re-established. It was abandoned again between 1852 and 1870 when Napoleon III attempted to re-establish a French empire. After a transitional period, the Third Republic was formed in 1875. It had the full support of the monarchists. The Third

Table 2.1 The five French Republics

First Republic:	1793–1804
Second Republic:	1848–1852
Third Republic:	1871–1940
Fourth Republic:	1946–1958
Fifth Republic:	1958–

Republic provided the longest lasting Constitution so far (65 years), and it survived despite unstable governments formed by coalitions made between parties. From 1940, during the Second World War, there was in effect no Constitution. A new one was duly enacted in 1946 to create the Fourth Republic. The current Constitution, in force since 1958, has proved to be one of the most resilient, though it has been subject to many amendments, especially recently.

Failure of the Fourth Republic

Between October 1946 and May 1958 there were 21 governments lasting on average six months each, with long periods when there was no government at all. Voting was by proportional representation and highly unstable coalitions had to be formed: there were numerous political parties and none were able to master an overall majority in their own right. They failed to form solid alliances, and coalitions were built to pass particular measures and soon afterwards collapsed. The Constitution played its part in the instability, by making it difficult for the government to control Parliament, though the main causes were political. There were attempts at reform, to strengthen the position of the government, but ultimately the system failed to deal with the problem posed by the colonies seeking independence, and in particular the revolts in Algeria which started in 1954. Despite weak governments, because of the strength of the civil service and certain leading politicians, France managed, on the internal front, to carry out a reasonable programme of recovery from the damage of the Second World War. It also played a leading role in the formation of the new Common Market in 1957. The system failed to carry out full reforms of the financial services and of the general institutional framework. For all its flaws, the Fourth Republic might well, therefore, have survived had it not been for the catalyst of the situation in Algeria.

The role of General de Gaulle

On 13 May 1958, a crowd composed of Europeans and some Algerians and military personnel occupied Government House in Algiers, from which the French government ran Algeria. They asked for a new government to be formed in France, headed by General de Gaulle. While nobody's first choice, the General was able to capitalise on his famous silent retreat to his native village after the Second World War. No one knew what was his policy on Algeria, and both those in favour of keeping Algeria as a French colony and those seeking independence thought that he was on their side. After yet another resignation by the government of the day, on 28 May 1958, the President of the Republic proposed the General to Parliament as the next Prime Minister. He was duly elected on 1 June 1958 by a comfortable majority of both right and left wing parties (excluding only the communists). A precondition for agreeing to lead the government and returning to politics was that the Constitution would be reformed to increase the government's control of Parliament. Indeed, on 27 May 1958, de Gaulle had already stated that he had 'started the procedures necessary to establish a republican government'. An Act was duly passed on 3 June 1958 to start the procedures required for the passing of a new Constitution.

The creation of the Fifth Republic

General de Gaulle was not given a free hand in rewriting the Constitution. Parliament and members of the previous government laid down many conditions, both as to its form and its substance. This was done to avoid any repetition of what happened in the Second World War when Marshal Pétain had been given a free hand and effectively ended the Constitution of the Third Republic without replacing it with anything else.

Conditions as to form

The law of 3 June 1958 gave powers to the General's government elected on 1 June 1958. A special committee was constituted, on which Members of Parliament who had served under the Fourth Republic were well represented. This ensured that the final draft would not be dictated solely by the General but would also reflect their views. In addition, the draft had to be approved by the *Conseil d'Etat*, by the government and finally by referendum.

Conditions as to substance

The Constitution had to respect the principles of:

• universal suffrage;
• the separation of powers;
• government responsibility to Parliament.

In addition, the new Constitution was to regulate France's relationship with its associated countries, that is to say the colonies (soon to be ex-colonies).

Promulgation of the new Constitution

The final wording of the Constitution was a compromise between General de Gaulle who wanted to vest power firmly in the executive, and Members of the old Parliament who wished to retain parliamentary control. It created a modified type of parliamentary regime. General de Gaulle did win on one point, that Members of Parliament should give up their seats on being made members of the government. This made it clear that their power base and loyalty then lay with the latter. If they left the ministerial post they could not stand for re-election until the next election. The new Constitution was adopted by the government, and ratified by referendum with a comfortable majority on 28 September 1958. It was formally promulgated on 4 October 1958.

The main characteristics of the Fifth Republic

The central aim of the constitutional reforms was to establish a parliamentary regime, with a healthy relationship with the executive so that the country could be governed efficiently and effectively. The Constitution therefore established:

- A well-defined role for Parliament, so that it could not exceed the powers given by the Constitution. It no longer elected the President of the Republic, who therefore had an independent power base. While a vote of no confidence in the government was still possible, procedures had been set up to make this a measure to be used only exceptionally
- A strong role for the President of the Republic.
- A parliamentary regime, in that the government was answerable to Parliament.
- An independent judiciary.
- A body responsible for enforcing the Constitution, known as the *Conseil constitutionnel*. This was responsible for ensuring the proper running of elections, which had formerly been left to Parliament. It was also generally responsible for ensuring that the Constitution was respected. We will discuss its role more fully in Chapters 3 and 7.

Amending the Constitution

The Constitution has been subject to many revisions. The procedure is set out in article 89. Amendments may be proposed either by the President of the Republic on the proposal of the Prime Minister or by Members of Parliament. In practice the initiative lies with the President, when the parliamentary majority is supportive, or with the Prime Minister when the parliamentary majority is with opposition parties. The usual procedure is that the Bill proposing the amendment must be voted by both Houses of Parliament in identical terms (the two Houses of Parliament are the National Assembly and the Senate). This gives either House a power of veto, if it does not approve the Bill.

Once the Bill has been agreed it is then put to a referendum, so that the final decision is with the people. An alternative procedure, which avoids the need to put the matter to a vote by referendum, is to hold a special meeting of both Houses sitting together, (*le Congrès*) convened by the President of the Republic. In that case the Bill will be approved, if it is adopted by three fifths of the votes cast.

• •

PART II: THE PRESIDENT OF THE REPUBLIC

The President of the Republic under the 1958 Constitution is the product of General de Gaulle's vision. The holder of this office has many functions, and now plays a much more important role than predecessors under the Third and Fourth Republics. Central to this is his or her leading role in the government of the country.

Presidents are not chosen by Members of Parliament, and General de Gaulle clearly conceived the President as the leader of the country, above Parliament and all other organisations. In his speech at Bayeux on 16 June 1946, reflecting on French constitutional history, General de Gaulle said:

> executive power should not originate from a Parliament which comprises two chambers and exercises legislative power. If it does, there is a real risk of confusion of the two powers, with the government being no more than a collection of delegations [from parliamentary interest groups].

General de Gaulle genuinely saw increased presidential power as the way to stop the succession of weak and unstable governments. As foretold in this speech, the instability of governments was indeed one of the main characteristics of the Fourth Republic. Under the new Constitution, the President was accordingly to have a real role in the government of the country. We will study the method of choosing Presidents, the duration of their mandate and their functions.

The Constitution created a regime which is recognisably parliamentary – a parliamentary regime signifies that the executive is answerable to Parliament and may be toppled by Parliament. The first House of Parliament, the National Assembly, is elected by direct suffrage, while the second House of Parliament, the Senate, is elected by indirect suffrage. The government is answerable to Parliament, and Parliament can pass a motion of censure. Most law-making power resides with Parliament. However, in 1962 the Constitution was reformed. Originally, the President had been elected by indirect suffrage. This reform provided for his or her direct election, which significantly changed the balance of powers. The French regime is still not presidential, on the American model, since the essential features of parliamentary regime, mentioned above, have been preserved. The balance of power between the President, the executive and Parliament depends on the strength of the personalities involved, and most of all on the relationship between the majority parties in Parliament and those that supported the President, but one thing is sure: Parliament is not all powerful any more.

▶ Appointment of the President

Nomination of candidates

The law relating to the nomination of candidates allows for a very wide choice. Any French person aged 23 or over can stand though, since 1976, they must be nominated by 500 members of an electoral college made up of elected representatives from around the country. This is known as the godparent system. Thus, while in theory anyone can be a candidate, in practice they must be well connected with the political establishment. Most Presidents have been, at some point in their career, Members of Parliament or local government, with a power base within the political system. However, General de Gaulle came from outside the system after being in self-imposed exile for over 12 years before he came back into politics, and Pompidou was a banker before he became Prime Minister and then President.

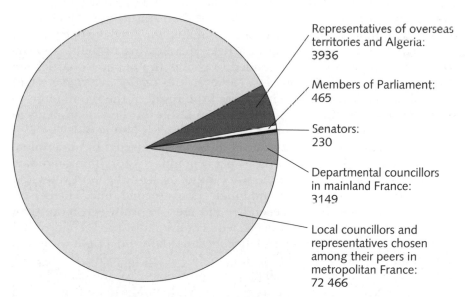

Representatives of overseas territories and Algeria: 3936

Members of Parliament: 465

Senators: 230

Departmental councillors in mainland France: 3149

Local councillors and representatives chosen among their peers in metropolitan France: 72 466

Fig. 2.1 The members of the first electoral college
(Source: Gouaud-Tandeau de Marsac, C. (2005), *Droit constitutionnel – La Vème République*, Paris: Ellipses)

Choosing the President

The law of 3 June 1958 provided for the President to be elected by a large electoral college of around 80,000 people (Fig. 2.1), which included Members of Parliament and representatives of local authorities and overseas territories. Members of Parliament, although part of the college, had less than 1 per cent of the votes.

This electoral process was only used once in the Fifth Republic, when General de Gaulle, without any serious rivals, won a landslide victory with nearly 80 per cent of the votes on 21 December 1958. In 1962, the Algerian crisis was resolved by giving the country independence. General de Gaulle then decided to dissolve the electoral college and to amend the Constitution to provide for election of the President directly by the people, a provision that is now contained in articles 6 and 7. This change was achieved controversially by a referendum initiated by the President of the Republic, who did not follow the ordinary procedure under article 89 of the Constitution. Since that would have required the approval of Parliament, General de Gaulle thought, probably correctly, that the amendment would not be successful. Instead, he chose to use the procedure entrenched in article 11 of the Constitution which allows the organisation of a public referendum for 'any bill which deals with the organisation of the public authorities' without necessitating prior approval by Parliament. The use of article 11 was criticised by most constitutional lawyers at the time, as this article was clearly not designed for such a purpose by the drafters of the Constitution. If it had been, it would have been included in title XVI of the Constitution which deals with constitutional amendments and contains one single article: article 89. Furthermore, the drafting of article 11, referring to 'bills', appears to indicate that it was only intended to enable the public to participate directly in the legislative process. However, the *Conseil constitutionnel*, in a decision of 6 November 1962, allowed the result of the referendum to stand on the basis that the popular will in favour of the amendments to the Constitution had legitimised the entire process (see p. 68).

The Constitution ensures that the President is elected by an absolute majority of votes (in other words, 50 per cent plus 1 vote). If no candidate obtains an absolute majority, the two candidates with the most votes and who are willing to take part stand for election a second time. The person with the most votes in this second round must logically win more than 50 per cent of the votes and is elected. Traditionally, the second round gives right to a battle between a left-wing candidate and a right-wing candidate, and the winner would lead by only a small majority. During the last presidential elections in 2002, however (Table 2.2), the candidate of the French National Front (a far right party), Jean-Marie Le Pen, caused a shock in French politics by finishing second in the first round, ahead of the socialist candidate, Lionel Jospin, and a mere 3 per cent behind

Table 2.2 The 2002 Presidential election results

First round, 21 April 2002:

Candidate	Votes	% of votes
Jacques Chirac (Rally for the Republic)	5 573 958	19.71
Jean-Marie Le Pen (National Front)	4 791 750	16.95
Lionel Jospin (Socialist / Labour Party)	4 558 554	16.12
Francois Bayrou (Union for French Democracy)	1 939 124	6.86
Arlette Laguiller (Lutte ouvrière)	1 625 169	5.75
Jean-Pierre Chevènement (Pole Republicain)	1 509 644	5.34
Noel Mamère (The Green Party)	1 484 238	5.25
Olivier Besancenot (Communist Revolutionary League)	1 206 782	4.27
Jean Saint-Josse (Hunting, Fishing, Nature and Traditions)	1 201 524	4.25
Alain Madelin (Liberal Democracy)	1 103 841	3.90
Robert Hue (Communist Party)	959 328	3.39
Bruno Mégret (National Republican Movement)	664 836	2.35
Christiane Taubira (Radical Left Party)	656 048	2.32
Corinne Lepage (Cap 21 Movement)	531 601	1.88
Christine Boutin (Independent candidate)	338 229	1.20
Daniel Gluckstein (Workers' Party)	132 335	0.47

27.86 % abstentions

3.40% blank votes

(Source: *Le Monde*, 23 April 2002)

Second Round, 5 May 2002:

Jacques Chirac	25 316 647	82.15
Jean-Marie Le Pen	5 502 314	17.85

19.86% abstentions

5.40% blank votes

(Source: *Le Monde*, 7 May 2002)

the incumbent president, Jacques Chirac. The entire left-wing electorate, socialists and communists, decided to vote against Jean-Marie Le Pen, and hence, by default, for their arch enemy Jacques Chirac, who ended up receiving more than 80 per cent of the votes in the second round.

Funding of elections and media publicity

Acts passed in January and May 1990 provided for equal television and radio time for all the parties and attempted to regulate political funding, by putting a cap, controlled by the *Conseil constitutionnel*, on electoral expenses. In the early years of the Fifth Republic the government of the day controlled the media and allocated itself most of the airtime, thereby saving itself money and putting rivals at a considerable disadvantage.

While the financial reforms have improved the situation for opposition parties, nonetheless, standing for the Presidency is an expensive business, and effectively limits the capacity of outsiders to mount a viable challenge. Certain doubts were raised during the 1995 presidential elections as to the electoral expenses of two of the candidates, Edouard Balladur and Jacques Chirac. One of the *Conseil constitutionnel*'s former members, Jacques Robert, told in his memoirs of suspicions that both candidates might have exceeded the permitted financial limits. The lack of investigating powers meant, however, that the *Conseil constitutionnel* was unable to check the veracity of the candidates' financial declarations and the election results were allowed to stand.

The presidential term in office

Following a constitutional amendment in 2000, the Presidential term was reduced from seven to five years. There is no limit to the number of times someone can stand, though so far only three Presidents have been elected for two consecutive terms and none for three terms.

Before 2000, many politicians had discussed the possibility of a five-year term (*le quinquennat*). Georges Pompidou, while President, even started in 1973 to introduce the constitutional reforms to make it possible, but dropped the idea because of insufficient parliamentary support. Thereafter, a familiar pattern emerged: while presidential candidates considered this an excellent idea, the same people once elected president thought this to be a very bad idea.

- Valéry Giscard d'Estaing, who had declared himself in favour of the reduction of the term at the very beginning of his presidency in July 1974, declared a few years later that 'the question is not at the top of my priorities any more.'
- Francois Mitterrand announced in his political manifesto in January 1981 that he would either reduce the presidential term to five years or make it a non-renewable seven-year term. However, in his 14 years

as President of the Republic, he did neither, indicating in 1985 that a change to the term was 'after all ... of no urgency any more.'

- Jacques Chirac, in favour of a five-year term in 1986, had changed his mind by the time he had become President in 1995. In July 1999 he stated 'the five-year term, in whatever shape, would be a mistake. I will therefore not sanction it.'

The idea was revived in May 2000 when the former President Valéry Giscard d'Estaing announced his intention to introduce a parliamentary proposal to allow the President of the Republic to sit for one five-year term only, banning presidents from standing for a second term. The Prime Minister, Lionel Jospin, a strong advocate of a five-year term, threatened to make the change, with or without the President's support. Under intense pressure, Jacques Chirac gave the green light for the process to be set in motion on 5 June of the same year. He used the procedure laid down in article 89 of the Constitution to make the constitutional amendment, after the National Assembly and the Senate had overwhelmingly voted in favour of the reforms. Jacques Chirac announced in a presidential decree that a referendum would be held on the subject a couple of months later. On 24 September, the French electorate was asked to answer by yes or no to the following question:

> Do you approve of the constitutional amendment setting the President of the Republic's term in office to five years?

Yet again, the answer was overwhelmingly in favour, with 73.15 per cent 'yes' votes. The electorate, however, showed little enthusiasm to participate in the vote, with less than a third going to vote, and 15 per cent of those who turned up leaving their voting form blank. The main reason was that the result was never seriously in doubt, with all the main parties in favour of a five-year term. This was the end of the original seven-year period, which had been carried over from the Third and Fourth Republics, and had lasted for 127 years.

▶ Cohabitation

In the past, the parliamentary majority sometimes changed during a presidency and the President had to operate with a government from a different party. This situation, known as *la cohabitation*, was made possible because of a shorter parliamentary term (5 years) than the 7-year presidential term. An unpopular president, forced with the elections for a new Parliament in the middle of his term, could thus lose the majority in Parliament. Such a situation occurred twice while Mitterrand was President, and lasted for two years on each occasion. It happened again in 1997, when President Chirac still had five years of his term to run.

One expected consequence of the change in the new presidential term

Table 2.3 French presidential and parliamentary elections

Presidential elections		Parliamentary elections
✓	1981	✓
	1982	
	1983	
	1984	
	1985	
	1986	
	1987	
✓	1988	✓
	1989	
	1990	
	1991	
	1992	
	1993	✓
	1994	
✓	1995	✓
	1996	
	1997	✓
	1998	
	1999	
	2000	
	2001	
✓	2002	✓
	2003	
	2004	
	2005	

is that it will provide more stability to the French parliamentary régime by making it less likely that the President and the Prime Minister will come from different parties. Many people consider that a recurrence of *cohabitation* is not impossible, but highly unlikely, in the future. The President's term being now on a par with Parliament's, and the two elections taking place within a month of one another, the President is expected to be able to work with a stable parliamentary majority during his entire term. Dates of coincident presidential and parliamentary elections appear in Table 2.3.

There is no doubt that *cohabitation*, described as a 'period of permanent conflict between the President and the Prime Minister', is an oddity in the French constitutional landscape, with the President having no clear duties, and unable to make use of his one real power, to dissolve the National Assembly, as this is unlikely to produce a sympathetic majority.

Opinion polls seem to suggest that the voters rather like the untidiness of *cohabitation*, as it ensures that the President cannot run the country as an elected dictator, which General de Gaulle was accused of doing, and nor can the Prime Minister, as he must work with a President of a different political persuasion (see p. 38).

▶ The functions of the President

As well as traditional ceremonial functions, such as receiving foreign dignitaries, and a general role as 'guardian of the Constitution and guarantor of national independence', the President has a large number of specific functions, which make him a cornerstone of the government process.

General functions

Article 5 of the Constitution can be read as a sort of mission statement for the President. It does not give any specific powers, but the language clearly shows that the role of the President is to be more than that of a ceremonial head of state:

> The President of the Republic is the guardian of the Constitution. By arbitration, the President ensures the proper operation of public authorities and the continuity of the State. The President guarantees national independence, territorial integrity, and respect for treaties.

Guardian of the Constitution
This is a role which the President now shares with the *Conseil constitutionnel*. We will see in Chapter 7 that, since 1974, this institution has taken an active and effective, if occasionally controversial, role in ensuring that the Constitution is respected. Nonetheless, the functions of the *Conseil constitutionnel* are limited and the residual role of the President is still important.

Arbitrator
This term is splendidly elastic, and clearly allows for different degrees of interference with the operations of government and the civil service. The exact nature of the involvement will depend largely on whether the President and the government are supported by the same parties. Even when they are not, the Constitution does not envisage just a figurehead President. Arbitration is a fairly active occupation. Even if the function is interpreted as neutrally as possible, it means ensuring that the rules are observed, and pointing out when they are not.

Guarantor of national independence
This ensures that the President, even in periods of *cohabitation*, plays an active part in foreign policy. The exact nature of this role will depend to a large extent on the personalities involved. The President is, however, a separate, independent voice and not a mere figurehead or spokesperson for the government.

Specific functions

As well as the general role outlined under article 5, the President also enjoys a number of specific powers. Article 19 divides these into powers exercised by the President alone, and those shared with the Prime Minister and members of the government which require a countersignature from the appropriate member of the government for their exercise.

Powers exercised by the President alone

The President has a considerable range of powers under the Fifth Republic which he or she can carry out alone. These include the power to:

• Article 8: Appoint the Prime Minister

Article 8 of the Constitution provides that the President appoints the Prime Minister. The President is not required to consult anyone, or to endorse nominations made by other parties, so in effect the President chooses the Prime Minister. This choice is one of the cornerstones of the Constitution of the Fifth Republic, ensuring that Prime Ministers derive their powers from the President and not from Parliament. The President needs to ensure, however, that the chosen Prime Minister can command a majority in the National Assembly, so that legislation can be passed and the dangers of a motion of censure avoided (art. 49). Mitterrand declared on television shortly after the 1986 parliamentary elections which resulted in the first government by a right-wing coalition and a left-wing President that 'No one, other than me, will choose the Prime Minister. Of course I must appoint someone who has every prospect of commanding a majority in Parliament, especially if there is any prospect of a motion of censure or a motion of no confidence.' When the President and the parliamentary majority are political allies, the former is the senior partner in every respect and the choice of a Prime Minister will be entirely his or her own, as was made clear with the appointments of Georges Pompidou and more recently Dominique de Villepin as both had never held an electoral mandate prior to being appointed Prime Minister. Prime Ministers from the same party as the President owe their powers to the President and will act in partnership with the President, on the terms chosen by the President. However, when the President is of a different party from the parliamentary majority, he or she will lose any freedom of choice and be, in effect, under an obligation to appoint the person supported by Parliament.

During the last *cohabitation* between a right-wing President and a left-wing majority in Parliament, Jacques Chirac had no option open to him other than to choose the leader of the largest left-wing party, Lionel Jospin.

• Article 11: Call a referendum

The President may submit government Bills dealing with a fairly wide range of matters to a referendum, in accordance with article 11 as

Table 2.4 The use of artice 11 to organise a referendum during the Fifth Republic

Date	Subject	Vote
8 January 1961	Right to self-determination for Algeria	Yes
8 April 1962	Evian agreements	Yes
28 October 1962	President elected by direct universal suffrage	Yes
27 April 1969	Amendment to the Senate and the French Region	No
23 April 1972	Enable the United Kingdom, Ireland and Denmark to join the European Economic Community	Yes
6 November 1988	Right to self-determination for New Caledonia	Yes
20 September 1992	Authorisation to ratify Maastricht Treaty	Yes
29 May 2005	The European Constitutional Treaty	No

amended by an Act of 4 August 1995. Table 2.4 lists the referenda under article 11 which have been called during the Fifth Republic.

This power to call a referendum was frequently used by General de Gaulle, and by no means only within the limited scope of article 11. In particular, he put to the people the proposal that the President should be directly elected, and obtained the necessary endorsement. Article 11 clearly reinforces the President's power, by giving an autonomous way of making major changes without involving the government.

- Article 12: Dissolve the National Assembly

The central role of the President is enshrined in the Constitution by giving the President sole authority to dissolve the National Assembly before the end of the full five-year term. The decree of dissolution is signed by the President, with no countersignature being required. The Prime Minister and the Presidents of both Houses of Parliament must be consulted, but their advice need not be followed. The historical reason for giving this right to the President was to avoid the frequent dissolutions of Parliament during the Third and especially the Fourth Republic. This right was in effect controlled by the parliamentary majority of the time and the government. It was often misused simply as a means to put pressure on warring parliamentarians. It was therefore taken away by the Constitution of the Fifth Republic and it is up to the President to decide whether dissolution is essential, because Parliament is no longer capable of legislating and carrying out its functions. Overall, the Constitution of the Fifth Republic has been successful in breaking the previous pattern of frequent changes of government, which were due to the government's inability to control Parliament under the Constitution of the Fourth Republic.

The main use of the right of dissolution is to resolve conflicts or potential conflicts between the President and Parliament. General de Gaulle dissolved Parliament in two extreme cases: in 1962 after Parliament had forced his Prime Minister, Georges Pompidou, along with the rest of his government, to resign following a motion of censure (article 49, para. 2), and in May 1968 after general strikes had brought France to a standstill. Mitterrand dissolved Parliament soon after he was elected in 1981 and 1988, and the elections produced a result favourable to Members of Parliament who supported him. Presidents can even choose a date for the parliamentary elections because they think it will produce a more favourable result than waiting for the expiry of the full five-year term. President Chirac did this in 1997, and failed as the electorate chose a Parliament with a majority of opposition left-wing members. He did not resign, choosing instead to remain in office while relying on the precedent of the previous two-year *cohabitation* governments. Arguably the situations were different as clearly being only short-term. It is questionable whether it is desirable to allow a long-term abdication of power by the President. However, it is clear that the institutions of the Fifth Republic are capable of surviving such an abdication, as the Constitution has already demonstrated its extreme flexibility.

To stop abuse of the power to dissolve Parliament, the elections for the new Parliament must be completed within 40 days, and there can be no further dissolution of Parliament for a year. These measures are designed to stop a President operating in effect without Parliament, by ordering frequent dissolutions.

- Article 10: Promulgation of Acts of Parliament

All legislation must be promulgated by the President (article 10). This is a function carried out by most heads of state. In the United Kingdom the equivalent procedure is that all Acts of Parliament must receive the Royal Assent. It is unheard-of for the President to refuse to promulgate, in the same way as no king or queen has refused the Royal Assent since Queen Anne refused her assent to the Scottish Militia Bill in 1708. Presidents are, however, given a period of 15 days in which to promulgate the law and can exercise some rights during that time. These include the right to:

1 Refer an Act to the *Conseil constitutionnel* (article 61). It will check whether the Act complies with the Constitution – a prerogative power discussed at p. 136 below. The law will not be promulgated until the *Conseil constitutionnel* has given its verdict and the wording of any subsequent promulgation will include details of the referral.
2 Resubmit the Act to Parliament. The President asks Parliament to reconsider the statute. This power has rarely been used, but it does in practice enable the President to ensure that a decision is delayed or indeed changed. It was used by the President, for instance, in 1983 to stop a law for a universal exhibition in 1989, when it became clear that the expense could not be warranted in difficult economic times. The referral enabled Parliament to change its mind, which it seemed, on that occasion, very willing to do.

- Article 13: Countersignature of *ordonnances* and decrees emanating
from the government

While the Constitution requires the President to promulgate laws, subject
to the limited rights mentioned above, the position for *ordonnances* (discussed more fully in Part V of Chapter 3) is not so clear. *Ordonnances* were
designed to enable government to legislate without the time constraints
of the full parliamentary procedure required for Acts of Parliament. The
President's signature of these *ordonnances* has been interpreted by most
constitutional lawyers as being a pure formality with the president having
little choice but to sign what is put in front of him or her. During the first
cohabitation of the Fifth Republic, the right-wing government was keen to
reverse some of the more controversial measures of the previous government. To do so it passed *ordonnances* on the privatisation of 65 enterprises
and on working conditions. President Mitterrand, however, refused to
sign them, forcing the government to pass Acts of Parliament instead
which were referred to the *Conseil constitutionnel*. It pronounced these laws
constitutional, but imposed conditions for their application.

It is unlikely that a President would again proceed in the same manner.
As *ordonnances* must be countersigned by the Prime Minister, it seems
that the better view is that a President who refuses to sign is acting
unconstitutionally.

Decrees relating to matters within article 37 which have been debated by
the government also require countersignature, under article 13. This has not
led to controversy during periods of *cohabitation* as such decrees have so far
related to relatively uncontroversial matters. However, when the President
and the Prime Minister are from the same party, the practice has been for the
President to initiate a number of decrees, merely obtaining the countersignature of the Prime Minister. The latter simply exercised personal discretion
by waiving deliberation by the government. Routine decrees, which have not
been debated by the government, do not require the President's signature.

- Article 16: Use emergency powers

Article 16 of the Constitution gives the President the right to suspend the
operation of the normal organs of government and to run the country. It
contains precise conditions for its use, with the President being required
to consult a number of bodies, including the *Conseil constitutionnel*, but
not being obliged to follow their advice. The President's powers are also
limited as to time: they must last no longer than the shortest possible
time to resolve the crisis. The only specific obligation is a prohibition on
dissolving Parliament, which is seen as a guarantee against a dictatorship.
That said, the powers are very wide, as the President may 'take such measures as are required in the circumstances'. These include carrying out the
functions of the government, Parliament and the judiciary, if required.
They are not easily controllable, and there is much debate as to whether
they should be abolished or modified, as the President's almost unlimited
powers have led some academics to talk of a 'temporary dictatorship'.

These powers have been used only once, during the Algerian crisis, which must have been very much on the mind of those responsible for the drafting of the Constitution in 1958. As mentioned earlier, the arrival of de Gaulle and the creation of the Fifth Republic were occasioned by the Algerian independence war. It was not therefore surprising that article 16 was used, for five months from April 1961 to September 1961. There was no doubt that the first condition for implementation applied – namely a serious and immediate threat to the institutions of the Republic. At that time the Republic included Algeria, and a group of French military personnel had rebelled against the Government in Alger. The second condition is the suspension of orderly operations of the Republic. This could be argued as applying in Algeria, a part of the French territory, where the military rebels had seized power and proposed to overthrow the French government. Unsurprisingly, the *Conseil constitutionnel* stated in its decision of 23 April 1961 that article 16 had been correctly invoked, and that both conditions were satisfied. The President received 16 additional advisory opinions by the *Conseil constitutionnel* on measures carried out while article 16 was in force, but they remained confidential and were not published. On the whole, the implementation of article 16 was accepted by public opinion. What is even more debatable is the length during which article 16 powers were used by the President. The rebellion was essentially quelled by the end of April 1961, yet the powers were exercised for a further five months. A possible reform would be to give the *Conseil constitutionnel* the right to pronounce on the appropriate time for termination of the measures.

- Articles 54, 56 and 61: Make decisions in relation to the *Conseil constitutionnel*

The French President nominates three of the members of the *Conseil constitutionnel* including its President. The President of the National Assembly and the President of the Senate nominate three each (article 56). This gives the French President some considerable indirect power over this institution. The role of the President is particularly important as, under article 5, it includes the role of guardian of the Constitution. It is accordingly essential that the *Conseil constitutionnel* and the President can work together. While the President's power under article 5 is very broad, it is clear that the President may not interfere directly with the *Conseil constitutionnel*'s exercise of its own more limited powers. He or she does have the right to submit to the *Conseil constitutionnel* a bill (article 61), or a treaty (article 54).

- Article 18: Deliver messages to Parliament

This right is contained in article 18 of the Constitution, but has rarely been used, as most Presidents prefer instead to express their views via the media, generally the television. President Mitterrand did this on numerous occasions in relation to the first Gulf War in 1991. Some of these messages have been of major importance, as was the case when President Mitterrand delivered a message to Parliament containing his views on the question of the first *cohabitation* of the Fifth Republic, in 1986.

- Miscellaneous powers

The President has the power to grant presidential pardons (article 17) and to guarantee the independence of the judiciary (article 64). In addition, he or she can negotiate and ratify treaties (article 52), which is of particular importance during periods of *cohabitation* as it gives the President full power in this reserved area of foreign policy.

Shared powers

Even though the Constitution seems very clear on the subject, the provisions on the President's powers which are shared with the Prime Minister have often been interpreted very broadly, or even been given an entirely new interpretation by the President. This is possible, as the President's misinterpretation of the Constitution cannot be punished by the *Conseil constitutionnel* as it does not have the power to do this (see Chapter 7).

- Article 8: Nomination of members of the government

The President can nominate ministers after a proposal has been received by the Prime Minister (article 8). This is a power of validation of the Prime Minister's choice. There may well be preliminary consultations, and if the Prime Minister and the President are of the same party, undoubtedly the President will influence the choice. The Constitution allows for complete flexibility in this regard. Once the formal proposal is made, the President is, however, bound to endorse it. During a period of *cohabitation* it was thought that the President would have no say in the selection of ministers, other than the all-important nomination of the Prime Minister. President Mitterrand, however, refused to endorse two nominations put forward by Jacques Chirac during the first *cohabitation* in 1986, for the positions of Foreign Affairs Minister and Defence Secretary.

- Article 15 : Heading the armed forces

The President heads the armed forces. The Constitution specifies, however, that he shares military decision-making powers with the Prime Minister, who, according to article 21, is responsible for military defence. The President has traditionally been the voice of France in relation to its military operations in the world. It was, for instance, President Chirac who took over the responsibility of expressing, at the United Nations and in the media, France's reluctance to allow the USA and the United Kingdom to go to war in Iraq in 2003.

- Article 13: Making senior civil and military appointments

The Constitution has entrusted both the President, in its article 13, and the Prime Minister, in its article 21, to make appointments to the top civil and military positions. During the first *cohabitation* (1986–8), President François Mitterrand refused to endorse several of the Prime Minister's choices.

- Article 30: Convening extraordinary sessions in Parliament

The President is entrusted, by article 30 of the Constitution, with the task of opening and closing by decree extraordinary Parliamentary sessions. The Constitution clearly indicates that this is purely a formality, as article 29 of the Constitution specifies that such sessions take place upon a request by the Prime Minister or a majority of Parliament. General de Gaulle refused to comply with a request of a majority of the Members of Parliament for an extraordinary session in 1960. François Mitterrand used this as a precedent to refuse a similar request on two occasions, in 1987 and 1993. He explained his decision in 1993 by declaring that 'the Government is not entitled to decide the convening of an extraordinary session [in Parliament], or decide on its agenda. Only the President of the Republic has the power to do this.'

The President's immunity

It is traditionally a country's constitution which determines the extent to which a Head of State may be subject to prosecution. In France, the relevant provisions are contained in article 68 of the Constitution:

> The President of the Republic is only responsible for acts committed in the course of his office if these amount to high treason. He may only be indicted by both Houses, if an absolute majority of members of both Houses vote for identical decisions in an open ballot. He shall be tried by the High Court of Justice.

Thus, article 68 lays down the principle that the President of the Republic is immune from any prosecution. It also imposes a limitation on his or her immunity by stating that the President may face prosecution for high treason regarding actions carried out in his official capacity. A trial of this nature would be the French equivalent of the American impeachment proceedings. High treason is generally interpreted as involving a serious breach of the President's official functions, though no definition is provided of the key concept of 'high treason', either in the Constitution or in the Criminal Code, nor is there any mention of the penalties that will be imposed following a conviction.

Article 68 specifies that the High Court of Justice (*Haute Cour de Justice*) is the relevant court to hear accusations of high treason. The court has never heard a case against the President, though there were rumours that it might be asked to consider some of General de Gaulle's more adventurous uses of the Constitution, such as the calling of a referendum under article 11 to approve legislation allowing for direct election of the President (see p. 26 above).

The question of the President's immunity has made the newspaper headlines on a regular basis since 1998. A commentary by the left-wing Minister of Justice that the right-wing President of the Republic, Jacques Chirac, was not above the law sparked off this debate. Thereafter, in a judgment of 22 January 1999, the *Conseil constitutionnel* stated *obiter* that:

> The President of the Republic, for any actions carried out in his official capacity, and except in the case of high treason, benefits from an immunity ... furthermore, while in office, he may only be judged for any criminal liability, by the High Court of Justice.

Thus, the *Conseil constitutionnel* effectively decided that the President's immunity provides an exemption from any prosecution while in office with the notable exception of the case of high treason. It thereby excluded any ordinary court's jurisdiction in prosecuting an incumbent President of the Republic. This point was made to emphasise the limitation of the jurisdiction of the International Criminal Court, in so far as it concerns the President, and to ensure that the treaty signed in Rome in 1998, recognising the future international court, left intact the protection granted by the Constitution to the President. The judgment caused much debate in France, as President Chirac was allegedly implicated in various criminal matters which took place before he became President of the Republic, while he was mayor of Paris and leader of the Gaullist RPR political party. The statement by the *Conseil constitutionnel* certainly influenced Jacques Chirac's decision in December 2000 to refuse to be questioned in a judicial investigation into his party's illegal financing. He argued in a television interview that his constitutional status prevented him from appearing as a witness, claiming that he would have liked to put an end to rumours, but that unfortunately he was prevented by the Constitution from doing so. Declaring 'I am the permanent victim in this case', he asked for the judiciary to provide some clarification on his status. After the Public Prosecutor at Nanterre decided on 22 March 1999 that he had no authority to prosecute a case against the President in the criminal courts, it was the *Cour de cassation*'s turn to express its views in a full sitting of the Court on 10 October 2001. It held that:

> The High Court of Justice can only judge the President of the Republic for actions of high treason while in office. Prosecution for all other offences by ordinary criminal courts can, thus, not take place during the presidential term ...

Thus, the *Cour de cassation* agreed partially with the *Conseil constitutionnel*, by recognising the President's absolute immunity while in office, except in the case of high treason. It went, however, further than the *Conseil constitutionnel* by making three additional points not expressly mentioned by the *Conseil*. Firstly, it pointed out that Presidents become, after completing their term in office, ordinary citizens again, judged by ordinary criminal courts. Secondly, while in office the President cannot be called as a witness in a criminal investigation and trial. Thirdly, the limitation period that applies to criminal proceedings is suspended while the President is in office.

Following his victory at the presidential elections in 2002, Jacques Chirac announced shortly afterwards the creation of a commission to review the President's immunity. The commission (known as the Avril Commission) was composed of twelve members: seven constitutional law specialists, one criminal law specialist, three judges, and one practising lawyer. It published a report in December 2002, suggesting that several amendments should be made to the Constitution. It recommended that article 68 should be redrafted to replace the term 'high treason' with the expression 'behaviour obviously incompatible with his presidential mandate'. Commission of such behaviour could lead to the President's removal from office. Louis Favoreu, one of the commission's members, explained that the term 'high treason' was ill conceived as it has not been properly defined and includes criminal and political elements, when all that is required is to ascertain whether the President should remain in office, which is a purely political matter. The new criteria would include any act that would affect the President's ability to exercise his or her functions, which might have occurred before the President was elected or in the President's private capacity (such as seriously injuring his wife during a domestic row). Having had to step down, the President could then face prosecution before the ordinary courts, just like any other member of the public.

The Avril Commission also recommended that the Constitution should confirm the president's immunity, while in office, from both prosecution and the obligation to appear as a witness. It also proposed that the High Court of Justice, composed of senators and deputies, should be replaced by a High Court (*Haute Cour*). The new High Court would bring together all the members of the National Assembly and all the senators to vote on whether or not the President should be forced to stand down.

The Avril Commission was criticised because its members were chosen by one of Jacques Chirac's closest aides among people who had already previously publicly expressed their preference for keeping an incumbent President's immunity. The report, however, does not appear to be biased. The members of the Commission included heavyweight constitutional lawyers (such as Pierre Avril, Louis Favoreu, Didier Maus, Guy Carcassonne and François Luchaire). The Report's conclusions were influenced by the approach taken to Heads of State in the Constitutions of other countries, including the USA, Italy and Germany, where senior politicians benefit from immunity while in office, but not afterwards (Fig. 2.2). The Avril Commission's recommendations have not yet been imple-

Fig. 2.2 Jacques Chirac's immunity and the judges. The caption can be translated: 'We will come back when you are less busy.'
Source: *Le Monde*, 12 October 2001, p.10.

mented and the President remains immune from prosecution while in office, except in the case of high treason.

PART III: THE GOVERNMENT

▶ Introduction

Under the 1958 Constitution, executive power is shared between the President, the Prime Minister and the other ministers who form the government. One of the fundamental principles of the Fifth Republic is that the executive power should not be founded on parliamentary power, as was the case under the Third and Fourth Republics. Since 1962, the power of the President derives from direct elections by the French people. The

Prime Minister acquires power through the President, who chooses and appoints him (article 8). Other members of the government are chosen by the Prime Minister and derive their power from that office. The choice must be ratified by the President under article 8, thereby emphasising that the minister's power does not emanate from Parliament. While party allegiance plays a part, some ministers have been appointed on the strength of personality or even their closeness to the Prime Minister alone, and have no roots in Parliament. Having ensured that the government has a power base other than temporary coalitions between parties, the Constitution further reinforces the government's position in relation to Parliament by stating unequivocally in article 20 that the government determines and conducts national policy. To achieve this it has at its disposal both the civil service and the armed forces (article 20).

▶ The role of the Prime Minister

The Prime Minister is a key figure in the Constitution. The most important article of the Constitution in this context is article 21, which delineates the role of the Prime Minister. In addition, article 49 paragraph 1 provides that the Prime Minister pledges the responsibility of the government before the National Assembly; article 39 gives the Prime Minister the right to propose legislation and article 16 determines his or her role when the President is exercising emergency powers.

Leader of the government

Prime Ministers lead the government (article 21). While the Constitution states that they can be chosen and appointed by the President, their selection must bear in mind the practical imperative that they have to be able to command a majority in Parliament. Originally, under the Third Republic there was no Prime Minister as such, merely a minister with his own portfolio and the role of leader, known as the *Président du Conseil.* Under the Fifth Republic, Prime Ministers do not have their own departments. They concentrate exclusively on coordinating and leading other ministers. They preside over inter-ministerial meetings, have their own advisers and lead the debates of the *Conseil des ministres*, the equivalent of the British Cabinet.

Responsible for national defence

National defence is according to the Constitution shared between the President who is the head of the armed forces, the government which has the armed forces at its disposition, and the Prime Minister who has the ultimate responsibility for national defence (article 21). It is therefore clear that on this important subject all branches of the executive must cooperate. Only in times of emergency, when article 16 is in use, are all powers vested in one pair of hands, those of the President.

Representative of the government in Parliament

Prime Ministers are traditionally seen as having the role of representing the government in Parliament. Article 49 para. 1 states that they pledge this responsibility, which is a much weaker requirement than that under the Third and Fourth Republics, where the government could not even take office until it had so pledged its responsibility. Reflecting partly the fact that government power does not derive from the National Assembly, various governments and Prime Ministers have taken different views on the timing of this event. It quite often takes place shortly after the government has been appointed, as was the case recently with Prime Minister Dominique de Villepin. It remains, however, at the Prime Minister's discretion. Edith Cresson formed a government in 1991, and failed to arrange to make the pledge before she had ceased to hold office a mere ten months later. Parliament can refuse to accept the government by a simple majority.

Holder of regulatory powers

The Prime Minister has the power to make both primary and secondary legislation (article 21). It is one of the novel and unique features of the Fifth Republic that law-making powers are shared between Parliament and government, a fact that is discussed in more detail in Chapter 3. There are two types of primary regulatory powers exercised by the government. First, matters classified as not being within the scope of parliamentary legislation are subject to legislation by government decrees under article 37. Secondly, Parliament can delegate the power to make laws under article 38, so as to enable important and urgent legislation to be enacted quickly. In relation to article 37, legislation concerning matters of low importance will not be discussed by the Cabinet and will come within the exclusive power of the Prime Minister; legislation concerning more important matters will be discussed by the Cabinet, and will require the countersignature of the President. As regards article 38, legislation by *ordonnances* is, arguably, within the exclusive power of the government (see p. 28).

In relation to regulatory powers, as is usual in most mature democratic systems, Acts of Parliament are implemented by the government, and can be supplemented by secondary legislation to facilitate this. Most of this secondary legislation is the sole responsibility of the Prime Minister, though he or she will in practice consult the ministers responsible.

Presenter of Bills

Prime Ministers can put forward Bills to Parliament. This right is shared with other members of the government (article 39). About three quarters of all Bills are currently introduced by the Government.

Adviser to the President

Presidents must consult the Prime Minister before they can exercise many of their most important powers (see p. 31). While the ultimate decision is made by the President, the need for consultation is no mere formality, given the status of the Prime Minister. Instances would include the dissolution of the National Assembly under article 12 and the exercise of emergency powers under article 16.

The working relationship between the President and Prime Minister

In practice, the role of Prime Minister and his or her relationship with the President is very different when they are backed by the same parties (the usual situation) than when they are not (during *cohabitation*). Table 2.5 lists the Presidents and Prime Ministers of the Fifth Republic. When Presidents have a majority in Parliament they behave like the leader of their party and are entirely free to appoint a Prime Minister of their own choosing. On the other hand, in case of *cohabitation*, there is a hostile majority in Parliament and Parliament will impose its choice of Prime Minister on the President. The balance of power between the two heads of the executive will vary greatly, depending on the existence or not of a *cohabitation*. In the absence of *cohabitation*, Presidents play both the role of head of state, as mentioned in the Constitution, and head of government, not expressly mentioned in the Constitution. They become all powerful, and have often been compared to a republican monarch. They outline the government's policy which the Prime Minister, ordinarily a person the President can trust, then attempts to carry out. That the balance of power is so much in favour of the President was acknowledged by Jean-Pierre Raffarin, who had just been chosen by Chirac to be his Prime Minister in May 2002, when he said that 'Chirac will form the Government, I will not necessarily have my say.' Again in 2004 he said that 'the strength of a Prime Minister, nowadays, is not his independence, but his influence ... I am at the same time number two of the executive [behind the President] and number one of the Parliamentary majority. I don't have any problem with this situation.' At about the same time, a member of Raffarin's government, Patrick Devedjian, expressed the same views: 'the President provides his very precise and rigorous instructions, and the Prime Minister follows and applies them.' Jacques Chirac, while he was Prime Minister under Valéry Giscard d'Estaing, deplored his lack

Table 2.5 Presidents and Prime Ministers of France: Fifth Republic

The Presidents of the Fifth Republic	The Prime Ministers of the Fifth Republic
Charles de Gaulle 1958–1969	Michel Debré 1959–1962 Georges Pompidou 1962–1968 Maurice Couve de Murville 1968–1969
Georges Pompidou 1969–1974	Jacques Chaban-Delmas 1969–1972 Pierre Messmer 1972–1974
Valéry Giscard d'Estaing 1974–1981	Jacques Chirac 1974–1976 Raymond Barre 1976–1981
François Mitterand 1981–1995	Pierre Mauroy 1981–1984 Laurent Fabius 1984–1986 Jacques Chirac 1986–1988* Michel Rocard 1988–1991 Edith Cresson 1991–1992 Pierre Bérégovoy 1992–1993 Edouard Balladur 1993–1995*
Jacques Chirac 1995–	Alain Juppé 1995–1997 Lionel Jospin 1997–2002* Jean-Pierre Raffarin 2002–2005 Dominique de Villepin 2005–

*indicates a period of *cohabitation*

of independence in carrying out the government's policies, and decided to resign in 1976, after only a couple of years.

In case of *cohabitation*, however, the balance of power shifts dramatically in favour of the Prime Minister, who ceases to be in a position of dependence upon the President and becomes the genuine head of government. This enables him or her to carry out his or her own policies without having to refer them to the President first for approval. When President Chirac contended in 1997, at the beginning of the last *cohabitation*, that 'the Constitution gives the President a pre-eminent role [over the Prime Minister], and ultimately, the final say,' his opposition Prime Minister at the time, Lionel Jospin, replied angrily that 'there is no domain of French politics where the President would have the final say.' Lionel Jospin reiterated these views in 2000, saying that 'the President can always say, but can't do.'

The existence of a *cohabitation* is not only of importance in determining how the powers are shared between the President and the Prime Minister, but also when the Prime Minister leaves office. Article 8 of the Constitution specifies that the Prime Minister offers his resignation to the President. General de Gaulle, one of the main influences on the Constitution, explained on 8 August 1958, before the new Constitution had come into force, that the Prime Minister was 'under no circumstances accountable towards the President,' and hence could not be forced by the President to resign. This interpretation was ignored by successive Presidents, who sacked their Prime Ministers at will. When Michel Rocard was forced against his will to stand down as Prime Minister in 1991, he stated: 'I have been sacked.' In order to avoid being seen as breaching the Constitution, Presidents traditionally ask their Prime Ministers to offer their letter of resignation. Presidents will usually get rid of Prime Ministers if they do not appear to have the backing of the electorate any more. President Mitterrand replaced his Prime Minister Michel Rocard in 1991 by the first woman Prime Minister, Edith Cresson, only to get rid of her a few months later because of her lack of popularity. More recently, President Chirac replaced Jean-Pierre Raffarin by Dominique de Villepin, as his Prime Minister's lack of popularity was starting to have an implication on his own popularity. In case of *cohabitation*, however, the President will not have any influence on the Prime Minister and will not be able to remove him or her from office. It comes therefore as no surprise that one of the longest serving Prime Ministers was Lionel Jospin, who held office for five years during a period of *cohabitation*.

▶ Ministers

Members of the government must resign their parliamentary seats on appointment under article 23. Their parliamentary functions are carried out by a substitute. The political reasoning is that members of government are likely to be more loyal to the government and less likely to resign if they cannot simply, as in Westminster, continue to represent their constituency in Parliament as ordinary members. The Constitution does not, however, forbid members of the government from holding local or regional appointments. Traditionally, in order to keep in touch with their constituents, they often combined their ministerial position with that of being an elected mayor or regional official. However, Lionel Jospin created a precedent by requiring all the members of his government to resign from any local or regional appointments to focus on their ministerial functions. The two following Prime Ministers, Jean-Pierre Raffarin and Dominique de Villepin, decided to follow suit.

Article 23 also forbids ministers from exercising any professional activity or employment in the public sector or any position of professional representation at national level. This has led to members of government holding a number of posts which are not within the prohibited categories including, as mentioned above, posts in local politics, but also posts at European level as Members of the European Parliament. This practice is under review and constitutional reforms have been proposed.

Ranking of ministers

Though the Constitution makes no reference to this, in practice four different types of ministers exist:

1 Ministers of State. Their number has varied enormously according to the personalities involved, but there are rarely more than five. These may be ministers of an important department, but the title can also be an honorary one. Under de Gaulle, the writer, André Malraux, was regularly both Minister of Cultural Affairs (even in France a minor post) and Minister of State to mark his closeness to the President.
2 Ministers of a department.
3 Auxiliary ministers. These are known as *ministres délégués* and assist the other ministers to carry out their responsibilities.
4 Junior ministers. These are appointed to help a particular ministry and are the only ones that are not a member of the Cabinet. They fall outside article 23 and are usually Members of Parliament.

The Cabinet

Ministers usually meet once a week, traditionally on a Wednesday. This meeting is chaired by the President of the Republic and is held at the President's official residence, the *Elysée Palace*. Only exceptionally can the Prime Minister be authorised to chair the meeting as deputy for the President, and then only for a specific, predetermined agenda. It is clear that the function of the President as chair is not a purely symbolic one. The manner in which this function is exercised depends on the personalities involved, and even more so on whether they are backed by the same parliamentary parties. On 14 February 2001 President Chirac refused to allow a Bill relating to the status of Corsica to be discussed in Cabinet. He justified his decision by pointing out that the *Conseil d'Etat* had criticised the bill in a previous advisory opinion. The Bill, which allowed Corsica to be exempt from several French statutes and introduced the right to learn the Corsican language at nursery school, was seen as clashing with France's constitutional principle of an indivisible, united Republic. This was only temporary, however, as Jacques Chirac agreed for the Bill to be put on the agenda of the following Cabinet meeting.

That said, as is inevitable, much real work in political terms is done before the Cabinet meeting takes place, and in times of *cohabitation* such work will receive no input from the President's party. The Cabinet has many functions, some constitutional, and some set down in various laws. In particular, it plays a crucial role in ensuring that government legislation passes smoothly through the parliamentary channels, and is responsible for regulations made under article 37. It may also, exceptionally, be responsible for passing a particular type of law known as *ordonnances*, which we will study further in Chapter 3. Furthermore, the Prime Minister is entitled to organise regular meetings with the members of his government outside Cabinet, without the presence of the President of the Republic. These meetings have taken place regularly during times of *cohabitation*.

• •

PART IV: PARLIAMENT

▶ Introduction

The Parliament of the Fifth Republic exercises legislative powers, and acts as a check on government action. There are two Houses of Parliament, the National Assembly and the Senate (Table 2.6). The National Assembly is the more important, reflecting the fact that it is directly elected. While laws are normally debated and agreed by both Houses of Parliament, if the Senate ultimately disagrees with the National Assembly it has only limited powers to delay the passing of the law. Like the House of Lords, the Senate ensures that there is an independent scrutiny of parliamentary legislation, and that controversial Bills are fully debated. As to the role of keeping a check on the government, this is exercised on a day-to-day basis in ways which have developed through practice. Parliament may also pass a motion of censure (article 49). Unlike the legislative power which is shared between the two Houses, the motion of censure can only be voted by the National Assembly.

Table 2.6 The French Parliament: the two houses

National Assembly	Senate
Lower House	Upper House
577 deputies	Currently 331 senators (341 in 2007, 346 in 2010)
Term: 5 years	Term: 6 years
Candidates' minimum age: 23	Candidates' minimum age: 30
Direct elections, every 5 years	Indirect elections of a half of all senators every 3 years
Each constituency elects one deputy	Elected by an electoral college (consists of members of the NA & local representatives taken from various levels)
President presides over the Congress	President replaces the President of the Republic in case of vacancy
Dissolution possible after decision by President	
Can hold the Prime Minister and his Government accountable through a motion of censure	

▶ Members of Parliament

The National Assembly has 577 members and sits in the *Palais Bourbon* in Paris. Members of the National Assembly are directly elected by the voters in their parliamentary constituency. However, unlike Members of Parliament in the United Kingdom who represent their constituents, their French counterparts collectively and individually represent all French people and not specifically their constituents. They are elected for a five-year term, though the President may dissolve the National Assembly and call an election before the end of this period (article 12).

There are 331 senators who sit at the *Palais du Luxembourg* in Paris. They are indirectly elected by a college of mayors and local councillors. Candidates must be at least 30 years old and are elected for a period of six years. Membership of the Senate rotates, with half the senators standing for re-election every three years. The President of the Senate replaces the President of the Republic in case of vacancy. This has taken place twice since 1958: in 1969 after General de Gaulle's resignation from the Presidency, and in 1974 following Georges Pompidou's death.

The current electoral system is biased in favour of rural communities and small towns. Senators elected in such areas represent far fewer inhabitants than those in large towns. The Senate was subject to some important reforms in July 2003; reform proposals had been on the agenda since the 1980s. In 1998, the Prime Minister at the time, Lionel Jospin, had publicly criticised the Senate and pointed out the need for reforms in an article in *Le Monde*, by declaring that '[a] chamber like the Senate, with so many powers, where a change of power is never possible, which is not elected directly by the people and which is not even based on a federation – since we have a unitary State ... is an anomaly among democracies.'

The original nine-year mandate was the longest of any political mandates in Europe and was considered by the original drafters of the Constitution as a necessary element of stability for a place where reflection and caution is paramount. But the Socialist government felt that stability should not mean stagnation. This had in practice been the case with the right-wing political parties having always had a permanent majority since 1958 and the same President, Alain Poher, for 24 years, re-elected a final time at the age of 80. In June 1999 the President of the Senate, Christian Poncelet, agreed in principle to consider some changes, but made it clear that the proposed reforms should not threaten the independence of the Senate, and should allow it to continue to control parliamentary legislation. He set up a think-tank in November 2001 to consider possible reforms to modernise the Senate. Its report, adopted by the Senate in July 2002, was the basis for the reforms that followed in 2003. The most important reform was to reduce the senators' mandate from nine years to six years, with half the Senate being renewed every three years instead of a third every three years. A second symbolic measure taken was to reduce the minimum age for Senatorial candidates from 35 to 30 years, to give it a more modern image, in touch with the younger members of society. It is, however, worth noticing that it is not yet on a par with the National Assembly, where the minimum age for candidates is 23 years, as some experience of a mandate at a local level is seen as beneficial before becoming a senator. Finally, the number of senators was increased, mainly in the urban areas to take into account demographical changes, so that there will be 346 senators by 2010.

In order to ensure the politicians' independence, there are strict rules on outside interests. In particular, Members of Parliament cannot also be members of the government, or of the *Conseil constitutionnel*, or sit in both Houses of Parliament, nor can they be civil servants. While in principle employment or self-employment in the private sector is allowed and even encouraged, a number of restrictions have been made. The most important provisions are contained in Acts of 1958 and 1972, which prohibit the holding of senior posts in public companies or private companies with substantial dealings with the government. Members are allowed to hold unpaid local government posts. The vast majority of Members of the National Assembly in fact have such a post in order to reinforce links with their constituency. In the UK, and in many other countries, such double mandates are not allowed. In France it has led to some concern, in that having both a national and a local mandate can lead to overwork, but it can also lead to a person being overpaid for the work they are actually doing. An Act of 30 December 1985 attempted to cut down on abuses of the system by restricting the number of mandates that could be held by a single person to two. At the time of writing, Bills are being debated by both Houses of Parliament proposing the abolition of such dual mandates. The new legislation would also affect the Senate, as many senators hold other elected posts, as well as their seat in the Senate. Paragraph 4 of article 46 of the Constitution states that constitutional statutes affecting the Senate must be voted in identical terms by both Houses. This gives the Senate a power of veto. It is expected that the Senate will use this in order to ensure that the proposed reform on dual mandates, and the reform on the method of election of the Senate mentioned above, take its views into account.

Members of Parliament are also required to make confidential statements as to their assets. They still have far more privacy in such matters than their British or North American counterparts, but in this area too, the situation is changing, and there is pressure for the law to be reformed.

The government sometimes addresses Parliament, though there is no fixed time for this, unlike the Queen's speech in the Parliament at Westminster which takes place at the beginning of each parliamentary session. The control of Parliament is very much a formal control exercised over the legislative Bills, and the day-to-day dialogue with the ruling party and the opposition does not take place in the same way as in the United Kingdom. Parliament may pass a motion of censure, following the procedure in article 49. The provisions have been carefully drafted to avoid the excessive use of the parliamentary motion of censure which was a characteristic of the Fourth Republic. The motion will only be passed if an absolute majority of members of the National Assembly votes in favour of it, and each member is restricted to signing three motions of censure in each ordinary session of Parliament.

Members of both the National Assembly and the Senate are not accountable for any activity carried out as part of their parliamentary duties. Before 1995, Members of Parliament also benefited from immunity from criminal prosecution, whether or not the prosecution related to acts concerned with the carrying out of their duties. Such immunity could be lifted, and this happened on two occasions in relation to Bernard Tapie, a high-profile businessman and politician, who was subsequently convicted of fraud. Since 1995, Members of Parliament no longer benefit from this immunity from criminal prosecution, except in relation to acts done in the carrying out of their duties.

▶ Acts of Parliament

The procedure for making an Act of Parliament is set out in articles 39 to 45 of the Constitution. Article 39 provides that the Prime Minister can make recommendations for government Bills. These must be approved by the *Conseil d'Etat* and the Cabinet (*Conseil des ministres*). Members of Parliament can also make suggestions for legislation, embodied in private members' Bills. With priority being given during Parliamentary sessions to the agenda established by Government (art. 48), except for one session every month, most proposals emanate from the government itself, and there is little chance that individual members' Bills will complete the law-making process detailed below, unless they have government support. They will not be given priority and will not receive help in speeding them along. Another limitation imposed on individual members' Bills, specified in article 40 of the Constitution, prevents these Bills from either reducing public revenues or increasing expenditures. The Bill abolishing the death penalty in 1981, for example, had to originate from a Government proposal as a prisoner sentenced for life is more expensive than a prisoner sentenced to death.

The general rule is that statutes must be approved by both Houses of Parliament. Following reforms in 1995, there is one ordinary Parliamentary session, taking place between October and June, with Parliament sitting for a maximum of 120 days. The process can begin in either House (article 42) and article 45 sets out the procedures to be followed to reach agreement between the two Houses. Once the originating House has approved the original draft, it will send it for debate by the other, which will in due course return it, usually with amendments. This procedure, known as the shuttle (*la navette*), can continue until both Houses of Parliament agree on the final wording, and there is no time limit imposed on this process. Acts (*lois ordinaires*) must be voted by a simple majority of members (but there is a different procedure for certain special types of Act, see below). The Constitution requires that votes be made in person, to cut down on absenteeism.

Prime Ministers are given the power, under article 45, to refer disputed laws to a special committee, known as *la commission mixte paritaire*, composed of seven people nominated from each House. They are not obliged to use this power, and in practice they do allow minor pieces of legislation to run their course – about two thirds of Bills are passed without the intervention of the commission. For urgent legislation, this referral can be made if agreement has not been reached after the first reading in each House, otherwise the referral can only be made after two readings have taken place. Once the commission has been appointed, the equality of the Houses of Parliament is replaced by the clear predominance of the National Assembly. If the commission agrees to the Bill being passed, this will then be approved by both the National Assembly and the Senate. If it does not, the Bill will be debated by the National Assembly only, and the version agreed by it will become law. Accordingly, the Senate can delay matters, and if the government chooses not to appoint the commission, the delay can be considerable. It cannot however stop a Bill from being passed altogether. The government can further speed up the passing of Bills by requiring that measures be either vetoed or voted as drawn (article 44 paragraph 3). This procedure is known as *bloc voté* and has been much used (or abused) by minority governments. It is a blunter instrument than the English guillotine procedure (which imposes time limits on debates), as it simply enables the government to push through Bills. Even more draconian is the procedure of the vote of confidence under article 49 paragraph 3 (Fig. 2.3), which simply gives Parliament the choice of vetoing the Bill, precipitating a general election, or passing it without debate.

In a recent study, the academic Raymond Ferretti identified three different reasons why a government might want to use article 49 paragraph 3:

- In some circumstances, even though its party has the majority in Parliament, the Government will want to pass a Bill via article 49 paragraph 3 that is not necessarily to the liking of all the members of its party. This was the traditional use of the motion of censure in the first years of the Fifth Republic.

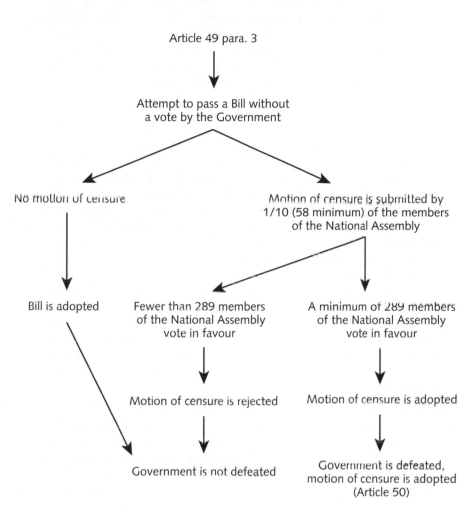

Fig. 2.3 Article 49 paragraph 3: how the Government may be defeated

- In other cases, the opposition in Parliament might attempt to disrupt the Government's work in Parliament by introducing a disproportionately high number of amendments to a Bill discussed in Parliament. The Prime Minister, Jean-Pierre Raffarin, resorted to article 49 paragraph 3 in February 2003 after the socialist party presented 12,500 amendments to a Government Bill aiming to reform the electoral system in European and local elections. A few years earlier, the Prime Minister at the time, Lionel Jospin, vowed never to use article 49 paragraph 3, out of respect for Parliament's work. The result was that numerous bills took an awfully long time to go through Parliament because of the large number of amendments introduced by the opposition. The most striking example was a Bill aiming to introduce a civil pact giving couples, even same sex couples, some of the benefits and responsibilities of marriage. This Bill took a whole year and a hundred hours of debate before finally being adopted by Parliament. Article 49 paragraph 3 signifies that no debate will take place, and that the Bill will almost immediately be ready to be promulgated by the President of the Republic.

- Finally, the Government's lack of an absolute majority in Parliament might justify the use of article 49 paragraph 3 in order to allow the Government to carry out its Parliamentary activities. During François Mitterrand's second Presidency, his socialist party gained 48% of the seats at the National Assembly. The communist party, with 4.5% of the seats, refused to join in a coalition with the socialists, but declared that it would not attempt to topple the Government using article 49 paragraph 3. The Socialist Government made the most of this situation, and each time that it could not get a Bill passed in Parliament, it resorted to article 49 paragraph 3 as it knew perfectly well that the Government could not be toppled without votes from the Socialist and Communist parties. The Prime Minister, Michel Rocard, made the most use of article 49 paragraph 3, using it 27 times between 1988 and 1991. His Government, in 1990, came to within five votes of being toppled.

Parliamentary powers are further curtailed in that its standing orders must be approved by the *Conseil constitutionnel* under article 61 paragraph 1.

There are certain special types of Act which require a stricter procedure to be followed for their adoption. These include Finance Acts, Social Security Finance Acts and Acts authorising the ratification of a treaty. Finance Acts annually fix the revenue and expenditure of the state. The procedure to be followed for their adoption is specified in article 47 and the *ordonnance* of 2 January 1959. Article 47 requires the examination and vote of a Finance Act to take place within 70 days. If Parliament has not voted it within this time the budget can be settled by an *ordonnance* passed by the government.

The Act of 22 February 1996 reformed the Constitution and created the Social Security Finance Acts, which follow a procedure laid down by a constitutional Act of 22 July 1996. This procedure is very close to that applicable to Finance Acts. They must be examined within 50 days, and failure to do so allows the government to introduce a Bill by means of an *ordonnance*.

Once laws have been voted by Parliament, they must be both promulgated and published before they become enforceable against ordinary citizens.

Promulgation

Presidents are responsible for promulgating Acts under article 10 of the Constitution. They have two weeks to decide to:

- require the legislation to be debated again by Parliament (rarely used in practice); or
- refer the legislation to the *Conseil constitutionnel* to check its constitutionality (never used in practice).

Once this time limit has passed, or once the *Conseil constitutionnel* has confirmed that the legislation complies with the Constitution or any parliamentary debate requested by the President has been completed, the Act must be promulgated. Standard terms are used to express the fact that the Act has been promulgated, and will include mention of references to the *Conseil constitutionnel* or the additional parliamentary debate as appropriate (Decree of 8 March 1990). The kernel of the wording is a statement by the President that the Act has been adopted by the National Assembly and the Senate, or by the French people, following a referendum. The President, in other words, confirms that a new Act of Parliament has come into existence.

Publication

Publication takes place in the Official Journal and for legislation of the European Union, in the Official Journal of the European Communities.

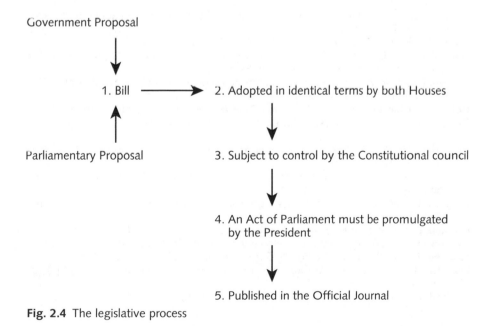

Fig. 2.4 The legislative process

An Act is binding one whole day after its publication. For example, an Act which is placed in the Official Journal appearing on 1 May is binding in Paris from the early morning hours of 3 May. Through publication everyone is presumed to have been informed of the text, so that it may subsequently be justly enforced against members of the public. Sometimes the legislation itself lays down rules specifying when a particular Act will come into force, and fixes a date later than publication, considering the text to be too complex to come into force immediately. Figure 2.4 summarises the passage of a piece of legislation from proposal to publication.

• •

BIBLIOGRAPHY FOR CHAPTER 2

Bastien, F. (2000), *Quinquennat – Conséquences politiques*, Paris: Economica

Beaud, O. and Lauvaux, P. (2003), 'Sur le soi-disant *"impeachment* à la française"', *D.* 2003, 2646

Bell, J. (1995), *French Constitutional Law*, Oxford: Clarendon Press

Brachet, B. (2000), *Droit constitutionnel et administratif: capacité en droit, DEUG droit*, Paris: A.E.S.

Bréhier, T. (1997), 'Une lecture stricte de la Constitution', *Le Monde*, 3 June 1997

Bremner, C. (2002), 'Poll victory gives Chirac complete control', *The Times*, 18 June 2002

Burdeau, G., Hamon, F. and Troper, M. (2001), *Droit constitutionnel*, Paris: Librairie générale de droit et de jurisprudence

Chagnollaud, D. (2004), *Droit constitutionnel contemporain, tome 2 (Histoire constitutionnelle – La Vème République)*, Paris: Dalloz–Armand Colin, 2nd edn

Chantebout, B. (2005), *Droit consitutionnel et science politique*, Paris: Armand Colin Editeur

Chemin, A. (2002), 'Jacques Chirac est réélu à l'Elysée grâce à la gauche mobilisée', *Le Monde*, 7 May 2002

Cohendet, M.-A. (2002), *Le président de la République*, Paris: Dalloz

Colombani, J.-M. (2000), 'La réduction du mandat présidentiel est approuvée à une majorité des deux tiers', *Le Monde*, 25 September 2000

Constitution de la République française (2005), texte présenté par Ferdinand Mélin-Soucramanien, Paris: Armand Colin

Debbasch, Charles (2004), *Constitution – Vème République*, Paris: Dalloz, 4th edn

De La Gorce, P.-M. and Moschetto, B. (2005), *La Vème République, Que Sais-je?*, Paris: PUF, 10th edn

De Virieu, H. (1998), 'Les élections sénatoriales, une affaire de "professionnels"', *Le Monde*, 13 August 1998

Documents d'études, Le Gouvernement de la Cinquième République (2002), La Documentation Française

Dreyfus, F. and d'Arcy, F. (1997), *Les institutions politiques et administratives de la France*, Paris: Economica

Duhamel, O. (2002), 'Osons la VIème République', *Le Monde*, 5/6 May 2002

Favoreu, L. (2003), 'Le statut pénal du chef de l'Etat', *D.* 2003, 430

Favoreu, L. and Philip, L. (2005), *Le Conseil constitutionnel, Que sais-je?*, Paris: PUF

Ferretti, R. (2003), 'Le retour du 49.3', http://www.rajf.org/article.php3?id_article=1518

Foillard, P. (2004), *Droit constitutionnel*, Orléans: Paradigmes – CPU

Formery, S.-L. (1996), *La Constitution commentée – article par article*, Paris: Hachette Supérieur

François, B. and Montebourg, A. (2005), 'Une nouvelle Constitution: la fin de l'exception française' *D.* 2005, 2473

Gattegno, H. (2002), 'Sur le statut pénal du président, dires d'experts', 7–8 July 2002

Gattegno, H. and Ridet, P. (2002), 'Le duel Chirac–Le Pen provoque un séisme politique', *Le Monde*, 23 April 2002

Gouaud-Tandeau de Marsac, C. (2005), *Droit constitutionnel – la Vème République*, Paris: Ellipses

Jackson, V. and Tushnet, M. (1999), *Comparative Constitutional Law*, St. Paul, MN: Foundation Press

Mathieu, B. (2003), 'Les propositions de la 'commission Avril' relatives au statut juridictionnel du Président de la République', *JCP* 2003, 53

Maus, D. (1998), *Les grands textes de la pratique institutionelle de la Cinquième République*, Paris: Documentation française

Pactet, P. and Mélin-Soucramanien, F. (2004), *Droit constitutionnel*, Paris: Dalloz–Armand Colin

Piastra, R. (2004), 'Les 46 ans de la Ve République', *D.* 2004, 3147

Piastra, R. (2004), 'Quelques propos sur l'article 49–3 de la Constitution', *D.* 2004, 2659

Portelli, H. (2005), *Droit constitutionnel*, Paris: Dalloz

Prevost, J.-F. (1987), 'L'éclipse partielle du chef de l'Etat en cas de cohabitation', *Le Monde*, 3 February 1987

Robert-Diard, P. (2005), Jacques Chirac, l'absent de son procès, *Le Monde*, 7 July 2005

Rousseau, D. (1998), 'Les transformations du droit constitutionnel sous la Vème République, *Revue du droit public* 1998, 1780

Zarka, J.-C. (2003), 'La réforme du Sénat', *JCP* 2003, 1341

Web Resources

Website: www.assemblee-nationale.fr: The National Assembly. Includes some text in English.

Website: www.elysee.fr: The President of the Republic. Includes some text in English

Website: www.journal-officiel.gouv.fr: Internet version of the Official Journal

Website: www.premier-ministre.gouv.fr: The Prime Minister. Includes some text in English

Website: www.vie-publique.fr: An official government website providing general information on the Constitution and administration of France

Website: www.rajf.org: *Revue de l'actualité juridique française*

Website: www.senat.fr: The Senate

Written sources of law

INTRODUCTION

A distinction can be drawn between written and unwritten sources of law. Written sources are those which are laid down by a public authority; unwritten sources may still be written down but not by a public authority. The former will be studied in this chapter and the latter in Chapter 4. The different written sources will be considered according to their position in the hierarchy of legal sources (also known as the hierarchy of norms) (Fig. 3.1).

It is important to know the rank of the different sources, as those lower in the hierarchy must conform to those with a higher status. We shall start with the highest source of law: the Constitution.

The 'constitutional block' Constitution of 1958 Preamble to the 1958 Constitution Declaration of Human and Civil Rights of 1789 Preamble to the 1946 Constitution The fundamental principles recognised by the laws of the Republic Charter for the Environment of 2004
International sources Treaties European Law
Constitutional Statutes
Parliamentary Statutes
***Ordonnances* and Regulations**

Fig. 3.1 The hierarchy of sources of law

••••••••••••••••••••••••••

PART I: THE CONSTITUTION

The present French Constitution, which established the Fifth Republic, is at the top of the hierarchy of the French sources of law. It was passed in 1958 and was masterminded by General de Gaulle. He considered that constitutional reform was necessary to increase the powers of the executive, especially the President, to govern the country effectively, and in particular to bring an end to the war in Algeria.

▶ The 'constitutional block'

In law, the Constitution is not simply the 1958 text, but also:

- the preamble to the 1958 Constitution;
- the Declaration of Human and Civil Rights of 1789;
- the preamble to the 1946 Constitution;
- the fundamental principles recognised by the laws of the Republic and referred to by the 1946 preamble;
- the Charter for the Environment of 2004.

Together these are known as the 'constitutional block' (*le bloc de con stitutionnalité*). This approach stems from the decision of the *Conseil constitutionnel* of 16 July 1971 which arose from an action brought by Simone de Beauvoir following the social unrest in 1968. Simone de Beauvoir had, with others, established a group called the *Association des Amis de la Cause du Peuple*. It aimed to provide legal and moral support for those who had found themselves in difficulty as a result of their participation in the political movement. The local Prefect had refused to allow this group to register its existence, without which formality it could not function effectively. The refusal had been issued on an order from the Minister of the Interior, who was anxious to fight what he felt was a threat of subversion. An action was initially brought against this refusal before an administrative court, which quashed the Prefect's refusal as illegal. The Minister realised that as the law stood at the time the refusal had been illegal, but decided to legislate to enable such decisions to be made in the future. On 30 June 1971 the National Assembly voted in favour of an Act which would have allowed a Prefect to suspend its decision on whether or not to register an association until a court had ruled on that organisation's legality. The President of the Senate submitted the Act to the scrutiny of the *Conseil constitutionnel*. In its deliberations it pointed out that the Act had to comply with the Constitution but also with the preamble to the 1958 Constitution. Under the preamble to the 1958 Constitution:

> The French people solemnly proclaim their commitment to human rights and to Rights of Man and the principles of national sovereignty defined in the Declaration of 1789 and confirmed and completed by the Preamble to the Constitution of 1946.

The *Conseil constitutionnel* took these references to the 1789 Declaration and the 1946 preamble and said that they were by implication part of the Constitution – despite the fact that the latter did not have this status under the Fourth Republic. The 1946 preamble itself refers to the '... fundamental principles recognised by the laws of the Republic'. While its original drafters were probably simply intending to pay homage to the work of the Third Republic, the *Conseil constitutionnel* used this vague statement to justify its opinion that these 'fundamental principles' also formed part of the Constitution.

The Constitution was given this broad interpretation because the document of 1958 was primarily concerned with laying down the relative powers of the government institutions and did not mention the rights of French citizens. The 1789 Declaration clearly does lay down these rights, particularly the traditional freedoms of an individual, such as freedom of movement and freedom of speech. The 1946 preamble – written at a time when the communists had considerable influence in France – contains social and economic rights such as the right to join a trade union, freedom to strike, the right to work and the right to asylum.

The 'fundamental principles recognised by the laws of the Republic' referred to by the 1946 preamble are a very vague concept. They allow the *Conseil constitutionnel* to look at Acts that have been passed before 1946 and extract from them their underlying fundamental principles. This gives the *Conseil constitutionnel* a very free hand as there is no definitive list of what these fundamental principles are and they exist only inasmuch as the *Conseil constitutionnel* declares that they do in its decisions. The principles tend to be founded on legislation laying down rights and freedoms under the Third Republic (1875–1940), which was an important period of social liberalism in France. The *Conseil constitutionnel* draws a clear distinction between the underlying principle in the text which has constitutional status, and the text itself which does not. These fundamental principles have been found to include the right to strike, freedom of information, the principle of equality and the right to a hearing. In the judgment of 16 July 1971 the *Conseil constitutionnel* confirmed that freedom of association was one of these fundamental principles which could be extracted from an ordinary Act of Parliament of 1 July 1901. As the Bill being considered by the *Conseil constitutionnel* was found to breach the principle of the 1901 Act, it was held to be partly unconstitutional.

In 2005, the preamble to the Constitution was amended to refer to a new Charter for the Environment. The inclusion of this Charter in the constitutional block is intended to highlight the growing importance of environmental issues for the future of France. Any future legislation should now be compatible with this Charter.

▶ Application of the constitutional provisions

Certain provisions of the 'constitutional block' are not clear enough to constitute legal rules that can be applied in practice. Where they amount to a simple declaration of intention on the part of those drafting the Constitution – for example, the right to work or the guarantee of rest and leisure time laid down in the 1946 preamble – the constitutional value of this principle, while undisputed, will be of very little real use to the citizen. For example, the *Conseil d'Etat* has on occasion found the protection of the right to asylum in the 1946 preamble to be too vague to be applied (C.E. 27 September 1985, *France Terre d'Asile*). On the other hand, the *Conseil constitutionnel* has found it to be sufficiently clear to annul certain provisions of a law on immigration (Cons. const. 13 August 1993). This decision led the government to limit the scope of the preamble on the issue of asylum, by adding article 53-1 to the Constitution by an Act of 25 November 1993.

The different elements of the 'constitutional block' all have to conform with the 1958 text. It is more difficult to determine which rule should take priority where a conflict arises between sources other than the 1958 text. Conflicts can arise particularly between the principles laid down in the 1789 Declaration and the 1946 preamble, which were written in different centuries with a very different philosophical inspiration. While the former lays down the rights of the individual, the latter is concerned with economic and social rights. The right to property, for example, is considered to be an untouchable, sacred right in article 17 of the 1789 Declaration, but is submitted to various restrictions by the 1946 preamble. The *Conseil constitutionnel* seeks to deal with such problems on a case-by-case basis. Thus, for example, the fundamental principle of 'continuity of public service' is interpreted as allowing certain restrictions on the right to strike which is expressly protected by the 1946 preamble (Cons. const. 25 July 1979), while in 1991 preference was given to the right to the protection of one's health laid down in 1946 over the freedom of the individual and the freedom of commerce and industry protected by the 1789 Declaration (Cons. const. 8 January 1991).

• •

PART II: INTERNATIONAL SOURCES

▶ Integration into national law

Part VI of the Constitution is concerned with treaties and international agreements, terms which will be used here interchangeably except where we are considering their procedural differences. There are two possible approaches that countries can take to international law. Under the dualist system, an international treaty to which a country is a signatory does not automatically become law in that country. Instead a national law must first be passed to introduce it into domestic law and it then has the same legal status as that legislation. This is the approach taken by the United Kingdom. Under the monist approach the treaty automatically becomes law in the country on its signature, with a higher legal status than ordinary Acts of Parliament. This is essentially the approach taken by France, though in a limited number of cases listed in article 53, ratification or approval must be authorised by an Act of Parliament. These are peace treaties, trade agreements, treaties relating to international organisations, state finances, amending legislation directly affecting private individuals, or giving rise to the transfer, exchange or appendage of territory. In addition, a government can seek the approval of Parliament even where not obliged by law to do so. This happened in relation to the decision of the European Council in 1976 for the election of European Members of Parliament by universal suffrage: although not bound to do so by article 53, the government chose to refer the matter to Parliament which gave its authorisation by an Act of 30 June 1977.

Under article 11, the President of the Republic can submit to a referendum an Act 'aiming to authorise the ratification of a treaty which, without being contrary to the Constitution, would affect the functioning of its institutions'. These provisions allow the President, if he or she wishes, to seek authorisation directly from the people rather than from their representatives in Parliament. This provision was used by President Pompidou, who organised a referendum in 1972 on the ratification of the Brussels Treaty of the same year on the admission of the United Kingdom to the European Economic Community.

▶ International treaties

The principle of the superiority of international treaties over legal norms other than the Constitution has been clearly laid down by the Constitution, but the judges have sometimes been hesitant to apply this principle in practice. The main rules on the question can be found in article 55:

> Treaties or agreements regularly ratified or approved have, from
> the date of their publication, an authority superior to that of Acts of
> Parliament, provided that, for each agreement or treaty, it is being
> applied by the other party.

This article expressly states that international treaties and agreements are
of a higher status than ordinary parliamentary legislation. International
law applies automatically in France if the three following conditions are
satisfied:

1 it has been ratified or approved;
2 published; and
3 applied by the other signatories.

Each of these conditions will be considered in turn. On the first requirement, French law draws a distinction between formal treaties and
simplified agreements. The former are made according to a lengthy
procedure in the name of the President. After having been signed, they
need to be formally ratified, a procedure under which those with the
real authority to make the treaty express France's agreement to be bound
by it, by the exchange of letters of ratification confirming the signature
already given by their diplomatic representatives. It is this procedure
which brings the treaty into force. For example, a treaty establishing
an International Criminal Court was signed by France in July 1998 and
finally ratified in June 2000.

The agreements in a simplified form are concluded in the name of the
government, merely need to be approved rather than ratified, and come
into force on being signed. Approval results from letters of approval or
a decree publishing the agreement. It is very different from ratification
since the state is bound from the time of signature of the agreement and
cannot refuse to give its approval. In practice, the distinction between
ratification and approval is less clear cut, as French courts require the
same proof for both procedures: a decree of publication. While over
three quarters of the conventions entered into by France take the form
of simplified agreements, there are no rational criteria which determine whether a particular agreement requires the formal or simplified
form. Thus very important agreements can be made under the latter
procedure.

The second condition, requiring publication, only applies to treaties
and agreements that would affect the rights and obligations of individuals. Other international undertakings do not need to be published
as they are addressed to public authorities who have impliedly been
informed of their existence as they work under the executive authorities who made them. As a result not all treaties concluded by France are
published. Publication is usually in the Official Journal, though those
produced by international organisations, particularly the European

Union, are binding in France on publication in the Official Journal of the European Communities.

The third requirement is known as the principle of reciprocity. The judges cannot themselves decide that this condition has not been satisfied, and where a serious argument is presented on this matter, they have to seek, and are bound by, the opinion of the Minister of Foreign Affairs. However, this final condition of reciprocity is not absolute: on 22 January 1999, the *Conseil constitutionnel* decided that the condition of reciprocity is not applicable in relation to some multilateral treaties, especially when a country's obligations do not depend on another country's performance of its obligations. The *Conseil constitutionnel* was asked by the President of the Republic and the Prime Minister to confirm the constitutionality of the Treaty establishing the International Criminal Court before ratification. It decided that, among others, article 27 of the Treaty was contrary to the Constitution:

1 This Statute shall apply equally to all persons without any distinction based on official capacity. In particular, official capacity as a Head of State or Government, a member of a Government or parliament, an elected representative or a government official shall in no case exempt a person from criminal responsibility under this Statute, nor shall it, in and of itself, constitute a ground for reduction of sentence.
2 Immunities or special procedural rules which may attach to the official capacity of a person, whether under national or international law, shall not bar the Court from exercising its jurisdiction over such a person.

This provision was in direct contradiction with article 68 of the Constitution which enables the President of the Republic to enjoy immunity from prosecution while in office. It led to the creation of an additional article in the Constitution (article 53-2)

While the *Conseil constitutionnel* is prepared to make sure that a treaty does not conflict with the Constitution, it stated in its decision of 15 January 1975 that it is not within its powers to check whether an Act conforms with a treaty. An Act on abortion had been submitted to the *Conseil constitutionnel* by 60 Members of Parliament with a request that the court verify its conformity with the Constitution. One of the grounds for this application was that it breached article 2 of the European Convention on Human Rights and, in consequence, breached article 55 of the Constitution. However the *Conseil constitutionnel* concluded that 'an Act which is contrary to a treaty will not automatically be contrary to the Constitution'. It justified this analysis by pointing out that as treaties were only applicable if the principle of reciprocity had been satisfied, their superiority to Acts of Parliament was only 'relative and conditional'. This gave them a status that was unsuitable for protection by the *Conseil constitutionnel* since its decisions were 'final and absolute'.

As the *Conseil constitutionnel* would not accept the role of controlling the conformity of statutes with treaties, it has been left to the ordinary courts to exercise this control. On occasion, during legal proceedings provisions of an international undertaking and of domestic law may be simultaneously relied upon and prove to contain conflicting terms. It is then up to the court hearing the case to determine the text that is applicable and to do so in the light of article 55, that is to say by giving a preference to the international text provided that the condition of reciprocity is satisfied. The highest civil and criminal court, the *Cour de cassation*, and the highest administrative court, the *Conseil d'Etat*, have only recently taken the same stance on this question.

Following the *Conseil constitutionnel*'s decision, the *Cour de cassation* was quick to apply article 55: in the *Société Jacques Vabre* decision of 24 May 1975 it was faced with a conflict between the provisions of an international undertaking (the Treaty of Rome of 25 March 1957) and a later legislative text of 1966 (article 265 of the Customs Code). It held that only the first was applicable, despite the fact that the latter postdated it.

For a long time the *Conseil d'Etat* refused to give preference to international undertakings conflicting with a later Act of Parliament, despite considerable criticism from academics. It recognised the primacy of treaties over older Acts of Parliament in the *Croissant* decision of 7 July 1978, but refused to do so over Acts of Parliament enacted after a treaty's ratification in the *Syndicat général des fabricants de semoule de France* of 1 March 1968. It took the view that to apply a treaty rather than a later Act of Parliament would amount to censoring the legislator in breach of the principles of the sovereignty of Parliament. The more recent statute repeals the older conflicting statute, by applying the more recent of the two conflicting norms. However, it eventually abandoned this stance, and fell into line with the *Cour de cassation* in its *Nicolo* decision of 20 October 1989.

The *Conseil constitutionnel* is, however, required to control the constitutional legality of Acts of Parliament that implement treaty provisions (article 54). This legal activism has the broad support of academics, but has on occasion provoked considerable discontent among politicians. The Schengen Convention of 19 June 1990 confers on any Member State of the European Community, which receives the first request for asylum, the exclusive competence to decide whether or not to grant asylum. This Convention was approved by the *Conseil constitutionnel* in 1991. An Act of 1993 on immigration aimed to implement the terms of this Convention into national law. This Act was submitted to the *Conseil constitutionnel* to determine its conformity with the Constitution. It held, in its decision of 13 August 1993 and amending its previous case law on the issue, that the Act breached the Constitution as, under the 1946 preamble, France was bound to examine systematically all requests for asylum, whether or not the case had already been considered by another country. As a result, the Constitution had to be amended, a reform which was introduced by the Act of 25 November 1993 inserting a new article 53-1 into the Constitution. This expressly allows France to enter into agreements with European states to determine their respective competence for the examination of asylum requests, while reaffirming that France 'always has the right to grant asylum to any persecuted foreigner'.

▶ European law

Title XV of the Constitution considers the question of the European Community and the European Union. Although European law is still covered by article 55 of the Constitution, it requires particular attention due to its practical importance and its specific characteristics.

A distinction should be drawn between primary and secondary European Community law. Primary European legislation consists of the treaties establishing and amending the Communities. It includes the Treaty of Paris of 18 April 1951 setting up the European Community of Coal and Steel, the Treaty of Rome of 25 March 1957 establishing the European Economic Community and the European Community of Atomic Energy, the Maastricht Treaty of 7 February 1992 creating the European Union, the Amsterdam Treaty of 2 October 1997 and the Nice Treaty of 26 February 2001.

Secondary European legislation is an important new development for international law. It consists of the rules unilaterally made by the Community institutions, particularly the European Council following proposals from the European Commission, under the powers given to them by the European treaties. It includes regulations, directives and the majority of the decisions of the Council of Ministers (article 249 EC Treaty). Integration of this legislation takes place under different conditions depending on the category of norm. Regulations are the European equivalent of Acts of Parliament, since they are of a general nature, binding and automatically enforceable in all Member States. The *Conseil constitutionnel* held, in a decision of 30 December 1977, that it was not within its jurisdiction to determine whether a European regulation complies with the Constitution. There was a fundamental difference in nature between a regulation, directly applicable in a Member State, and an International Treaty, as mentioned by article 55 of the Constitution, necessitating ratification before entering into force. It therefore excluded regulations from article 55's scope. Directives are addressed to those to whom they refer, and impose a result to be attained, while leaving it to Member States to choose the means of reaching this result, through domestic legislation, within a certain time limit. The European Court of Justice has stated that certain directives may give rights to individuals against the State. Decisions are binding but only concern those to whom they are addressed.

In a recent decision of 10 June 2004, the *Conseil constitutionnel* decided that it was not within its remit to check the constitutionality of an Act of Parliament transposing a directive into French Law.

Soon after the *Nicolo* decision, the French *Conseil d'Etat* accepted in its *Boisdet* decision of 24 September 1990 that European law, including secondary European law, has a higher authority than domestic Acts of Parliament. Thus, it accepted in the case that a European regulation prevailed over a later national Act of Parliament. The *Conseil d'Etat*'s decision of *Rothmans France* of 28 February 1992 specified that Acts of Parliament that are contrary to a European directive should not be applied by the administration. In this case, the plaintiff, the tobacco company Rothmans, had been denied by the French Ministry of Finance the right to raise the price of imported tobacco. French legislation determined that the price of imported tobacco sold in France should be fixed by the Government. Rothmans claimed that the legislation was contrary to a European directive which allowed the price of tobacco to be decided by the tobacco companies. The *Conseil d'Etat* agreed with Rothmans.

The *Cour de cassation* has concluded that the issue of reciprocity cannot be successfully argued in the context of the European Community, despite the terms of the new article 88-2 which makes specific reference to this requirement. Apart from directives, European Community law automatically takes effect in France on publication in the Official Journal of the European Communities.

Title XV was to be amended to make the French Constitution compatible with the proposed European Constitution. While Parliament passed relevant legislation on this subject, these provisions will only be brought into force if the European Constitution is itself established. As this currently looks unlikely, following the rejection of the European Constitutional Treaty in the French and Dutch referenda, the provisions will probably remain unchanged.

The relationship between international treaties and the Constitution

If a treaty conflicts with the Constitution, article 54 specifies that the latter must be amended before any treaty ratification can take place:

> If on reference by the President of the Republic, the Prime Minister, the President of the National Assembly, the President of the Senate or sixty members of one of the Houses of Parliament, the *Conseil constitutionnel* rules that an international agreement contains a clause contrary to the Constitution, its ratification or approval may be authorised only after the Constitution has been amended.

Thus it is the *Conseil constitutionnel*'s task to determine the compatibility of international treaties and the Constitution. The *Conseil constitutionnel* confirmed in a decision of 9 April 1992 that, once a treaty has been ratified, it may not be submitted to any check as to its constitutionality. In practice, the *Conseil constitutionnel* attempts to interpret treaties in a constitutional 'friendly' way (*l'interprétation neutralisante*) in order to enable ratification without the need for constitutional amendment. The Constitution has only been amended to comply with international treaties in very limited cases:

- On 25 June 1992, following the Treaty of Maastricht, articles 88-1 to 88-4 were included and articles 2, 54 and 74 had to be amended;
- On 25 November 1993, following the Schengen Agreement, a new article 53-1 was included;
- On 25 January 1999, following the Treaty of Amsterdam, articles 88-2 and 88-4 had to be amended;
- On 8 July 1999, following the Statute establishing the International Criminal Court, a new article 53-2 was included;
- On 25 March 2003, following the creation of the European Arrest Warrant, article 88-2 was amended.

On 1 March 2005, the French Parliament passed an Act to amend the French Constitution in the light of the planned European Constitution. It is now unlikely that the latter will come into force and therefore the Constitution will remain unchanged. The *Conseil d'Etat*, implicitly in the *Koné* decision of 3 July 1996, and expressly in the *Sarran* decision of 30 October 1998, held that the Constitution should have primacy over international treaties. In the *Sarran* case the *Conseil d'Etat* was seized by a number of French citizens who had been denied the right to vote at a referendum organised in the French overseas territory of New Caledonia. A French statute enacted to enforce article 76(2) of the Constitution made the right to vote conditional upon having resided on the island for 10 years. The claimants argued that this created two types of French citizen with unequal rights and was contrary to certain international treaties. The *Conseil d'Etat* declared the French statute to have acquired Constitutional status by enforcing a provision of the Constitution. It therefore dismissed the claim as the French Constitution had a higher status than the international treaties it appeared to conflict with. Soon afterwards the *Cour de cassation* espoused a similar view in the *Fraisse* decision of 2 June 2000. The two cases used similar wording, explaining that 'the supremacy [conferred by article 55] to international treaties, does not apply, in domestic law, to Constitutional sources of law.' This point of view was welcomed by a majority of French legal writers and could be explained by the fact that a treaty which conflicts with the Constitution will not come into force unless the Constitution is amended, hence giving the Constitution the upper hand. The Constitution is and should remain the fundamental norm in French Law, from which all other sources derive their legitimacy, including treaties. It is worth noting that this view contradicts the European Court of Justice's view in the *Costa* decision of 15 July 1964 that European Law should be supreme (over the entire national law of every Member State).

The *Conseil constitutionnel* was asked in 2004 to determine the conformity of the European Constitutional Treaty to the Constitution. The main bone of contention was article I-6 of the Treaty which reaffirms European Law's supremacy over the national laws of every Member State:

> The Constitution and law adopted by the institutions of the Union in exercising competences conferred on it shall have primacy over the law of the Member States.

This provision could be viewed as directly contradicting the *Sarran* and *Fraisse* rulings by France's two supreme courts, which had recognised the supremacy of the French Constitution. In a decision of 19 November 2004, the *Conseil constitutionnel* decided that the French Constitution remained supreme. It based its decision on the fact that article I-6 could not be understood in isolation, but had to be interpreted in the context of the general aims of the Treaty. The common intention of the Member States could be found in the preparatory works to the Treaty and showed a clear intention not to change the existing legal order.

PART III: CONSTITUTIONAL STATUTES

It is important not to confuse the term *lois constitutionnelles* with *lois organiques*:

*   *Lois constitutionnelles* amend the Constitution. For example, the *Loi constitutionnelle* of 25 June 1992 inserted a new title in the Constitution regarding the European Community and the European Union.
*   *Lois organiques* (which for convenience will be translated as 'constitutional statutes'), flesh out the details of the Constitution, though they do not form part of it. For example, the organisation and rules of procedure of the *Conseil constitutionnel* have been explained in greater length in the Constitutional statute of 7 November 1958, amended several times since.

Constitutional statutes can only be used where the Constitution so provides. Thus, article 63 of the Constitution states:

> A constitutional statute lays down the rules concerning the organisation and functioning of the *Conseil constitutionnel*, the procedure that is followed before it, and particularly the time limits for the submission of applications.

Articles 46 and 61 provide special procedures that have to be followed for the making of such statutes. They must be laid before Parliament for at least 15 days before any vote can be taken. The National Assembly can only pass the statute without the support of the Senate if it is voted with an absolute majority of its members; though where the statute concerns the Senate, it must be voted in identical terms by both Houses of Parliament. Before being promulgated, constitutional statutes must be submitted to the *Conseil constitutionnel* to check that they do not conflict with the Constitution.

$$\bullet\;\bullet\;\bullet\;\bullet\;\bullet\;\bullet\;\bullet\;\bullet\;\bullet\;\bullet\;\bullet\;\bullet\;\bullet\;\bullet\;\bullet\;\bullet\;\bullet\;\bullet\;\bullet\;\bullet$$

PART IV: STATUTES

Technically French statutes are much lower in the legal hierarchy than in the United Kingdom. They can be divided into two types: those voted directly by the people in a referendum and those voted by the people's representatives in Parliament. The former are not higher in the hierarchy than the latter, which can amend and repeal them. It is well known that a lot of French law has been codified since the days of Napoleon Bonaparte in the eighteenh century. These codes fall within this discussion as they are really just the product of a single or several long parliamentary Acts. As part of its efforts to improve access to the law, the French government has recently undertaken a programme of codification. The legislative powers to carry out this programme of codification were contained in an Act of 16 July 1999.

In the United Kingdom, an Act tends to be given a name according to its subject matter, for example, the Police and Criminal Evidence Act 1984. In France, Acts of Parliament are usually referred to by the date on which they were passed and by a number reflecting the year in which they were passed, for example, Act no. 95-880 of 4 August 1995. In practice the Act is often simply referred to by its date.

▶ Statutes resulting from a referendum

The power to call a referendum

The power to make these statutes is provided for in article 11 of the Constitution. The scope of article 11 was extended by an Act of 4 August 1995 reforming the Constitution. This article now states:

> When Parliament is in session, the President of the Republic may on
> the recommendation of the government, submit to a referendum
> any Bill which deals with the organisation of public authorities,
> or reforms relating to national economic or social policy and the
> institutions which administer it, or calls for authorisation to ratify

a treaty and which, while not being contrary to the Constitution, would affect the operation of its institutions. Recommendations for a referendum may also be made on the joint motion of the two Houses of Parliament, published in the Official Journal.

If the referendum is called on the government's recommendation, it will make a declaration in the two Houses of Parliament, followed by a debate.

If the Bill is approved by referendum, the President of the Republic shall promulgate it, within fifteen days from the date when the result is announced.

Thus the President can submit directly to the nation a Bill that concerns one of three subjects:

1 the organisation of public powers;
2 the reforming of the economic or social policy of the nation and public services associated with it; or
3 the ratification of a treaty affecting the constitutional institutions.

The few referendums called during the Fifth Republic are listed in Table 3.1.

The first subject area was the ground for two referendums under de Gaulle on the Algerian question: on 8 January 1961 and 8 April 1962. The referendum of 8 January 1961 asked the French people to vote on the text giving Algeria the means to move towards autonomy by the acceptance of the policy of auto-determination. The referendum of 8 April 1962 concerned the approval of the Evian agreement to resolve the Algerian crisis.

Table 3.1 Referendums during the Fifth Republic

Date	Subject	Provision of the Constitution used	Result
8 January 1961	Self-determination in Algeria	Art. 11	Yes
8 April 1962	Evian agreement on the Algerian crisis	Art. 11	Yes
28 October 1962	Election of the President of the Republic through direct elections	Art. 11	Yes
27 April 1969	Reforming the Senate and regionalisation	Art. 11	No
23 April 1972	Entrance of the UK into the EEC	Art. 11	Yes
6 November 1988	Status of New Caledonia	Art. 11	Yes
20 September 1992	Ratification of the Maastricht Treaty	Art. 11	Yes
24 September 2000	Changing the duration of the presidential term	Art. 89	Yes
29 May 2005	Ratification of European Constitution	Art. 11	No

The second subject area was added by the Act of 4 August 1995. This Act also repealed the provisions relating to the holding of referendums concerning France and its ex-colonies in Africa, which had become redundant once these countries had gained independence in the 1960s.

The third subject area for a referendum has been applied three times. Firstly, when it served as the basis for the consultation on 23 April 1972 on the entrance of the United Kingdom into the European Economic Community. Secondly, on 20 September 1992, to allow the President to ratify the Maastricht Treaty. Thirdly, on 29 May 2005, to determine whether the European Constitutional Treaty should be ratified.

The power to call referendums gives the President a real initiative in the making of Acts while restricting the role of Parliament in the process. Referendums were particularly used by President de Gaulle as a tool of government. He defended a mixed conception of democracy which left a place for the direct intervention of the people to make decisions by means of a referendum alongside the representative democracy of Parliament. This dualist conception is expressed in article 3 paragraph 1 of the Constitution which states:

> National sovereignty belongs to the French people who exercise it through its representatives and through referendums.

At the same time, for de Gaulle a referendum was a vote of confidence in the President, whereby the public were asked to give him a new popular investiture during difficult times, with a positive vote being made a condition of his remaining in office. When a negative vote was given following his fourth consultation by referendum in April 1969 he therefore chose to resign.

Since de Gaulle's time, the use of the referendum procedure is generally felt to have been less successful. Participation in the 1972 referendum on the admission of the United Kingdom into the European Economic Community was poor, and the referendum of 6 November 1988 concerning the future status of New Caledonia was marked by a record level of abstentions – more than 65% – which deprived it of much of its political authority. The most recent referendum on the European Constitution, however, had a higher level of participation with 70% of the population turning out to vote.

General de Gaulle used the referendum procedure in order to amend the Constitution, in particular in 1962, so that the President would be directly elected by the people and thereby increase his status and power. This was very controversial as many felt that article 11 could not be used in this way, pointing to article 89 which specifically provides for reform of the Constitution by parliamentary Acts. There were practical reasons for General de Gaulle to prefer to rely on the article 11 procedure. Article 89 imposes that the Bill be voted, in identical terms and with a majority of the votes made, by the National Assembly and the Senate. In 1962 de

Gaulle no longer had a majority in the two Houses of Parliament, and in 1969 the Senate was very hostile to the proposed reform. The use of article 89 to call a referendum has only been used once since 1958: on 24 September 2000, a referendum was organised proposing to reduce the presidential term from 7 years to 5 years. This proposal, which had the backing of the French president, Prime Minister, and Parliament, was overwhelmingly approved by the electorate and amended article 6 of the Constitution accordingly.

Originally President Mitterrand was opposed to the use of article 11 in this way. But once elected he adopted a very different position, considering that '... the use established and approved by the people can now be considered as one of the means of reform, concurrently with article 89' (*Revue des Pouvoirs*, 1988, p. 131. F. Mitterrand: 'Sur les institutions. Entretiens du Président de la République avec le Professeur O. Duhamel'). The practice was repeated to amend the Constitution in the light of the Maastricht Treaty. A committee set up by the government to consider matters of constitutional reform, known as the Vedel Committee, considered however, in a report of 15 February 1993, that this practice was unconstitutional. It is therefore regrettable that the Act of 4 August 1995, which completed and amended article 11, did not provide the necessary clarification on this point.

Procedure

The power to call a referendum belongs exclusively to the President. A proposal to the President to hold a referendum can be delivered either jointly from the National Assembly and the Senate or from the government, when Parliament is sitting. Following a reform of the Act of 4 August 1995, where a President is proposing to hold a referendum a debate must take place in both Houses of Parliament. Logically, if the referendum was proposed on the joint initiative of the Senate and the National Assembly, they would already have had a debate on the subject, so a parliamentary debate will always follow the President's decision. This debate must not be followed by a vote, as this would restrict the President's own freedom to decide.

On receipt of the proposal, it is the President who actually decides independently whether or not to hold a referendum, and no countersignature of the Prime Minister or members of the government is required. To date, referendums have only taken place on a proposal from the government, but in practice the real initiative has mostly come from the President: the government has simply been rubber stamping this initiative to conform with the spirit, if not the letter, of article 11 of the Constitution.

Arguments were put forward at the time of the 1995 reforms in favour of extending the rules of procedure for a referendum which could be decided, and not simply proposed, by Parliament, or on the initiative of the people. Both of these proposals were rejected by the legislature.

The *Conseil constitutionnel* centralises the results of the referendum and the Act is promulgated within two weeks following their announcement by the *Conseil constitutionnel*.

Litigation arising from the referendum

The President's decision to call a referendum is not susceptible to any legal action before the courts. The *Conseil constitutionnel* pronounces on any possible irregularities in the voting operations, which, if serious, can lead to the referendum being declared as either partially or completely void according to article 50 of the Constitutional statute of 7 November 1958.

Once the statute has been adopted, it is unusual in that it cannot be submitted to the *Conseil constitutionnel* to control its constitutionality. Following the referendum of 28 October 1962, the President of the Senate applied to the *Conseil constitutionnel* against the resulting Act allowing the President to be elected by direct suffrage, which had been voted by a strong majority but had not yet been promulgated. The application was rejected, in a decision of 6 November 1962, on the basis that the *Conseil constitutionnel* only had the power to scrutinise Acts of Parliament and not Acts resulting from a referendum, as they constituted the direct expression of national sovereignty. This stance was confirmed by the decision of the *Conseil constitutionnel* which was concerned with the ratification of the Maastricht Treaty (Decision of 23 September 1992). Due to this case law, many lawyers have argued that such Bills should be submitted to the control of the *Conseil constitutionnel* before being submitted to the public, but this reform was rejected by Parliament in 1995. At the time many parliamentarians felt that the *Conseil constitutionnel* had become too intrusive and were happy to see its powers curtailed in this way. These statutes rank equally with statutes made by Parliament in the hierarchy of the sources of law and, hence, can be amended or repealed by ordinary Acts of Parliament.

❭ Statutes made by Parliament

Historical background

In the United Kingdom there is a system based on the supremacy of Parliament. This was essentially the position in France after its Revolution in 1789, when parliamentary legislation was considered to constitute an extremely important source of law, second only to the Constitution. Parliament could legislate on any subject as the only limitations imposed on its legislative powers were procedural. This position was presented by Rousseau in his work *Du contrat social* (1762), and accepted because Parliament was considered to represent the nation, allowing citizens to express their will through their representatives. Inspired by this reasoning, article 6 of the Declaration of Human and Civil Rights declares: 'Acts of Parliament are the expression of the general will'. The executive, by contrast, and as its name suggests, was merely there to execute parliamentary legislation. Thus, in principle, Parliament had a general competence to pass any legislation it wished, while the executive could only make regulations to enforce the legislation. While legislation would be of a general nature laying down the broad rules, regulations made by the executive would be more specific, applying the general rules to the precise situations of everyday life. The executive would only lay down general rules if these were necessary for carrying out its administrative functions.

This was the theory; the practice was slightly different. The legislature itself developed the habit of passing Acts to authorise the executive to make legislative decrees (*décrets-lois*) which could alter or rescind existing Acts of Parliament. This led to a profound overturning of the legal hierarchy, because the regulatory power was thereby temporarily placed on an equal footing with its legislative counterpart.

Gradually, the evolution of constitutional law put into question the supremacy of parliamentary legislation, at first timidly under the Third and Fourth Republics, and then blatantly under the Fifth Republic. Parliament progressively lost the monopoly for laying down rules of a general nature, delegating the same power to the government – despite the fact that this was expressly forbidden by the Constitutions of the Third and Fourth Republics. Thus, under the Third Republic, article 1 of the constitutional law of 25 February 1874 forbade Parliament to delegate its legislative powers. This provision was first ignored on budgetary matters by an Act of 14 December 1879 and then in relation to taxes by Acts in 1892 and 1897. It was again breached by legislative decrees for reasons of efficiency during the war preparations: for example, the Act of 19 March 1939 gave the government the power to make legislative decrees adopting measures necessary for the defence of the country.

This practice became established under the Fourth Republic, even though article 13 of the Constitution unequivocally stated: 'The National Assembly alone votes Statutes. It cannot delegate this power.' Despite the very clear terms of the Constitution, the *Conseil d'Etat* ruled that in certain circumstances Parliament could delegate its legislative power. Under the Vichy régime during the Second World War, all legislation emanated from the head of state.

Apart from the specific issues relating to the Vichy government, the reason why the practice differed from the theoretical framework laid down by the Constitution was because, while Parliament had been given considerable powers, it was full of small parties that were unable to agree with each other to make effective use of those powers. Very little legislation was actually passed because a majority could not be found to vote in its favour. This was a particular problem in the 1950s because the struggle for Algerian independence was reaching a head and the politicians were unable to agree how to deal with the crisis. When de Gaulle was invited to form a government and produce a new Constitution, he had a clear view that the way forward was to increase the powers of the executive, particularly the President, and decrease the powers of Parliament. This is reflected in the role that the 1958 Constitution gives to parliamentary legislation.

▶ Parliamentary statutes in the Fifth Republic

Today, Parliament can only legislate on a limited number of subjects, which are primarily listed in article 34 of the Constitution, creating the legislative domain. The terms of article 34 distinguish between where the legislature fixes the rules and where it merely determines the fundamental principles. This distinction was only respected during the first few years and is now of little significance. Article 37 states that all other topics are to be regulated by the executive, not Parliament, as they fall within the regulatory domain. In the words of article 37: 'Subjects other than those which are in the legislative domain have a regulatory character.' Thus, parliamentary legislation is the exception: everything that is not legislative is regulatory. Certain other articles of the Constitution, such as article 66 paragraph 2 on the protection of the freedom of individuals and article 72 paragraph 2 on the administration of local communities, also refer to the requirement that legislation be in the form of Acts of Parliament. However, these latter articles are of limited scope and on the whole merely duplicate the broader provisions in article 34.

In fact, the Constitution has subsequently been interpreted to allow legislation to be made in subject areas that go well beyond the limits of article 34. It is up to the *Conseil constitutionnel* to make sure that articles 34 and 37 are respected, but in its decision of 30 July 1982 it took the view that these articles were not intended to strike down automatically as unconstitutional a provision of a regulatory nature contained in an Act of Parliament. Instead it considered that they simply provide an opportunity for the government to protect its regulatory domain. Thus, only the government can complain to the *Conseil constitutionnel* that a piece of legislation enters into its domain, and not Members of Parliament. If the government choose to turn a blind eye, an Act can cover regulatory subject areas and Members of Parliament can do nothing about it. Since this decision, it can be said that the regulatory domain has become a shared domain, including provisions of statutes and regulations, but with priority to regulations. In the 1982 case, the action had been brought by

Members of Parliament, who had argued that an Act freezing prices and wages infringed on the regulatory domain and therefore breached the Constitution. Their application was rejected as applying the principles mentioned above; the *Conseil constitutionnel* held that only the government could bring such an action to protect its regulatory domain.

This decision has to be understood in its practical context. Opposition Members of Parliament were systematically using the *Conseil constitutionnel* to obstruct the work of Parliament, a process which was both tarnishing the public image of the *Conseil constitutionnel* and creating practical difficulties in the functioning of the court, faced with such a heavy workload. More importantly, given the quantity of regulatory provisions in the legislation being passed, such applications, if allowed, could have crippled the legislative process. By firmly closing the door on these cases, a political and constitutional crisis was avoided.

Since 1982, the interventions of Parliament in what was previously the regulatory domain have multiplied. By laying down rules in the form of statutes, the government avoids the requirement to respect the general principles of law imposed by the *Conseil d'Etat* on government regulations. This is the case, in particular, for Acts having retrospective effect that the *Conseil d'Etat* might annul. Also, by introducing regulatory provisions into an Act, the government is able to submit to debate a more homogeneous text and to align its majority more closely with it.

In addition, following the decision of 16 July 1971 which recognised the existence of the 'constitutional block', the *Conseil constitutionnel* was able to add to the list in article 34 new legislative subject areas which, under the Declaration of Human and Civil Rights of 1789 and the 1946 preamble, must be regulated by Parliament. This approach was first taken in a decision of 28 November 1973. This case was concerned with whether the executive or Parliament had the power to make rules concerning minor offences. No reference to these offences was made in article 34, which refers only to major and serious offences as falling within the legislative domain. Despite this, the *Conseil constitutionnel* declared that minor offences and their punishments fell within the legislative domain when, rather than being limited to the imposition of a fine, they could deprive an individual of his or her freedom. In reaching this conclusion it relied not on article 34, but notably on the Declaration of 1789. The legal point of this case remains important though its facts are no longer relevant, as the new Criminal Code of 1994 prevents minor offences from giving rise to a custodial sentence.

A historical analysis of the Constitution suggests that the approach taken by the *Conseil constitutionnel* accurately reflects the intention of its writers. Article 37 was originally drafted in the following terms: 'The subject areas other than those referred to by article 31 [which subsequently became article 34] have a regulatory character.' This direct reference to the equivalent provision of article 34 was later removed, which suggests that the writers of the Constitution did not want to limit the legislative domain only to the subjects listed in that article.

The constitutional reform of 22 February 1996 has further increased the legislative domain. This added the supervision and control of the 'general conditions for the financial balance of the Social Security budget'. Although, in budgetary matters, the expenses determine the receipts, it is here foreseen that this should be reversed so that, taking into account the predicted receipts, the Finance Acts will annually fix the expenditure goals. This is an ambitious attempt to try to control state spending.

In conclusion, the legislative domain is far from being as narrowly delimited as was originally thought when the Constitution was voted in 1958, having been extended by the limited controls exercised by the *Conseil constitutionnel*, the development of the 'constitutional block' and subsequent constitutional reform.

PART V: *ORDONNANCES* AND REGULATIONS

Under the Fifth Republic, a considerable amount of law emanates not from Parliament but from the executive. We will consider the two possible types of laws that can be made by the executive: *ordonnances* and regulations.

▶ *Ordonnances*

It is not possible to translate this term into English as there is no direct equivalent in the English legal system. An *ordonnance* is a special form of delegated legislation and constitutes the direct descendant of the legislative decrees which were used under the Third and Fourth Republics. Whilst under these earlier constitutions such measures may have been in breach of the Constitution, the legality of *ordonnances* under the 1958 Constitution is not open to debate. The main provision for these can now be found at article 38, which states:

> In order to carry out its programme, the government may ask Parliament to authorise it for a limited period to take measures which are normally within the legislative domain by means of *ordonnances* instead of the usual procedure.
>
> They shall be adopted by the Cabinet after consultation with the *Conseil d'Etat*. They shall come into force on publication, but shall lapse if the government Bill calling for ratification is not laid before Parliament by the date specified in the enabling Act.
>
> At the expiry of the time limit referred to in the first paragraph of this article, *ordonnances* on subjects within the legislative domain may be modified only by parliamentary legislation.

Thus Parliament can pass an enabling Act allowing the government to make *ordonnances* on a particular subject which is normally within the legislative domain, for a limited period of time. The enabling Act must specify in some detail the type of measures that can be taken (C.E. 12 January 1977).

As to their form, they must have been the object of an opinion of the *Conseil d'Etat*, have been discussed in Cabinet, be signed by the President and countersigned by the Prime Minister and the ministers responsible. The requirement that the President sign these measures gave rise to controversy during the first period of *cohabitation* in 1986. The President claimed the right to refuse to sign, relying, it seems, on article 13 para-graph 1, which provides for the signature of both *ordonnances* and decrees discussed in Cabinet. It is accepted that the President can choose whether or not to sign decrees, so it was argued that this should also be true of the signing of *ordonnances*, which are cited in the same sentence of the same article. Relying on this argument the President refused to sign several *ordonnances* that had been drawn up by the government of the day (which was of a different political affiliation from himself).

The enabling Act contains two successive time limits. First, the Act fixes a period during which the government is authorised to make *ordonnances*. Secondly, there is a longer time limit for the government to deposit a Bill in order to ratify the *ordonnances* that it has made. These measures have a hybrid character, because they initially have the status of a regulation. On the expiry of the second time limit there are two possible situations. either the government has failed to deposit a Bill to ratify the measures, in which case they become invalid. Alternatively, if the government has deposited the Bill, then the subsequent conduct of Parliament has to be considered. Where the Bill was never submitted to a debate, the *ordonnances* simply keep their regulatory character. If the Bill was discussed, but Parliament refused to ratify it, then it is invalid. Lastly, Parliament may have ratified the *ordonnances*, either expressly by voting in favour of the Bill, or impliedly by referring to them in a legislative text. If ratified they have the status of an Act of Parliament, with retroac-tive effect from the date of their creation (Cons. const. 10 March 1966; C.E. 19 December 1969, *dame Picard*). In practice, governments regularly deposit *ordonnances* before Parliament by the date laid down, but fail to register them for a debate which might have proved politically sensitive. From 1959 to 1 January 1994, 25 enabling Acts were passed. Of the 187 *ordonnances* which resulted, only 35 were expressly ratified.

In addition to those referred to in article 38, there are also three other categories of *ordonnances*. First, article 92 of the 1958 Constitution provided for the taking of 'legislative measures necessary for the setting up of the institutions' judged to be 'necessary for the life of the nation, the protection of citizens and the safeguard of freedoms'. These provi-sions were to have the force of Acts of Parliament and were destined to remedy the gap in the legislative power during the transitory period. In fact, the government abused this article, widely applying it to publish 300 *ordonnances* in the four months that followed the promulgation of the Constitution, profoundly changing the nation's legal foundations. Many have the status of constitutional Acts, which are known as an *ordonnance organique* or *ordonnance portant loi organique*. Having become redundant, the article has now been repealed by the constitutional reform implemented by the Act of 4 August 1995, though the texts to which it served as a legal base remain in force.

Secondly, we saw that there are *ordonnances* which concern the budget and the Social Security Finance Acts. If Parliament has not pronounced on the proposed Bill within the time allotted, the provisions of the proposal can be brought into force by an *ordonnance*. These provisions have not been relied upon to date.

Thirdly, de Gaulle used a referendum on 8 April 1962 to seek the authority to make *ordonnances* to resolve the Algerian problem. Although nothing in this text referred to the need for these *ordonnances* to be submitted for ratification by Parliament, the *Conseil d'Etat*, anxious to have the opportunity to control their legality, decided they had a regulatory nature and they were in consequence submitted to its censure (C.E. 19 October 1962, *Canal*). As a result of this judgment, the government had these *ordonnances* ratified as a block by Parliament by the Act of 15 January 1963.

Regulations

These are made by the executive and the administration. Under the Fifth Republic they have become an increasingly important source of law, highlighted by the broad provisions of article 37. The existence of a domain in which the government can do what it wants without the intervention of Parliament is difficult to reconcile with the requirements of democracy, and the rise in the role of regulations has been criticised by many. Until 1981, the government carried out a major construction programme of nuclear power stations, while refusing any parliamentary debate on the subject.

During the early years of the Fifth Republic, a distinction was drawn between those regulations made under article 37 of the Constitution, called *règlements autonomes,* and those made to implement an Act, called *règlements d'application*, which are recognised by article 21, and fall as a result within the scope of article 34 and the legislative domain. This distinction has been undermined by the *Conseil constitutionnel*'s case law allowing infringements of the legislature into the autonomous regulatory domain provided that it is not opposed by the government, and indeed never had any practical importance as the same legal regime has always been applied to the two types of regulation.

Different categories of regulations exist, depending on their author. Ordinary regulations made by the President or the Prime Minister are known as decrees. In times of emergency the President can issue decisions under article 16 – these emergency powers were used by President de Gaulle following the military putsch in Algeria from 23 April to 30 September 1961. Regulations made by lower bodies such as ministers, mayors and local councils are known as orders (*arrêtés*). The more senior the author of the regulation in the administrative hierarchy, the higher the status of the regulation as a source of law. Thus a decree of the President discussed by the Cabinet is superior to a decree of the Prime Minister. In the same way, a decision of a minister is superior to an order issued by a mayor.

Despite the usual pre-eminence of the President under the Fifth Republic, the main power to make regulations belongs to the Prime Minister (article 21). These decrees must be countersigned, where appropriate, by the ministers given the responsibility for their application. If the Prime Minister is the only person responsible for the execution, there will be no countersignature. The President also has at his disposal a power to make regulations since, according to article 13, he or she must sign the decrees discussed in the Cabinet, which are then countersigned by the Prime Minister and the ministers responsible. By contrast, ministers do not benefit from a general power to make regulations, but can only issue orders for the organisation of their services (*Conseil d'Etat* 7 February 1936, *Jamart*) or under a special power given to them by an Act of Parliament. Finally, other administrative authorities (for example, the Prefect and the mayor) and private associations (such as sports federations) can be given a power to make regulations.

All regulations must be published and those which emanate from the executive are published in the Official Journal.

While the *Conseil constitutionnel* controls the constitutionality of statutes, the administrative courts control the constitutionality of administrative legislation. This is known as the *principe de légalité* . This means that for regulations there is a process of judicial review open to private citizens, which is not the case for Acts of Parliament. In addition, individuals can also, if a regulation is invoked against them in the course of legal proceedings before any court, raise a defence that the regulation is illegal.

· ·
BIBLIOGRAPHY FOR CHAPTER 3

Aubert, J.-L. (2004), *Introduction au droit*, Paris: Armand Colin
Beignier, B. and Mouton, S. (2001), 'La Constitution et la Convention européenne des droits de l'homme, rang et fonction', *D.* 2001, 1636
Carbonnier, J. (2002), *Droit civil – Introduction*, Thémis, Presses
Chagnollaud, D. (2005), 'La Constitution française ne peut être révisée par voie de directives ...', *D.* 2005, 100

Dubois, L. (1999), 'Les trois logiques de la jurisprudence Sarran', *Revue française de droit administratif* 1999, 57

Feldman, J.-P. (2004), 'Le projet de loi constitutionnelle relative à la Charte de l'environnement', *D.* 2004, 970

Jestaz, P. (2005), *Les sources du droit*, Paris: Dalloz

Mathieu, B. (2004), 'Le Conseil constitutionnel conforte la construction européenne en s'appuyant sur les exigences constitutionnelles nationales', D. 2004, at 1739

Mathieu, B. (2004), 'La 'Constitution' européenne ne menace pas la République', *D.* 2004, 3075

Pontier, J.-M. (2000), 'A quoi servent les lois?', *D.*2000, 57

Puig, P. (2001), 'Hiérarchie des normes: du système au principe', *RTD civ.* 2001, at 749

Terré, F. (2003), *Introduction générale au droit*, Paris: Dalloz

Verpeaux, M. (2004), 'Les Principes fondamentaux reconnus par les lois de la République ont-ils encore un avenir?', *D.* 2004, 1537

Verpeaux, M. (2005), 'La loi constitutionnelle du 1er mars 2005 modifiant le titre XV de la Constitution, ou la révision', *D.* 2005, 2485

Zarka, J.-C. (2005), 'A propos de l'inflation législative', *D.* 2005, 660

Web Resources

Website: www.assemblee-nat.fr: The National Assembly

Website: www.conseil-etat.fr: The *Conseil d'Etat*

Website: www.courdecassation.fr: The *Cour de cassation*

Website: www.journal-officiel.gouv.fr: Internet version of the Official Journal

Website: www.ladocfrancaise.gouv.fr: La documentation française

Website: www.legifrance.gouv.fr: Légifrance. Includes some legislation in English.

Website: www.senat.fr: The Senate

4 Unwritten sources of law

Unwritten sources of law are those sources which do not emanate from a public authority (and may actually be written). There are three unwritten sources of law in France: judicial decisions, custom and academic writing. Each of these will be discussed in turn.

PART I: JUDICIAL DECISIONS

In the United Kingdom, under the common law system, court judgments are an important source of law. Before the 1789 Revolution, French case law was accepted as an important source of law and French judges had a lot of power. After the Revolution, those who had been involved in its instigation were anxious that the power of the judges should be reduced as it was felt that they supported the old régime. The revolutionaries were also keen supporters of the principle of the separation of powers and therefore tried to reduce the judges' powers to the mere application and interpretation of the law, which would primarily be found in the new codes, and forbade judges from creating legal rules. Thus, article 5 of the Civil Code states:

> Judges are forbidden to give a judgment in general and regulatory terms in the cases which are submitted to them.

Judges were simply to decide the case they were hearing, rather than to try and establish a precedent for the future. This is reinforced by article 1351 of the Civil Code which provides:

> A judgment only binds the object of the judgment. The thing requested must be the same; the request must be based on the same case; the request must be between the same parties, and brought by them and against them in the same capacity.

Thus a judgment can only be applied in another case if the parties are identical and the issues raised are exactly the same. As a result, in French law a court is not technically bound to follow a previous decision, whether handed down by itself or another court. This means that there is no system of binding precedent in French law. This is the reason why judicial decisions are merely seen as secondary sources of law. As a result, the judiciary is in a very difficult position. They are only supposed to apply the law and are not allowed to create it. At the same time article 4 of the Civil Code states:

> The judge who refuses to judge under the pretext of the silence, obscurity or insufficiency of the law, can be prosecuted for causing a miscarriage of justice.

In other words, if judges fail to decide a case at all, on the basis that there is no law on the question, they will be guilty of a criminal offence, for which they can be fined or banned from carrying out their judicial functions for up to 20 years. The law can be found in the codes, but these have been drafted very broadly, unlike the more detailed drafting of legislation in the United Kingdom, leaving a lot of unanswered questions.

In practice, article 4 has had important consequences: courts have had to interpret the codes creatively. The whole law of tort was, until recently, based on five short articles of the Civil Code, 1382 to 1386, and has been almost entirely developed by judicial decisions. For instance, the French Civil Code specifies in its article 1384 that a person may be tortiously liable for his own acts, but also for 'things which are in his custody'. The courts have had to determine who is liable for damage caused by a stolen car: the actual owner of the car or the car thief? In the famous *Franck* affair, the French *Cour de cassation* decided on 2 December 1941 that it should be the actual owner. A few years later, it held that the thief was liable if he or she had the use and control of the stolen item.

While in theory judicial decisions are not a source of law because they do not have normative force, in practice they have become increasingly influential, especially those of the *Cour de cassation* (the highest civil court) and *Conseil d'Etat* (the highest administrative court). Every legal system needs to be consistent in order to be just and therefore it would be dangerous for judges to ignore what the other courts around them in the country were deciding. Initially, after codification, textbooks simply discussed the articles of the new codes and made no reference to any case law. Now, gradually, textbooks are placing more emphasis on judicial decisions, though still not as much as British textbooks do, and often primarily in the footnotes rather than in the main text. A judicial decision can still not be based solely on a previous decision: some other legal source must be cited as the grounds for the judgment. (Judges can never cite a previous judicial decision as the basis for their own judgment.) French academic writers and courts still rarely cite a single case as a legal authority, preferring instead to point out that judges consistently decide in a certain way on the same facts, using very often the same legal terminology, (or that conflicting judgments are handed down on a certain issue). Inevitably, the decisions of the highest courts carry more weight than those of the lower courts and can become highly influential. It is, indeed, the function of the top courts to maintain a certain consistency in the interpretation of the law. Furthermore, in case of doubt, lower courts can now ask the *Conseil d'Etat* and the *Cour de cassation* for a non-binding advisory opinion on an unsettled point of law (see p. 104).

Unlike England, with the Interpretation Act of 20 July 1978, France does not have any general rules of statutory interpretation. The French *Cour de cassation,* in a recent decision of 29 January 2002, confirmed that lower courts are free to use the method of interpretation of the law they want and their decisions may not be quashed on the pretext that no reference was made to the 'travaux préparatoires' when interpreting the law. While technically a lower court is not bound by a higher court, courts prefer to follow earlier judgments so that like cases are treated alike, allowing justice to be done. What is important in this context is not the factual decision of the court, but the legal reasons on which it relied.

Judicial decisions on administrative law

The decisions of the *Conseil d'Etat* are particularly important as administrative law has not been codified and the gaps in the legislation have been filled by the *Conseil d'Etat* developing general principles of law. For example, the *Conseil d'Etat* developed a general principle of sex equality in the *Demoiselle Bobard et autres* decision of 1936. Some general principles are actually quite precise: for example, there is a general principle that a company cannot make a pregnant woman redundant following the *Dame Pynet* case of the *Conseil d'Etat* in 1973. This has led some academics to claim that judicial decisions are genuine sources of administrative law.

The importance of foreign judicial decisions

In recent years, the French judiciary has been increasingly exposed to foreign decisions. French judges sometimes have to apply foreign case law, particularly decisions of the European Court of Justice and the European Court of Human Rights. The French judiciary has also started looking at the way law is applied and interpreted in other countries. One of the reasons for this is the increasing influence of large foreign law firms (mainly American and British) in France.

In certain types of case, French judges may be influenced by the way law is applied and interpreted in other countries. For example, in extradition cases, a rule of international law requires that the defendant has committed a crime in the country requesting extradition and the country holding the offender in detention. The French judge will therefore look at the foreign legal system to ascertain whether the relevant conduct amounts to a crime in that country.

The French *Cour de cassation*, in a decision of 13 March 2001, had to decide whether to allow President Gadaffi, suspected of being involved in bombing a French plane, immunity from prosecution. In deciding this issue the Court looked at the interpretation of the concept of immunity by other foreign courts, most notably by the House of Lords in the General Pinochet case. The *Cour de cassation* was unable to find a rule of international law enabling a national court to lift a foreign Head of State's immunity following the crime of terrorism. Thus, it concluded that Gaddafi, as an incumbent Head of State, was protected by the principle of immunity.

The French *Conseil d'Etat* made explicit mention of a foreign judicial decision for the first time in the *Techna* decision of 29 October 2003. This case was concerned with a very specific legal issue: a European directive required food producers to state the ingredients and exact quantities in their food products. This requirement conflicted with the producers' desire to keep these matters secret from their competitors. The French court looked at the way other countries coped with this problem. It noted that the application of the directive had been suspended in some countries (Holland, Germany and Britain). The Conseil d'Etat, citing among others the English High Court, decided to do the same in order to make sure that French producers should not be put at a disadvantage in comparison to producers from these countries.

PART II: CUSTOM

A custom is a practice that has become binding, and thus has gained the status of a legal rule. Before the 1789 Revolution, this was the predominant source of law. With the Revolution its role was significantly reduced to make way for parliamentary legislation. The Civil Code was passed in 1804 in order to replace all general and local customs. In the nineteenth century, academic writing tended to deny that custom was a source of law at all. In fact, the revolutionaries had merely repealed the written customs while custom as a generic source of law continued to exist. Now it is accepted as a source of law, though only a minor one. It continues to play a role because it has the advantage of being flexible and adaptable, though this also means that it can be imprecise and unreliable.

Material and psychological elements

According to the classical analysis, custom has two components: the one being material, the other being psychological. The material element is also described as objective. It consists of a practice that has been repeatedly and constantly followed by the individuals concerned over a period of time.

The psychological element is described as the subjective element. This consists of the belief held by the people involved that the conduct comprising the material element is binding. This element allows one to differentiate custom from practices which have no legal character but are simply habits carried out for convenience. For example, a common practice allows a married woman to take her husband's family name. This rule is not legally binding, and the married woman can choose to continue to use her maiden name.

Popular custom and scholarly custom

A distinction is drawn by the influential French academic Carbonnier between custom that genuinely has a popular origin, deriving from a practice followed by the masses, and custom that has a scholarly origin, having been developed by the lawyers with the implied approval of the masses, which has become established over time. There are two forms of scholarly custom: legal maxims and general principles of law. Legal maxims can also be described as legal proverbs or sayings. They were created by academics and judges a long time ago, in order to condense and render more memorable the rules of law. These sayings are often in Latin and sometimes in ancient French. Some have passed into the Civil Code and therefore no longer pose any difficulty because the Code provides their legal foundation: for example, the maxim 'as regards movcable property, possession is title' can now be found in article 2279 of the Code. Many others have remained outside the legislative field, but continue to be considered as rules of law, and the *Cour de cassation* sometimes expressly refers to them in its judgments.

The general principles of law are those principles that have been described by legal writers and judges. They are not considered to have created these principles, but to have put into words what was implied by the spirit of the law, as revealed to them in the different texts. For example, it is a general principle of law that every promise of marriage is void as breaching the absolute freedom which must prevail in the formation of the conjugal relationship, a principle underlying article 1460 of the Civil Code.

But the difference is more in the form than in the substance: depending on whether one insists on the external formula or on its content, one is faced with a legal maxim or a general principle of law. Not all the general principles of law are expressed as legal maxims, but all legal maxims can be expressed as general principles of law.

In fact, in developed legal systems the distinction between popular and scholarly custom is rather artificial as all laws tend to be the product of a lawyer or a technocrat. The professional practices which Carbonnier qualifies as customs that are popular in origin are much more the product of the leaders of the professional groups than of their participants, while the habit that is really popular never gives rise to litigation.

The relationship between custom and statutes

Three important issues need to be discussed as regards the relationship between custom and statutes:

- Custom can be expressly mentioned by a statute. Acts of Parliament refer back to custom to clarify legal expressions concerned with morality and current practice which change too subtly to be given a fixed definition in written rules. This is known as a custom *secundum legem.* Article 389-3 of the French Civil Code mentions that minors may in general not become parties to a contract, except if allowed by law or accepted by custom. The meaning of the concept of 'fault', mentioned in the Civil Code in relation to tortious liability, relies more on custom than an Act of Parliament. Notions such as 'acting in good faith' or 'in the public interest' evolve with time and are understood with the help of custom.

  Statutes sometimes refer to local practices, particularly in rural areas where the desire for legislative unity and centralisation in France in 1804 came up against the local and regional differences in the country. For example, article 645 of the Civil Code refers to local practices in the context of the use of water.
- Custom may apply in the absence of a statutory regulation. This is known as custom *praeter legem.* Custom will fill a gap left by legislation. Portalis, one of the original drafters of the Civil Code, acknowledged the existence of such rules in his preliminary speech for the Civil Code.
- Some rules, developed through custom, may directly contradict a statute. These are in general very rare and merely constitute an exception to the written rule. This type of custom is known as *contra legem.* For example, article 931 of the Civil Code requires donations made to private individuals to be confirmed by a written document drafted by a Notary. However, a practice which accepts the validity of donations unconfirmed by a Notary has developed into a custom accepted by the courts. Article L 442-1 of the Commercial Code and article L 122-1 of the Consumer Code expressly forbid a contract for the sale of goods to be made conditional upon the purchase of a minimum quantity. Despite this, the commercial courts have accepted that in compliance with commercial practice, for certain goods (such as matchsticks) a minimum purchase quantity can be imposed.

The role of custom in commercial law

Custom continues to play an important role in the commercial sector. These customs come from the practices habitually followed by the contracting parties in a given commercial field, such as the shipping industry.

Speed is of the essence, and custom is seen as a more flexible source than written legislation. Courts accept that the existence of such practices can be confirmed by the chambers of commerce, experts or other professional bodies. To facilitate this, a registry of professional practices (*bureau de dépot des usages professionnels*) was set up at the Paris Commercial Court in 1983. Customs are often applied by the arbitration courts created by professional bodies.

PART III: ACADEMIC WRITING

The opinions on the law developed by academics in their writing are not strictly a source of law, but constitute a powerful influence on its development. It is known in France as *la doctrine*. It can be taken into account by the judges when interpreting the law, and for the practitioner these writings provide assistance with interpretation rather than a legal authority. Such writing can be found in the *répertoires*, which are alphabetically listed encyclopedias of law, for example *Le Répertoire Dalloz*. *Traités* are books written by leading academics, often when they were preparing their PhDs. They are very detailed, but are often left out of date because they cover several volumes and are expensive to produce. Books described as *précis*, *thémis* and *manuels* are student textbooks, while *mémentos* are very short guides to a subject, most suitable for exam revision.

French cases are clear and concise; the legal issue is hardly ever mentioned in more than two or three paragraphs, especially in cases handed down by the two highest courts: the *Cour de cassation* and the *Conseil d'Etat*. Interpretation and understanding of these short cases is often provided by legal academics, in the case commentaries found in legal journals.

Academic writing is most influential when the case law is not yet settled. An interpretation will be provided by a legal writer and may be adopted by the case law.

BIBLIOGRAPHY FOR CHAPTER 4

Aubert, J.-L. (2004), *Introduction au droit*, Paris: Armand Colin
Bénabent, A. (2005), 'Doctrine ou Dallas?', *D.* 2005, 852
Cachard, O. (2004), 'Aux grands arrêts, les juristes reconnaissants …', *D.* 2004, 429
Code civil (2005), Paris: Dalloz
Carbonnier, J. (2002), *Droit civil – Introduction*, Paris: Thémis
Jestaz, P. (2005), *Les sources du droit*, Paris: Dalloz
Morvan, P. (2005), 'Le revirement de jurisprudence pour l'avenir: humble adresse aux magistrats ayant franchi le Rubicon', *D.* 2005, 247
Terré, F. (2003), *Introduction générale au droit*, Paris: Dalloz
Tricot, D. (2004), 'L'élaboration d'un arrêt de la Cour de cassation', Doctrine, *JCP* 2004, 225

5 The civil and criminal court system

PART I: AN INTRODUCTION TO THE CIVIL AND CRIMINAL COURTS

In France there are two separate court systems, the civil and criminal court system and the administrative court system. In addition, there are a small number of courts that do not belong to either system. In the United Kingdom, by contrast, there is only one court system.

In this chapter we will study the civil and criminal court system which is known as *l'ordre judiciaire*. First, we need to understand why there is more than one system and how they relate to each other, and to the courts outside the two systems.

▶ Historical evolution of the two court systems

The intermediate law of the revolutionary and post-revolutionary period is credited with the passing of laws forbidding the civil and criminal courts to judge cases involving the government, other public authorities and the administration generally. The first law was an Act of 16-24 August 1790. This included in article 13 a prohibition on judges interfering in any manner whatsoever with the actions of the administration. Any judge breaching this prohibition would incur criminal liability. This was confirmed in a subsequent law passed in August 1795, which contained an even wider general prohibition on the civil and criminal courts having any dealings whatsoever with the acts of the administration. This law is still in force.

The intermediate law also sought to apply the principle of the separation of powers, expounded in 1748 by Montesquieu in his book *De l'esprit des lois*. The author distinguished three functions of the state: that of creating law (the legislative power), that of executing public decisions (the executive power), and that of judging crimes and disputes between individuals (the judicial power). Liberty would be promoted by ensuring that the three powers were not concentrated in one body. The definition of the judicial power only covers judging crimes and disputes between individuals; it does not include judging the acts of the administration. Therefore, he argued that the body to which judicial power is devolved, the civil and criminal court system, should not judge the acts of the administration.

After the 1789 Revolution, though the ordinary courts no longer had the power to judge the administration, no administrative court system was created. As mentioned in Chapter 1, intermediary law created the *Conseil d'Etat*, which originally only had advisory powers but, in time, became the focus of a fully fledged administrative court system. The administrative court system will be studied more fully in Chapter 6.

The courts and the Constitution

The current Constitution of 1958 does not refer to the administrative court system in its text. It does refer to, and guarantee the independence of, the civil and criminal court system in Title VIII. However, both academic writing and the *Conseil constitutionnel* have confirmed that the existence of a separate administrative court system is a fundamental principle of the Republic.

Other systems, like those of the United Kingdom and the United States, have not evolved a separate court system for administrative law. UK law even considers the ordinary courts' power to hear cases involving the administration, in particular the various powers of judicial review of administrative acts, to be a fundamental pillar of constitutional law. The modern justification for the existence of a separate court system is simply that it works. Arguably, the modern French administrative court system exercises its functions as impartially as the English and Welsh courts, and more efficiently since it allows for specialisation at all levels. In comparison a large number of specialised administrative tribunals exist in the United Kingdom for tax and other administrative matters, at lower levels only, leaving the ordinary courts to deal with complicated appeals on points of law or cases of abuse of power.

Courts of general jurisdiction and specialised courts

Within each system specialised courts have been created (and more and more are still being created to cope with the increased complexities of human affairs). Examples of specialised courts within the civil and criminal system are employment and commercial courts. Within the administrative system, there is the Audit Court (*la Cour des comptes*). Specialised courts can only hear matters within the specific remit of the court.

All other courts in each system are called courts of general jurisdiction and can hear cases relating to all matters within the system, other than those which are within the competence of a specialised court. Most of the courts in the civil and criminal system share the same judges and administration. For ease of exposition we will study civil and criminal courts separately. Courts of appeal, as in the United Kingdom, hear appeals from all courts within the system.

▶ Consideration of facts and/or law

A fundamental distinction is drawn in the civil and criminal system between those courts which consider the facts and the law of a case and those which consider points of law only. All courts other than the *Cour de cassation* decide what facts have been proved and what alleged facts have been shown to be untrue. They also apply the law to the facts. The highest court in the system is the *Cour de cassation*. It does not rejudge the facts but merely considers whether the law has been correctly applied and whether the grounds for the decision were correctly set out.

PART II: THE CIVIL COURTS

The main legislative provisions regulating the civil courts are contained in the *Code de l'organisation judiciaire* (COJ). The civil courts of first instance and of appeal will be considered in turn. Table 5.1 sets out the civil courts' jurisdiction since 2002, related to the amount claimed.

▶ Courts of first instance

Eight important courts of first instance will be studied in detail: the *tribunaux de grande instance* (TGI), the *tribunaux d'instance* (TI), the neigh-

Table 5.1 The jurisdiction of the civil courts since 2002 based on the value of the claim

	Jurisdiction before 9 September 2002	Jurisdiction from September 2002 to January 2005	Current jurisdiction
TGI	Claims above €7,800	Claims above €7,800	Claims above €10,000
TI	Claims below €7,800	Claims between €1,500 and €7,800	Claims between €4,000 and €10,000
Neighbourhood court	N/A	Claims up to €1,500	Claims up to €4,000

bourhood courts, the commercial courts, the employment tribunals, the agricultural tenancy tribunals, the social security tribunals and the disability disputes tribunals.

Tribunaux de grande instance

Jurisdiction

The *tribunaux de grande instance* (TGI) have general jurisdiction. Legislative provision is made for them in articles L 311-1 and L 311-2 (COJ). In civil matters they hear all cases, if the claim is in excess of €10,000, except those specifically allocated to specialist courts, such as the commercial courts and employment tribunals. This is the main reason why the TGI is the busiest type of court in France, hearing in excess of 615 000 cases in 2003.

The TGI also have exclusive jurisdiction in a small number of matters such as family law (marriage, divorce, adoption), property law, intellectual property and inheritance law. The TGI is the only civil court at first instance where legal representation is mandatory.

Organisation

The legislative provisions for the administrative organisation of the TGI can be found in the Act of 22 December 1958. For administrative purposes France is divided into sections known as *départements*, for which there is no direct English equivalent, but for ease of reference this term will be translated below as a 'department'. Each department has at least one TGI, but the number increases for departments with larger populations. The *Nord* department (in the North of France) has, for instance, seven TGI. There are a total of 181 TGI.

Each TGI is headed by a President. The number of judges based in each court varies according to its size. In small courts with five judges or fewer, judges do not specialise and will hear whatever case is allocated to them. Larger courts are organised into specialist divisions, including civil and criminal divisions. The Paris TGI is, for example, divided into 31 divisions. Judges will rotate between divisions every few years so as to remain non specialists.

The Act of 8 February 1995 allows TGI to set up divisions operating in locations outside the court buildings so as to hear cases closer to where the parties live. Such divisions are not required to specialise and can deal with any matter within the jurisdiction of the TGI.

The number of judges hearing a case is always uneven, with the smallest court having at least three judges under article L 311-8 (COJ). This allows for the majority view to prevail where there is a disagreement on how to decide a case. The judgment is that of the court, not of the individuals, and the judges are not named. Majority judgments, with two of one opinion and the third disagreeing, are believed to be quite common. The dissenting judge will agree to the judgment and will not reveal his or her original dissent.

Since the Act of 10 July 1970 most matters can be heard by a single judge, if the President of the court decides so and the parties agree, in order to relieve pressure of work. Certain legislative provisions also provide that for certain matters a case should be heard by a single judge. For example, a single judge deals with pre-trial matters, car accidents, and with most family law matters (including divorces).

The President has administrative and disciplinary functions. Since the Act of 23 December 1983, he or she is advised by assemblies of judges and clerks of the tribunal. These are designed to involve the various members in the running of the tribunal, to make it more democratic and less auto-cratic. In particular, judges make proposals as to how the work should be distributed, though the President still makes the final decision.

Tribunaux d'instance

Jurisdiction

The *tribunaux d'instance* (TI) are specialist courts, and as such they can only hear matters specifically allocated to them by the *Code d'organisation judiciaire* or other legislation. Their main remit, following an Act of 26 January 2005 amending article L 321-2 COJ, is small civil cases worth between €4,000 and 10,000. Certain other matters also fall within their jurisdiction. For example, while cases concerning land are not as a rule within their jurisdiction, they hear matters relating to the lease of land and buildings up to the financial limits mentioned above (article R 321-2), and various agricultural disputes (article R 321-7). The court also has specific powers (without financial limit) to deal with certain disputes relating to the conduct of elections (article R 321-20). The civil partnerships that couples (of same or different gender) are entitled to make since an Act of 15 November 1999, in order to provide them with similar rights to married couples, must be registered at the TI. In fact, the list of cases that may be referred to the TI is long and varied, and consists of litigation suited to resolution by a local court.

If a matter comes within the jurisdiction of a TI, the usual rule (but subject to many exceptions) is that the case will be heard by the tribunal which is closest to the defendant's home.

Organisation

The TI in their present form are a relatively new creation, having been established by the Act of 22 December 1958. At the time, 455 TI replaced the 2092 *justices de paix*. The *justices de paix* were a much more locally based jurisdiction, which shared some features with the English and Welsh magistrates' courts, with their emphasis on community links.

There are currently 473 TI in France. The general rule is that each *arrondissement*, roughly equivalent to an English local authority district, has its own TI. Some have more than one. Cases will usually be heard by one professional judge only (article L 321-4 of the COJ). The courts have their own buildings and clerk. The TI can also hear cases outside their court buildings in order to be closer to where the parties live (article R 321-32 of the COJ).

The TI are closely linked to the local TGI (discussed above). For example, the TGI will provide the judges, who are lent to the TI for three years. The President of the TGI is also, in effect, president of all the TI within its area. The President is advised on matters relating to the TI by a special assembly of TI staff, created by a law of 23 December 1983. The TI is in many ways simply a division of the TGI, dealing with small cases at first instance. There is no appeal to the TGI. Appeals are made directly to the court of appeal.

The conciliation role of the Tribunaux d'instance

In addition to their traditional role in the resolution of litigation discussed above, the TI also have a much under-used role in achieving conciliation. The court's predecessor, the *justices de paix*, used to require parties to try to achieve a negotiated settlement before they proceeded to full-blown litigation. Their role was compared by Treilhard, one of the drafters of the Civil Procedure Code, to that of a father trying to encourage his two children to make up after a fight. Although this service has not been compulsory since 1958, Parliamentary Acts of 20 March 1978 and 18 May 1981 were passed allowing the court to appoint conciliators to help parties settle cases. Conciliators are not judges and can only facilitate the reaching of an agreement between the parties. They can operate outside the court at locations closer to where the parties live. This development has brought the court nearer to its historical roots, which was run by a lay justice of the peace with no legal qualification. As a further step to making the court more closely connected with the ordinary citizen, an Act of 19 January 1995 provides for the appointment of part-time judges for a period of seven years. They are allowed to continue practising another profession. The procedure is lighter and quicker than in the TGI, and parties are under no obligation to have legal representation in court.

The neighbourhood courts

The most recent of all French courts were created by an Act of 9 September 2002. They are known in French as *les juridictions de proximité*, which we have translated here as neighbourhood courts. They were created to relieve the TI of some of their workload and to be closer to the people.

Jurisdiction

These courts are entitled to hear small civil claims by private individuals worth up to €4,000 (article L 331-2 COJ), with no right to appeal to the Appeal Court.

Organisation

Neighbourhood courts are not staffed by career judges but by people with a degree of experience in the legal profession, such as lawyers, retired professional judges, law lecturers or certain categories of civil servants. They are nominated for seven years and must be over 35 years old (Decree of 15 May 2003). Every new applicant has to follow a five-day legal training course, acquire work experience in a court, and undertake a number of hours of continuing education every year. It is only a fractional appointment (one day per week) and, in most cases, judges are entitled to continue to exercise simultaneously another profession. By the end of 2004, approximately 300 judges had been appointed and by 2007 this is expected to have increased to 3300. Serious efforts have been made to help recruitment, for example, the French Employment Agency advertised in April 2005 for people to become judges in the neighbourhood courts. Cases are heard by single judges. A judge from the TI may intervene if the neighbourhood court is faced with a difficult legal or factual issue.

Criticism

There has been considerable criticism of the creation of these new courts. The *Ecole Nationale de la Magistrature* expressed doubts as to the court's capacity to dispense fair and just judgments. It considered the training of the neighbourhood judges as totally insufficient, and called instead for an increase in career judges. The *Conseil constitutionnel* dismissed these concerns in two decisions of 29 August 2002 and 20 January 2005 (see Chapter 7 for the role of the *Conseil constitutionnel*).

Following protests by the first judges appointed to these courts, the Government decided in December 2004 to increase the court's jurisdiction. It enabled the court to hear cases of up to €4,000 (see Table 5.1) and also decided that companies, as well as private individuals, should be allowed to bring proceedings before this court.

▶ Commercial courts

Since the middle ages, in France and in most of Europe, laws relating to business transactions were developed to facilitate trade. In France disputes were heard in separate commercial courts. France still has commercial law which relates to business dealings only, and separate courts of first instance. These commercial courts were officially established in a royal edict of 1563, and were the only courts to survive the 1789 Revolution. Their existence was confirmed in an Act of 16-24 August 1790.

Jurisdiction

The jurisdiction of commercial courts (*tribunaux de commerce*) is set out in articles L411-1 to L414-7 and R411-1 to R414-21 of the COJ. It is a specialist court with jurisdiction over three main areas:

- disputes between traders, merchants and bankers relating to their respective businesses. It is worth noting that the French definition of business is narrow. The activity must essentially relate to money or money's worth and no more. Farmers and lawyers are not considered to be in business and their disputes will be heard in the local TGI;
- disputes between business partners;
- disputes relating to commercial transactions. The Commercial Code lists these in considerable detail, but the list is not exhaustive. Most usual business activities, such as sale, purchase, transport and banking operations are included. If the defendant is involved in a commercial activity, but the claimant is not, then the claimant may choose between bringing the proceedings before the commercial court or the TGI;
- in some cases of receivership and compulsory liquidation.

For very small transactions having a value of no more than €4,000, there is no right of appeal. For transactions above that amount there is a right of appeal to a court of appeal, and for all cases the right to refer points of law to the *Cour de cassation*. The higher courts have commercial divisions, but there are no separate commercial appeal courts.

As with other courts of first instance, cases will normally be heard by the court nearest to the defendant's home.

Organisation

The number of courts in each department depends on the amount of commercial activity. Rural areas do not usually have a commercial court, and two rural departments, Lozère and Haute Savoie, have none. In areas where there is no commercial court the local TGI will hear commercial cases, following the commercial courts' rules of procedure. There is a special system for the overseas departments (Guyana, Martinique, Guadeloupe, and Réunion) and for Alsace–Lorraine, which was annexed by Germany between 1871 and 1919 and has kept some different legal institutions. At the time of writing, there are 191 commercial courts in France.

Each court has a president, a vice president and its own administration. As in the TGIs, most judgments are given by at least three judges. Larger courts, such as the Paris Commercial court which is staffed by 172 lay judges, are divided into specialist divisions.

The judges of commercial courts are all lay judges, except in Alsace–Lorraine and in the Overseas department where lay judges sit with a professional qualified judge. The judges are advised by a legally qualified clerk (in the same way that lay magistrates in England and Wales can call on the services of a qualified court clerk when hearing criminal cases). Judges are not paid. They are elected by the local business community, unlike magistrates in England and Wales who are appointed by the Minister for Constitutional Affairs from a list of suitable candidates. The election procedure, which dates back to 1883, is complex, but designed to ensure the widest possible representation. It is worth mentioning that women have been entitled to vote in these elections since 1898, almost half a century before they got the political vote. Local businesses elect an electoral college every three years and this elects the judges. Judges must:

- be French;
- be at least 30 years old;
- have been in business for five years;
- not have been the subject of bankruptcy proceedings.

As cases become increasingly complex, and judges are not paid, it has become quite difficult to find enough judges of the right calibre. Judges can remain in office for very long periods. The only rules are that on first election they must stand for re-election after two years. Thereafter, subject to re-election every four years, they can continue indefinitely provided they take a year off every 14 years. Some courts are limited to hearing only smaller cases, but most courts still hear all cases, which is a heavy workload for unpaid lay people.

Since an Act of 16 July 1987, cases are necessarily heard by an uneven number of judges. The number is usually three, but a single judge can sit alone in some cases. The court procedure is more informal than for many of the other civil courts. Commercial courts undoubtedly provide a relatively cheap, quick and flexible method of dealing with small disputes. Parties are under no obligation to have legal representation. For claims whose value does not exceed €3,800, there is no appeal. For long and complex cases, the party which loses can, and very often does, appeal. The first stage in the commercial court at least gives parties a chance to settle the matter in relatively informal surroundings. However, in the increasingly complex modern business world, it is undoubtedly felt by some to be an unsuitable system. It is also open to abuse, as the temptation by judges to use information gained in court for their private business advantage can often be too great to resist.

An aborted reform

Following a parliamentary report (the *Montebourg* report) published on 2 July 1998, the Minister of Justice announced his intention to introduce a radical reform of the commercial courts. The reforms contained two main objectives:

- The location of the commercial courts had to be reformed. There was an over-representation in rural areas and an under-representation in large towns. A report of the Paris Chamber of Commerce in June 1997 pointed out that 10 per cent of commercial courts dealt with half the total number of cases. The number of courts was reduced from 227 to 191 by a decree of 30 July 1999, the smaller courts being closed down.
- The proposed reform also wanted to require professionally qualified judges to preside over the traditional lay judges in cases of public importance, such as matters involving the liquidation of companies, mergers and acquisitions. This system of mixing professional and lay judges in commercial courts already exists in numerous European countries such as Germany, Belgium and Norway. Traditional lay judges would be allowed to sit alone on minor cases. The professional judges would be required to take courses in economics and business matters, while lay judges would have to improve their knowledge of the relevant law. The lay judges would be obliged to declare their business assets and commercial interests so that a register of interests could be compiled. This requirement was designed to enable lay judges to be controlled, and to ensure that they did not judge matters in which they had an interest. There had been a number of recent cases involving corrupt judges misusing their role to ensure advantages for their businesses. This proposal for reform was not welcomed by everybody. During the period prior to the announcement, there was considerable opposition by many lay judges, in small towns and rural areas, who are important in the local business community. Twenty per cent of all lay judges resigned in protest following the announcement to introduce these changes. This, coupled with the fact that it would have required an additional 350 professionally qualified judges, and that it had been an idea put forward by the socialist government, led the newly-formed conservative government to announce on 22 November 2002 that it had decided not to introduce these changes.

Employment tribunals

Employment tribunals, known as the *conseils de prud'hommes*, were established by Napoleon in 1806, first in Lyon and then nationwide in 1809. They had a role both as a forum for conciliation of industrial and employment disputes and as a court. Over the years, their role has developed and they have been reformed regularly. Until 1979, these tribunals were set up in a very random way: some had only jurisdiction for a limited number of professions, and some parts of the country were without any employment tribunal at all, forcing the *tribunaux d'instance* to deal with employment disputes. The Act of 19 January 1979 increased the number of tribunals, so that they are to be found all over France and not just in the more industrial areas. There are currently 271 such tribunals (article L 511-3 of the Employment Code).

Jurisdiction

This is a specialist court whose jurisdiction is set out in article L 511-1 onwards of the Employment Code, and reproduced in the COJ, in article L 421-1 onwards. Tribunals hear all disputes relating to individual contracts of employment in the private sector. These include actions relating to unfair dismissal and redundancy. The jurisdiction of these tribunals is wider than that of British employment tribunals, since they cover all individual claims, and not just those under specified legislation. They do not, however, hear disputes relating to collective bargaining, which are referred to the local TGI, or most disputes involving civil servants, which fall within the jurisdiction of the administrative courts.

Cases will normally be heard in the tribunal nearest to the employee's place of employment. The employee, however, is also entitled to choose the tribunal nearest to the place where the employment contract was concluded or where the employer is based (article R 517-1 of the Employment Code).

For small disputes worth €4,000 or less, there is no right of appeal. For larger claims, there is a full right of appeal to the court of appeal. A special division of this court, the social division, hears appeals from employment tribunals and two other tribunals briefly mentioned below, the agricultural tenancies tribunal and the social security tribunal. Parties also have the usual right to refer points of law to the *Cour de cassation*.

Organisation

The number of courts in an area depends on the amount of industrial activity, but there is at least one employment tribunal in each department.

The judges of employment tribunals are lay people. They must attend a six-week legal training course before being allowed to hear cases. The French *Cour de cassation* has on a number of occasions held that the composition of the employment tribunal could be contrary to the right to a fair trial as enshrined in article 6 of the European Convention on Human Rights: the condition of having an impartial court was judged, in a decision of 2 July 2002, to have been breached when a judge heard a claim where he had provided legal advice to one of the parties in earlier litigation. A court must not only be impartial but also appear to be impartial. On the other hand, the *Cour de cassation* did not find a breach of article 6 in a decision of 19 December 2003 when one of the judges was a member of the same trade union as one of the parties.

The tribunals are all divided up into five sections with eight judges each, half representing employers, and half employees. Four sections cover management, industry, commerce and agriculture and a fifth section covers all other activities.

All cases must first be heard by two judges: one employee and one employer, who will try to help the parties negotiate a solution. Parties may choose to be represented by a lawyer, but are under no obligation to do so. Only a very limited number of cases, fewer than 10 per cent, come to an end following conciliation. If conciliation has failed, cases are heard in a more formal environment by four judges: two employers and two employees.

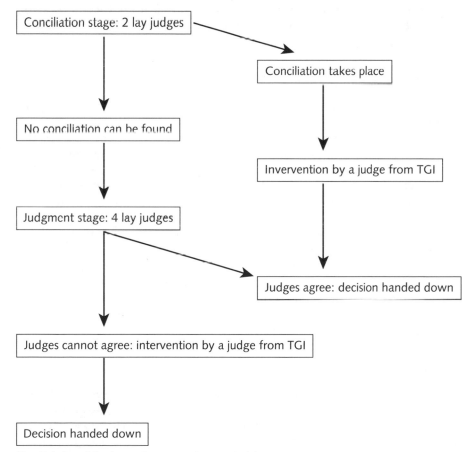

Fig. 5.1 Possible stages to an employment claim

Since the number of judges sitting in a case is even, if the judges cannot agree on a decision, a judge from the local TGI (*le juge departiteur*) will help the four lay judges and break the deadlock (article L 515-3 of the Employment Code). The possible stages of an employment claim are set out in Figure 5.1.

Each section has a president and vice president and benefits from the services of the tribunal's administration. The president and vice president are elected for a one-year term, by the judges. The holders of these offices alternate each year between employers and employees to avoid bias.

Like the commercial court judges, employment tribunal judges are elected. All workers and employers aged 16 or over within the area of the tribunal, including foreign nationals and the unemployed, can vote. Judges must be French and at least 21 years old, and either employees or employers. While the electoral college comprises basically all the economically active adult population (other than the self-employed), the turn-out is very low. Judges are elected for a five-year term. Both employees and employers receive some remuneration for their work. Employees must be granted leave by their employers. Nonetheless it is difficult to find enough candidates.

Agricultural tenancy tribunals

These tribunals, known as the *tribunaux paritaires des baux ruraux*, were created by Parliament on 4 December 1944, and deal with disputes relating to agricultural tenancies. The structure and organisation of the 431 current tribunals dates back to a 1958 reform. The law governing these tribunals is now contained in articles L 441-1 to L 444-1 of the COJ. The tribunals operate from the local TI. The hearings are presided over by the judge of the local TI, who sits with four elected lay judges, two representing tenants and two representing landowners. Lay judges are elected for six years, must be French, at least 26 years old, and must have been tenants or landowners for at least five years.

There is no right of appeal for small-value disputes of €4,000 or less. For all other cases parties have the right to appeal to the social division of the court of appeal. These tribunals do not function on a permanent basis because of the scarcity of cases. Every tribunal deals, on average, with fewer than nine cases each year.

Social security tribunals

These tribunals, known as *tribunaux des affaires de Sécurité Sociale,* are another post-war creation. Social security legislation was passed in 1945, and specialised tribunals to deal with the inevitable disputes followed shortly afterwards in 1946. The current law dealing with the organisation and jurisdiction of these 116 tribunals is set out in the COJ in articles

L 451-1 and R 451-1 and in the Social Security Code. They operate from the local TGI. Cases are heard by the President of the TGI who sits with two lay judges: one representing employees, the other representing employers. The lay judges are not elected. This is because the subject matter is not so close to the interested parties and is more technical. Lay judges are nominated for three years by the president of the local court of appeal. There is no right of appeal for small value matters of €4,000 or less. For other cases, parties have the right to appeal to the social division of the local court of appeal.

Disability disputes tribunals

Jurisdiction
These tribunals, known as *tribunaux du contentieux de l'incapacité*, deal with disputes between private individuals and the social security office regarding their level of disability, and are staffed by both professional and lay judges. Lay judges are selected by the Ministry of Justice and the President of the court of appeal. They include employers, self-employed people and employees' representatives. The organisation and jurisdiction of these tribunals is determined by the COJ in its article R 452-1 and by the Social Security Code, article L 143-2 to article L 143-4. Appeals are sent to a special court, the national disability disputes appeal court (the *Cour nationale de l'incapacité et de la tarification de l'assurance des accidents du travail*) which is based in Amiens.

The rules regarding staffing of the disability disputes tribunals and the disability disputes appeal courts had to be amended in 2002 and 2003. The *Cour de cassation*, in a decision of 9 March 2000, criticised the tribunal's staffing as it was headed by a civil servant working for the social security office, who had no security of tenure and was seen as lacking independence and impartiality. His or her position therefore breached the requirement of a fair trial which is enshrined in article 6 of the European Convention on Human Rights. The national disability appeal court was criticised for the same reasons in five decisions of the *Cour de cassation* of 22 December 2000 (and because an important piece of evidence – the medical appraisal – was not being disclosed to claimants). Each of these courts is today headed by a professional judge.

Conclusion

There is undoubtedly scope for the creation of further specialist tribunals to cope with the increasing complexity of modern society. If these were to be created, a right of appeal to the local court of appeal would also need to be provided.

▶ Courts of appeal

Cour d'appel

The appeal system provides a way of correcting cases that were wrongly decided by the first instance courts, whether due to an error of fact, law or procedure. The courts of appeal (*Cours d'appel*) proceed by way of retrial and re-examine witnesses. They are known as courts of second instance as they re-judge the facts and the law examined by courts of first instance. They also have reasonable discretion to judge additional facts which have come to light since the case was heard at first instance. The courts of appeal were established after the Revolution. There are 35 in total, so geographically they are reasonably close to the parties. Their geographical location is mainly based on historical factors and does not adequately reflect the current demographic and economic distribution in France. This means that their workloads vary significantly. The Paris court of appeal is larger than the others as it covers six departments and deals with approximately 35 000 cases per year as opposed to other courts, like Bastia, which cover only two departments and deal with fewer than 2000 cases a year. The number of appeals is also much higher than in England, with a high proportion of the disputes involving relatively large amounts of money proceeding to appeal. In 2003, almost 200,000 cases were heard by the courts of appeal.

Jurisdiction
Each court of appeal hears appeals from all first-instance civil courts in its area, except:

- small claims;
- cases from the disability disputes tribunal heard by the national disability dispute court;
- a limited number of cases excluded by legislation, for example, appeals against decisions by the *juge des tutelles* are heard by the TGI due to article 1215 of the Civil Procedure Code.

It also hears appeals from the criminal divisions of the TI and TGI, which we look at in more detail at p. 106.

Organisation
Each court of appeal is headed by a president. In order to cope with the large number of specialist appeals, courts are divided into a number of divisions: civil, criminal, social, commercial and others. The number and type of divisions is decided by each court in accordance with its size and the particular demand in the area. The judges are known as *conseillers*. Each division has its own president. As in the TGIs, the policy is for judges to rotate among the divisions every few years so that they do not become too specialist.

Judgments are given by either three or five judges according to the importance of the case. For very important cases, judges from two different divisions will sit to ensure more breadth and objectivity. Only the judgment of the court is published, as agreed by all the judges. Any dissenting opinions are kept private.

The president of each court of appeal has administrative and disciplinary functions both over the court of appeal and, to some extent, over first instance courts in their area. As for the TGIs, assemblies of judges and clerks are consulted on administrative matters. The court also hears disciplinary cases against lawyers and clerks of the court. To hear such cases representatives from the most important divisions sit together to form '*l'assemblée des chambres*'.

▶ Cour de cassation

This court is the successor of the revolutionary *tribunal de cassation* created in 1790. It is the only central court for the whole of the civil and criminal system. Its role is to 'judge the judgments' of the appeal courts and of courts that have decided matters from which there is no right of appeal. Parties who are unhappy with a decision from any of these courts may apply to the *Cour de cassation* to quash the case on a point of law. The *Cour de cassation* does not retry the case. It does not examine facts and is therefore not a court of third instance (article L 111-2 COJ and article 604 of the New Code of Civil Procedure). In this it differs from the House of Lords and the Supreme Court of many other jurisdictions. However, like the House of Lords, the main role of the *Cour de cassation* is to ensure a consistent interpretation of the law.

The *Cour de cassation* is not bound by its own decisions but it does try to be consistent. As there is no doctrine of precedent, it cannot ensure that the other courts will follow the same line, though the court does undoubtedly have considerable influence. Until recently, every case could be brought to the attention of the *Cour de cassation* and a very large number were (21,394 civil cases and an additional 8,714 criminal cases in 1995). By contrast, the UK legal system manages to limit appeals to the House of Lords, which hears about 60 appeals a year, restricting leave to appeal to cases which are of great legal importance. It then relies on the doctrine of precedent to ensure consistency.

Organisation

The *Cour de cassation* sits in the centre of Paris, in the same building as the Paris court of appeal, the *Palais de Justice*. It is the highest court of the civil and criminal system.

The court is presided over by a judge known as the 'First President'. This is the highest-ranking post in the judiciary. He or she does not judge

The special formations of the *Cour de cassation*:

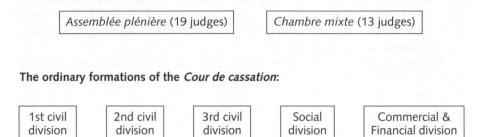

The ordinary formations of the *Cour de cassation*:

| 1st civil division | 2nd civil division | 3rd civil division | Social division | Commercial & Financial division |

Fig. 5.2 Civil formations of the *Cour de cassation*

matters, but is the head of the court's administration and participates in drafting the most important judgments. The court consists of five civil divisions and a criminal division (Fig. 5.2). The civil divisions consist of a commercial and financial division, a social division and three general divisions. The first of the general divisions deals with contracts, insurance and international law, the second with divorce and civil procedure, and the third with property and planning law. Each division has its own division president. At the time of writing, there are 88 full judges (known as *conseillers*), 65 assistant judges (known as *conseillers référendaires*), and a further 8 newly-qualified judges acting as administrative assistants (known as *auditeurs*). The main function of assistant judges is to prepare reports on the case for consideration by the judges, but they can also, when necessary, take part in judging a case when their presence is necessary to make up a quorum. They also assist the judges by carrying out various administrative tasks.

Normally judgments are given by at least five judges from the same division, article L131-6-1 COJ. The Division President, or the First President, can decide to reduce the number to three for more straightforward cases. Parties have the right to object and require a full sitting. To ensure fairness and consistency, judgments in matters involving more than one division, such as a problem involving both contract and land law, will normally be heard by a joint bench (*Chambre mixte*) consisting of a minimum of 13 judges from at least three divisions. The decision to refer the matter to the joint bench in such cases can be made either by the First President or by the division originally allocated the matter where there is a risk of an incompatible judgment. The state representative, the public prosecutor (*procureur général*), can also require that a matter be transferred to the joint bench.

Since an Act of 3 January 1979 (article L 131-2 COJ), either the First President, the public prosecutor, or the court originally referred to can decide that a case involves an important point of law on which there has been a history of inconsistent judgments by lower courts. They then have the power to refer the case to a special formation of the court, known as the *Assemblée plénière*, comprising 19 judges, three from each of the six divisions presided over by the First President. This is unusual and is still considered an innovative procedure in this context.

Judges used to rotate annually among the divisions. This practice has been stopped, to encourage a degree of specialisation among the judiciary. This also makes for stability and consistency in judgments. Nonetheless commentators have noted that a change of Division President can have a marked effect on the content of the judgments of the court.

The appeal mechanism

As mentioned above, appeals to the *Cour de cassation* can only be made on points of law. Appeals will usually be made against a decision of a local court of appeal, but can also be made against a decision of a first instance court where there is no right of appeal to the court of appeal. The latter are rare, as they involve small amounts of money, and the cost of referring a matter to the *Cour de cassation* is high. Ordinary procedures of the civil court system are illustrated in Figure 5.3.

When an appeal is made and the *Cour de cassation* decides that it agrees with the judgment that is the subject of the appeal, it gives a decision rejecting the appeal, called an *arrêt de rejet*. No further recourse is possible, and the judgment is upheld. If it decides that the judgment which is the subject of the appeal involved an error in law, it will quash that decision. Since it cannot rehear the case, as a normal court of appeal would (and as the House of Lords does), it usually remits the case for retrial by another court of the same level as the one that made the error, normally another court of appeal (article L 131-4 COJ). That court will fully retry the case. Parties can then refer the matter once again to the *Cour de cassation*. This time the matter may be heard either by the special sitting of 19 judges (*Assemblée plénière*) described above, or by a joint bench, or simply by another division of the *Cour de cassation*, depending on the importance of the points of law at issue. The court will then make a final decision on the law, against which there is no appeal. It may agree with the judgment of the retrial court, which will end the proceedings. If it considers that the retrial court made an error of law, it will pronounce on the law definitively. However, as the *Cour de cassation* cannot hear the facts of the case, the matter is usually referred to another court of the same level as the original one which will apply the law as stated by the *Cour de cassation* to the facts and make a judgment accordingly.

In exceptional circumstances, the *Cour de cassation* is allowed to quash a case without referral to another court of the same level as that which made the wrong decision – for instance, if the claim is statute barred (article L. 131-5). This procedure is very time-consuming and expensive, and causes great inconvenience to the parties who are left in a state of uncertainty until the third court of appeal has pronounced judgment, following

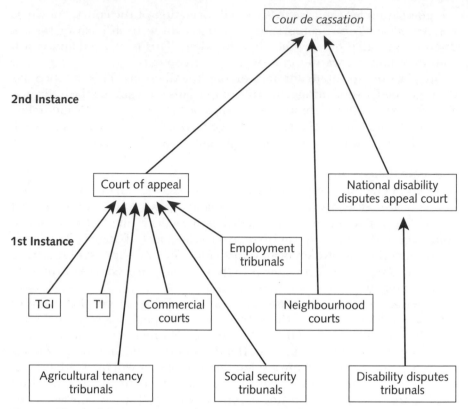

Fig. 5.3 The Civil Court system: ordinary procedures
Note, there is no appeal to the Court of Appeal where the case is only concerned with a small sum; instead the case goes directly to the *Cour de cassation*.

the law as stated by the *Assemblée plénière*. Nonetheless, some cases involving both considerable amounts of money and points of principle do progress through all these stages. As the system stands at present there is little to stop determined and rich losers from continuing the process until the second referral to a court of appeal by the *Cour de cassation*.

A brief look at a famous case known as *l'affaire Poussin* can help to give a flavour of the operation of the system (Table 5.2). The parties, who lost at first instance, kept on with the process until the *Assemblée plénière* decided the law in their favour. From the first case at the local TGI in 1972 to the hearing at the last court of appeal at Versailles in 1987, this particular case took 15 years. A family owned a painting which, according to family legend, had been painted by a famous painter called Nicolas Poussin, whose work commanded high prices and was collected by museums. When the family decided to sell the painting, they obtained expert opinion, on which they relied, that the painting was not in fact by Poussin. They then proceeded to sell it at an auction in 1968 for a fairly nominal sum of 2,200 FF. The Louvre, the famous museum in Paris, has a right to buy French paintings in certain circumstances, which they exercised in this case. It then, shortly afterwards, exhibited the painting as a genuine Poussin. The family sued the original purchaser and was successful at the local TGI, which decided the sale was voidable for mistake. The Louvre and other interested parties appealed at the Paris court of appeal, which held that the contract was valid, and in particular that mistake on the part of the seller had no effect on the contract. The family then referred the question of the voidability of the contract to the *Cour de cassation* for the first time. The court quashed the judgment of the Paris court and remitted the case for retrial at the Amiens court of appeal. This court came to the same conclusion as the Paris court of appeal and the family referred the same point of law again to the *Cour de cassation*. As this was a second referral, the matter was heard again by the *Cour de cassation* which agreed with its original views and interpreted the law so that the contract was voidable for mistake. The case was referred to another court of appeal in Versailles, but this time the court had to follow the law as stated by the *Cour de cassation*. The Versailles court accordingly judged that the contract was voidable and the Louvre returned the picture to the family. The painting was sold shortly afterwards for 7.4 million FF. In monetary terms, at least, in this case the 15-year wait was worthwhile.

The procedure described amounts to a compromise between the need to respect the independence of each court and the need to impose some consistency. If the full procedure is followed, the relevant lower court must, just this once, follow the law as stated by the *Cour de cassation*. No other court is then strictly bound to follow in other cases the law as stated, although if only to avoid the need to go through this lengthy procedure, courts do tend to take into account the rulings of the *Cour de cassation*.

Table 5.2 *L'affaire Poussin* at a glance

1968 (21 February): Sale of the painting	
1972 (13 December): Decision of the TGI	– cancelled the sale
1976 (2 February): Decision of the Court of Appeal of Paris	– held that the sale was valid
1978 (22 February): Decision of the *Cour de cassation*	– invalidated the Court of Appeal decision
1982 (1 February): Decision of the Court of Appeal of Amiens	– confirmed the validity of the sale
1983 (13 December): Decision of the *Cour de cassation*	– invalidated the Court of Appeal decision
1987 (7 January): Decision of the Court of Appeal of Versailles	– cancelled the sale

It is possible, in certain cases, as mentioned above, for the process to be shortened by referral straight to the *Assemblée plénière*. This must clearly be an exceptional procedure involving a hearing of the case by 19 judges, first time round, rather than the normal five. In cases which are very likely to continue to the second referral stage this procedure can save both time and money. However, an approach aimed at reducing the court's caseload was successfully introduced by an Act of 15 May 1991. This allows lower courts, before passing judgment, to ask for an advisory opinion from a special formation of the *Cour de cassation* on a point of law, if it is new, complex, and likely to occur frequently (article L 151-1 COJ). It was considered vital that the special formation of the court should consist of senior members of the judiciary whose opinion would be respected and followed by other courts. Accordingly, a large number of judges is required – at least nine, including the First President, the President of each of the six divisions of the court and two judges from each of the divisions concerned with the particular point of law. Once the opinion has been referred to the court which applied for it, there is no obligation on that court to follow the opinion, and the parties have the right to refer the point again to the *Cour de cassation* after the court of appeal has made its judgment. The procedure is still in the experimental stage. The restricted right to refer, which is available to the court only and not to the parties, and the need for the advice to be given by such a large number of judges, combined with the freedom of the parties and the courts to ignore the advice, has meant that it has only rarely been used. It clearly can be developed to ensure that the referring court will be subject to a requirement to follow the opinion of the *Cour de cassation*, in the same way as national courts are required to follow interpretations of the European Court of Justice on points of European law. There is scope for the extremely narrow current remit to be broadened to include all important or complex points of law, and in due course this could well become the normal method of using the services of the *Cour de cassation*.

Furthermore, since 1979, article L 131-5 (COJ) allows the *Cour de cassation* to judge a matter definitively without referral to another court of appeal, in the exceptional cases where it considers that the facts as stated by the court of appeal allow it to apply the law to the facts itself.

The most logical reform of installing a filtering system to allow only the most important cases to proceed to the *Cour de cassation* was strongly resisted until 2001. In the past, a special division did indeed vet all cases referred to the court and only allowed cases it considered serious to proceed to judgment. This division was abolished in 1947, partly so that its judges could be redeployed to hearing cases and partly because the division was seen as blocking cases unnecessarily for long periods by examining each case in depth. In 1994 there was a plan to copy the reforms of the top administrative court, the *Conseil d'Etat*, which has successfully set up a filtering procedure reducing its workload by 65 per cent, but this plan was later dropped.

Finally, a filtering procedure was introduced at the *Cour de cassation* following an Act of 25 June 2001 which amended article L 131-6 (COJ). Every case heard by one of the civil chambers of the *Cour de cassation* is first examined by a reduced chamber of three judges. This reduced chamber has then a choice of three solutions: reject the case, decide the case itself or send the case to an ordinary chamber of five judges. In 2004, the reduced chamber rejected more than five thousand cases.

• •

PART III: THE CRIMINAL COURTS

▶ Introduction

French criminal procedure is divided into three stages:

1 the police investigation,
2 the judicial investigation, known as *l'instruction*, and
3 the judgment.

The three stages will be discussed fully in Chapter 10, which is concerned with criminal procedure. It is during the second stage that the French system differs most from the English and Welsh system: for serious offences the criminal investigation is pursued by an investigating judge, known as *le juge d'instruction*, while in England and Wales the whole investigation would be carried out by the police and the defendant's representatives. At the third stage the French judge often simply rubber stamps the findings of the pre-trial investigation, while in England and Wales all decisions as to both fact and law are made at the trial itself where the parties present their own version of events. While the first stage of the criminal procedure takes place outside the court system, both the second and third stages have their own hierarchy within the court system.

Most of the legislative provisions relating to the criminal courts are contained in the Code on Criminal Procedure, *le Code de procédure pénale*, and it will be abbreviated in the rest of this chapter as 'CPP'.

▶ First instance courts concerned with the criminal investigation

For serious offences, a judge (*le juge d'instruction*) is appointed to investigate the matter, by collecting evidence, interviewing witnesses and appointing experts. He or she is a judge of the local *tribunal de grande instance* (TGI) appointed for this purpose for a limited period. There is no equivalent to these judges in the English system. They do not decide the accused's guilt or innocence, which is the task of the trial court. When making

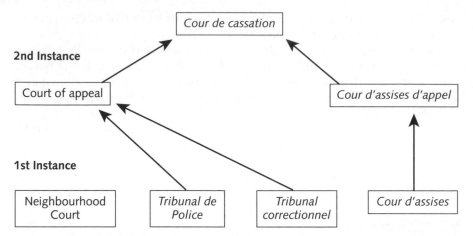

Fig. 5.4 The criminal trial court system: ordinary procedures
Note, there is no appeal to the Court of Appeal where the case is only concerned with minor offences, instead the case goes directly to the *Cour de cassation*

judicial decisions, such as whether or not to release a person being held on remand, the investigating judge is technically sitting as a court.

Some powers, particularly relating to the decision whether or not to place a person in custody on remand, have recently been withdrawn from the investigating judge and given to a new judge called the judge of freedom and detention (*le juge des libertés et de la détention*). This new judge is discussed in detail at p. 212.

First instance criminal trial courts

There are three courts of general jurisdiction: the *tribunal de police,* the *tribunal correctionnel* and the *Cour d'assises.* Each hears trials relating to a different type of offence. The first two operate from the same buildings as the courts hearing civil cases and share the same judges and administration (see Part I of this chapter). The third court, for the most serious offences, is unique in many ways (see *Cour d'assises* below). It does however also share personnel and has close connections with the other courts. Ordinary procedures of the criminal trial court system are illustrated in Figure 5.4

Tribunal de police

Minor offences, known as *contraventions*, are tried before a *tribunal de police*, which is a special formation of the *tribunal d'instance* (TI). This court only has limited sentencing powers, such as to impose fines not exceeding €3,000 and to seize stolen goods (article 521 CPP). The very minor offences, for instance most driving offences attracting a penalty short of a temporary disqualification from driving, are not subject to appeal (article 546 CPP). Both the accused and the prosecutor have a right of appeal in other cases.

Tribunal correctionnel

Major offences, *délits*, are all offences which are not serious offences, *crimes*, and which can be sentenced by imprisonment or have a maximum fine of at least €3,750. Such offences are triable in a special formation of the TGI known as the *tribunal correctionnel* (article 381 CPP). The more serious offences must be tried by three judges (article 398-3 (CPP)). If necessary judges from another tribunal or the court of appeal can be lent to make up numbers, and lay judges from the neighbourhood courts are also entitled to sit in this court (Act of 26 January 2005). An Act of 8 February 1995 provides that a number of less important offences (about half of the cases heard) must, subject to limited exceptions, be tried by a single judge (article 398 CPP). These include many traffic offences, those relating to misuse of credit cards or cheques, or the use of soft drugs.

In order to cope with the increasing complexity of offences involving business and financial matters, a series of laws (set out in article 704 CPP) provide for such matters to be tried in a specialist division of certain designated TGIs. The trial judges allocated to the division are experts in the field, and there is at least one such special division in the area covered by each court of appeal. The investigating judge allocated to the case will also be a specialist, as will the prosecutor. In the small number of cases of this type, where the penalty is not going to exceed the limits of the *tribunal de police*, the matter will be remitted for trial to the *tribunal de police* after prosecution and investigation by officials of the TGI. In many ways these divisions operate in practice as separate courts, but the French legal system is wary of setting up separate courts for trying special types of crime. Precedents, mostly connected with periods of unrest, such as the fight for Algerian independence, have acquired a poor reputation. The current increase in crimes involving business and financial matters has accordingly been accommodated within the existing courts. Given the high-profile nature of these cases, it has not been possible to avoid considerable publicity, and the judges involved have become well known to the general public.

Eight *tribunaux correctionnels* were given wider territorial jurisdiction extending across several regions by the Act of 9 March 2004. These eight courts are Bordeaux, Fort-de-France, Lille, Lyon, Marseille, Nancy, Paris and Rennes. The aim of this reform is to help fight organised crime more effectively.

Cour d'assises

The *Cour d'assises* is the court in which the most serious offences, known as *crimes*, are tried. It has jurisdiction over offences with a maximum sentence of at least ten years and can impose life imprisonment. The death penalty has been abolished in France. A jury, consisting of nine jurors, hears cases in this court, sitting alongside three professional judges. The jurors are chosen by random selection from an election list. They must be French nationals, aged over 23, and know how to read and write. They take an oath at the beginning of the trial promising to examine and decide according to their conscience and their personal conviction (article 353 CPP). The judges and jurors deliberate and vote together on the facts, the law and the punishment. These deliberations take place immediately after the prosecution and defence cases have been heard, and must not be interrupted, but continue until a decision is reached. Eight votes are necessary for any decision unfavourable to the accused. This entails at least five jurors, that is the majority, being in agreement, a requirement that exists in principle to prevent the professional judges exerting undue influence over their lay counterparts.

The *Cour d'assises* was established by an Act of 16-26 September 1791. The inspiration was the Assize Courts in England and Wales (now abolished) which had been greatly admired by Voltaire, but the *Cour d'assises* has developed in a unique way.

The *Cour d'assises* sits in sessions normally of 15 days' duration, so that members of the jury are not kept from carrying out their usual occupations for too long. Additional sittings can be ordered. In Paris the court sits nearly continuously, but in other towns it only convenes once a quarter.

There is one *Cour d'assises* per department (article 232 CPP), but it does not usually have its own buildings. It is run from the nearest court of appeal and in most instances it sits in the department's chief town. Where the town boasts a court of appeal, it shares buildings with it. In other towns it will normally share buildings with the TGI. The court has jurisdiction where the accused either lives in the department where the court is situated, or committed the crime or was arrested in that department.

The President of the nearest appeal court chooses a president for the *Cour d'assises*. The appointment is limited to one session. The President is chosen from the judges of the court of appeal, including division Presidents (article 247 CPP). The President is assisted by two judges called *assesseurs*. They are appointed from among judges of either the court of appeal or the TGI. Additional assistant judges may be appointed as necessary.

▶ Specialist criminal courts

The courts we have studied so far are all courts of general jurisdiction. There are also an increasing number of specialist courts created by Parliament. In Chapter 7, we will study courts with the special remit of judging the President of the Republic if he or she is suspected of high treason, and members of the government suspected of committing offences.

The Act of 9 September 2002 created neighbourhood courts (*les juridictions de proximité*). This court was created to facilitate access and to reduce delay. It consists of a lay judge who is selected on the basis of his or her skills or experience, and is usually a former judge or lawyer recruited on short-term contracts. The court only has jurisdiction over certain minor offences (article 706-72 CPP) of which the list is fixed by decree (Decree 23 June 2003, article R-53-40 CPP). Before this court was created, these cases would have been heard by the *tribunal de police*. It hears, in particular, minor non-fatal offences against the person and minor criminal damage cases. It has the same territorial jurisdiction as the *tribunal de police*. The neighbourhood courts can also ratify formal plea bargains (*la composition pénale*) if this power has been delegated to them by the president of the *tribunal de grande instance*.

A specialist court has been established to hear terrorist cases (article 706-18 CPP), a court that specialises in organised crime (article 706-75 CPP, Act of 9 March 2004), and a court responsible for hearing cases involving maritime pollution (article 706-107 CPP, Act of 9 March 2004). There are some specialist courts for members of the armed forces including courts for those posted abroad and specialist divisions of the normal courts including the *Cour d'assises*.

Young people have the benefit of a separate criminal system. Serious crimes committed by young persons aged 16 or 17 are tried in a special juvenile formation of the *Cour d'assises* and the procedure is similar to that for adults. Custodial sentences are lighter but similar to adult sentences. The main difference from the procedure for adults is that at least two judges are specialist children's judges and proceedings are not always open to the public.

Where the juvenile formation of the *Cour d'assises* does not have jurisdiction, the court system for criminal charges against young people under the age of 18 runs parallel to that for adults, and uses the same court buildings. The adult system has been carefully adapted for young people, except for very minor offences tried in the *tribunal de police*, where there is no special procedure. Investigation is carried out either by a judge or by an investigating judge specialising in dealing with young offenders. On the whole, less serious offences are investigated by a specialist judge. When the investigation is completed, the judge can refer the matter to trial or can decide to deal with the matter without a trial and pronounce a non-custodial sentence, such as a warning or a supervision order. Since the law of 2 February 1995, the judge can now choose to impose detention for no more than five years at a specialist institution. Where the investigation is carried out by an investigating judge, the procedure is similar to an investigation for crimes committed by adults.

If the result of the investigation phase is that the matter should proceed to trial, the case will be heard by a special formation of the TGI. The tribunal is headed by a children's judge nominated by the President of the TGI, assisted by two lay magistrates nominated for a period of four years.

Since the Act of 15 June 2000 establishing appeals against decisions of the *Cour d'assises*, there exists a *Cour d'assises d'appel des mineurs* which however is only different from that at first instance by the number of jurors: 12 instead of 9.

Criminal appeals relating to the investigation

The Judicial Investigation Division

Each local court of appeal (*Cour d'appel*) has a permanent Judicial Investigation Division (*Chambre de l'instruction*). Appeals relating to decisions of a judicial nature handed down by the investigating judge and the judge of freedom and detention can be made to the Judicial Investigation Division. Such appeals can be made by the prosecution and, in limited circumstances, by the private parties.

Until the Act of 15 June 2000, this was known as the *chambre d'accusation*. This Division consists of a president and two judges of the court of appeal. It hears appeals relating to the judicial investigation. These appeals can relate to decisions taken by the investigating judge and the judge of freedom and detention (articles 173, 185, 186, 187, 206 and 207 CCP). As well as providing a forum for the person being investigated to appeal on the conduct of the investigation, the Judicial Investigation Division is available to the public prosecutor's office, if it is unhappy with the conduct of the investigation. The investigating judges are jealous of their independence and often resent any such appeal which can be seen as interference.

In the past, if the offence was a serious offence (*un crime*), the Division automatically reviewed all judicial investigations, and the case only proceeded to trial in the *Cour d'assises* if the Division agreed it should do so. This automatic review was no longer considered necessary when a full right of appeal against decisions of the *Cour d'assises* was introduced. Investigating judges now unilaterally take the decision that a case should proceed to trial and send cases directly to the *Cour d'assises*.

Article 221-1 of the Code of Criminal Procedure provides that, whatever the offence committed, the Judicial Investigation Division may review the case if no substantial progress has been made after four months. It can even refer the matter to a different investigating judge.

The Division also hears some appeals relating to procedures not concerned with the judicial investigation, including extradition procedures, the European arrest warrant and police disciplinary matters.

Cour de cassation

A further appeal on points of law is possible before the *Cour de cassation*.

▶ Criminal appeals relating to judgments

Three main courts hear appeals against criminal court judgments: the court of appeal, the *cour d'assises d'appel* and the criminal division of the *Cour de cassation*. Each of these will be considered in turn.

Court of appeal

Appeals are heard by the criminal division of the local court of appeal (*Cour d'appel*), which hears both civil and criminal appeals. As with civil cases, appeal is by way of a retrial. There is one constraint on the freedom of a court of appeal: it cannot increase the sentence against an accused who has made an appeal. The court can only increase a sentence if the appeal is made by the prosecution.

Each court of appeal hears appeals from the *tribunaux de police* (except for minor offences), and the *tribunaux correctionnels*. They do not hear appeals from decisions of the *Cour d'assises*. The busiest courts of appeal have a specialist criminal division (*la chambre des appels correctionnels*). Less busy courts sit on alternate days as civil or criminal courts. Cases are usually heard by the President of the court of appeal and assisted by two other judges (article 510 CPP). Following a reform introduced by the Act of 9 March 2004, appeals relating to certain minor offences can be heard by a single judge.

Appeals relating to young offenders are heard by a specialist division of the court of appeal, headed by a specialist judge appointed for three years.

Cour d'assises d'appel

Historically, judgments of the *Cour d'assises* could not be the subject of an appeal on the facts, but only on points of law, to the criminal division of the *Cour de cassation*. This lack of a full right of appeal risked breaching the

European Convention on Human Rights, which specifies that 'every person declared guilty of a criminal offence by a court has the right to have examined by a higher court the declaration of guilt or the conviction'. Three justifications were frequently given to explain this absence of an ordinary appeal. First, it was pointed out that through the jury the verdict had been reached by the people, who are sovereign. Secondly, rights of appeal were available in relation to the judicial investigation that preceded the trial. Finally, Protocol 7 of the European Convention provides that there need be no right of appeal where a person has been tried by the highest court, and it was argued that the *Cour d'assises* was such a court.

The right to appeal against any decision to convict of the *Cour d'assises* has now been introduced by the Act of 15 June 2000 (article 380-1 and 380-2 CPP). The Act of 4 March 2002 gave the prosecution the right to appeal against an acquittal. These appeals are heard by another *Cour d'assises*, designated by the criminal division of the *Cour de cassation*, and acting as an appeal court. Thus it is an appeal before another court of the same type and level, though it has a slightly different membership. Under article 698-6 CPP, the *Cour d'assises d'appel* consists of 12 jurors instead of 9, a president and 8 wing members (9 professional judges in total). The majority required to establish guilt or to issue the maximum sentence is increased to 10 out of 12 (an absolute majority), though 8 jurors are sufficient to give a lesser sentence.

Decisions of the *Cour d'assises d'appel* can be the subject of a further appeal to the criminal division of the *Cour de cassation*.

Appeals against a decision of the *Cour d'assises* relating to the civil action alone will be heard not by another *Cour d'assises*, but by the criminal division of the *Cour de cassation*.

Criminal division of the *Cour de cassation*

There is only one criminal division of the *Cour de cassation*, which is consequently seriously overworked. The criminal division, like the others, is presided over by its own president. Both the division President and the President of the *Cour de cassation* can decree that more straightforward cases are heard by three judges and not the full complement of five. Any judge chosen to hear the case can ask for it to be heard by the full complement of five judges and the request will be granted. Parties to the case can also ask for the case to be heard by five judges, with leave of the judges allocated to the case (article L131-6 of the COJ).

Parties can refer points of law to the court, with a view to having the judgment of the appropriate lower court quashed or confirmed. The procedure is similar to that for civil cases discussed above. The court hears cases referred from all the lower criminal courts.

The *Cour de cassation* can exceptionally act as a full appeal court, if, owing to new evidence of fact, there is a prima facie case that a factual error has been committed. In order to proceed on this ground the accused must obtain leave from a special commission consisting of five judges. If leave is granted, the criminal division of the *Cour de cassation* will hear the case as a court of appeal (article 622 CPP).

Following the Act of 25 June 2001 the Criminal Division can be asked for an opinion on a point of law by any criminal court apart from the courts concerned with the criminal investigation and the *Cour d'assises* (article 706-64 CPP). The procedure is also not available where defendants are being held in custody on remand or on conditional bail. The application can only be considered if the issue of law:

• is new,
• poses serious difficulties,
• is relevant to a large number of cases.

This opinion is given before the lower court hands down its judgment in the case, and within three months of the request. The lower court is not technically bound by the opinion given by the *Cour de cassation*. Until 2001 this power had only been available in relation to civil matters, but it has now been extended to criminal matters.

The Act of 15 June 2000 established an appeal against criminal decisions which the European Court of Human Rights has found a breach of the European Convention, where the breach is so serious that the European Court's judgment has not put an end to its harmful consequences for the convicted person. An application has to be made within a year of the European Court's decision. A commission of seven judges of the *Cour de cassation* will sit in public and consider a request for such an appeal to be heard. The commission can send back the matter before a court of the same level and type that originally convicted the defendant (article 626-1 onwards CPP). Alternatively, if a retrial can no longer be organised (for example, if the convicted person has died) then the case will be referred to a full sitting of the *Cour de cassation* which can affirm or quash the conviction. The Commission's decisions cannot themselves be the subject of an appeal.

If on the completion of the procedure convicted persons are found to be innocent, they can receive damages and request a publication of the decision to put the record straight.

BIBLIOGRAPHY FOR CHAPTER 5

Aubert, J.-L. (2005), 'La distinction du fait et du droit dans le pourvoi en cassation en matière civile', *D.* 2005, 1115

Beauvalet, C. and Cirendini, O. (2004), *Cour d'Assises*, Paris: Jalan

Boré, L. and De Salve de Bruneton, J. (2005), 'Quelques idées sur le pourvoi en cassation', *D.* 2005, 180

Canivet, G. (2002), 'La procédure d'admission des pourvois en cassation: bilan d'un semestre d'application de l'article L 131-6 du COJ', *D.* 2002, 2195

Le conseil de prud'hommes (2002), Ministère des affaires sociales, du travail et de la solidarité, Paris: La documentation française

Cottin, M. (2002), 'La Cour de cassation se dote d'une procédure d'admission des pourvois en cassation', *D.* 2002, 748

Gondouin, G. and Rouxel, S. (2004), *Les institutions juridictionnelles*, Presses Universitaires de Grenoble

Héraud, A. and Maurin, A. (2002), *Institutions judiciaires*, Paris: Sirey

Kernaleguen, F. (2003), *Institutions judiciaires*, Paris: LexisNexis / Litec

Lebreton, M.-C. (2004), 'La justice de proximité: un premier bilan pessimiste', *D.* 2004, 2809

Martin, R. (2004), 'Vous avez dit proximité?', *D.* 2004, 507

Morvan, P. (2004), "Partisane' mais paritaire donc impartiale: la juridiction prud'homale', Aperçu rapide, Actualité, *JCP* 2004, 269

Perrot, R. (2004), *Institutions judiciaires*, Paris: Montchrestien

Rancé, P. (2001), 'Interview de Christophe Pettiti, La Cour nationale de l'incapacité et de la tarification', *D.* 2001, 789

Rancé, P. (2002), 'La réforme des tribunaux de commerce', *D.* 2002, 1050

Ruel, F. (2005), 'La juridiction de proximité: retouchée mais pas encore coulée', *JCP* 2005, 417

Scarano, J.-P. (2005), *Institutions Juridictionnelles*, Ellipses

Vincent, J., Guinchard, S., Montagnier, G. and Varinard, A. (2005), *Institutions judiciaires*, Paris: Dalloz

Zenati, F. (1992), 'La saisine pour avis de la Cour de cassation', *D.* 1992, 247

Web resources

Website: www.ca-paris.justice.fr: Paris Court of Appeal

Website: www.courdecassation.fr: The *Cour de cassation*. Includes some text in English

Website: www.justice.gouv.fr: The Ministry of Justice. Includes some text in English

Website: www.tgi-angouleme.justice.fr: The TGI in Angoulême

Website: www.tgi-macon.justice.fr: The TGI in Macon

6 The administrative courts

PART I: THE *CONSEIL D'ETAT*

▶ History

The administrative courts are concerned with litigation involving the administration, and are completely separate from the civil and criminal court structure. The *Conseil d'Etat* is the highest administrative court. It was created under Napoleon by article 52 of the Constitution of 13 December 1799. Initially, its sole role was to advise the administration, but an Imperial decree of 11 June 1806 created the Litigation Committee (*la commission du contentieux*) inside the *Conseil d'Etat,* and between 1806 and 1831 it gradually developed its judicial role. During this period it had no autonomous power to make decisions, and instead had to present its verdicts for approval to the head of the executive. This requirement was abolished by the Act of 24 May 1872. Following this Act, the *Conseil d'Etat* confirmed in the *Cadot* decision of 13 December 1889 that it had become a genuinely independent court.

The *Conseil d'Etat* was for many years the sole administrative court with general jurisdiction so that cases were heard by it unless they were specifically allocated to another court. By 1953, there was a four-year waiting list of 26,000 cases for the *Conseil d'Etat* and a major reform was therefore undertaken to try and reduce the *Conseil*'s workload. It heard fewer cases at first instance with the creation of the administrative courts (*tribunaux administratifs*), while the latter were given general jurisdiction to hear cases at first instance.

After the 1953 reform the waiting list for the *Conseil d'Etat* decreased, falling to 4,800 by 1968. But the amount of administrative litigation was increasing rapidly, with 9,800 cases being submitted for a hearing before the administrative courts in 1987 compared to 2,500 in 1954. While the *Conseil d'Etat* had succeeded in increasing its efficiency, so that in 1987 it was hearing three times as many cases as it had done 15 years earlier, the waiting list was still growing. By 1987 the average wait for a trial before the *Conseil d'Etat* was three years and five months and 25,000 cases were waiting to be heard – the effects of the 1953 reform had disappeared. The waiting list of cases to be heard by the *Conseil d'Etat* had increased from a low point of 4,800 in 1968 to 25,000 in 1987. Since 1987, waiting times have again increased to pre-1953 reform levels.

Further reform was necessary. An initial proposal would simply have created new posts in the litigation division for individuals recruited from the prestigious *Ecole Nationale d'Administration* (ENA, discussed at p. 262), who would have helped in the investigation and trial of cases. This was rejected by Parliament in 1981. A second proposal which would have created three specialist sub-divisions to hear cases concerning tax, the civil service, and public works, was rejected by Parliament in 1985. Neither of these reforms would have affected the role of the *Conseil d'Etat*, they would simply have tried to help it deal with its workload. It was the third, and more ambitious, attempt at reform that was successful with the passing of the Act of 31 December 1987, which came into force on 1 January 1989. This Act sandwiched an intermediary court structure between the administrative courts and the *Conseil d'Etat*: the administrative courts of appeal (*cours administratives d'appel*). These were given much of the power to hear appeals of fact and law that had previously been held by the *Conseil d'Etat*. As a result of these reforms the *Conseil d'Etat* has been progressively transformed into primarily a final court of appeal on points of law only. The *Conseil d'Etat* continues to play a central role in the administrative court system. With 15% of cases being appealed from the administrative courts and 15% being taken from the administrative courts of appeal, one in every 100 cases eventually finds its way before the *Conseil d'Etat*. Unfortunately, the problems of delay have still not been beaten: in 1995, while 36% of cases were heard by the *Conseil d'Etat* within one year, 29% still took more than three years. The 1987 Act established the admissions committee for appeals on points of law. This serves as a filter preventing the pursuit of actions before the Litigation Division that are inadmissible or manifestly ill-founded, to try and prevent the *Conseil d'Etat* from becoming overloaded. About two thirds of all actions are declared inadmissible.

▶ The organisation of the *Conseil d'Etat*

The *Conseil d'Etat* is governed by the Code of Administrative Justice (*Code de justice administrative*). It currently has 310 members, of which only two thirds are working inside the *Conseil d'Etat* at any one time. The majority of members are recruited from the *Ecole Nationale d'Administration*. They are generally considered to be part of the country's elite and the privileges that come with membership are causing increasing displeasure among the general population. Most controversially, members can be seconded for a certain duration to work in the administration or the private sector; this was the case for the bank *Crédit Lyonnais* at the time of its collapse. There has been much comment in the media as to how far these individuals' experience in the *Conseil d'Etat* actually equips them for such positions.

The Prime Minister is officially the President of the *Conseil d'Etat*. This is largely a ceremonial role, and in practice the President's functions are carried out by the Vice President.

The *Conseil d'Etat* is organised in six divisions, each headed by a President. Five of these divisions have a purely administrative function and are the divisions for home affairs, finance, public works, welfare, and report and research. Finally there is the litigation division which fulfils the *Conseil d'Etat*'s judicial functions. This is itself divided into ten sections. As well as the President at its head, the litigation division has three deputy presidents and a president of each section.

Traditionally members of the *Conseil d'Etat* are members both of the litigation division and an administrative division, a principle that can be found in the decree of 30 July 1963. This has the advantage of allowing the judges to have first-hand experience of the day-to-day work of the administration. On the other hand, in the light of recent pronouncements of the European Court of Human Rights, it may be that this practice breaches the European Convention and will have to be reviewed at some future date. The European Court of Human Rights looked at the question in the context of the *Conseil d'Etat* of Luxembourg, which is organised on very similar lines to its French counterpart. It ruled in the *Procola v Luxembourg* decision of 28 September 1995 that dual membership risks being in breach of article 6(1) of the European Convention which lays down the right for cases to be heard by an independent and impartial court.

There are four possible types of hearing, depending on the importance and complexity of the case. A decision from the two more senior court formations will have greater weight in practice than one from the two lower formations. The most common formation consists simply of three judges of a single section sitting alone. Alternatively, nine judges from two sections can sit together. Where the case is of particular importance it can be heard before a more extensive and senior selection of judges. A formation of the litigation division, known as the *section du contentieux*, gathers 17 judges – the President and three Vice Presidents of the division, the ten Presidents of the sections, the reporting judge (*le rapporteur*) and two members from the administrative divisions.

The full sitting, known as the *Assemblée du contentieux,* is the highest formation and deals with litigation of extreme importance, including cases involving the election of national and European Members of Parliament. It consists of 12 judges of the highest rank drawn from all the divisions, including the Vice President of the *Conseil d'Etat*, the six Presidents of the divisions, the three Deputy Presidents of the litigation division, the President of the section that investigated the matter, and the reporting judge. The Vice President of the *Conseil d'Etat* presides over the hearing and has the casting vote should the judges be equally divided on a case.

▌ The powers of the *Conseil d'Etat*

The *Conseil d'Etat* exercises both advisory and judicial functions.

The advisory powers

The advisory role of the *Conseil d'Etat* represents an important part of its activity. This role has been a feature of the *Conseil d'Etat* since its creation, and was increased by the 1958 Constitution. For example, it must be consulted before decrees in the legislative domain are amended, delegated legislation is made (*ordonnances*), and government Bills are adopted by the Cabinet (articles 37, 38 and 39 of the Constitution respectively). While in such situations the government is bound to seek this advice, it is not bound to follow it. In addition, the government has a wide discretion to seek the *Conseil d'Etat*'s advice when confronted by an administrative problem. Thus, for example, it advised on the wearing of Islamic headscarves in schools (27 November 1989), the creation of an international criminal court (29 February 1996) and the effects of a European arrest warrant on the French Consitution (26 September 2002). The *Conseil d'Etat* can also undertake studies at the request of the Prime Minister or on its own initiative. Each year the report and research division prepares a report suggesting areas in need of reform.

The judicial powers

The judicial role of the *Conseil d'Etat* has significantly changed with the creation of the administrative courts and the administrative courts of appeal. It can hear cases at first instance, appeals on facts and law, or appeals on points of law only. Finally, it can give advice on points of law.

Court of first instance

When the *Conseil d'Etat* acts as a court of first instance it also by definition acts as a court of last instance, because it is the highest administrative court from which there is no further right of appeal. Since the reform of 1953, it only acts as a court of first instance in a very small number of cases that are considered to be too important to be judged by any other court, or too difficult to link to the territorial jurisdiction of any particular court. The former include applications for judicial review against decrees (which emanate from the President and the Prime Minister) and delegated legislation (*ordonnances*); cases concerning the individual situation of senior civil servants nominated by presidential decree, and litigation arising from regional elections. The latter includes actions against administrative acts which apply in the jurisdiction of more than one administrative court, or arising from conduct outside France. This amounts to approximately 3,000 cases a year.

Appeals on facts and law

With the reform of 1987, much of the *Conseil d'Etat*'s role in hearing appeals on facts and law has gradually been transferred to the administrative courts of appeal. These have general jurisdiction to hear such cases, leaving the *Conseil d'Etat* with this function only where it has been specifically invested with it. This is the case for litigation arising from certain local elections and repatriation orders.

Appeals on points of law only

Until 1988 such cases only represented 5% of the *Conseil d'Etat*'s workload. With the transfer of jurisdiction to the new administrative courts, this is set to become its main judicial function, which befits the court sitting at the head of the administrative system. In 1995 this had become 17.4% of its workload and, with the final transfer of ordinary appeals on facts and law to the administrative courts of appeal, this was set to increase further. Through these cases the *Conseil d'Etat* is able to impose consistency in the system's case law. In the past, it merely heard such appeals from the specialist administrative courts where there was no right of appeal on the facts of the case. Now, such appeals come from both these courts and the new administrative courts of appeal. When exercising this function, the *Conseil d'Etat* rules on the legal regularity of the decision. When it finds that the law has been breached it quashes the decision, and sends the case back to a lower court to be heard again. Exceptionally, since the Act of 31 December 1987, the *Conseil d'Etat* can itself decide the case if this is found to be in the interests of justice.

Advice on points of law

The administrative courts and the administrative courts of appeal can seek the advice of the *Conseil d'Etat* on a point of law (article L113-1 of the Code of Administrative Justice). This is possible where a new point of law has arisen that is widely occurring and presents serious difficulty. The trial of the case is suspended while the referral is being made. The *Conseil d'Etat* gives its opinion on the point of law within three months. This opinion is not binding, and no appeal is available. The procedure was inspired by one that exists for the European Court of Justice and the aim is to save time and to achieve consistency in judicial decisions.

• •

PART II: COURTS WITH GENERAL JURISDICTION AND SPECIALIST COURTS

▶ Administrative courts

In the past the *Conseils de préfecture* heard some minor administrative litigation. They had been created in 1800, but they only had limited jurisdiction and, while their role had been increased in 1934, most first instance cases were still heard by the *Conseil d'Etat*. The increase in cases involving the administration made this arrangement impractical and was leading to considerable delays before cases were being heard. After the Second World War the *Conseils de préfecture* were proving to be conspicuously unsatisfactory in coping with the increased demands of administrative litigation. In consequence, a decree of 30 September 1953 replaced them with the administrative courts (*tribunaux administratifs*). The relevant legislation governing both the administrative courts and the administrative courts of appeal (discussed below) can be found in the Code of Administrative Justice.

There are currently 37 administrative courts, which heard more than 155,000 cases in 2005. Each court is headed by a president and has at least three ordinary judges. The larger administrative courts are organised into divisions, the biggest being in Paris with 13 divisions. Normally divisions hear cases separately, but occasionally for complex cases they can sit together.

Powers

The administrative courts are now courts of first instance with general jurisdiction, so that cases are brought before them unless they are specifically allocated to another court. We have seen that the *Conseil d'Etat* has reserved a limited power to hear cases at first instance, and the failure to transfer these last cases to the administrative courts almost 50 years after their creation undermines the administrative courts' status in a way that is no longer justifiable or acceptable.

The territorial competence of the administrative courts is governed by the place where the authority that took the decision or signed the contract giving rise to the litigation has its legal base. This leads to a very similar outcome as for civil litigation, as the administration is usually the defendant in legal proceedings before the administrative courts. This general principle initially led to the majority of cases being brought before the administrative court of Paris because most branches of the administration were based in the capital. So a considerable number of exceptions have been developed, to decentralise the litigation as far as possible. For example, litigation concerning immovable property is allocated according to the geographical position of the property concerned.

Unfortunately, the workload of the administrative courts has continued to increase. While the number of judges has been increased and productivity improved there is still an average waiting period of 22 months.

A controversial development in their jurisdiction has been the result of the Act of 15 March 2004. This Act bans the wearing of ostentatious religious symbols in State schools. If a student is excluded from school on the basis that this Act has been breached, they can appeal to the administrative courts.

In addition to their judicial functions, the administrative courts also have a very limited advisory role.

Administrative courts of appeal

History

Initially appeals on fact and law from the administrative courts were heard by the *Conseil d'Etat*. Gradually, the effects of the 1953 reform disappeared under the weight of rapidly increasing administrative litigation. The number of actions registered before the administrative courts progressed from 20,000 in 1971 to 62,000 in 1987; in other words it tripled in 16 years. The Act of 31 December 1987 created the administrative courts of appeal. The legislation left intact the general jurisdiction at first instance of the administrative courts and the *Conseil d'Etat*'s limited jurisdiction to hear cases at first and last instance; the intention being primarily to impact on existing appeal procedures. The Act initially created five courts in Bordeaux, Lyon, Nancy, Nantes and Paris. Since then, another three courts have been created in Marseilles, Versailles and Douai as some of the courts were struggling with large geographical jurisdictions.

The President of an administrative court of appeal is generally a member of the *Conseil d'Etat*. Each court contains two to four divisions. Usually five judges from a single division hear a case. A special formation of seven judges drawn from all the divisions can be summoned to hear the most important cases.

Powers

The administrative courts of appeal have the power to hear appeals on points of fact and law against most decisions of the administrative courts in their territorial jurisdiction, though as we have seen, the right to hear a limited number of these appeals has been reserved for the *Conseil d'Etat*. To reduce the workload of the administrative courts of appeal, the Act of 1 September 2003 provides that some cases heard by the administrative courts of first instance involving small sums of money can no longer be the subject of an appeal to these courts. Instead, such cases go directly to the *Conseil d'Etat*. As a result, the caseload of the *Conseil d'Etat* increased by 22 per cent in 2004. The administrative courts of appeal also have a small advisory role.

▶ Specialist administrative courts

There are approximately 50 specialist administrative courts hearing 20,000 cases a year, concerned with litigation arising from such matters as public finances, social welfare payments and immigration. Some have their own specialist appeal courts to hear appeals on fact and law. All these courts are controlled by the *Conseil d'Etat* through the appeal process. Of particular interest are the Audit Court (*Cour des comptes*) and the Regional Audit Court (*Cour régional des comptes*).

Audit court

The Audit Court (*Cour des comptes*) was created by an Act of 16 September 1807 under Napoleon, replacing the *Chambre des comptes* that had existed before the 1789 Revolution. It was responsible for placing the public accounts under judicial scrutiny. Like the *Conseil d'Etat* it developed both judicial and administrative functions. With the decentralisation reforms in 1982, the Audit Court became an appeal court hearing appeals on fact and law from the newly created Regional Audit Courts. It also remains a court of first instance for scrutinising certain public accounts. As regards its administrative functions, it assists Parliament and the government in the enforcement of legislation dealing with public finances and publishes a yearly report. It is governed since 1994 by a Code for the Financial Courts (*Code des juridictions financières*).

Recruitment to this court is the same as for the *Conseil d'Etat*. Thus many of its officers are selected from the *Ecole Nationale d'Administration* (ENA), with the Audit Court tending to be third in the choice of places to be employed after the *Conseil d'Etat* and the Finance Inspectorate. Others are selected after they have gained experience in other parts of the administration, and without having to sit a competitive examination.

At its head is a president who is responsible for allocating the cases to its different divisions. Unlike the *Conseil d'Etat*, the *ministère public* (see p. 241) is employed in both this and the Regional Audit Court. Its role is to make sure that the appropriate procedures are followed, for example that the accounts are submitted on time.

In the past, the Audit Court had remained silent about frauds concerning European funds. From 1999, following pressure from Europe, it will inform the European Commission of any such frauds that come to its attention.

Regional Audit Courts

Until 1982, the local accounts were controlled either by the Audit Court or, for the smaller communities, by accountants in the Treasury. The Regional Audit Courts were created by the Act of 2 March 1982 following decentralisation, with one court being based in each region. The more detailed rules applying to these courts can be found in the Code for the Financial Courts. Much of the jurisdiction that had previously belonged to the national Audit Court was transferred to the Regional Audit Courts along with some of the work of the Treasury accountants. The aim was to transfer this work to independent bodies which were geographically close to the institutions being controlled.

The Regional Audit Courts have three main functions: to check the accounts of the local government authority in their area, watch over its financial management and monitor its budget. The first is a judicial function, while the latter functions are primarily administrative in nature. These courts are extremely important, not least because the local authorities manage and spend vast annual budgets. The courts hand down approximately 30,000 judgments and 1,000 opinions on budgetary control every year.

Looking at the first of these three functions, the courts check the accounts of the public accountants in their area and of organisations receiving public funding. These accounts have to be submitted annually for inspection and any delay in doing so can lead to the payment of a fine. Where appropriate the public accountant can be made personally responsible for any deficit in the accounts, and will have to cover any loss into the public account from their private finances.

When looking at the financial management of the local authority, the court is looking at its cost efficiency, and does not seek to evaluate the policies behind the spending decisions. This is potentially a very extensive power, which it is difficult to delineate. Unlike the previous control, it is not automatic, but carried out at the discretion of the court. In exercising this function, it cannot issue any binding decision, but simply issues observations.

Finally, the Regional Audit Courts control local budgets. This was the main innovation of the 1982 Act, and its most controversial provision. The budget should normally be prepared by 15 April and submitted to the court by the public accountant. Failure to fix a budget will lead to the intervention of the court. If the budget does not balance and represents a 10% overspend (or 5% if the population is under 20,000) then the Prefect (the chief administrative officer of the *département*) will contact the court. It will make proposals for balancing the budget within a month of this

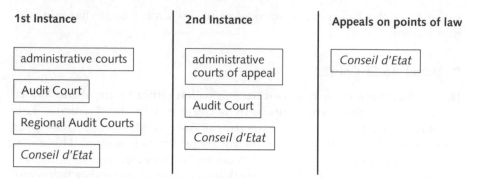

Fig. 6.1 The administrative court system at a glance

communication. The local council will discuss these proposals within a month. If it fails to do so, or fails to reach a satisfactory agreement, the Prefect will reach a decision on the matter and must give reasons, should it differ in any way from the proposals of the court. If the budget fails to allow for payment of debts that must be paid in law, then the court can be contacted and it will issue a warning that it may take action against the council. If after a month the council has not acted upon this warning the Prefect is instructed to act unilaterally, and his or her failure to do so constitutes a civil wrong which can lead to the payment of damages.

The procedure before these courts is quite unusual as, for example, there is no need for an application from a third party to begin proceedings: it automatically intervenes each year to judge the accounts of the local authority. Through their work serious cases of corruption of high-profile local politicians have been brought to light, bringing the role of these courts very much into the media spotlight. Generally, it is felt that so far they have done an excellent job.

▶ A comparison between the *Conseil d'Etat* and the *Cour de cassation*

Through the legislative reforms introduced during the twentieth century, the administrative court structure has moved closer to that of the civil and criminal courts. However, differences still remain, the main one being that the role of the *Conseil d'Etat* remains much more varied than the narrow function of the *Cour de cassation*.

The *Conseil d'Etat* will in certain cases act like a court of second instance, judging both on the facts and the law (Fig. 6.1), whereas the *Cour de cassation* focuses on the law only (see p. 99).

The *Conseil d'Etat* participates in the legislative process and acts as a special adviser to the government. The *Cour de cassation*'s functions remain purely judicial in order to respect the principle of the separation of powers. The academic Roger Perrot argues that this should be changed, and that role of the *Cour de cassation* should be extended to include an advisory role to the government as well. In his opinion, nobody is better placed to help in the legislative process of a civil law Bill than the judge from the highest civil court in the country. By contrast, it makes little sense to consult the *Conseil d'Etat* on matters of private law. In recent years, the *Cour de cassation* has attempted to influence the government indirectly by publishing an annual report where it highlights what it believes to be gaps or imperfections in the law (art. R 131-13 COJ). Numerous statutes have also been influenced by judgments handed down by the *Cour de cassation*. For example, courts declared contracts with surrogate mothers illegal at the beginning of the 1990s. A statute of 29 July 1994 introduced subsequently new provisions in the Civil Code, art. 16-7, which confirmed the courts' position.

Appointment to the *Cour de cassation* represents the pinnacle of a judge's career and can only be achieved after having first gained experience in the lower courts. It is also a great honour for a judge to be appointed to the *Conseil d'Etat*, but such a person can exercise their entire judicial career at the *Conseil d'Etat* and progress through the internal hierarchy of the court.

Sometimes the decisions of the *Conseil d'Etat* and the *Cour de cassation* conflict. An example of this arose from litigation following the birth of a disabled child. Doctors had failed to detect the disability during the pregnancy so the parents were unable to make an informed decision as to whether to continue with the pregnancy or to have an abortion. The *Cour de cassation* ruled on 17 November 2000 that the disabled child was entitled to compensation for the mere fact of being born in these circumstances. By contrast, the *Conseil d'Etat* ruled in the *Quarez* decision of 14 February 1997 that the parents were entitled to compensation but not the child. The government intervened by enacting the Act of 4 March 2002, of which article 1 precludes any right to compensation for the birth of a child.

• •

BIBLIOGRAPHY FOR CHAPTER 6

Bell, J. (2000), 'Celebrating 200 years of the *Conseil d'Etat*', *International and Comparative Law Quarterly*, at 660

Brachet, B. (2000), *Droit constitutionnel et administratif: capacité en droit*, DEUG droit, Paris: A.E.S.

Brown, L. N. and Bell, J. (1998), *French Administrative Law*, Oxford: Oxford University Press

Drago, P. (1988), 'Les Cours administratives d'appel', *Revue française de droit administratif*, 1988, 196

Gondouin, G. and Rouxel, S. (2004), *Les institutions juridictionnelles*, Presses Universitaires de Grenoble

Héraud, A. and Maurin, A. (2002), *Institutions judiciaires*, Paris: Sirey

Idriss, M. (2005), 'Laïcité and the banning of the 'hijab' in France', *Legal Studies* vol. 25, 260

Kernaleguen, F. (2003), *Institutions judiciaires*, Paris: LexisNexis / Litec

Long, M. (1988), 'Une réforme pour préparer l'avenir', *Revue française de droit administratif,* 1988, 163

Perrot, R. (2004), Institutions judiciaires, Paris: Montchrestien

Scarano, J.-P. (2005), *Institutions Juridictionnelles*, Paris: Ellipses

Stirn, B. (1987), 'La situation des tribunaux administratifs', *Revue française de droit administrative,* 1987, 437

Vincent, J., Guinchard, S., Montagnier, G. and Varinard, A. (2005), *Institutions judiciaires*, Paris: Dalloz

Web resources

Website: www.caa-paris.juradm.fr/caa/paris/index.shtml: Paris Administrative Court of Appeal

Website: www.justice.gouv.fr/chiffres/chiffres.htm: judicial statistics

Website: www.conseil-etat.fr: The *Conseil d'Etat*

Website: www.conseil-etat.fr/ce/organi/index_or_or01.shtml: Diagram showing the organisational structure of the *Conseil d'Etat*

Website: www.ccomptes.fr: the Audit Court website which includes some text in English

7 Miscellaneous courts

INTRODUCTION

The existence of two separate court systems, for civil and criminal matters on the one hand and administrative matters on the other, throws up the potential for jurisdiction disputes between the two systems. A Jurisdiction Disputes Court (*le Tribunal des conflits*) has been created to resolve these conflicts, which will be considered in Part I below. We will also study three courts with close political connections which are also outside the two court systems, the *Conseil constitutionnel* (see Part II below), and the High Court of Justice and the Court of Justice of the Republic (see Part III below). Additionally, since 1982 there is a military tribunal (*tribunal aux armées*) with very limited jurisdiction over cases involving French military personnel operating outside France. It is felt that in times of peace, no other type of military tribunal is needed. The Code of Military Justice (*Code de justice militaire*) makes provision for the creation of military tribunals with a more extensive jurisdiction during times of war.

PART I: JURISDICTION DISPUTES COURT

▶ Jurisdiction

It is a basic principle of the French legal system that civil and criminal courts have no jurisdiction over the administration. A tribunal was established between 1849 and 1851 and reinstated in 1872 to settle jurisdiction disputes. Before this tribunal existed, the administration simply decided that a particular matter was one of administrative law and was not suitable for the ordinary courts. As we will see, the current system still bears traces of this and is not entirely evenly balanced between the ordinary and administrative courts.

▶ Positive conflict

If the administration considers a case in which it is involved has improperly been brought to the ordinary courts, it will draw the matter to the attention of a local government official, known as the Prefect (*préfet*). The official will endeavour to reach an agreement with the court on the issue, but if no agreement is reached, the matter is referred to the Jurisdiction Disputes Court. That court must rule on the issue within three months. If the Jurisdiction Disputes Court decides that the case does not fall within administrative law, the original court will continue its hearing of the case and will pronounce judgment. If it agrees that the case should be heard by the administrative courts, it will be remitted to the appropriate administrative court. While the procedure for referral of cases is undoubtedly biased in favour of the administration, the court itself is impartial and often decides that the referred case should continue in the ordinary courts. For example, in 1961 a case was brought in the local *tribunal d'instance* by an association of ex-soldiers who had suffered head injuries while in service. They had submitted claims for compensation to the government through the postal service, but these claims had not been delivered in time and their claims were rejected. They then proceeded to bring actions against the post office, complaining that it had failed to deal appropriately with the various letters and parcels that had been sent. The local authority thought the matter should be heard by the administrative courts, as the post office was owned by the state. It referred the case to the Jurisdiction Disputes Court, which gave judgment on the case on 20 November 1961. The court held that legislation passed in 1905 and 1958 required all matters relating to the relevant post office services to be heard by the ordinary courts. It accordingly held that the case should be heard by the ordinary courts and referred it back to the local *tribunal d'instance* for judgment.

▶ Negative conflict

It is also possible that neither court considers itself competent. In the past a jurisdictional dispute could only be brought to the attention of the Jurisdiction Disputes Court after the litigation had been fully heard by a court in each court system. This was very time-consuming and, while this right still exists, a quicker procedure was introduced by the Decree of 25 July 1960. This provides that if a court decides that it is not competent it must refer the matter to the Jurisdiction Disputes Court to determine the appropriate court to hear the litigation. Both these procedures can be used at first instance and appeal, but not on referral to the *Cour de cassation* which does not, strictly speaking, hear a case.

▶ Mixed cases

Litigation can arise which involves issues of both administrative law and civil or criminal liability, and separate actions can be brought in the courts of each system relating to the appropriate aspects of the case. It is quite possible that these courts will reach conclusions which are incompatible with each other, for instance if they reach differing views of the factual circumstances giving rise to the litigation. An Act of 20 April 1932 provides that the Jurisdiction Disputes Court can be asked to judge the facts of the matter and the judgment will be binding on the courts in both systems. This Act has only been used on a very few occasions.

A good example of the use of this law is the case which prompted its enactment, the case of *Rosay* (8 May 1933). In 1932, M. Rosay was injured in a collision between a private car and a car belonging to the administration. He brought an action before the local *tribunal de grande instance* against the driver of the private car. This court decided that the driver of the other car was responsible. According to the law in force at the time, cases against a driver of a government car had to be brought before the administrative courts. The claimant then brought a case before the local administrative court which decided that the driver of the private car was responsible. The new Act of 1932 was used to refer the conflict to the Jurisdiction Disputes Court, which was asked to decide who caused the accident. By a judgment of 8 May 1933 it decided that both the private driver and the government driver were responsible and ordered each to pay half the damages. This decision was binding on both the TGI and the administrative court. If the same litigation was to arise today, it would not be necessary to refer the matter to the Jurisdiction Disputes Court, since an Act of 31 December 1957 states that all claims relating to accidents involving government cars are to be heard by the ordinary courts.

▶ Organisation

The Jurisdiction Disputes Court sits in the *Palais Royal*, where the *Conseil d'Etat*, the highest administrative court, is also based. The physical proximity of the two courts perhaps indicates that where there is a conflict of jurisdiction, the administrative court system may have a slight, if unacknowledged, advantage, even though the two systems are regarded as equal. The court has eight judges, three of which come from the *Cour de cassation* and have been elected by their peers, and three are from the *Conseil d'Etat* who have been posted to this court. Those six judges elect another two, invariably one from each court. As the number of judges is even, in case of a failure to reach agreement, the court reconvenes with the Minister of Justice, who has a casting vote. While this is somewhat unusual, a casting vote is sometimes necessary and it would not be acceptable if this power were exercised by a person belonging to either court system.

. . . .
PART II: THE *CONSEIL CONSTITUTIONNEL*

The *Conseil constitutionnel* has many functions but its most important is to enforce compliance with the Constitution. As such, it carries out many of the functions of the constitutional courts in countries such as the United States and Germany, though its jurisdiction is more limited than these courts.

❱ Historical background

The intermediate law of the revolutionary and post-revolutionary periods forbade judges from interfering with the government, because of the principle of the separation of powers. This included a prohibition, contained in the Acts of 16-24 August 1790, on taking any action in relation to laws passed by Parliament. While the Constitution was held to be the highest order of law and superior to ordinary laws, there was no effective mechanism for ensuring that ordinary legislation complied with the Constitution. Neither the courts within the civil and criminal system nor the administrative courts could pronounce on the matter.

The 1946 Constitution of the Fourth Republic created the Constitutional Committee, which enjoyed only a very limited designated jurisdiction, mostly concerned with protecting the powers of the Senate. Even within its sphere of influence it could not really enforce its decisions. If it considered a law was unconstitutional, it could only suspend the law, until the government chose to revise the Constitution. It only attempted to do this once, and did not even then use its limited powers as a compromise was reached. The Committee can nonetheless be seen as the predecessor of the current *Conseil constitutionnel*.

The founders of the Fifth Republic saw the creation of the new *Conseil constitutionnel* as a useful tool in the constitutional armoury for ensuring that the power of Parliament was kept under control. The 1958 Constitution limited the law-making powers of Parliament to specified areas (article 34) and provided that the government could create laws in matters outside the scope of the reserved matters (article 37). The writers of the Constitution thought that the main function of the new body would be to ensure that Parliament did not trespass on the area reserved to the government.

▶ Membership

Membership of the *Conseil constitutionnel* is determined by article 56 of the 1958 Constitution. All members are known colloquially as 'the wise' (*les sages*). Past presidents are life members. During the first few years, when the role of the new body was still thought to be fairly limited, it was considered that past presidents would play a useful role, and two ex-presidents of the Fourth Republic (Vincent Aurial and René Coty) did occasionally sit. Valéry Giscard d'Estaing was the first former President of the Fifth Republic to decide to use this right in June 2004, at the age of 78, after having lost his political mandate as a regional councillor. There has been some discussion about reforming the Constitution to abolish this right, and to enable Parliament to benefit from the political experience of former presidents instead by giving them a position for life in the Senate.

The regular members are the nine chosen members who sit for a single term of nine years, with one third of the membership being renewed every three years. Membership at the time of going to press is set out in Table 7.1.

There is no requirement that judges of the *Conseil* be legally qualified, though in recent years a large number have been. The appointments are all made by politicians: three by the President of the Republic, three by the President of the National Assembly and three by the President of the

Table 7.1 The current ten members of the *Conseil constitutionnel*

Member	Chosen by	Mandate
Valéry GISCARD D'ESTAING	N/A	Life member
Pierre MAZEAUD, President	the President of the Republic	1998–2007
Simone VEIL	the President of the Senate	1998–2007
Jean-Claude COLLIARD	the President of the National Assembly	1998–2007
Olivier DUTHEILLET de LAMOTHE	the President of the Republic	2001–2010
Dominique SCHNAPPER	the President of the Senate	2001–2010
Pierre JOXE	the President of the National Assembly	2001–2010
Pierre STEINMETZ	the President of the Republic	2004–2013
Jacqueline de GUILLENSCHMIDT	the President of the Senate	2004–2013
Jean-Louis PEZANT	the President of the National Assembly	2004–2013

Senate. On the whole, the mechanisms for appointment and for renewal of membership ensure that not all are appointed under the influence of one person. The fact that these members are being chosen by three of the most important personalities of French political life has led to questions being asked about their independence. Many members have in effect been appointed on the basis of their political allegiance or friendship. The *Conseil constitutionnel* was slow to make a legal impact following its creation, partly because its first President, M. Noel, had few qualifications for the post, other than being a friend of President de Gaulle and a member of the ineffective Constitutional Committee of the Fourth Republic. In fact none of the initial members of the court were legally qualified. It was not until 1981 that a judge supporting the socialist party was appointed to the court. During his presidency, François Mitterrand appointed two of his former ministers, Robert Badinter, former minister for justice, and Roland Dumas, former foreign affairs minister as presidents of the *Conseil constitutionnel*.

While no qualifications are required for membership of the *Conseil constitutionnel*, since 1995 members must not hold any elected office (Act of 19 January 1995), in order to respect the principle of the separation of powers. Before 1995, the *Conseil constitutionnel* was heavily criticised for allowing their members to have a political mandate while sitting at the *Conseil constitutionnel*. Some of its members, for instance, presided at the same time in regional or local councils. Many professions are also incompatible, but these do not include that of professor of law, a position that several members have exercised concurrently with their office. While no legal qualifications are required, in practice many of the most eminent constitutional lawyers have been members of the *Conseil constitutionnel*, for example, Luchaire, Vedel, Cassin, Badinter and Waline.

Once appointed, the members have privileges similar to ordinary judges, in that they can only be removed from office if they become physically incapable of working, hold an elected office or are deprived of their civil and political rights. In 1998, the then president of the *Conseil constitutionnel*, Roland Dumas, chose to temporarily stand down from office early when he came under suspicion of having been involved in corrupt practices (involving the improper use of money belonging to the ELF Oil Company). M. Dumas initially stopped acting as president on 6 March 1998 when it was clear that he would be formally charged with these offences, but he returned to the presidency on 20 May 1998 and took part in the celebration of the fortieth anniversary of the *Conseil constitutionnel* in October 1998. During this period, the *Conseil constitutionnel* also made the controversial pronouncement, which appeared to exonerate the President of the Republic from prosecution for crimes committed before he became president, a decision which significantly benefited President Chirac for the reasons mentioned at p. 32. Roland Dumas' presidency nevertheless became increasingly precarious, with the *Conseil constitutionnel* seriously hampered and its reputation damaged, and after significant media pressure he was forced by the eight other judges to take administrative leave on 24 March 1999. He finally resigned from office in February 2000, as his position had become untenable and pressure had been placed on him by the other judges of the *Conseil*. He was immediately replaced by Yves Guéna, who was the oldest member of the court, and who had been carrying out the presidential functions during the interim period prior to Dumas' resignation.

Cases must be heard by a minimum of seven judges. The majority view prevails. Dissenting opinions are not published, which has been criticised by the lawyers Rousseau and Spitz, who believe more transparency would lead to greater legitimacy and increased trust by the public. On the other hand, the former judges, Vedel and Luchaire, have argued that the publication of dissenting judgments would compromise the *Conseil constitutionnel's* united front. The impression of secrecy is increased by the judges' obligation to abstain from publicly commenting on any topic which will be or has been debated by the *Conseil constitutionnel*, in order not to compromise the dignity or independence of their position. The former President of the Republic, Valéry Giscard d'Estaing, publicly disclosed his views on the European Constitutional Treaty in October 2004, in an article published in the newspaper *Le Monde*, one month before the *Conseil constitutionnel* was due to discuss the conformity of this document with the Constitution, and again at the beginning of 2005 on the French Radio Channels *Europe 1* and *France Inter*. Even though he decided to abstain from taking part in the decision-making process, he was criticised by many constitutional lawyers for his indiscretion.

The decision of the court is final as it cannot be subjected to any appeal and, according to article 62, is binding on the judiciary. This clearly indicates the special nature of the *Conseil constitutionnel* as there is traditionally no binding precedent in France. The civil and administrative courts have been slow in taking into account the *Conseil constitutionnel's* decisions interpreting the Constitution: the *Conseil d'Etat* explicitly acknowledged a decision of the *Conseil constitutionnel* for the first time in 1983 (the *Société des Etablissements Outters* decision of 20 December 1983). The *Cour de cassation* implicitly recognised the authority of a decision of the *Conseil constitutionnel* in 1985 (the *Bogdan and Vukovic* decision of 25 April 1985) and finally explicitly accepted it was bound by the *Conseil constitutionnel's* interpretation of the Constitution in a decision of 25 March 1998.

▶ Functions

The *Conseil constitutionnel* only has the powers given to it by the Constitution. This limitation on its powers was expressly acknowledged by the court in its decisions of 14 September 1961 and 26 March 2003. It does not possess any general authority to provide opinions on how the Constitution should be interpreted. In its decision of 26 March 2003, it held that 'the *Conseil constitutionnel*'s jurisdiction is strictly defined by the Constitution ... it is not entitled to provide any decision other than in the cases expressly provided by the Law.'

It has two main judicial roles:

- to supervise elections and judge any litigation resulting from elections;
- to judge the constitutionality of statutes, standing orders of Parliament and international treaties.

It also enjoys an important advisory role if the President uses emergency powers under article 16 (discussed at p. 29). This article requires the President to consult the *Conseil constitutionnel* when he or she decides to have resort to the powers contained in the article. The *Conseil's* advisory opinion must be published and decides whether the two necessary conditions were satisfied: the existence of a threat endangering the French Republic's institutions and the interruption of the constitutional public powers. These two conditions were found to be present following the rebellion of the French military in Algeria. The *Conseil* also subsequently provided 16 unpublished advisory opinions for Charles de Gaulle on each subsequent use of article 16 in 1961. Furthermore, the *Conseil constitutionnel*, as enshrined in article 7, has been entrusted with the task of determining the President of the Republic's inability to exercise his or her functions, temporarily or permanently. This may only take place by an absolute majority vote. The *Conseil constitutionnel* gave a broad interpretation to article 7 when it officially declared the office of President of the Republic was vacant on two occasions during the Fifth Republic: following Charles de Gaulle's resignation from the presidency in 1969, having lost the trust of the French people after a crashing referendum defeat, and following Georges Pompidou's death in 1974.

Elections

The Constitution provides that the *Conseil constitutionnel* is involved in the referendum process and the elections of the President of the Republic, senators, and Members of Parliament. It is, however, not involved in the elections to the European Parliament that are within the remit of the *Conseil d'Etat*.

For presidential elections (articles 7 and 58) and referendums (article 60) its role is supervisory, ensuring the regularity of the general procedures and the declaration of the results.

For the election of senators and Members of Parliament, article 59 requires the *Conseil constitutionnel* to act as a court, hearing any litigation that is referred to it by a registered elector or candidate – such referrals are quite frequent. The case of *Deval* v *Durand* of 5 January 1959 was the first to result in the annulment of an election. A friend of the victorious candidate had sent copies of a personal letter recommending members of a local business association to vote for the candidate and to ask their friends to vote for him. This was in breach of a law regulating election publicity and the election was held to be invalid. A more recent example was the *Le Chevallier v Casanova* decision of 28 July 1998. A joke made on television by a famous French comedian on the day of a Parliamentary election led to one of the results being cancelled. The comedian had jokingly encouraged people to go out voting in the Var department, pointing out that the National Front electorate would not forget to cast their vote. The electoral Code bans any political campaigning on voting day, and this was adjudged to constitute political propaganda that might have influenced the outcome of the election as the Labour candidate, Odette Casanova, only won by a slender margin of 33 votes. The elections were reorganised a few months later and were won by the Labour candidate by a comfortable majority.

In relation to the sanctions that the *Conseil constitutionnel* can impose, as well as annulling elections, as occurred in *Le Chevallier* and the *Deval* cases, it can also declare a candidate to be ineligible to stand for a specified period, to ensure that they are not re-elected at the subsequent by-election. This sanction has been imposed on several high-profile candidates of the French National Front Party. This type of case represents a very large part of the *Conseil constitutionnel*'s current workload, particularly following an Act passed in 1990 imposing limits on political campaign expenses: in 2003, out of 151 cases, 119 related to article 59.

Enforcing the Constitution

The Constitution contains five provisions which can be relied upon to enforce the Constitution through the intervention of the *Conseil constitutionnel*.

Article 41

The Constitution limits the areas in which Parliament can pass laws (see p. 44). The *Conseil constitutionnel* is required to police the division between the powers of Parliament and the executive to legislate, as laid down by articles 34 and 37. In case of dispute, article 41 requires the government and Parliament to endeavour to reach agreement. Failing this, either of the parties can refer the dispute to the *Conseil constitutionnel* which must rule on the matter within eight days. This was originally expected to be a key area of work for the *Conseil constitutionnel*. In fact over the last 20 years, while there have been many disputes between the government and Parliament where the procedure in this article has been used, a settlement has usually been reached without the need to refer the matter to the *Conseil constitutionnel*. Further, if Parliament chooses to pass a law outside the ambit of article 34, the *Conseil constitutionnel* has stated that this is not automatically invalid and indeed it will only look into the matter if the government asks it to do so (see p. 70).

An early decision of 27 November 1959, about a government decree limiting the price paid on the sale of agricultural tenancies, provides a good illustration of the early operation of this article. The government's decree was unpopular with farmers, and two Members of Parliament started the parliamentary procedure for a private member's Bill amending the provision. They argued that the government's decree interfered with fundamental principles of property law by restricting the basic right to dispose of property, and was therefore within the subject matter reserved to Parliament under article 34. The *Conseil constitutionnel* declared that the decree was properly concerned with points of detail on the calculation of the price of property, but not with any fundamental rights and was therefore outside article 34; it was suitable for government legislation under article 37. The decree was therefore affirmed and the proposed parliamentary legislation could not be pursued.

Article 41 can also be used where Parliament considers that the government has abused its power to legislate by *ordonnances*, for specified purposes and for a limited period of time under article 38.

Article 37

Occasionally the government decides it would like to amend a parliamentary statute without having to pass another Act of Parliament to do this. This is only possible if the statute is outside the sphere reserved to Parliament under article 34. For Acts passed before the 1958 Constitution came into effect, the government only needs to consult the *Conseil d'Etat* before amending the law through the passing of a regulation. For Acts which came into force after the new Constitution, it must refer the matter to the *Conseil constitutionnel* and obtain a ruling that the subject matter of the amendment to the law is outside the sphere reserved to Parliament. For example, in 1959 the government wanted to pass a decree to change the composition of the governing body of the organisation responsible for running public transport in Paris (the RATP). The *Conseil constitutionnel* ruled on 27 November of that year that, while an Act had been required to create the governing body, because the RATP was a state enterprise falling within article 34, changes to its composition could be done by a government decree.

Article 61

Under article 61, the *Conseil constitutionnel* judges the constitutionality of statutes passed by Parliament and standing orders of Parliament. The *Conseil constitutionnel* can then decide in several different ways:

- It may declare a provision to be in compliance with the Constitution, in which case it can be promulgated and enforced. Occasionally, the *Conseil constitutionnel* will pronounce a statute to be constitutional on the condition that it is interpreted in a specified way.
- It may declare that an unconstitutional provision cannot be promulgated or enforced, as mentioned by article 62. To get round this problem the government may choose to amend the Constitution so that the offending text can then be passed.
- Alternatively, it may declare a statute unconstitutional, but add that if specific amendments are made, the *Conseil constitutionnel* would consider that the defect had been remedied.

When deciding the conformity of a provision to the Constitution, the *Conseil constitutionnel* will be required to interpret the Constitution. For example, an Act relating to the future status of Corsica was referred to the *Conseil constitutionnel*. In a decision of 9 May 1991, the court cancelled the first article of the Act which had acknowledged the existence of the Corsican nation. This provision was considered to be contrary to article 1 of the Constitution which states:

> Art. 1: France is an indivisible, secular, democratic and social Republic.

The *Conseil constitutionnel* clearly thereby interpreted the Constitution as preventing there being any other Nation in France than the French nation.

Only constitutional statutes and parliamentary standing orders are automatically referred to the *Conseil constitutionnel*. Ordinary parliamentary legislation will only be considered by the *Conseil constitutionnel* if it has actually been referred to it by persons with authority to do so. Many Acts of Parliament are never referred, and their constitutionality cannot normally be contested once they have been promulgated.

This is the area where the role of the *Conseil constitutionnel* developed in ways which had not been foreseen by the creators of the Constitution. Until 1971, most of the work of the *Conseil* on the constitutionality of Acts of Parliament related to the division of law-making powers between Parliament and the government. Two important developments took place in the early 1970s, which resulted in the *Conseil constitutionnel* playing a very important role in developing constitutional law. The first was the creation of the 'constitutional block' in 1971 (discussed at p. 53). By enlarging the definition of the Constitution to include the Declaration of Human and Civil Rights of 1789, the preamble to the 1946 Constitution, and the fundamental principles recognised by the laws of the Republic, the *Conseil constitutionnel* dramatically increased the scope of its operations. This evolution was criticised by the former Prime Minister Edouard Balladur in 1993, when he mentioned that 'since the *Conseil constitutionnel* decided to include the Preamble within the "constitutional block", it has monitored the conformity of Acts of Parliaments with general principles, sometimes more philosophical and political than legal, sometimes contradictory, and, furthermore, conceived at different times from this one'.

The second milestone was the Act of 29 October 1974. It increased the ways in which a case on the constitutionality of legislation could be commenced. In the original draft of the Constitution, only the President of the Republic, the Prime Minister, the President of the National Assembly or the President of the Senate could refer legislation (article 61). After the 1974 amendment, 60 Members of the National Assembly or Senate could also do this. In effect, before 1974 only people close to the ruling government were entitled to refer cases, whereas now a group of opposition politicians can do so, and this happens regularly. This was vital to increase applications to the *Conseil constitutionnel* relating to the constitutionality of legislative Bills. Until this reform, and since 1958, only nine references had been made on the basis of article 61, with most emanating from the Prime Minister; the average since 1974 has been fifteen such references a year. Nowadays, 90 per cent of all cases are referred to the *Conseil constitutionnel* by Members of the National Assembly or the Senate, and this has, in effect, become an instrument for the opposition groups in Parliament to block the government's actions.

An early example of the combined effect of these two developments can be seen in the decision of 15 January 1975 on proposed legislation reforming the law on abortion. Under an Act of 1920, women had the right to an abortion where the pregnancy posed a danger to the health of the mother, or where the child would be severely disabled. It was proposed to add an additional justification for abortions which would be available during the first ten weeks of the pregnancy: that the pregnancy and birth would cause distress to the mother. The *Conseil constitutionnel* held that this legislation did not breach article 2 of the 1789 Declaration (protecting the right to life), nor any fundamental principles recognised by the laws of the Republic, nor the principle declared in paragraph 11 of the preamble to the 1946 Constitution (where the state guarantees to protect children's health). This case illustrates how the *Conseil constitutionnel* aims to balance potentially conflicting principles from a wide range of sources. It is also a good example of the independence of the *Conseil constitutionnel*, which it had little opportunity to demonstrate before 1974 because only the government or persons under its sphere of influence could refer cases to it. Since then, the majority of references have been made by groups of opposition Members of Parliament and it has had plenty of scope to develop its case law, handing down many important decisions.

Article 54

Following an amendment of the Constitution in 1992, under article 54 international agreements can be referred to the *Conseil constitutionnel* before they have been ratified by the same people who have this power under article 61 (see p. 138). To date nine international treaties only have been referred to the *Conseil constitutionnel*.

Article 77

Situated in the Pacific Ocean, East from Australia, New Caledonia is an island that was until recently part of the French overseas territories. Its status changed in the late 1990s following political unrest by local independence movements. An agreement was signed between all political parties and the State in 1998 to give New Caledonia a right to self determination and possibly to move towards independence. A local referendum has now been scheduled after 2014 to determine the final status of the island. In the meantime, the French State has transferred some of its powers to the local institutions, among them a local government and a local congress, and recognises for the first time New Caledonian citizenship. The local congress is entitled to make local laws, known as *lois du pays,* in a number of limited cases, as defined by a constitutional Act dated 19 March 1999.

A new title XIII has been included in the Constitution relating to the transitional status of the island. Article 77 of this Constitution, complemented by articles 104 and 105 of the constitutional statute, enable a *lois du pays* to be referred to the *Conseil constitutionnel* to control its conformity with the Constitution.

▶ Limitations of the *Conseil constitutionnel's* powers

There are five important limitations on the *Conseil constitutionnel*'s powers, which relate to the control of the constitutionality of certain statutes. These are Acts:

• passed after a referendum;
• which amend the Constitution (*lois constitutionnelles*);
• which are already promulgated;
• not actually referred to the *Conseil*; and
• incorporating European directives into French Law.

In addition, the *Conseil constitutionnel* will not look at the compatability of an Act with European law or an international treaty.

Acts passed following a referendum

By a decision of 6 November 1962, reconfirmed on 23 September 1992, the *Conseil constitutionnel* decided that it could not review the constitutionality of statutes approved by popular vote in a referendum. It held that its function under the Constitution was limited to the sphere of public authorities and did not include laws voted for by the French people. This is a serious limitation of power, as on the whole only important measures are the subject of referendums, though the number of such Acts is small.

Lois constitutionnelles

The *Conseil constitutionnel* decided in a decision of 26 March 2003 that no provision of the Constitution entitles it to review the constitutionality of statutes amending the Constitution (*lois constitutionnelles*). The *Conseil constitutionnel* refused in this case to examine whether the statute aiming to revise the Constitution in order to enable further decentralisation complied with the condition expressed in article 89 that the republican form of government cannot be amended.

Promulgated Acts

Once an Act of Parliament has been promulgated, no one, including the *Conseil constitutionnel*, can pronounce it to be unconstitutional. This rule, reaffirmed by the *Conseil constitutionnel* in a decision of 27 July 1978, considerably limits its powers and increases that of Parliament. A major drawback of this rule is that any pre-1958 statute is exempt from being referred to the *Conseil constitutionnel*, and will remain in force even though it might breach the Constitution. On the other hand, a clear advantage of this rule is the existence of legal certainty, as a promulgated statute may not be challenged for its unconstitutionality.

In many countries with constitutional courts, such as Germany and Italy, such a power is available. A Bill that would have allowed individuals to complain that a promulgated Act breached the Constitution was defeated by the Senate, and the legislation was not passed on two occasions, in 1990 and again in 1993. Government regulations can be the subject of judicial review in the administrative courts, but there is no equivalent procedure for parliamentary laws.

This, however, may be carried out indirectly in a limited number of cases: the *Conseil constitutionnel* recognised that it had the right to check conformity with the constitution of a statute that was already in force when new provisions modifying the existing statute were referred to the *Conseil constitutionnel* in a decision of 25 January 1985. It may be argued that the *Conseil* is acting, in these cases, beyond its remit, as this had certainly not been intended by the original drafters of the Constitution.

Absence of a referral

Another important limitation on the *Conseil constitutionnel*'s powers is that even though there has been an increase in the number of cases submitted since the reform of article 61 allowing 60 Members of Parliament to refer any legislation they choose to the *Conseil constitutionnel*, such submission is still not compulsory. The proportion of statutes submitted each year varies between 15 and 30 per cent of those voted, so the vast majority are not reviewed by the *Conseil constitutionnel* to determine their constitutionality.

Acts incorporating European directives into French law

Following a decision of 10 June 2004, which was confirmed by two decisions of 1 and 29 July 2004, the *Conseil constitutionnel* refused to determine the conformity of a Bill incorporating a European directive into French law with the Constitution. For a European directive to have any effect in a Member State, it normally requires domestic implementation (article 249 EC Treaty). Basing its decision on article 88-1 of the Constitution, which mentions that France is 'a member of the European Community and the European Union', it concluded that such incorporation is a constitutional obligation that can only be limited if the Bill is expressly contrary to the Constitution.

The independence of the *Conseil constitutionnel*

Because of the way its members are chosen, doubts have been raised as to the *Conseil constitutionnel*'s independence, especially when General de Gaulle was in office. It is an important issue, since a decision by five unelected members can prevent the will of Parliament, and thus indirectly the French people, from adopting an Act of Parliament which the *Conseil* deems contrary to the Constitution. These doubts seem to be confirmed by the declaration of the former President of the *Conseil constitutionnel*, Gaston Palewski, that 'while General de Gaulle was the head of State, it appeared to me to be difficult to have a different understanding of the Constitution than the actual author of the Constitution.' General de Gaulle was strongly opposed to the creation of a constitutional court, believing that in France 'the supreme court is the people'. It was also acknowledged by François Luchaire, one of its former members, that the *Conseil constitutionnel* extended its jurisdiction beyond what had been foreseen by the drafters of the Constitution after General de Gaulle's death in 1970, starting with the decision of 16 July 1971 (see p. 53). The *Conseil constitutionnel* has effectively since 1971 become the protector of human rights and has thus transformed itself into a genuine constitutional court.

It is clear, however, that the *Conseil constitutionnel* has always been concerned to maintain a unity within its case law, thus preventing any criticisms that sudden changes may be due to changes in its members.

It avoids favouring one political personality more than another, and has treated left-wing and right-wing politicians in a similar fashion. The *Conseil constitutionnel* has made itself equally unpopular among successive governments and Members of Parliament of left- or right-wing persuasion when declaring Acts of Parliament unconstitutional. This was shown in a recent study by Gouaud-Tandeau de Marsac when she compared the *Conseil constitutionnel*'s activity during a right-wing and a left-wing government. During four years of right-wing governments, between 1993 and 1997, out of 60 parliamentary statutes referred to the *Conseil constitutionnel*, 23 contained an unconstitutional provision and seven were declared entirely unconstitutional. In comparison, during the five following years of a Labour government, out of 67 statutes, 28 contained an unconstitutional provision and nine were declared entirely unconstitutional by the *Conseil constitutionnel*. Furthermore, it has never been in doubt that its decisions are always based on clear and logical, legal arguments.

PART III: THE HIGH COURT OF JUSTICE AND THE COURT OF JUSTICE OF THE REPUBLIC

The original Constitution of the Fifth Republic provided, in articles 67 and 68, for a special court, the High Court of Justice (*la Haute Cour de Justice*), to judge the President of the Republic and the members of the government for high treason. While in recent years various government scandals have come to the public's attention, none were brought before this court. As a result of its apparent ineffectiveness, it was decided in 1993 to reform the Constitution and its article 67. An Act was passed on 27 July 1993 which retained the High Court of Justice but restricted it to hearing cases of high treason committed by the President of the Republic. A new court was created, known as the Court of Justice of the Republic (*la Cour de Justice de la République*), for the trial of government ministers (new articles 68-1 to 68-3 of the Constitution). The latter is arguably part of the system of criminal courts, but as it is so closely connected with the High Court of Justice it will be studied in this chapter.

The High Court of Justice

Jurisdiction

The jurisdiction of the High Court of Justice is now limited to accusations of high treason committed by the President of the Republic. A trial of this nature would be the French equivalent of the American impeachment proceedings. No definition is provided of the key concept of 'high treason', either in the Constitution or in the Criminal Code of 1994. It is likely to be interpreted to include any civil wrong committed in breach of his or her duties as guardian of the Constitution, a possible example being abuse of the emergency powers given under article 16. The court has never heard a case against the President, though there were rumours that it might be asked to consider some of General de Gaulle's more adventurous uses of the Constitution, such as the calling of a referendum under article 11 to approve the law allowing for direct election of the President (see p. 26). However imprecise the notion of high treason, it is the only ground for referral to the High Court of Justice. The referral to the High Court of Justice may only be made by Parliament if it is the wish of an absolute majority of the members in each House; private individuals are not entitled to make referral to the High Court of Justice.

Organisation

As mentioned in the constitutional statute of 23 November 1993, the court is made up of 24 judges and 12 back-up judges, half of whom come from the National Assembly and the other half from the Senate. They are elected by their peers by a secret ballot. The judges elected by the National Assembly are replaced every time there is an election, and the judges elected by the Senate are replaced periodically as new senators are nominated. There is therefore a close connection between the judges and the respective majorities in Parliament and the Senate. At the time when the High Court of Justice also had jurisdiction to consider cases against members of the government, this provoked accusations that it was not always impartial. Of particular concern were cases that had originally been brought against members of minority parties but were dropped after an election put the parties of those accused back in the majority. The existing composition of the court was kept for the restricted jurisdiction put in place by the 1993 constitutional reform, on the basis that the President is above party politics.

Procedure

A motion to bring charges must be signed by at least 10 per cent of the members of both the National Assembly and the Senate before it can be put to the vote. The prosecution of a case is then commenced when Parliament passes a resolution to bring charges. This resolution must be voted in identical terms by an absolute majority of both Houses of Parliament. This stage of the procedure was reached in cases involving scandals implicating members of the government when the court still had its wider jurisdiction. It has been used in particular since 1992, in a number of cases against people who were ministers in 1985 at the time of the scandal concerning blood transfusions with blood contaminated by the AIDS virus. The ministers concerned were Laurent Fabius (Prime

Minister), Georgina Dufoix (Minister of Social Affairs), and Edmond Hervé (Minister of Health). Parliament voted to bring charges of failure to assist persons in danger, which is an offence under French law.

Once Parliament has voted a resolution to bring charges, the matter is referred to the committee appointed to open a judicial investigation into it. The members of this committee are five judges of the *Cour de cassation* and two Members of Parliament acting as judges for the High Court of Justice and chosen by their peers. They hold office for a year.

In the contaminated blood case, the committee declared that the proposed charge was time-barred. It then proceeded to investigate the possibility that the accused were guilty of manslaughter – prosecution for this offence would not be time-barred in certain circumstances. It became clear that the procedure was too slow and unlikely to come to fruition in the form of a hearing before the High Court of Justice.

Where a matter actually proceeds to a hearing, the case will be heard by the elected parliamentarians acting as judges. There is no appeal against the verdict reached, which is voted on in secret.

This court operates in a unique way, but it is connected with the ordinary system in that the judges who are members of the committee conducting the investigation are judges of the *Cour de cassation*.

The Court of Justice of the Republic

The Court of Justice of the Republic (*la Cour de Justice de la République*) was created by adding a new Title X to the Constitution, entitled 'Criminal liability of members of the government'. It shares some features in common with the High Court of Justice and a few features which connect it more closely to the civil and criminal court system. Its first case was the continuation of the contaminated blood litigation and we will look at this experience to illustrate aspects of the court's operation.

Jurisdiction

As mentioned by article 68-1 of the Constitution, the court's jurisdiction is limited to offences committed by members of the government in the exercise of their duties. Whereas before 1993, the jurisdiction of the High Court of Justice was limited to cases of high treason, the jurisdiction of the Court of Justice of the Republic has been extended to include crimes and major criminal offences. If the offences are not deemed to have been exercised as part of a ministerial duty, ordinary courts will take over jurisdiction, even if the offences were committed while in office. The link between the offence and the State functions will become the determining factor when deciding jurisdiction, as was established following the decisions of the *Tribunal correctionnel* of Lyon on 20 April 1995 and the *Cour de cassation* on 27 June 1995. The Court of Justice of the Republic declared itself unable to exercise jurisdiction, in a decision of 10 November 1999 relating to suspicions of corruption and fraud against Michel Noir while he was a member of the Chirac Government between 1986 and 1988, as this link between the offence and the state function was not established.

Furthermore, and very unusual in the French legal system, article 68-3 of the Constitution contains a proviso giving the Court retrospective jurisdiction with regard to matters that took place before its creation.

Membership

Three members of the court are judges of the *Cour de cassation*, elected by their peers for three years. The other 12 judges are Members of Parliament elected by their peers in a similar way to the election of judges for the High Court of Justice (article 68-2 of the Constitution). While parliamentarians are still a clear majority, the views of the three professional judges will have the weight of judicial experience, and the President of the court is a professional judge. The judges must give grounds for their verdict and their decision can be referred on points of law and procedure to the *Cour de cassation* by the accused.

Procedure

The second paragraph of article 68-2 enables the Public prosecutor of the *Cour de cassation*, or people who consider that they have been the victims of an offence committed by a member of the government while carrying out their duties, to bring an action in the Court of Justice of the Republic. The type of case it deals with means that it has greater similarities to a civil or criminal court than the High Court of Justice. A Constitutional statute of 23 November 1993 regulates the procedures that apply to the Court of Justice of the Republic. A special commission (*la commission des requêtes*) investigates all claims and only those approved by that commission will go any further, so its role is vital. This commission dismissed a recent referral by five families against three former Ministers for Health, Jean-François Mattei, Bernard Kouchner and Philippe Douste-Blazy. The claim concerned a vaccination campaign to fight hepatitis B that had been instigated by the Ministry for Health. The families claimed that there was clear evidence that the occurrence of terminal diseases, among them multiple sclerosis, was due to the use of the vaccine. The special commission declared, in its decision of 24 March 2005, that the link between the vaccine and the diseases was not sufficiently established to warrant further investigation.

The commission consists of three judges from the *Cour de cassation*, two from the *Conseil d'Etat*, and two from the Audit Court – thus the four administrative judges have a majority of votes. They are all elected by their peers, and hold office for a term of five years (there being no renewal at election time). This composition is designed to ensure the independence of the body.

At the time of writing, the commission of the Court of Justice of the Republic is investigating allegations of corruption against Charles Pasqua while he was in office as Home Secretary between 1993 and 1995.

Cases which have cleared this hurdle are referred to the committee responsible for opening a judicial investigation for this court. The committee consists of three judges of the *Cour de cassation* and holds office for a three-year term. The committee can order an acquittal or decide that sufficient charges exist for the case to be decided by the 15 members of the Court. Decisions of the Court are subject to appeal to the *assemblée plénière* of the *Cour de cassation*.

In 1997 the Minister for Education, Ségolène Royal, was sued by two professors from a veterinary school in Marseilles for defamation. Cases of institutionalised bullying had taken place in that school and the minister commented that there was clear evidence that some staff members had been complicit in the matter. Medical and veterinary schools have traditionally always been infamous for particularly degrading initiation procedures which led to legislation banning these practices. The *Cour de cassation* established the Court's jurisdiction in a decision of 23 December 1999. The Court acquitted Ségolène Royal in a decision of 16 May 2000 as there was clear evidence available to back up her declarations.

The former Secretary of State for the disabled, Michel Gillibert, was sentenced to a three-year suspended prison sentence and €20,000 fine by the Court in 2004 for having embezzled funds between 1989 and 1990 while in office. This money should have been used to set up and run a charity for the disabled in France. The Court's sentence, on 7 July 2004, was relatively lenient as it took into account the culprit's ailing health which would have made it 'nearly incompatible with a prison detention'.

▶ The contaminated blood scandal

The Court of Justice of the Republic sat for the first time in order to hear the case against the three former ministers, Laurent Fabius, Georgina Dufoix and Edmond Hervé, in the contaminated blood scandal. Up to thirteen times more people in France were contaminated with the AIDS virus following a blood transfusion than in any other European country. The prosecution was primarily concerned with looking at liability for the infection of people, including haemophiliacs, who had had blood transfusions before October 1985, or after that date, due to contact with such blood products. The state had been judged responsible for contaminations between November 1984 and October 1985 under administrative law, by a decision of the *Conseil d'Etat* on 9 April 1993. The *Conseil d'Etat* considered that from 20 November 1984 the public authorities should have put into effect regulatory measures after the Advisory Commission for Blood Transfusions had received vital information about the health risks. By 20 October 1985 it considered adequate measures for the safety of blood products had been put into place.

The case against the ministers concerned the way the government had exercised its powers to supervise the health service. The complainants argued that there were several measures that they had failed or been slow to order during their time in office, and the resulting delays had caused the victims to be contaminated with AIDS:

- There had been a failure to select blood donors, and in particular blood had continued to be collected from inappropriate places, such as red-light districts and prisons. The proportion of drug addicts among detainees who were infected by hepatitis C and AIDS was very significant. In 1985, the collections in prison represented 0.37% of blood donations but were responsible for 25% of contaminations. Back in June 1983 a circular had been issued advising that a selection process should be introduced for blood donors, but this was not generally applied by the French medical profession.
- Donors had not been tested for the AIDS virus, and an American AIDS test had been blocked in order to favour the development of a French test by Diagnostics Pasteur, for economic reasons. The first official report into the contamination of haemophiliacs was carried out in 1991 by Michel Lucas, head of the general inspectorate of social affairs. This revealed that an inter-ministerial meeting on 9 May 1985 had taken place, in which the Prime Minister's office had demanded to 'hold back for a little longer' the file on registering the American AIDS test.
- Blood products for haemophiliacs that risked being contaminated with AIDS had not been withdrawn and replaced with heated products which were safe, until October 1985.
- People who had received blood transfusions between 1980 and 1985 had not been recalled so that they could be offered an AIDS test, to prevent their sexual partners or unborn children being contaminated. According to the compensation fund, 81 people close to haemophiliacs and 309 close to blood transfusion patients were subsequently contaminated as a result of this failure.

Correspondence between the Minister of Social Affairs, Claude Evin, and his technical adviser, Jean-Paul Jean, from June 1988 to May 1991, sheds some light on these matters. A note dated 30 March 1989 from the adviser to the minister states:

> Some inactivated American products were available on the market in 1985. It seems that the choice was made to defend the system of French blood production, at the [National Centre for Blood

Transfusions]. The stocks that were known to be contaminated would have continued to be used in particular for haemophiliacs already treated for several years with un-heated products ... Today, everybody is looking for the State, and for the minister in particular, to deal with a dramatic problem: the death in the short term of thousands of people contaminated at a time when, for certain of them, it could have been avoided by an emergency plan which was not made.

A further note dated 17 November 1989 states:

It is true that there were at the time some debatable political decisions, between March and October 1985 (refusal to import on a large scale heated products and to destroy the stocks, delay in putting into place the testing to benefit the Pasteur test).

At the preliminary committee stage the prosecutor, Jean François Burgelin, on two occasions sought a ruling that there was no case to answer (March 1997 and June 1998). On 17 July 1998 the committee dismissed 17 of the complaints. Several days before their ruling the criminal division of the *Cour de cassation* had handed down a judgment giving a narrow definition of the crime of poisoning or complicity to poison. In the ministers' case, the committee subsequently rejected the charge of aiding and abetting a poisoning and decided to charge them instead with involuntary manslaughter and assault on a person's integrity. M. Fabius and Mme Dufoix were sent for trial on three charges of involuntary manslaughter and two charges of assault on a person's integrity. M. Hervé was charged with three offences of involuntary manslaughter and four assaults on a person's integrity. The maximum sentence that could be imposed for these offences was three years' imprisonment or a fine of 300,000 FF.

The victims of the offences included Paul Pérard, who died after being infected with AIDS in May 1985 during an open heart operation; Charles-Edouard Pernot-Cochin, a baby who died after being infected in May 1985 by a blood transfusion carried out at birth; Sylvie Rouy, 36 years old, contaminated when she was given a blood transfusion while giving birth in August 1985 with blood that had been collected in July 1985 and not tested for the virus; and Sarah Malik who contracted AIDS while an unborn foetus and died at the age of two – her mother had been given a blood transfusion in April 1985 and had not been recalled to advise her of the risk of infection.

The majority of the complaints for which the ministers were sent for trial concerned people contaminated by the AIDS virus following blood transfusions. With the exception of one case, all the complaints relating to haemophiliacs were dismissed by the committee, on the simple ground that it was impossible to prove that blood products used during the minister's period of responsibility had caused the AIDS infection – the victim might have already been infected. The only case of a haemophiliac which was allowed to proceed was against M. Hervé alone, and concerned Pierre Roustan, a 60-year-old haemophiliac who died in May 1993. HIV negative at the time of a test carried out on 10 May 1985, he was declared HIV positive by a test on 13 November 1985. He had been infected at some point between these two tests by blood derivatives that had not been heated.

The trial that ensued before the Court of Justice of the Republic was highly controversial. Twenty-four political judges were selected, 12 of whom actually tried the case and the other 12 were available as substitutes in case any needed to be replaced. These judges were chosen by their peers, in proportion to the political groups in the National Assembly (majority on the left), and of the Senate (majority on the right). Thus, of the 12 judges who actually tried the case, five were on the left and seven were on the right, while the defendants had been members of the socialist government. Among these judges there were three doctors, two *avocats*, two former ministers, two lawyers, one Prefect, a former judge and an ex-businessman.

In addition there were three professional judges from the *Cour de cassation*. In 1997, the President of the criminal division of the *Cour de cassation*, Christian Le Gunehec, was elected by his peers at the age of 68 to the presidency of the Court of Justice of the Republic.

The 1993 Act established the court had left some practical issues unanswered which had to be resolved at preliminary meetings of the judges, including the substitutes, before the trial actually took place. For example, the legislation made no reference to how the judges should dress for the trial. The judges on the right favoured wearing the black gowns of the *tribunal correctionnel*. Those on the left were divided on the issue. Some wanted the professional judges to wear black robes and the parliamentarians to wear civilian clothes, while others wanted all the judges to wear civilian clothes. The issue was resolved by a secret ballot on 24 November 1998 which decided that all the judges would wear black robes. A distinction between the professional and parliamentary judges was however drawn by the table plan adopted by M. Le Gunehec. The three professional judges sat at the centre. The other judges were distributed according to a protocol which took into account the date of their election to the court, their age and the length of time they had been in Parliament. The parliamentary judges were not paid any additional sum for working as judges, but they continued to receive their salaries as Members of Parliament.

Problems arose from the fact that alongside the prosecution of the former ministers in the Court of Justice of the Republic, separate criminal proceedings against their advisers were being brought before the ordinary criminal courts. Many of the potential defendants in the latter proceedings were summoned to be witnesses in the trial of the ministers. This raised the question of whether the witnesses should be forced to give evidence against their will and whether they should be obliged to give their evidence on oath when they would not be obliged to do so at their own trial. It was argued by some of the witnesses that an obligation to give evidence on oath would be in breach of their defence rights. They clearly feared that their testimonies might be used against them at their own subsequent trial. This situation is not foreseen by the Code of Criminal Procedure. Prior to the trial at the Court of Justice of the Republic some of the witnesses made it clear that they would not attend, which could have made them liable to the payment of a fine. Following the recommendations of the President of the court, the judges decided at a preliminary meeting on 9 February 1999 that the witnesses would not be obliged to give evidence on oath. As for those who refused to appear, the court would decide, case by case, whether they would be required to do so. As a result, at the trial some witnesses did not give their evidence on oath; some gave evidence but relied heavily on written notes or even a pre-written text, in breach of the usual rules of criminal procedure; others, such as doctor Claude Weisselberg, ex-adviser to Edmond Hervé, simply refused to give evidence.

The 1993 Act creating the court was ambiguous on whether it should hand down a simple verdict of guilty or not guilty (like the *Cour d'assises*) or whether it had to give reasons for its verdict as is the case for the *tribunal correctionnel*. On the one hand, article 26 of the Act states that 'except where it is otherwise provided, the rules concerning the debates and judgments for cases before the *tribunal correctionnel* apply before the Court of Justice of the Republic'. On the other hand, article 32 of the Act refers to the procedures of the *Cour d'assises* in relation to the deliberations and judgment. Eventually the judges decided that they would give reasons for their judgment.

The court sat at the International Conference Centre in Paris. On the fourth day of the trial, President Le Gunehec gave a short clarification of his personal vision of the procedure before the court:

> The hearing takes place according to the rules of the *tribunal correctionnel*, that is to say the judges are judges who rule on both the facts and the law, and not jurors. We are in a public trial, not in a trial made for the public. The only aim is that the judges should reach a verdict.

The victims were not allowed to be civil parties to the criminal process, and they could not therefore have access to the file and be legally represented in the proceedings, but could only be heard as witnesses. They were left feeling powerless as the trial progressed, and placed themselves in the front row of the public gallery, throwing insults at the suspects and defence witnesses as they gave evidence. The victims were heavily reliant on the prosecution to put their case, but the senior public prosecutor, Jean-François Burgelin, had submitted on two previous occasions applications that the prosecution should not proceed. He asked no questions of the defendants nor of their three witnesses when they gave evidence. At the trial he requested that all three ministers should be acquitted and receive a 'reprimand', a notion that is in fact unknown to French criminal law, but which seemed to be a gesture to satisfy public opinion. He justified this approach on the basis that convictions would criminalise political life, and drew attention to the risk of confusing criminal responsibility with political responsibility. This was a view that had been taken by M. Pierre Mazeaud, a member of the *Conseil constitutionnel* (*Le Monde*, 22 February 1999), who argued that this error had been made by the original committee responsible for referring cases to the court. In its referral the court had stated:

> Every fault that is not intentional is of a nature to give rise to criminal responsibility, not only of the person who is directly at the origin of the harm, but equally of the person who, at different degrees, from close or from far, contributed to it.

In a similar vein, the two junior prosecutors, Jean-François Burgelin and Roger Lucas, pointed to the fact that there had been a general failure of governmental structures that had caused this human tragedy, rather than any individual failing. They argued that there had been a dilution of information as it rose up the hierarchy of the ministries. Roger Lucas did suggest that M. Hervé had delegated too much power to his advisers so as to spend more time on his position as Mayor of Rennes. However, at the same time he drew attention to the inefficiency of the consultative organs, and observed the failure to communicate which reigned between the administrations. Finally, he highlighted the disastrous gap between the awareness of the health risk and the financial decision-making on public health issues. With the absence of any civil parties to the proceedings and the reluctance of the prosecutors to prosecute, the trial lacked a balance between the prosecution and the defence.

During the first days of the trial, the media criticised the President of the court, Christian Le Gunehec, for being inadequately prepared for the hearing. There were suggestions that he might be having difficulty making the transition from the *Cour de cassation*, which dealt with appeals on the law only, to the Court of Justice of the Republic, which was a court of first instance, hearing issues of fact and law and requiring the examination of witnesses.

The parliamentary judges could not ask questions directly to the witnesses; instead they had to pass their written questions to the President, who would ask the questions on their behalf. Le Gunehec was criticised for not asking all of these questions. At one stage, half a dozen parliamentary judges from the right threatened to resign if the President did not get his act together. There were even hopes that Le Gunehec might withdraw on the basis of ill health.

The hearing ended on 26 February 1999 when the judges withdrew to deliberate their verdict. These deliberations took place on 2 March 1999. The substitute judges did not participate in the final deliberations of the court. A secret ballot was taken to determine by a simple majority the guilt or innocence of each defendant. On conviction, a second secret ballot determined the sentence. This is the same procedure as that used by the *Cour d'assises*. Under article 2 of the 1993 Act the deliberations should have been kept secret. This article provides that:

> [O]n their election, the parliamentary judges take an oath before the Assembly that appointed them … They swear and promise to well and loyally fulfil their functions, to keep the secret of the deliberations and votes and to conduct themselves always as honourable and loyal judges.

But the secret was breached and information leaked to the press. Apparently *Le Monde* knew the outcome of the deliberations before the verdict had even been read out in open court, but decided not to publish as this could have been a ground for a successful appeal to the *Cour de cassation*.

The discussions only lasted a few hours. It seems that the parliamentary judges on the left had always favoured an acquittal, while the right remained divided throughout the trial, being worried about how public opinion would react to any verdict to acquit. The judges agreed relatively quickly to acquit Laurent Fabius by 12 votes to three. The parliamentary judges did not deny that the government might have wanted to carry out a strategy favourable to Diagnostics Pasteur, but they almost all recognised that the concern to help French businesses was in effect a duty for politicians. In fact, they concluded that the decision to institute compulsory testing had been 'rapid' and 'reasonable'. One judge on the right had pleaded for the unique responsibility of M. Fabius as Prime Minister at the relevant time, and two judges (a parliamentarian on the right and a professional judge) made known their opinion in favour of imposing liability on all three former ministers.

Mme Dufoix was acquitted by ten votes to five. The longest deliberations were over Edmond Hervé. He was convicted of one charge of involuntary manslaughter for failing to recall Sarah Malik's mother after a blood transfusion in April 1985; and one charge for a non-fatal offence against Sylvie Rouy for failing to order the testing of the blood that had been collected before compulsory testing was introduced. At the time of the trial Sylvie Rouy was extremely ill but she attended the proceedings in a wheelchair and her evidence to the court had made a strong impression on the judges. The parliamentary judges on the left and one judge on the right pleaded in vain that a conviction on this basis would give rise to the possibility of all the subsequent Ministers for Health being liable until 1992 when patients had been recalled. The vote was very close – eight votes to seven – and was divided on political lines. The five judges on the left rallied to the acquittal, along with one judge on the right and a professional judge. The second vote, to determine the punishment, showed the difficulty the judges had in convicting the accused. Only three judges voted in favour of a suspended prison sentence, the 12 others voting in favour of a conviction without sentence.

A sub-group of half a dozen judges, of a mix of right- and left-wing politics, was then selected to write the text of the judgment the next day. This was read out in court on 9 March 1999 and was 23 pages long. The judgment stated that Laurent Fabius had actually made a 'rapid' and 'reasonable' response on the issue of testing blood donors, and had thereby contributed to accelerating the decision in 1985 to introduce these tests. It also observed that Georgina Dufoix had promptly ruled on the financial aspects of putting into place the government measures.

The victims and their representatives were in the courtroom to hear the judgment and reacted angrily to the verdict, shouting 'Shame on the parliamentarians!', 'Shame on this parody of justice!', 'You have blood on your hands, M. Hervé!' Outside the court, Sylvie Rouy, sitting in her wheelchair, said:

> This verdict destroys us a second time. Edmond Hervé is not the only person responsible, but he is the only one convicted. This is not fair. We wait now for the second trial of this case, that of the advisers. This time our lawyers will be there. (*Le Monde*, 10 March 1999)

The *Association française des hémophiles* and the *Association française des transfusés* denounced the proceedings as a 'sham trial' and declared that they hoped the trial of the ministers' advisers would allow them indirectly to prove the guilt of the ministers.

Lawyers have criticised the legal foundations of the judgment and are particularly dissatisfied with the dispensation from punishment accorded to Edmond Hervé. The relevant legislative provisions are contained in article 469-1 of the Code of Criminal Procedure. A dispensation is granted very rarely, and then only for minor offences. It can only be ordered 'when it appears that the rehabilitation of the guilty person has been achieved, that the damage caused has been repaired and that the trouble resulting from the offence has ceased'. But the judgment made no reference to these conditions being satisfied, instead invoking the context of the case and stating that Edmond Hervé had not totally benefited from the presumption of innocence, inasmuch as his case had been severely prejudiced and prejudged before he came to trial. In the words of the court:

> Fifteen years have passed since the facts and five years since the commencement of the prosecution by the *commission des requêtes* of the Court of Justice of the Republic and the judgment of the three

former members of the government …; during these years numerous theses have been put forward in the contaminated blood affair, making accusations on the responsibility of the ministers without them being in a position to defend themselves; in such a context, Edmond Hervé could not benefit totally from the presumption of innocence, and was submitted, before judgment, to excessive prejudgment, as is too often the case for many parties to legal proceedings.

Dominique Matagrin, the President of the *Association professionnelle des magistrats*, was of the view that:

This is not law, since the grounds for the decision that they give bear no relation to the dispensation from sentence, it is political polemic. (*Le Monde*, 11 March 1999)

A professor from Paris II University, Elisabeth Cartier, further commented that:

To invoke the presumption of innocence in a decision whilst, at the same time, one pronounces guilt is highly contestable … Either the court recognised the guilt, but was only applying the dispensation from punishment because the legal conditions were satisfied, which is not the situation in the case, or it recognised the innocence of the accused and acquitted. In any case, a decision with such legal reasoning can only give rise to the censure of the *Cour de cassation*. (*Le Monde*, 11 March 1999)

The verdict has not managed to put an end to the controversy surrounding the contaminated blood scandal. On 13 March, four days after the verdict, one of the political judges, M. Autain, told the newspaper *Presse Océan* that he had voted in favour of the acquittal of M. Hervé. Complaints to the state prosecutor were made by other members of the court that this breached the judge's oath to keep secret the deliberations of the court. The prosecutor in Paris has now opened an investigation into the matter and the judge has been charged with violating his obligation to remain silent about the court's deliberations. Edmond Hervé reacted to his conviction by stating that the court was political and had handed down a biased judgment (*Le Monde*, 11 March 1999).

The former socialist Minister for Health, Claude Evin, was charged on 18 June 1999 with involuntary manslaughter in relation to his failure to recall people between 1989 and 1991 who had had blood transfusions before August 1985. The complaint had been submitted by the *Association française des transfusés* and by Henri and Madeleine Aloncle, parents of Catherine Aloncle, a young woman who died in 1991 after being allegedly contaminated by a blood transfusion in 1984. According to the complainants, instead of recalling the patients, M. Evin put into place a compensation fund for haemophiliacs and people contaminated from transfusions, in April 1989, to dissuade them from trying to find out who was responsible for the contaminations. The decision of the committee to charge the former minister was based on the precedent created by the conviction of Edmond Hervé. Claude Evin was acquitted by the Court on 6 November 2003 as there was no evidence that he had acted negligently. Furthermore, it was not possible for the Court to establish that Catherine Aloncle had received blood from a contaminated sample.

In the light of the trial, there have been calls to reform the Court of Justice of the Republic, opinion being that it was created in too much haste in 1993. The inclusion of politicians as judges means that there is a real danger that any judgment it reaches will be viewed as having been decided through political expediency rather than to achieve justice. Whenever it acquits, the public may think that the politicians are simply protecting each other. The presence of political judges also means that judges will frequently know the accused personally. In the trial of the three former ministers, the judges were frequently coming into contact with the defendants before their trial. Thus each week the socialist judges would rub shoulders with M. Hervé and M. Fabius in a socialist group meeting of the National Assembly; one of the judges, Charles de Courson, sat three seats away from M. Hervé at the Finance Commission; M. Ollier, a judge of the court, was a vice president of the National Assembly and met M. Fabius once a week at the meeting of the Presidents of the National Assembly and the Senate – M. Fabius only stood down as President of the National Assembly for the duration of the trial. The judges claimed to have been careful throughout not to discuss the case with the accused but the situation did not inspire confidence in the public.

Two leading constitutional lawyers, Olivier Duhamel and Georges Vedel, have argued that all politicians should be tried by the ordinary criminal courts. The justification for the current position is the principle of the separation of powers and the fear of giving the professional judges too much power. But they argue that the court should no longer differ according to whether you are a minister or an ordinary citizen of France. They suggest that there could still be a commission responsible for filtering unfounded complaints against politicians. An advantage of such a reform would be that the ministers' alleged accomplices could be tried in the same proceedings (*Le Monde*, 3 March 1999). But the successive governments have reacted cautiously to these demands, and no change has yet taken place.

•••••••••••••••••••••••••••••

BIBLIOGRAPHY FOR CHAPTER 7

Bailleul, D. (2004), 'Quand le juge ressemble au constituant', *D.* 2004, 3089

Bell, J. (1995), *French Constitutional Law*, Oxford: Clarendon Press

Bréhier, T. (1999), 'Roland Dumas est isolé à la présidence du Conseil constitutionnel', *Le Monde*, 23 March 1999

Chagnollaud, D. (2004), Dr*oit constitutionnel contemporain, tome 2 (Histoire constitutionnelle – La Vème République)*, Paris: Dalloz – Armand Colin, 2004

Constitution de la République française (2005), texte présenté par Ferdinand Mélin-Soucramanien, Paris: Armand Colin

Courtois, G. (1999), 'Son président par intérim assure que le Conseil constitutionnel fonctionne "normalement" ', *Le Monde*, 14 May 1999

Courtois, G. (2000), 'Le Conseil constitutionnel est invité à trancher la situation de M. Dumas', *Le Monde*, 21 February 2000

Courtois, G. (2000), 'Roland Dumas annonce sa démission du Conseil constitutionnel', *Le Monde*, 11 March 2000

Debbasch, C. (2004), *Constitution – Vème République*, Paris: Dalloz

De La Gorce, P.-M. and Moschetto, B. (2005), *La Vème République, Que Sais-je?*, Paris: PUF

Dubourg-Lavroff, P. A. (1994), *Les décisions essentielles du Conseil constitutionnel: des origines à nos jours*, Paris: L'Harmattan.,

Favoreu, L. (2001), 'L'application de l'article 62, al. 2, de la Constitution par la Cour de cassation', *D.* 2001, 2683

Favoreu, L. et Philip, L. (2003), *Les Grandes Décisions du Conseil Constitutionnel*, 12th edn, Paris: Dalloz

Favoreu, L. and Philip, L. (2005), *Le Conseil constitutionnel, Que sais-je?*, Paris: PUF

Foillard, P. (2004), *Droit Constitutionnel*, Orléans: Paradigmes – CPU

Formery, S.-L. (1996), *La Constitution Commentée – Article par Article*, Paris: Hachette Supérieur,

Gondouin, G. and Rouxel, S. (2004), *Les Institutions Juridictionnelles*, Presses Universitaires de Grenoble

Gouaud-Tandeau de Marsac, C. (2005), *Droit Constitutionnel – la Vème République*, Paris: Ellipses

Héraud, A. and Maurin, A. (2002), *Institutions Judiciaires*, Paris: Sirey

Jackson, V. and Tushnet, M. (1999), *Comparative Constitutional Law*, St. Paul, MN: Foundation Press

Kernaleguen, F. (2003), *Institutions Judiciaires*, Paris: LexisNexis / Litec

Mathieu, B. (2005), 'Le respect de la Constitution: risque ou exigence?', *D.* 2005, 2401

Moutouh, H. (2003), 'Le contrôle de constitutionalité des lois constitutionnelles: suite et fin', *D.* 2003, 1099

Pactet, P. and Mélin-Soucramanien, F. (2004), *Droit Constitutionnel*, Paris : Dalloz-Armand Colin

Perrot, R. (2004), *Institutions Judiciaires*, Paris: Montchrestien

Piastra, R. (2005), 'Du devoir de réserve des conseillers constitutionnels …', *D.* 2005, 233

Portelli, H. (2005), *Droit Constutionnel*, Paris: Dalloz

Rousseau, D. (2004), *Le Conseil Constitutionnel en Questions*, Paris : L'Harmattan

Rousseau, D. and Spitz, E. (2001), 'Le crépuscule du Conseil constitutionnel', *Le Monde*, 7 December 2001

Roussillon, H. (2001), *Le Conseil Constitutionnel*, Paris: Dalloz

Scarano, Jean-Pierre (2004), *Institutions Juridictionnelles*, Paris: Ellipses

Turpin, D. (1995), *Le Conseil Constitutionnel – Son Rôle, sa Jurisprudence,* Paris: Hachette Supérieur

Wacquet, P. (2002), 'Regard sur le Tribunal des conflits', *D.* 2002, 742

Web resources

Website: www.conseil-constitutionnel.fr: The *Conseil constitutionnel.* Includes some text in English

Website: www.jurist.law.pitt.edu/world/france.htm: Materials on French constitutional law provided by the University of Pittsburgh

Website: www.droitpublic.net: website on public law

Website: www.ucl.ac.uk/laws/global_law: Institute of Global Law, contains cases by the *Conseil constitutionnel* translated into English

8 Judgments

PART I: DRAFTING OF JUDGMENTS

Every judgment consists of a syllogism. This consists of a major state-ment affirming a general legal rule, a minor statement exposing the facts of the case, and the application of the former to the latter leading to the verdict. It comes always as a surprise to lawyers from common law systems to see that French judgments are very short compared to the judg-ments of common law courts, often fitting on a single page. Dissenting opinions are never published.

During the 1970s, a Commission for the Modernisation of Legal Language was created to make such language more accessible to the general public. At the time, there was a real danger that ordinary litigants were unable to understand the judgments that had been handed out against them. This was particularly worrying in the lower courts as the lit-igant might not be represented by a lawyer who would have explained its meaning. The Commission reported in 1977 and significantly influenced the drafting of judgments handed down by first instance and ordinary appeal courts, while the decisions, particularly of the *Cour de cassation*, the administrative courts and the *Conseil constitutionnel*, have remained largely unchanged. The drive towards modernisation and simplifica-tion has thus led to a diversification in drafting styles, and a distinction therefore needs to be drawn between the traditional way of drafting judg-ments and the more modern style of drafting.

▶ Traditional drafting of judgments

An example of a traditional judgment can be found on p. 164 below. It consists grammatically of a single sentence with only one full stop, to be found at the end. The subject of the sentence is the court that gave its verdict. The danger is that where the facts and reasoning of the case are complex the result can be an extremely lengthy sentence, which may be punctuated with only a few commas and semi-colons – something that would never be acceptable in any other context. The judgment is divided into two parts: the grounds for the court's decisions (the *motifs*) and the court's verdict (the *dispositif*). It is only in this last part of the judgment that the verbs are put into the present indicative, forming the action verbs for the single sentence of the judgment.

Each paragraph belonging to the *motifs* starts with the phrase *attendu que*, meaning 'whereas' or 'given that', and these paragraphs are individually known as an *attendu*. Within a paragraph the phrase '*attendu que*' can be replaced by the single word *que*, simply to avoid repetition. The administrative courts, the *Conseil constitutionnel* and some courts of appeal, such as the one in Paris, prefer the phrase *considérant que* (considering that, in view of). The phrase *par ces motifs* (for these reasons) introduces the verdict. It is this verdict that constitutes the most important part of the judgment for the litigants, while it is the *attendu* containing the specific reasoning of the court which is the most important for lawyers. The court will only rely on a single reason for its judgment, as to provide secondary reasons would suggest that it could have made a mistake with the first. The judgment is very short compared to the judgments of common law courts, as described above, often fitting on a single page.

▶ The judgments of the *Cour de cassation*

The *Cour de cassation* hands down two principal types of judgment: final judgments rejecting the appeal and judgments allowing the appeal. These will be considered in turn, on the assumption that there was a single ground for the appeal. The *motifs* of such a judgment will start with the phrase *Sur le moyen unique*. In practice, several grounds may be considered by the court in its judgment or a single ground may be sub-divided, with each being discussed separately under different subheadings, such as *Sur le premier moyen* or *Sur le deuxième moyen, pris en sa première branche*. In this case the layout is much the same as discussed below, since the judgment of the *Cour de cassation* essentially consists of successive decisions, placed next to each other and recapitulated finally in one single verdict. A judgment by the *Cour de cassation* is especially short, rarely longer than two or three paragraphs. As the *Cour de cassation* only rules on the law and not the facts, its judgments focus on the legal issues and include just a very short explanation of the facts necessary to understand the issues at hand.

Judgment rejecting the appeal

The first *attendu* relates the facts of the litigation and repeats the view taken by the court of appeal (or the relevant court against whose decision the appeal is being made). The second *attendu* states all the legal arguments that have been presented by the appellant in support of his or her appeal, in compliance with article 455 of the New Code of Civil Procedure of 1975 (the defendant's arguments are not normally given). This includes the words *alors que*, in phrases such as *Attendu qu'il est fait grief à l'arrêt attaqué d'avoir ainsi statué alors que* ... (Whereas the views of the Court of Appeal are attacked on the grounds that ...). This specific terminology serves as a useful reminder not to confuse what is stated here with the actual reasoning of the court. This *attendu* simply reproduces or summarises the words of, or the grounds, contained in the application. When the grounds are badly written, the drafter of the judgment of the *Cour de cassation* may copy out the exact words, but place them in quotation marks, to make it clear that they do not approve of the poor drafting.

In relation to the second *attendu*, there are a range of grounds on which an appeal can be brought before the *Cour de cassation*, all of which concern appeals on points of law. These include:

- breach of the law (this is the ground most frequently relied upon, and includes the argument that the judgment lacks legal basis (*manque de base légale*) because the law has been misinterpreted or misapplied; and disciplinary grounds which attack, not the verdict, but the way the decision has been written or given, with the latter being a procedural irregularity. The most important disciplinary ground is the failure to give reasons in breach of article 455 of the New Code of Civil Procedure of 1975);
- a conflict between judgments (where the execution of one judgment would conflict with another, thus the conflict is between the verdicts, rather than their legal reasoning);
- a denial of justice (if a court has failed to adjudicate a matter on purpose);
- an exceeding of a court's powers;
- an absence of jurisdiction;
- a lack of legal foundation (for example, where a document that was relied upon has subsequently been found to be a fraud, or where a ministerial decree has been declared void).

The third *attendu* always starts with the phrase *mais attendu que* and contains the rejection of these arguments. This 'but' constitutes the start of the actual reasoning of the *Cour de cassation* and is a very important part of the judgment. If the case is particularly straightforward, these paragraphs will be contracted into one, while keeping the three *attendu que*. The verdict then follows.

Judgment allowing the appeal

These are generally shorter than judgments rejecting the appeal, but tend in law to be of more importance as they positively affirm a legal position.

The judgment starts by referring to the legal text or texts on which the verdict is based, in accordance with article 1020 of the New Code of Civil Procedure of 1975. The texts referred to may be, for example, legislation, regulations or administrative decisions and are usually those on which the appeal was based. Where reference is made to several texts, these will be listed in descending order according to the authority attached to them in the hierarchy of sources; thus an article of the Civil Code will be cited before a regulation. Some texts are extremely broad and frequently relied upon (such as article 1110 of the Civil Code making the contract voidable for mistake, or article 1382 of the Civil Code imposing a general rule of tortious liability), though where there is a more specific text this will generally be preferred. Where there is no text that can be relied upon, the court will refer instead to a general principle of law or a rule of customary law (this is more frequent for the administrative courts where the law has not been codified). This first section of the judgment is known as the *visa* and each paragraph within it starts with the word *Vu*. There then follow two to four *attendus,* with the arguments given by the lower court. Thereafter, in a final *attendu*, the *Cour de cassation* provides an explanation of what the lower court did wrong. Finally, the court indicates that the appeal was successful.

A classic verdict allowing the appeal is:

Par ces motifs:
Casse et annule, dans toutes ses dispositions, l'arrêt rendu le ... entre les parties, par la cour d'appel de ..., remet en conséquence la cause et les parties dans l'état où elles se trouvaient avant le dit arrêt et, pour être fait droit, les renvoie devant la cour d'appel de ...
(Accordingly:
The appeal against the decision of the court of appeal of ... dated ... is granted, the parties and their case are returned to the state in which they were before the decision was made and in order for justice to be achieved the matter is referred back to the court of appeal of ...)

Of particular interest are the leading judgments which either lay down the position of the *Cour de cassation* on a legal issue for the first time, or reverse a previous stance taken by the court. Such cases are frequently heard by a hearing of the full court (*Assemblée plénière*) or by the joint bench (*Chambre mixte*), and tend to be judgments allowing the appeal. They often include immediately after the *visa* a general statement of the legal principle that has been applied and which is the reason why the judgment is of interest to a lawyer. This is known as the *chapeau*, meaning literally 'the hat'. It will start with the phrase *attendu que* and may consist either of quoting word for word the relevant article relied upon, or give the court's interpretation of this article. For example:

Vu l'art. 1382 c.civ;
Attendu que ce texte ordonnant que l'auteur de tout fait ayant causé
un dommage à autrui sera tenu de le réparer, n'exige pas, en cas de
décès, l'existence d'un lien de droit entre le défunt et le demandeur en
indemnisation; ...
(Given article 1382 of the Civil Code,
Whereas the text ordering that all human acts which cause damage
to another, obliges the person by whose fault the damage occurred
to make amends, it does not, where death ensues, require the
existence of a close link between the plaintiff and the deceased; ...)

▶ Modern drafting of judgments

The modern style of drafting judgments is less formal, with most notably
the first part of the judgment recounting the facts, the procedure and
the claims of the parties, as a narrative, so breaking the tradition that
the whole judgment should be a single sentence. The use of the term
attendu que refers to the legal reasoning of the court itself. Such judgments may also be divided to deal with each element of the claim
separately. The result is that these decisions are generally clearer than
they were in the past, though they may still not be comprehensible to
many litigants.

PART II: CITATION OF JUDGMENTS

In common law countries, the judgments take the names of the parties
to the litigation; whilst in France, one indicates the name of the court
which gave the decision, followed by the name of its town and the date
that the judgment was handed down. The name of the court is usually
abbreviated (see Table 8.1).

For example:

TGI, 27 July 2004

A judgment of the *tribunal de grande instance* of Bordeaux of 27 July
2004.

Court of appeal judgments are named after the town in which the court
sits and the relevant date. For example:

Lyon, 18 janv. 1999

A decision of the court of appeal in Lyon of 18 January 1999.

If it is a decision of the *Cour de cassation*, the name of the division which
gave the decision is added. For example:

Table 8.1 Abbreviations of court names

Court	Abbreviation
Conseil constitutionnel	C.C. / Cons. const.
Conseil d'Etat	C.E.
Conseil d'Etat, assemblée du contentieux	C.E. Ass. / CE, ass.
Conseil d'Etat, section du contentieux	C.E. Sect. / CE, sect.
Cour administrative d'appel	C.A.A.
Cour d'appel	C.A.
Cour de cassation	Cass.
Cour de cassation, Assemblée plénière	Cass., ass. plén. / Ass. plén.
Cour de cassation, chambre civile	Cass., civ. / Civ.
Cour de cassation, première chambre civile	Cass., 1ère civ. / Civ. 1ère
Cour de cassation, chambre criminelle	Cass., crim. / Crim.
Cour de cassation, chambre mixte	Cass., ch. mixte. / Ch. Mixte
Cour de cassation, chambre sociale	Cass., soc. / Soc.
Tribunal administratif	T.A. / Trib. admin.
Tribunal de commerce	T. com. / Trib. com.
Tribunal de grande instance	T.G.I. / Trib. grande inst.
Tribunal de police	T. pol. / Trib. pol.
Tribunal des conflits	T.C. / T. confl. / Trib. confl.
Tribunal d'instance	T.I. / Trib. Inst.

Cass, 2e civ. 20 sept. 1999 or Civ. 2ème, 20 sept. 1999

A decision of the second civil division of the *Cour de cassation* of 20 September 1999.

Cass, comm. 13 avr. 1998 or Comm., 13 avr. 1998

A decision of the commercial division of the *Cour de cassation* of 13 April 1998.

The names of the decisions of the administrative courts include the name of the plaintiff. For example:

C.E, 20 oct. 1989, *Nicolo*

A decision of the *Conseil d'Etat* of 20 October 1989. The plaintiff was called Nicolo.

Table 8.2 Abbreviations of legal journals

Legal journal	Abbreviation
Gazette du Palais	*Gaz. Pal.*
Semaine juridique: also *called Juris-Classeur périodique*	*JCP*
Recueil Dalloz	*D.*
Revue française de droit administratif	*RFDA*
Revue française de droit constitutionnel	*RFD const.*
Revue trimestrielle de droit civil	*RTD civ.*

C.E., Ass 30 oct. 1998, *Sarran*

A decision by the full sitting of the *Conseil d'Etat* of 30 October 1998. The plaintiff was called Sarran.

Well-known administrative decisions are often cited by referring only to the name of the plaintiff. For example:

arrêt Nicolo

arrêt Sarran.

The reference to the journal or journals where the decision is reported (Table 8.2) follows the case name and at the end the page number is indicated. For example:

Ass. plén., 17 nov. 2000, D.2001, 332

TGI, 18 December 2003, D.2004, 2675.

▶ Example of a judgment of the *Cour de cassation*

This judgment arose from a civil dispute and the *Cour de cassation* dismissed the appeal on the law.

Cour de cassation, Ass. plén. 5 mai 1984

LA COUR; – Sur le moyen unique: – *Attendu*[1], selon *l'arrêt attaqué*[2] (Agen, 12 mai 1980), que[1] le 30 juin 1975, l'enfant Eric Gabillet, alors âgé de 3 ans, en tombant d'une balançoire improvisée constituée par une planche qui se rompit, éborgna son camarade Philippe Noye avec un bâton qu'il tenait à la main; que[3] M. Lucien Noye, agissant en qualité d'administrateur légal des biens de son fils, assigna ses parents, les époux Gabillet, en tant qu'exerçant leur droit de garde, en responsabilité de l'accident ainsi survenu; – *Attendu que*[4] les époux Gabillet font grief à l'arrêt d'avoir déclaré Eric Gabillet responsable sur le fondement de l'art. 1384. al. 1er, c.civ., *alors*[5], selon le *moyen*[6], que[5] l'imputation d'une responsabilité présumée implique la faculté de discernement; que la cour d'appel a donc violé par fausse application l'alinéa. 1er de l'art. 1384 c.civ.;

} Facts

} Legal arguments

} The grounds for the court's decision (*les motifs*)

Mais attendu que[7]' en retenant que le jeune Eric avait l'usage, la direction et le contrôle du bâton, la cour d'appel, qui n'avait pas, malgré le très jeune âge de ce mineur, à rechercher si celui-ci avait un discernement, a *légalement justifié*[8] sa décision;

} Upholding of the court of appeal's decision

Par ces motifs[9], rejette[10].

} The verdict (*le dispositif*)

1 The first *attendu que*. These two words are often separated in the sentence.
2 It is the decision of the court of appeal which the plaintiff is seeking to quash.
3 A synonym for *attendu que*.
4 The second *attendu que*.
5 The term *alors que* always introduces the arguments of the plaintiff when these have been rejected.
6 The argument of the plaintiff.
7 The third *attendu* of a decision of the *Cour de cassation* rejecting the appeal starts with this phrase *mais attendu que* and contains the rejection of the plaintiff's claim.
8 A formula often used in a judgment rejecting the appeal.
9 A traditional formula introducing the verdict.
10 Verdict to reject.

Translation of example
WHEREAS according to the judgment made at Agen on 12 MAY 1990, which is the subject of this appeal, on 30 June 1975, the child Eric Gabillet, then aged 3, blinded his friend Philippe Noye in one eye with a stick held by him, in the course of a fall from an improvised swing made from a plank of wood; and WHEREAS Mr Lucien Noye, acting as legal administrator of his son's property, sued Eric Gabillet's parents, Mr and Mrs Gabillet, on the ground that as his legal guardians, they were responsible for the accident caused by their son; and WHEREAS Mr and Mrs Gabillet attacked the decision that Eric was responsible for damage on the basis of article 1384, on the ground that Eric could not be held responsible unless he had the ability to reason and that accordingly article 1384 of the Civil Code was not correctly applied by the court of appeal.

But WHEREAS having established that young Eric had the use, direction and control of the stick, the court of appeal was not required to establish that this very young child had the ability to reason, and has fully justified its judgment;

Accordingly the appeal is dismissed.

BIBLIOGRAPHY FOR CHAPTER 8

Ancel, P. (1994), *Travaux dirigés d'introduction au droit et droit civil*, Paris: Litec
Bocquillon, J-F. and Mariage, M. (2001), *Droit*, Paris: Dunod
Cachard, O. (2004), 'Aux grands arrêts, les juristes reconnaissants ...', D. 2004, 429
Cohendet, M-A. (1994), *Méthodes de travail, droit public*, Paris: Montchrestien
Defrénois-Souleau, I. (2004), *Je veux réussir mon droit. Méthodes de travail et clés du succès*, Paris: Colin

Elliott, C, Geirnaert, C. and Houssais, F. (1998), *French Legal System and Legal Language*, London: Longman

Frison-Roche, M.-A. (1994), *Introduction générale au droit*, Paris: Dalloz

Goubeau, Gilles and Bihr, Philippe (1993), *Les epreuves écrites du droit civil*, Paris: LGDJ, 1993

Lobry, C. (1995), *Droit: BTS. Tome 1*. Paris: Techniplus

Mendegris, R. and Vermelle, G. (2004), *Le commentaire d'arrêt en droit privé*, Paris: Dalloz

Mimin, P. (1927), *Le style des jugements*, Paris: Juris-classeurs – Godde

Pansier, F.-J. (2005), *Méthodologie du droit*, Paris: LexisNexis / Litec

Steiner, J. (2002), *French Legal Method*, Oxford: OUP

Terré, F., Lequette, Y. and Capitant, H. (2000), *Les grands arrêts de la jurisprudence Civile, Tome 2*, Paris: Dalloz

Tricot, D. (2004), 'L'élaboration d'un arrêt de la Cour de cassation', Doctrine, JCP 2004, 225

Web resources

Website: www.conseil-etat.fr: The *Conseil d'Etat*

Website: www.courdecassation.fr: The *Cour de cassation*. Includes some text in English

Website: www.ucl.ac.uk/laws/global_law: Institute of Global Law, contains French cases and Statutes translated into English

Civil procedure

INTRODUCTION

This chapter looks in detail at the rules of procedure applied in civil courts of first instance. We will consider how proceedings are commenced (Part I), the pre-trial procedures (Part II), the hearing and the judgment (Part III). For each of these stages, the New Civil Procedure Code of 1975 (NCPC) sets out both procedures and principles common to all civil courts (Book 1 articles 1 to 749) and procedures specific to each court (Book 2 articles 750 to 1037). Unless stated otherwise, any articles referred to in this chapter are from this Code. The NCPC contains rules which primarily refer to the *tribunal de grande instance* (TGI), the first instance court of general jurisdiction, rather than the specialist courts. We will also concentrate chiefly on the rules of the TGI, as these serve as a model for those of the specialist courts such as the *tribunal d'instance* (TI), the commercial court and employment tribunals, and merely note points of procedure specific to the specialist tribunals, when relevant. Part IV below contains a brief discussion of the procedure before the courts of appeal and the *Cour de cassation*.

PART I: COMMENCING PROCEEDINGS

▶ Historical background

In 1806, during the period of *le droit intermédiaire* (intermediate law) mentioned in Chapter 1, a code of procedure was enacted which, subject to amendments, was in force for nearly 170 years. It placed great emphasis on compliance with formalities, to the extent that formal irregularities could result in annulment of the action, since they could not be corrected.

This was increasingly seen as unsuitable to the more complex and flexible world of the late twentieth century. In 1969, a commission, presided over by the then Minister of Justice, Jean Foyer, prepared a major reform, increasing flexibility, promoting conciliation and emphasising the principle of giving due hearing to the parties. It took six years to bear fruit with the passing of the first two Books of the New Code of Civil Procedure of 1975.

The first Book lays down general rules which apply to all courts and the second Book provides special rules which apply to certain courts. We will limit our study of civil procedure to these two Books of the Code. Two additional Books were added in 1981: the third dealing with particular subjects such as persons, goods and matrimonial property, and the fourth relating to arbitration. A fifth, relating to enforcement, is currently being drafted. The 1806 Code is still in force in relation to matters not covered by the NCPC, in particular with regard to enforcement of judgments.

While the NCPC did implement a thorough revision of procedure on the lines mentioned above, the increase in litigation since the early years has been so great that further reform was considered necessary including reforms to speed up procedure, cut down on the number of appeals and encourage parties to settle cases. A decree of 28 December 1998 implemented some of the measures required. Most of the provisions are on points of detail beyond the scope of this book, but we will mention the more important ones as appropriate.

▶ The right to bring and defend an action: a fundamental principle

The right to bring and defend an action is a fundamental principle of the French Constitution. The principle is also one of the general principles of law enforced within the European Union and enshrined in a number of treaties and conventions to which the French government is a signatory, including the European Convention on Human Rights.

Most civil actions are brought by private claimants, either individuals or companies. The first article of the NCPC spells this out. Judges can take the initiative to bring a case, but this is rare. Article 30 also states that:

- claimants have the right to be heard on the merits of their claims;
- defendants have the right to dispute the validity of claims.

The judge will pronounce authoritatively on the merits of an application, and declare whether or not it is well founded.

Most rights are enforceable in case of breach. For instance, under a simple contract for the sale of goods, there is a right to receive payment for goods in exchange for delivering goods of merchantable quality. Agreements not to use a right to sue in a particular instance will only be valid if limited to specified matters, and a general declaration that a person will not avail themselves of the right to go to court will have no legal force.

▶ Abuse of right

Not all claimants are successful, but they have exercised a right and cannot be penalised for doing so. The courts may still order parties to pay costs, but no fine can be imposed. The only exception to this general principle is that parties may be penalised if they are deemed to have abused their right. Article 32-1 (and article 559 in relation to appeals) provides for payment of a fine if an action is brought in a dilatory or abusive manner. Any party affected by such conduct may also bring a claim for damages. Traditionally, courts would only award damages for the wrongful conduct of a case if the defendant had shown malice or bad faith or a serious fault. However, the *Cour de cassation* has broadened the scope of this right to include, for example, the mere pursuit of a claim through all available means beyond what was reasonable given the matter of the dispute.

Thus, in *Durand v Commune de Bizonet* (*Cour de cassation*, 5 July 1965), M. Durand had brought an action claiming that he owned land over which a public highway had been built. This claim was rejected by the TGI, and M. Durand brought an appeal on certain points of law and procedure to the *Cour de cassation*, in particular complaining that the TGI had not fully investigated the claim. The *Cour de cassation* did not accept any of the points made and dismissed the appeal. M. Durand had been pursuing the matter for 27 years and, as well as eventually losing his claim, had to pay damages to the commune for pursuing the claim for so long.

▶ Conditions for commencing the action

If a party has the right to bring an action and chooses to do so, they will begin by issuing a statement of claim. The NCPC spells out clearly that 'procedure is a servant of rights' and that an action can only be commenced to defend rights. English civil procedure is seen as an independent body of rules administered by the courts, which have a right to dismiss obviously frivolous, groundless, or vexatious claims, under the Supreme Court Act 1981. While under English law parties can commence civil cases by following the procedural rules, subject to the court's right to stay or dismiss the case, in French law, the right to bring an action in a civil case depends on rules of *locus standi* which depend largely on the legitimacy of the claim. Article 31 provides that 'Anybody with a legitimate interest in the success or failure of a claim may commence an action'. It adds that sometimes the law lays down rules, reserving the authority to bring or defend a claim to certain people. The law interprets these limitations as set out below.

Legitimate interest

The first and most important hurdle faced by claimants is the need to satisfy the court that they have a legitimate interest. For instance, only a married couple can bring an action for divorce, it does not concern their relatives or any other parties who might personally consider they have an interest in the matter. Not all cases are as straightforward, but even in complex and contentious matters, it is the lower courts which determine whether the parties have a legitimate interest in the case. Their decision on the issue is not subject to appeal, though the *Cour de cassation* can be seized if it can be argued that the original court did not interpret the law correctly when making its decision. For example, the extent, if any, to which an unmarried partner had any claim against someone who had caused the death of their partner had been the subject of many conflicting decisions since the 1870s. Most decisions held that relationships other than marriage were too volatile to confer any financial interest to the unmarried partner. The relationship could be broken at will, and therefore a remaining partner did not have a legitimate interest enabling them to bring a case for compensation. The *Cour de cassation* settled the matter in *Gaudras v Dangereux* (27 February 1970) when it decided that such persons had a legitimate interest, if the relationship had been stable. They were therefore entitled to financial compensation from the person responsible for the car accident which caused the death of their partner.

Date of interest

The interest must exist at the date of the court case. Cases may be brought to defend existing rights, but not to ascertain the existence of rights. For instance, a case brought with a view to forcing a beneficiary to declare whether or not he or she wished to accept a bequest would not be legitimate. This rule is subject to some statutory exceptions such as article 1040 which implicitly allows actions to be brought with a view to determining whether someone has French nationality.

Personal interest

The claimant must have a personal interest in the outcome of a case. Trade unions and professional associations can bring proceedings to defend their collective interests (for example, to fair pay), but not the interests of individual members (for example, in connection with dismissal). Even charities and societies formed to promote various worthy aims cannot bring cases designed to promote these aims, since they are deemed to reflect a general interest and not a personal interest of the parties.

Qualification to bring the action

Finally, claimants are required to prove that they are qualified to bring the action. It will usually be sufficient to prove that the claimant has a legitimate, direct and personal interest in the matter. In family law, in particular, certain classes of people are designated as having exclusive rights to bring cases in certain matters; for example, children have a right to bring an action to declare who their father is, and that right is not available to other interested relatives.

▶ Issuing the claim form

Having drafted the statement of claim, the claimant must then arrange for the claim form to be issued by a court official known as a *huissier*, who has a monopoly on serving claim forms (article 55). Article 56 states that the claim form must contain:

- the name of the court or tribunal;
- a statement of claim, including relevant facts and law;
- a statement that if the defendant does not respond, judgment will be made solely on the basis of the information provided by the claimant;
- a list of documents relevant to the action.

For cases brought before the TGI, article 752 provides that in addition the claimant must appoint a lawyer, and the claim form must mention the time limit for the making of the appointment.

▶ Service of the claim form

The claim form must be served either by post, in person or through the defendant's lawyer (articles 665 to 674). If service is made by post, it is deemed to have been received by the defendant on the date on which the receipt is signed. For the purpose of complying with any relevant time limits, it is deemed to have been made on the date of posting (as evidenced by the postmark). In some cases it must be made in person (article 654) by the *huissier*.

▶ Substituted service

When the claimant fails to serve a claim successfully, the NCPC provides for substituted service, usually at the defendant's last known address. The claimant does not need to make an application to court (as would be necessary in England), since the procedures are simply set out in the NCPC and are not prescribed by a court official in the light of the particular case. This can lead to non-residents, particularly foreigners, being served with claim forms without their knowledge, as there is no control of the reliability of the claimant's information as to the defendant's last known address, or the circumstances of the case.

▶ Time limit

In most cases the defendant must respond within two weeks (article 755), but where the claim form has not been served personally the defendant may have up to two months (article 643). In practice, the court may be flexible about a late response by the defendant and may, in certain circumstances, accept a response that is only submitted at the court hearing.

▶ Joint petition

Alternatively, parties may make a joint petition signed by both parties setting out their respective positions (articles 793 to 796). This procedure is clearly designed to save money and is suitable where there are only a few points at issue and the parties are agreed on most matters. It is particularly suitable where the parties are aiming for conciliation (articles 12 and 58) or where the matters are straightforward and the parties choose to have them decided by a single judge (article 794).

▶ Alternative methods of dispute resolution

In recent years increased emphasis has been placed on trying to resolve disputes through the use of alternative methods of dispute resolution. The aim is to improve the efficiency of the civil justice system to cope with the considerable increase in litigation over the past 30 years (around 75%). M. Coulon, a senior judge, prepared an influential report on the subject in the 1990s. He recommended that the number of cases should be reduced by encouraging the settlement of cases. He also aimed to make procedures for cases that reach the courts more efficient, to avoid continuing and unacceptable delays. The main aim of the subsequent reforms that have been introduced is to try to create a settlement culture similar to that which exists in England and Wales, where far more claims are settled before all available appeals have been exhausted.

Conciliation will be attempted if the parties have expressed a desire to try to settle the case in this way (art. 830) or, where appropriate, by obliging the parties to attempt conciliation (art. 829). The consent of the parties to enter mediation is usually required, though the Decree of 23 June 2003 provides that the judge can order the parties to try mediation. This effort at settlement can take place either in front of the judge or a professional mediator. The parties are usually given one month to try to reach a settlement and the mediator will write to let the judge know the outcome of these efforts. Where a settlement is reached this will be written down in an agreement signed by the parties.

The specialist courts

So far we have studied the procedure before the TGI. Being the first instance court of general jurisdiction, this procedure serves as a model. A study of the procedure before the specialist courts is beyond the scope of this book, but a few general comments need to be made. Before these courts a mainly oral, rather than a written, procedure is usually followed. The parties can, if they choose, represent themselves or appoint designated lay persons to do so. More emphasis is placed on conciliation.

Tribunal d'instance (articles 827 to 847)

Preliminary attempts at conciliation are not compulsory, but are encouraged. The parties can commence actions in a variety of ways, including simply asking for the court to effect conciliation. However, the most usual way to state a claim at the TI is to serve a statement of claim which asks for conciliation and, if this fails, then to commence formal proceedings (articles 836 and 837). In an attempt to encourage greater use of the conciliation process, since March 1999, the judge, with the agreement of the parties, may appoint an informal negotiator with a view to enabling the parties to settle the dispute as quickly and simply as possible.

Neighbourhood courts (articles 827 to 847)

These courts were established in 2002 and are discussed at p. 89. As regards the procedures followed in these courts, they are essentially identical to those followed in the *tribunal d'instance*. Cases are heard by a single judge and as far as possible the procedures before the court are kept simple and quick.

Commercial courts (articles 853 to 878)

The main difference from the procedure before the TGI is that the parties can represent themselves and do not need to appoint a lawyer.

Employment tribunals (Employment Code, articles 516 to 518)

The procedure is very informal. The claimant can make a written demand or the parties may simply appear in person. Conciliation is compulsory (articles 516-13 to 516-20).

• •

PART II: PRE-TRIAL PROCEDURE

The preparatory phase of proceedings is designed to enable the parties to present their respective cases in a complete and orderly fashion, to allow the judges to reach their judgment in full knowledge of all relevant facts and law. The NCPC makes the parties clearly responsible for presenting issues of fact and law in the pleadings. Despite this, except in very straightforward cases, the French judiciary takes a more pro-active management role than English judges have traditionally done. Pre-trial procedure also includes carrying out a number of tasks, which, in England, would take place at the court hearing itself, such as interviewing witnesses and assessing experts' reports.

▌ Filing the statement of claim

To file a statement of claim, the claimant deposits a copy with the court office. This must be done within four months of the date of it being served on the defendant, otherwise service is invalid and the action annulled (article 757). The court office then lists the action, and allocates it a number. It enters the names of the parties and the cause of action and other details in its register (article 726). The President of the relevant court then sets the date for the final pre-trial hearing at which the matter is discussed with the parties' lawyers (article 759).

▌ Exchange of pleadings

The next step is that the parties proceed to exchange pleadings, which contain a statement of each party's claims and the arguments in support. They also arrange on their own initiative for production to the other party of all documents relevant to their case, including written evidence, such as letters and agreements, and, if relevant, written statements made by witnesses (article 132). The aim of this stage is to ensure that each party has disclosed the facts they intend to rely on, how they are going to prove them, and the relevant points of law (article 15). While the English legal system contains many rules about the form of proceedings and the manner of exchange of pleadings, French parties are given a relatively free rein on how they proceed to exchange pleadings provided they achieve the aim set out in article 15. Parties must be given time to consider and reply to pleadings but they can go on exchanging further pleadings until they are satisfied that all points have been raised, and that they comply with article 15. Pleadings are exchanged between lawyers and a copy filed at the court (articles 815 and 816). At the hearing the judge will decide whether the case is straightforward enough for it to be referred to trial, or whether further investigations are needed, to be conducted under judicial supervision.

▶ Defences

The three main types of defence available to the defendant are set out here.

Action inadmissible

The defendant may submit that the case should be struck out on the ground that the claimant had no right to bring the action. This is known as a *fin de non-recevoir* and is found in articles 122 to 126. This would be the case, for example, where the claimant lacks a legitimate interest (discussed in Part I above) or where the limitation period has expired.

Based on the merits of the case

In most cases, the defendant will try to deny the validity of the claimant's claim. Articles 71 and 72 of the NCPC simply refer to any defence which will defeat the claimant's claim after examination of the relevant law, without any attempt at classification of the types of defence available. For instance, in a simple case for breach of a contract for the sale of a car for €6,000, this could take the form of a plain denial: the defendant might simply deny the existence of a contract. It could also take the form of what is known, in English law, as a 'confession and avoidance'. For example, the defendant purchaser could admit that he had signed a contract, but avoid the claim for payment by saying he only signed the contract because the seller had falsified the mileage on the clock.

Based on a procedural irregularity

The NCPC contains detailed provisions for dismissing claims on the ground of procedural irregularity. Applications to dismiss claims on these grounds must be made separately, before any applications as to the substance of the claim are made (article 74). This plea includes where the court seized of the matter is not the appropriate court or where the matter is the subject of litigation in another court. Actions may also be struck out where there has been a failure to serve the statement of claim in accordance with the rules. The claimant would then need to commence a new action ensuring that the new pleadings are free of irregularity. In order to avoid this expense and inconvenience, the NCPC allows parties, in certain circumstances, to rectify irregularities, for instance where this would cause no injustice to the other party (articles 115 and 121).

▶ Claims made during the course of the action

Counterclaim

The defendant may make a counterclaim against the claimant (article 64). The counterclaim must relate to the claimant's claim (article 70) so that they can be heard together and judgment pronounced on both at the same time. For instance, where a wife is applying for a divorce, alleging faults committed by her husband, the latter could counterclaim by applying to divorce his wife on the ground of faults committed by her. As well as provisions for counterclaims, article 70 contains special rules regarding claims for a set-off (*demande en compensation*) which may be pleaded as to the whole, or part, of the action. For instance, in an action for payment for goods a claim for set-off may be made, due to the defective state of the goods.

Such claims do not need to be related to the original action, though the judge reserves the right to try the claim separately if it might cause undue delay to the original action.

Further claims

The claimant may make a further claim related to the original one during the course of exchange of pleadings (articles 65 and 70).

Third party notice

One of the parties, usually the defendant, may wish to join a third party to the action on the basis that they are entitled to relief from the third party because of an action connected to the original one. For instance, a tenant who is being sued in connection with a failure to comply with an obligation to decorate a flat may wish to join a sub-tenant who has accepted responsibility to the tenant for the obligation to decorate the flat. The third party then becomes a defendant in relation to the original defendant, and judgment on both cases is given together. It is also possible for third parties to apply voluntarily to be joined to the original action (article 66).

The preliminary hearing

The preliminary hearing known as an *appel des causes* takes place on the day appointed when the statement of claim was issued. A judge considers the progress made in preparing for the hearing, including the exchange of pleadings and the disclosure of documents. The judge then decides whether preparation has reached a stage where the matter can proceed to a court hearing, or whether additional work needs to be done. In practice, judges usually find that more preparation is needed and that it should be carried out under the close supervision of a judge.

Short procedure

In straightforward matters, or where the parties are exceptionally well prepared, the judge will make a closing order in respect of the preparation phase of the case, and will send the case to the court, to be heard on a date fixed by the President of the court (article 760).

Where judges decide that cases are not quite ready, but only minor items are required, which they trust the parties to comply with, they will fix a new date for the pre-trial hearing to consider the few missing items and will then send the case for trial (article 761).

Long procedure

Most cases will not be ready to proceed to the hearing on the date of the *appel des causes*, and will be referred to a judge of the relevant division who will take an active role in preparing the case. The judge is known as the *juge de la mise en état* and is given a number of powers to facilitate the completion of the preparation for trial, which the parties have not managed to complete on their own initiative. We will refer to this judge as the preparatory judge.

The preparatory judge will try to ensure that the work is done by the parties within a reasonable period of time, and will aim to keep his or her intervention to a minimum. The judge will endeavour to agree a list of items to be done before the hearing, such as pleadings to be answered, documents to be provided, witnesses to be examined, and will also arrange for the parties to agree a timetable for each step. If agreement cannot be reached, the judge has powers to invite the parties to complete the pleadings, or to produce documents or to take other necessary steps. If they fail to meet these requirements, the judge has the power to order them to do so (articles 763 to 765). The preparatory judge can order a case to be stayed, if both parties are dilatory (article 781). If one party is ready and prevented from having the case heard, because of undue delay of the other party, the judge may send the case to trial on the basis of the pleadings and documents provided (article 780).

Since March 1999, the President of the division where the hearing is scheduled may decide at any time that the case is ready to be heard. If he or she so decides, or if the matter is urgent, he or she may transfer the case to the short procedure, described above, and if appropriate will fix a date for the hearing. Parties may also request that the President take this action (article 910).

Within the above framework, the powers of the judge are varied and extensive. It would be beyond the scope of this book to discuss these powers in detail, but a few examples are given here to illustrate the considerable scope for initiative given to the judge.

Disclosure of documents (articles 132 to 142)

The judge may be asked by one or more parties to enforce disclosure of documents by the other parties, and may also order delivery of documents not in the parties' possession, or not signed by the parties but which are necessary to the case. The general rule is that the parties are only required to produce documents which they intend to rely on (and which are therefore likely to be favourable to their claim). There is no general duty on the parties to disclose all documents relating to the case, whether or not they are likely to further their particular claims. The only way in which someone can be made to disclose a document is if the judge expressly orders it, because it has happened to come to the judge's knowledge or that of the other party. Unfavourable documents can otherwise be kept secret.

Witness evidence and expert evidence (articles 199 to 284)

Judges can obtain both oral and written evidence, if necessary, on their own initiative (article 199). The NCPC lays down detailed formal requirements for written witness statements (article 202). The judge's powers concerning oral evidence are very wide, and extend to requiring witnesses to give evidence, unless they have a legitimate excuse. The judge may also conduct oral hearings and may ask questions during the proceedings. This is very different from the English and Welsh procedure where witnesses are often examined at the trial by both parties' lawyers, with the judge playing only a minor role. The French judge has even greater powers in connection with expert evidence, as the normal practice is for a single neutral expert to be appointed by the court. Parties do not normally appoint their own experts (articles 232 to 284).

▶ Closing order

When the judge considers that all preparations including exchange of pleadings, disclosure of documents, examination of witnesses, and other steps, have been carried out satisfactorily, a closing order will be made and a date set for the hearing.

▶ Pre-trial procedure in specialist courts

Tribunal d'instance (articles 843 and 844)

If attempts at conciliation fail, the procedure followed is a simplified version of that in the TGI. The procedure is oral and there is no formal requirement for written pleadings.

Commercial courts (article 661)

If conciliation fails the procedure followed is very closely based on that in the TGI, though more formal than that in the TI. Cases are less likely to be judged immediately, and there are provisions for the investigation and preparation of the case by the parties, closely supervised by the judge.

Employment tribunals (Employment Code, articles R516-21 to R516-25)

This court has its own form of pre-trial procedure. There is much emphasis on conciliation, but should this fail, the parties may proceed to prepare for the case in accordance with the above provisions of the Employment Code.

· ·

PART III: THE HEARING

Civil procedure in France, as in England and Wales, is based on adversarial principles. The parties bring, prepare and present their case on their own initiative. The judge plays no active part, merely serving as arbiter. As we have seen, the preparatory stage is still, in the simplest and most straightforward cases, conducted largely on this basis. The judge simply checks the materials prepared by the parties and decides whether the matter is ready for trial. However, in more complex cases, the judge takes a more active role in preparation. The procedure accordingly incorporates many inquisitorial elements. The judge tries to ensure that the parties do as much of the preparation as possible themselves. But, if necessary, the judge will interfere, interview witnesses, conduct expert investigations and do whatever is required to complete the investigation. The hearing on the other hand is always held on an adversarial basis. The parties present the findings of the investigation, present the file containing these findings and put forward their case. The procedure is oral and carried out in public.

The principle of giving due hearing to the parties

The principle of giving due hearing to the parties is a fundamental principle of the French legal system and of most legal systems from the civil and common law traditions. It applies to the preparatory stage as well as to the hearing. Article 14 of the NCPC sets out the principle that no one may be judged unless their case has been heard or they have at least been asked to put their case. While it is appreciated that default judgments may occasionally be necessary, parties should, at least, have been served with notice of proceedings, so that it can be said that they have been asked to put their case. Default judgments will be dealt with later. For other judgments, article 15, requires the parties to have put their case fully at the preparatory stage, so that each has an opportunity to answer all the points made. This is achieved by the lawyers for the claimant and the defendant exchanging pleadings. The rules of procedure also contain provisions as to time limits to ensure that parties have a reasonable time in preparing their case. No one should, in principle, make points in the hearing which have not been made at the preparatory stage, but the procedure is adversarial in the sense that all parties are given equal opportunity to present their case. The judge must also observe the principle of the parties' right to a hearing at all times and must, when making any decision, ensure that it is made on the basis of points which have been fully debated (article 16).

Right to a public hearing

The right to a public hearing is a basic principle of French law. This was confirmed in a case before the *Conseil d'Etat* of 4 October 1974. The principle is also enshrined in international conventions, such as article 5 of the UN Universal Declaration of Human Rights and article 6 of the European Convention on Human Rights. Publicity is seen as essential, so that justice can not only be done but can also be seen to be done. If the hearing is private, there is no means of checking independently what happened at the hearing, or of challenging the accuracy of reports of the case provided either by the court or by the parties concerned. The principle does not, however, apply to the preparatory stage of the proceedings, which it is felt is better dealt with in private.

Exceptions to the right to a public hearing

The NCPC affirms the principle of publicity at the hearing (articles 22 and 433), except where the relevant legislation provides otherwise. Many laws dealing with specialised subjects do indeed contain provisions for hearings relating to them to be heard in private, because of the sensitive nature of the subject matter. For instance, article 248 of the Civil Code provides for most divorce hearings to be private. The NCPC also contains provisions that some specified matters are to be heard in private, where the judge has no discretion in the matter. These include paternity cases in article 1149. However, article 435 extends the scope for exceptions to the rule considerably; such exceptions include the protection of privacy, public order and the wishes of the parties. The judge decides whether the exceptions apply and may also pronounce authoritatively on any question as to whether the court applied the exceptions correctly (article 437).

▶ Role of the press and other media

As in the United Kingdom, while members of the press have the right to be present at public hearings, they may not record proceedings by audio-visual means. The only exception, under an Act of 11 July 1985, is recording for historical purposes for deposit in archives which are not to be released to the public. This exception has not, so far, been used for civil trials. A number of statutes starting with the Act of 29 July 1881 also regulate the general rights of the press in relation to court reporting. The detail of these laws is beyond the scope of this book, but the subject is of practical importance as real publicity is largely carried out through the media, so effective publicity of court hearings is not ensured merely by a right to a public hearing.

▶ Oral debate

Civil cases are usually heard by the preparatory judge (whose role we discussed at p. 177 above) and two others, but can be heard by one judge with the consent of the parties. The hearing is designed to enable the parties to highlight the most important aspects of their case. In reality the written file recording the findings of the preparatory stage is the judges' main instrument in enabling them to reach their judgment. The file includes the statement of claim and defence, the witness statements, documentary evidence, experts' reports and all other relevant documentation. The lawyers will often conduct the hearing without calling the parties to give evidence, though they may do so if they consider it useful. Other witnesses will usually have been interviewed during the preparatory stage and will have provided witness statements which are part of the file. Exceptionally, witnesses can be called with the judges' agreement.

Sometimes, in particularly complex cases, the preparatory judge, or another judge, will have prepared a written report which fully analyses the relevant facts and law, referring to relevant previous cases and academic articles. If a report has been prepared, the hearing will start with the reading of the report. This is not a judgment. Very occasionally the report is published and in setting out the full facts of the case and issues of law and relevant previous cases dealing with the same points of law, it reads like the first part of a judgment of the English Court of Appeal. This information is not contained in the final judgment, which is very brief and concise (see p. 183). However, in most cases, the judges who attend the hearing will not have the benefit of such a report and must do the work for themselves by reading the files and relevant literature. The hearing starts with the claimant's lawyer presenting the case, including a summary of the salient facts and the most important propositions of law they are relying on to prove the case. The pleading is short and concise, and it is quite usual for the lawyer not to call their client. The defendant's lawyer will then answer the points made by the claimant's lawyer both in fact and law. The claimant's lawyer and the defendant's lawyer can, if the judge allows it, address the court to answer points made by the other. The parties can continue to conduct the proceedings in this fashion until the judge decides that the case has been fully debated. The judge is free to intervene to ask for clarification where necessary. If a member of the *ministère public* is present, they will normally make a statement at the end of the hearing giving their views on the issues involved and, in important cases, this is published along with the judgment. The statement must be heard by the judges, but it is not binding, and the judges are free to disagree with what it says.

▶ The judgment

Closing of oral submissions and deliberation by judges

The judge (or judges) will formally end the hearing and declare the closing of the oral submissions, when they consider that the issues have been fully debated. In very straightforward matters the judge may immediately give judgment, or do so after a short consultation among the judges in court. But in most civil cases the judges will take some time to deliberate and agree on the judgment, usually six weeks to two months. The date of the judgment will be announced at the end of the hearing and in most civil cases the final judgment will be given in public (articles 450 and 451). The judges will then meet in private to discuss issues and decide on their verdict, and the content of their deliberations is private (article 448).

Final judgment

The judgment pronounced will include a summary of the facts and a reasoned decision as to the law applicable to the facts in a concise form. The judgment is unanimous, and in a contested case is a final communiqué for public consumption. This may well be a compromise outcome of a heated debate among the bench, where differing views would have been strongly expressed before a consensus was reached. It is very different from a judgment of the High Court or Court of Appeal in England and Wales where all judges may state their own opinion. The judgment pronounced after the end of the hearing is known as a final judgment, to distinguish it from various interlocutory rulings during the earlier phases of the trial. These are also called judgments but are classified as interim or provisional judgments. There is normally no appeal against interim or provisional judgments, which include the many rulings made by the judge during the investigation phase. Most final judgments are subject to appeal. The final judgment is an authoritative statement of the rights of the parties in the matter and they cannot litigate again on the same matter (articles 480 to 482).

Enforceability of final judgments

When the judges have made their final judgment, the winning party must obtain a formal copy of the judgment (known as *une grosse*), with an endorsement certifying that it is enforceable. It must then be served on the party against whom the judgment has been made (articles 675 to 682). The judgment will, in most cases, only be enforceable if these formalities have been complied with. The other necessary condition is that no appeal has been made and the time limit for lodging it (usually one month) has expired.

The oldest and simplest method of enforcement for judgment debts is, as in England and Wales, the seizure of goods. This is carried out by a court official, the *huissier* (see Chapter 12). The modern law in this area was thoroughly revised by the Act of 31 July 1991 and a decree of 31 July 1992, both of which came into force on 1 January 1993. It is worth noting that the French system does not have an exact equivalent of injunctions, nor does it recognise the concept of contempt of court with the consequence of imprisonment. Apart from various forms of seizure of goods, the main method for enforcement, in particular of judgments ordering the defendant to do certain actions, is the imposition of a daily fine known as *une astreinte*, until the order has been complied with.

▶ Urgent interim or provisional measures

In certain cases, the claimant would be seriously prejudiced if the only way open was to bring an action according to the procedures described above, culminating with a judgment and enforcement. Accordingly, as in England and Wales, a number of methods are available to obtain urgent interim or provisional measures. These are usually undertaken by a single judge appointed by the President of the relevant court, known as *le juge des référés*. Such measures, for example an order for immediate payment of part of a debt, will only be granted where the situation is urgent, and where the claimant's case is beyond doubt. Any such orders are technically provisional (article 488) but since they will only be made where the claimant has a very strong case, they are not in practice very frequently overturned (articles 484 to 488).

▶ The specialist courts

Tribunal d'instance (articles 827 to 852)

The hearing is informal. There are no specific provisions in the NCPC.

Commercial courts (articles 853 to 878)

The hearing proceeds on the same lines as that in the TGI but in a less formal manner.

Employment tribunals (Employment Code, articles R 516-26 to 516-29)

The hearings are informal and oral. The lay bench then votes on the judgment. If a majority of the judges cannot agree, the bench simply retires and continues deliberation until a majority vote has been obtained (in much the same way as a lay jury reaches a verdict in the United Kingdom).

• •

PART IV: APPEALS TO THE COURT OF APPEAL AND REFERRALS TO THE *COUR DE CASSATION*

▶ **Appeals to the court of appeal**

As mentioned in Chapter 5, parties have a right of appeal to the relevant regional court of appeal, from the decisions of most courts of first instance, with limited exceptions for each court. The exceptions mostly relate to cases where small amounts of money are involved which are heard before the neighbourhood courts. As in first instance claims, parties may only bring an appeal if they have an interest in the case (article 546). Usually this right can solely be exercised by parties to the original judgment who are unhappy with the outcome. On rare occasions, third parties may be allowed to join in an appeal (article 544) or may even be required to do so (article 545). A person who guaranteed an agreement might, for instance, be joined to the appeal under these provisions even though they were not a party to the case at first instance.

Conditions for making an appeal

The conditions for making an appeal are simple. The appeal must be made within the time limit prescribed, usually one month (article 538). As for first instance actions, aggrieved parties' rights to bring an appeal are only really limited if they are deemed to be abusing the right of appeal (article 559, discussed at p. 169).

Scope of appeal

The courts of appeal proceed by way of retrial and can re-examine witnesses and generally proceed as if the case were being started afresh. In French law it is considered a matter of public policy that there should be a right of appeal to a court which hears all issues afresh. It is, however, usual for parties to limit the appeal to specific points, in which case the remit of the court of appeal is limited to those matters, and the original court's decision remains binding on the other issues (articles 561 and 562). Even where the appeal is limited to points raised, the French courts have a wider discretion than the courts in the United Kingdom with regard to judging new facts, and can examine evidence not previously provided. These new elements must, however, relate to the matters which were the subject of the original case (articles 563 to 566). The judgment of the court of first instance cannot be executed until the appeal has been heard, and it is also suspended during the rather brief period allowed for lodging appeals.

Procedure

As we will see in Chapter 12, much of the preparatory stage of the appeal is carried out by specialist lawyers known as *avoués* (article 899). This does not apply to cases which do not require parties to be represented by a lawyer, such as cases originally brought in the employment tribunal. *Avoués* work in collaboration with the parties' *avocats*, but the role of the *avocat* is largely limited to the hearing itself. The *avoués* are involved from the start of the proceedings, and must sign the initial notice of appeal lodged with the court's secretariat (articles 901 and 902). The appeal is lodged by the appellant and names the parties and the points of the appeal, if relevant. If none are mentioned, it is assumed the appellant requires the whole case to be tried afresh by the appeal court. The preparatory procedure is then carried out by the judge and the *avoués*. This is similar to that in the TGI, and the judge may, in straightforward cases, proceed directly to the hearing. In most cases there will be a *conseiller de la mise en état* who will supervise the preparation of the case, in a similar way to the preparatory judge at first instance (articles 910 to 915). The hearing itself is governed by the same general provisions as hearings in the lower courts (articles 430 to 435). The respondent may also make a cross appeal against the appellant. The procedure is the same as for the original appeal.

Setting aside default judgments

If a court made a default judgment, for example because the defendant did not receive the claim form and therefore failed to make an appearance, the NCPC allows an alternative procedure. This is a lodging of a formal objection to the judgment requiring that it be set aside, and the procedure is regulated by articles 571 to 578. The full conditions are set out in article 473. These are very restrictive, more so than an application to the High Court in England and Wales to set aside a claim form in similar circumstances. The aim is to try to stop parties using the procedure as a delaying technique. If the party applying complies with the provisions of article 473, the court will proceed to rehear the case and will give a new judgment. The normal time limit of one month (article 538) can be extended by application to the President of the relevant court and at their discretion, in the case of default judgments where the writ has not been served (article 540). The original judgment cannot be enforced if an application is made to set it aside.

▶ Referrals to the *Cour de cassation* and other actions

Lodging appeals or setting aside judgments are classified as ordinary procedures. In addition, a number of other methods are open to parties not satisfied with a judgment. Two methods that are only rarely used are the *recours en révision* and *tierce opposition*. The main method is referral to the *Cour de cassation*; see below and see Chapter 5 above. If successful these applications result in the original judgment being re-examined and revised, if appropriate. The original judgment can still be enforced, until such time as the new hearing has been completed.

Recours en révision (articles 593 to 603)

Where the time limit for lodging an appeal has expired, parties can still explore the possibility of applying to have the judgment set aside on a number of very limited specified grounds, such as fraud (article 595). The time limit for making the application is two months from the date of discovery of the fraud or other fact entitling the party to make the application (article 596).

Tierce opposition (articles 582 to 592)

Third parties affected by a judgment may apply for the case to be reheard. This procedure could be used, for instance, by the guarantor of a debt who was not joined in the original action. The time limit is 30 years (article 586).

▶ Referrals to the *Cour de cassation*

The *Cour de cassation* is not a court of appeal; its role is to 'judge the judgments' which are referred to it. These include judgments of the courts of appeal and judgments in respect of which there is no right of appeal (articles 605 and 606). The right to refer is limited to cases where it is argued that the relevant court has not applied the law correctly (article 604). As well as errors of law, this includes mistakes as to formalities, or as to the competence of a court to make the judgment. The one ground specifically mentioned is irreconcilable judgments. One of the main functions of the court is to ensure uniform application of the law. This is a very direct way in which the appeal courts' interpretation of the law can be challenged in particular cases, while preserving the right to judge new cases as they please, subject of course to new referrals to the *Cour de cassation*.

Procedure

The appellant files a statement setting out the grounds for the referral, with the court clerk's office (article 974), which arranges for it to be sent to the respondent. Parties must then appoint a lawyer with rights of audience in the *Cour de cassation* (article 973). The only exception, as with the duty to appoint lawyers at earlier stages in the procedure, is cases that started in a court which allows the parties to appear in person, such as the employment courts. The parties then exchange pleadings limited to points of law (articles 999 to 1015). Following an Act of 25 June 2001, after the exchange of pleadings, the case is initially examined by three judges who can decide that an application is inadmissible (for example, because it is trivial or because it has been issued out of time). If the case is admissible, it is referred for a full hearing of at least five judges.

The court appoints a *juge rapporteur* to report on the case at the hearing. When the preparatory stage is completed, the matter proceeds to a hearing. As the court only hears matters of law, it is quite common for the parties not to be represented at this stage. The court listens to the report of the *juge rapporteur* and the views of the representative of the *ministère public*, and then adjourns, returning at a later date to pronounce judgment (known as an *arrêt*).

Either the *Cour de cassation* agrees with the law as pronounced by the lower court, which ends the procedure, or if it disagrees with the law as expounded in the decision referred, the court may make an order for the matter to be retried at another court of the same level.

••••••••••••••••••••••••••••••

BIBLIOGRAPHY FOR CHAPTER 9

Couchez, G. (2004), *Procédure civile*, Paris: Armand Colin
Croze, H. (2004), *Le Procès civil*, Paris: Dalloz
Croze, H. and Morel, C. (2001), *Procédure civile*, Paris: PUF
Larguier, J. (2005), *Procédure civile: droit judiciaire privé*, Paris: Dalloz
Nouveau code de procédure civile (2005), Paris: Dalloz

10

Criminal procedure

PART I: INTRODUCTION

❯ The sources

French criminal procedure was originally codified in the *Code d'instruction criminelle* of 1808. This was replaced in 1958 by the Code of Criminal Procedure (*le Code de procédure pénale*, CPP) which is currently in force. Any articles referred to in this chapter will be to this Code unless specified otherwise. Under the 1958 Constitution, criminal procedure falls within the legislative domain of article 34, and therefore regulations play only a limited role in this area, primarily applying parliamentary legislation. Because of article 55 of the Constitution, legislation must conform with international treaties, which is particularly significant in this context due to the 1950 European Convention on Human Rights. This Convention has made an important contribution to the rules on criminal procedure. In particular, article 6 of the European Convention protects the right to a fair trial for those charged with criminal offences. This right is available from the time the person is charged with an offence to the end of the prosecution, and procedures such as on-the-spot penalty fines undermine this protection. In considering this right, the courts consider the overall fairness of the procedures, allowing the absence of one guarantee to be counterbalanced by the existence of another. In practice, the criminal division of the *Cour de cassation* generally takes the view that for matters of criminal procedure its principal source is the Code and the Convention is only of secondary importance.

❯ Three stages

In order to protect citizens from abuse, the rules on criminal procedure seek to avoid giving a single individual too much power, and instead limit their powers to one type of function. Thus the criminal process is divided into three stages, with different officials responsible for each stage of the procedure:

- the police investigation and the prosecution;
- the judicial investigation;
- the trial.

The distinction is slightly artificial between the first two stages, as in practice the investigating judge delegates most of the tasks of investigation to the police, thus the police play a key role during both phases.

The rules of criminal procedure have also developed around the distinction between the three classes of offence mentioned in Chapter 5, at p. 106–108 above: serious, major and minor offences. In particular, a judicial investigation only tends to be used where a serious offence has been committed.

An inquisitorial and adversarial system

A distinction can be drawn between inquisitorial and adversarial criminal systems. An inquisitorial system is characterised by a process that is not open to the public, the parties do not automatically have a right to be heard, the judges play an important and active role in gathering the evidence and an emphasis is placed on collecting written documentation to prove or disprove the case. Adversarial systems put an emphasis on public procedures, oral hearings, and giving an opportunity to the parties to put forward their case, while the judge is primarily limited to the role of an arbitrator ensuring that there is fair play. The first two stages of the French criminal procedure have traditionally been inquisitorial in nature, with particular emphasis being placed in the building up of a written file of the case containing all the statements, expert reports, and records of investigative procedures carried out. Elements of the adversarial process have been added in recent years, in an effort to give greater protection to the rights of the citizen and giving all parties opportunities to be heard. The trial hearing has always mixed elements of the inquisitorial and adversarial system, as it usually takes place in public with a limited opportunity for the parties to put their arguments orally, but the written file on the case prepared during the pre-trial investigation is central to the hearing.

Reform

Criminal procedure is an area that attracts considerable political attention and is frequently the subject of legislation. President Chirac established a Commission of Reflection on Justice (*la Commission de réflexion sur la Justice*) which was presided over by the then President of the *Cour de cassation*, Pierre Truche, and reported in July 1997 (the Truche Report). There were two main themes to this report: the protection of the presumption of innocence and the relationship between the public prosecutor's office and politicians. As a result seven Bills were presented to Parliament during 1998 and 1999 which sought to adopt many of the recommendations made in the Report. After much debate, some of this legislation was finally adopted by Parliament but some of its proposals fell by the wayside. Recent legislation has sought to increase the openness and transparency of the criminal system, reduce the powers of the investigating judge, and strengthen the independence of the public prosecutor. These changes were felt to be vital in order to regain the confidence of the French public, which had been lost in the aftermath of various political and financial scandals.

The presumption of innocence

Following the Act of 15 June 2000, a preliminary article to the Code of Criminal Procedure guarantees respect for the presumption of innocence. The inclusion of this provision was the implementation of a recommendation made in 1990 by the Commission on Criminal Justice and the Rights of Man, presided over by the leading criminal law academic, Madame Delmas-Marty.

To give effect to this presumption the system seeks to give certain guarantees to defendants and victims. They should benefit from a fair trial and the procedures should give due hearing to all the parties and achieve a balance between their rights, so that one party must not enjoy rights that the other party does not benefit from. If the media present a person who is the subject of a police or judicial investigation as guilty before a court conviction, the judge can put a stop to this by, for example, ordering the publication of a statement at the expense of the party at fault. The principle of the separation of the powers of prosecutor and judge is reinforced. The judges guarantee the rights of victims during the course of the whole criminal procedure. Defendants have the right to be informed of charges against them and to be assisted by a defence lawyer. Restrictions imposed on them must be monitored by a judge and be proportionate to the gravity of the offence and the necessities of the investigation. Defendants have a right to have their case heard within a reasonable time, a right that has been developed by the European Court of Human Rights. Any person convicted has the right to have their conviction examined by another court.

In a jury trial, the jurors are reminded that the defendants are innocent until proven guilty and that they must have the benefit of the doubt (article 304 Code of Criminal Procedure).

▶ Secrecy

Traditionally, the judicial and police investigations and judicial deliberations take place in secret, leaving only the trial hearing open to the public. Parliament has considered that the democratic principles of freedom of information and freedom of the press have to be balanced by the need to achieve justice. The secrecy of the early stages of the criminal procedure is justified on the ground that this is necessary so that investigations can be carried out without prior communications taking place between accomplices, relevant evidence being destroyed and pressure being placed on witnesses. It has been argued that this secrecy protects the presumption of innocence, by preventing the media from declaring guilt before a court has reached its judgment. The dangers of too much publicity were highlighted in 1997, when a high-profile operation was launched to arrest suspected members of a paedophile ring and several of those arrested subsequently committed suicide. Article 11 of the Code of Criminal Procedure provides:

> Except in the cases where the law provides otherwise, and without prejudice to the rights of the defence, the procedure during the police and judicial investigation is secret.
>   Any person who participates in this procedure is bound by professional secrecy and if breached can be punished under articles 226-13 and 226-14 of the Criminal Code.

In fact, only a limited number of people are bound by this secrecy provision, as article 11 refers simply to those who 'participate' in the procedure. This has been interpreted as referring to people whose profession or status mean they have a duty to be involved, such as the public prosecutor, the investigating judge, the police, experts, interpreters, court clerks and defence lawyers. The *Cour de cassation* had suggested that because of their professional duty to keep things secret, the defence lawyers could not pass to their clients documents from the case file that had been given to the lawyer for their exclusive use (*Assemblée Plénière*, 30 June 1995). This was strongly criticised as preventing defendants from effectively preparing their defence. The Act of 30 December 1996, amending article 114 of the Code of Criminal Procedure, was therefore passed allowing lawyers to give their clients copies of any documents from the file that they receive.

Article 11 does not bind the civil party and ordinary witnesses from disclosing what goes on before the criminal trial begins, as they are not treated as 'participating' in the procedure. In addition, the duty of secrecy only applies to certain elements of the file. For example, facts which are visible to the public, such as arrests and re-enactments, cease to be protected from disclosure, so that a witness is free to tell other people what he or she has seen. Certain acts, like police custody and the holding of a person on remand, cannot be covered by the secrecy requirement, as it would be dangerous to allow a person to be detained without another being informed. Information can also be released to the public where this is in the interests of the investigation, such as where there is a call for witnesses or a photo of the suspect is issued.

The Act of 9 March 2004 has introduced an article 11-1 of the Code of Criminal Procedure specifying that the prosecutor or investigating judge can authorise the communication of information about the criminal process to appropriate organisations, so that scientific investigations can be carried out to prevent a future accident or to compensate the victim. Employees of such organisations are, however, required to respect the professional secret.

The principle of secrecy is protected by criminal, civil and disciplinary sanctions. There is, for example, an offence of violating professional secrecy (articles 226-13 and 226-14 of the Criminal Code). A journalist can be convicted of the offence of handling if found to have obtained documents in breach of the professional secrecy provisions (*Cass. crim.* 3 April 1995). Proving the commission of these offences can be difficult, as journalists are not bound to reveal their sources (article 109 CPP). The courts have, though, been prepared to convict journalists for handling, when the exact identity of their source is not known but the court is confident that the original transfer of the information to the journalist must have been by a police officer in breach of article 11 (*Cass. crim.* 13 May 1991). The offence of defamation is also available (the Act on the Press of 29 July 1881). If no criminal investigation has been commenced, and the media have suggested that a person has committed a crime, that person is free to bring an action for defamation to clear his or her name. Such an action was successfully brought by the prominent politician, François Léotard, when a book was published suggesting that he was involved in the murder of a Member of Parliament in the South of France.

Public revelations in breach of the principle of secrecy during the police and judicial investigation do not, however, render the relevant procedure void (*Cass. crim.* 24 April 1984), unless this breach was detrimental to the interests of one of the parties (*Cass. crim.* 25 January 1996).

In recent years it has been accepted that too great an emphasis on secrecy during the criminal investigation can lead to an abuse of power, since it places the suspect in a very vulnerable position. As a result, the legislature has been progressively intervening to introduce greater openness and transparency to the system.

In practice, the media have obtained information on these pre-trial criminal procedures and have been prepared to publish it, despite possible infringements of the criminal law. Sometimes the investigating judges are themselves responsible for disseminating information, most markedly in the case of Jean-Michel Lambert, who was an investigating judge looking into the mysterious murder in 1984 of Gregory Villemin. He brought out a book about the murder while the criminal investigation was still ongoing. On the other hand, the investigating judges sometimes use media publicity to ensure that their investigations are not summarily curtailed by corrupt decision-makers higher up, who would wish to prevent political and financial scandals coming to light. It has indeed been suggested that using the media in this way ensured that criminal proceedings were pursued in the contaminated blood scandal case (allegations that blood contaminated with the AIDS virus had been used by the medical services for financial reasons, discussed at p. 146 above).

While the Truche Report accepted that the press fulfilled an important democratic function, it also felt that further restrictions on its powers needed to be imposed to encourage the press to behave ethically. The Act of 15 June 2000 has made it a criminal offence to publish pictures of a person in handcuffs or placed in custody on remand. The Truche Report recommended that generally there should be greater openness during the criminal investigation, with public hearings being held where important decisions affecting the freedom of individuals had to be made, which all the parties could attend. It also suggested that communications services be established by the courts, so that the public and journalists could receive more information about criminal cases through official channels.

While secrecy has in the past been the norm for the initial stages of the criminal procedure, it has been accepted that the trial hearing should take place in public. However, a recent decision of the Criminal Division of the *Cour de cassation* of 15 June 1999 refused to annul a decision of the court of appeal of Grenoble that was reached behind closed doors. In that case, the defendant had been ordered in January 1990 to demolish an illegal building within six months. A fine was imposed of 100 FF a day for each day that the defendant failed to do this after that date. When the defendant failed to demolish the building, in a private hearing the court of appeal increased the fine to 500 FF a day. The *Cour de cassation* accepted that it had been a mistake to hear the case behind closed doors, but the decision was allowed to stand as it had neither been established nor argued that the interests of the defendant had suffered as a result.

PART II: THE POLICE INVESTIGATION

There are two types of police in France: the crime prevention police (*la police administrative*) and the criminal investigation police (*la police judiciaire*). The former aim to stop the commission of offences, while the latter are responsible for finding the criminal after an offence has been committed. It is the criminal investigation police that we are concerned with in this chapter. This force is made up of two different kinds of police officer. First, the national police who work primarily in urban areas and belong to the Home Office. Secondly, the *gendarmes* who carry out their functions in the suburbs and in rural areas. Historically the *gendarmes* worked under the Ministry of Defence, but to try and achieve a more united police force, the Act of 29 August 2002 placed them under the operational authority of the Home Office, while still allowing them to retain their military status, to try and achieve a more united police force. The senior public prosecutors are responsible for watching over police investigations and must be kept informed by the police of the procedures carried out (articles 75-1 and 75-2 CPP).

As regards the methods of investigation, there are rules against entrapment, so that the police cannot themselves play a part in the commission of the offence in order to detect its commission, though there are exceptions for drug and customs offences and organised crime.

Having been informed of the commission of an offence, the police can carry out either an ordinary (articles 75 to 78 CPP) or an expedited (articles 53 to 74 CPP) investigation.

▶ The expedited investigation

Under article 53 of the Code of Criminal Procedure serious and major offences can give rise to an expedited investigation if:

* the suspect was caught red-handed or shortly after the commission of the offence,
* the suspect was found in possession of incriminating objects soon after the commission of the offence, or
* the suspect is the subject of public protest.

The advantage for the police of an expedited investigation is that they have increased powers which do not require the consent of those who are subjected to them. They can, for example, take external samples, including fingerprints and photographs (article 55-1 CPP), hear witnesses, and place a suspect in police custody (articles 63 to 65 CPP). The expedited investigation lasts for eight days but, following the Act of March 2004, it can be extended by a further eight days (article 53 CPP).

Having been informed of an offence, the police must immediately inform the public prosecutor (article 54 CPP) and then go directly to the scene of the crime to take all measures necessary to preserve any evidence. A suspect must be arrested where serious incriminating evidence justifies them being charged. A person's home can be searched without their consent where the occupier appears to have participated in the commission of an offence or to have documents or objects relating to an offence (article 56 CPP). Certain places, such as diplomatic buildings and university premises, benefit from special protection. In principle, the searches cannot be started before 6 am and after 9 pm (article 59 CPP). Where necessary, night searches are possible for investigations concerning terrorism, drug trafficking, procuring of prostitutes and organised crime (article 706-28, 706-35 and 706-89 CPP). The search must take place in the presence of the person in whose home it is carried out or, where this is impossible, by a representative of their choice. Failing this, two independent witnesses must be appointed by the police (article 57 CPP). The police must seize everything that could serve to reveal the truth (articles 54 and 56 CPP). Only the police and the qualified participants in the search can look at the papers and documents before they are seized. A statement describing the whole of the operation must be drawn up, if possible at the place where the search took place. The witnesses must sign the statement and any refusal to do so is mentioned in the statement.

Searches carried out in certain places can only be performed by a judge in the presence of a representative of the profession to which the subject of the search belongs. This is the case for searches in the offices or home of an *avocat*, which can only be carried out by a judge in the presence of the President of the local Bar or a person delegated to carry out this role by the President. This is also the position for searches of the offices of doctors, *notaires*, *avoués* and court bailiffs (article 56 CPP). If the President of the local Bar considers that a document is being removed unlawfully, it must be placed under seal and sent to the judge of freedom and detention to decide the matter. His or her decision cannot be the subject of an appeal (article 56-1 CPP). In order to protect the principle of freedom of information, searches of the offices of a newspaper or broadcaster can only be carried out by a judge. This judge makes sure that the investigations undertaken do not attack the free exercise of the journalist's profession and that they do not lead to an unjustified delay in the diffusion of information (article 56 CPP). If the rules on search are breached, the search is illegal and invalid.

▌ The ordinary police investigation

When the police carry out an ordinary police investigation, they only have three coercive powers: firstly, to carry out a search of property where the offence has a maximum sentence of at least five years and the judge of freedom and detention has agreed to it (article 76 CPP); secondly, to place suspects in police custody (article 77 CPP); and thirdly, to order witnesses to come to the police station to be questioned (article 78 CPP). Any other measures restricting the freedom of an individual require that person's consent, and in particular the police have no power of arrest.

▶ Police custody

The placing of a person in police custody is considered a vital part of the criminal process, providing an opportunity to interrogate a suspect, while preventing them from being able to communicate with members of the public, particularly possible accomplices. Until 1958 there was no legal provision for regulating police custody. This was a dangerous situation as it left scope for abuse by the police, and the passing of the 1958 Code of Criminal Procedure provided an opportunity to lay down a legal framework for this stage of the police investigation. The rules relating to police custody are the same whether it is carried out under an ordinary or an expedited investigation. Only people against whom there exists one or several plausible reasons to suspect that they have committed or attempted to commit an offence can be placed in police custody. In the past, both suspects and witnesses could be subjected to police custody, but since the Act of 4 January 1993, its use is now limited to suspects (article 63 CPP). Witnesses can only be detained for the time needed to take their statement and during this period they are not technically held in police custody.

A person can be placed in police custody for the purposes of interrogation for 24 hours. In certain circumstances this can be extended to 48 hours by the public prosecutor (articles 63 and 77 CPP).

There have been concerns over police violence during the custody procedure. The Committee for the Prevention of Torture, an organ of the Council of Europe sitting in Strasbourg, pointed in 1993 and again in 1998 to evidence of persistent bad treatment inflicted on people held in French police stations.

Between 25 and 29 November 1991 Ahmed Selmouni was held in police custody in Bobigny, which is on the outskirts of Paris. He had been arrested and was later convicted of being involved in the international traffic of heroin. It seems that during his detention he suffered serious abuse at the hands of five police officers. His hair was pulled, he was punched and kicked and received blows to his head with a baseball bat. Due to his injuries, he had to be taken to hospital as an emergency patient. On his return to the police station the next day, he again suffered ill-treatment.

The case was taken to the European Court of Human Rights by Ahmed Selmouni. He has joint Moroccan and Dutch nationality and the Netherlands took the exceptional decision of joining itself to the proceedings. Relying on the medical evidence, and in the absence of any plausible alternative explanation for the injuries he had suffered, France was condemned for torture, inhuman and degrading treatment under article 3 of the European Convention on 28 July 1999 by a unanimous verdict of 17 judges. France is only the second country in Europe, the first being Turkey, to be condemned for torture by the European Court of Human Rights. Ahmed Selmouni was awarded 500,000 FF damages.

France was also condemned by the European Court of Human Rights for not having given him a fair trial within a reasonable time. He had submitted his formal complaint on 15 March 1993, but the police officers were only brought before a trial court five and a half years later. The police officers were convicted and given prison sentences but submitted an appeal. This was heard by the court of appeal in Versailles in March 1999. The court upheld the police officers' convictions but significantly reduced their sentences. The sentence of the senior police officer, Bernard Hervé, was changed from four years in prison to 18 months, with 15 months suspended. The three months remaining had been covered by the time spent on remand and the automatic sentence reductions. So Bernard Hervé did not have to return to prison. All the other sentences to prison were reduced to suspended sentences. A further appeal could have been made to the *Cour de cassation*, and normally the European Court of Human Rights will not hear cases until all available proceedings before the national courts have been completed. However, case law developed in relation to the Kurds in Turkey by the European Court of Human Rights now sets the precedent that the court will only wait for the completion of national proceedings if they are efficient and available in practice and not just in theory. This case law was applied to France in the *Selmouni* case, which was found to have been too slow in prosecuting the matter.

The case has been deeply embarrassing to France, which prides itself on being a country which protects human rights, and raises questions not just about the violence in the police force but also about the relationship between the police and the judiciary, as the judges should be playing a key role in detecting and prosecuting such cases. Fabien Jobard, a researcher in the field of police violence, has commented on the problem of prosecuting the police for violence, unless it is very serious, as they can claim that injuries were caused by the victim violently resisting arrest (see *Le Monde*, 3 July 1999). The *Ligue des Droits de L'Homme* has asked for the creation of an independent administrative authority that would investigate police violence.

Following the Act of 4 January 1993, persons held in police custody benefit from a certain number of rights to protect them from abuse during their period in detention. They can have a close person informed by telephone that they are being held in police custody (article 63-2 CPP). To reduce the risk of physical abuse, they can be examined by a doctor (article 63-3 CPP). The suspect must be informed of their right to see a lawyer. A person placed in police custody should usually be immediately informed of their rights, though the police can delay informing a suspect of certain of their rights by up to three hours (article 63-1 CPP). Following the Act of 18 March 2003, a person is no longer informed of their right to remain silent.

This right to see a lawyer was only introduced in 1993 and represented a minor revolution in criminal procedure. The suspect's lawyer will be informed by the police of the nature of the alleged offence, but is not allowed to consult the file on the case, attend the formal acts of the police investigation, or tell anyone about the interview while the person is held in police custody. The lawyer can simply provide written observations to be added to the file. If police custody is extended, a new meeting with a lawyer can be requested at the start of this extension (in other words, after 24 hours in police custody).

The *Conseil constitutionnel* considers that the right to see a lawyer during police custody is an absolute right of the defence, though different rules can be laid down by the legislature according to the facts of the case, provided any differences do not arise from unjustified discrimination and do not affect the rights of the defence (*Cons. const.* 11 August 1993). Thus, in relation to terrorism, organised crime and drug trafficking the police can delay a person seeing a lawyer.

Affidavits must be prepared stating the time spent in police custody, the duration of the police questioning and the detainee's rest periods (article 64 CPP). Though there are no fixed time limits for police questioning, a circular specifies that the law aims to avoid questioning for lengthy periods. Research carried out in 1993 on behalf of the Royal Commission on Criminal Justice in the United Kingdom suggested that in practice such questioning could take place for oppressive lengths of time, until the detainee was emotionally broken (see Leigh and Zedner, 1993). The researchers questioned the reliability of any confession that was obtained in these circumstances.

Under article 41 of the Code of Criminal Procedure the whole process of police custody is placed under the control of the public prosecutor's office. Thus, when a person is placed in police custody, the police must inform a senior public prosecutor promptly (articles 63 and 77 CPP) who can subsequently authorise, where appropriate, the prolongation of custody for a further period of 24 hours. The role of the prosecutor is considered to provide an important protection for the detainee, but it may not satisfy the requirements of the European Convention on Human Rights. Article 5(3) of this Convention requires that a person who is arrested or detained must be immediately transferred before a judge who is empowered by the law to exercise judicial functions. Members of the public prosecutor's office are technically judges, being members of the same professional body and receiving the same training as the judges on the bench. The criminal division of the *Cour de cassation* has therefore judged that articles 63 and 77 of the Code of Criminal Procedure are not incompatible with the European Convention, considering that the senior public prosecutor is a judge 'empowered by the law to exercise judicial functions' (*Cass. crim.* 10 March 1992). However, the European Court of Human Rights ruled that local state prosecutors in Switzerland did not satisfy the criteria of article 5(3), as their impartiality could be questioned since they could subsequently bring a prosecution against the person placed in custody (*Huber v Suisse* (1990)). This judgment has influenced subsequent legislation so that the extension for a further 48 hours' police custody in relation to terrorist or drug offences must be authorised either by the President of a *Tribunal de Grande Instance* or a designated member of the bench.

While the 1990s saw an improvement of the rights of persons held in police custody, there is still scope for further progress: in particular, suspects are not informed of their right to remain silent and a suspect's lawyer is not present during the actual interrogation.

▶ The civil action

The victims of a crime can bring a civil action for damages before the criminal courts. This civil action will be decided during the criminal trial (articles 2 and 3 CPP). The commencing of civil proceedings in this way also triggers a criminal prosecution. The civil party can do this in one of three ways. First, by the issue of a summons to a known suspect to attend a trial court. This will be served by the court bailiff and is possible for minor or major offences where a judicial investigation is only discretionary. Secondly, the victim or their legal representative can make a complaint to an investigating judge. This procedure will be used where there is no known suspect or where a judicial investigation is either compulsory (see below) or felt to be useful on the facts. Thirdly, a request for damages made to a police officer during the course of a police investigation will trigger a civil action.

To be able to commence civil proceedings the individual must have suffered a personal and direct harm – including psychological harm – as a result of the offence. Where a crime causes no harm to an individual, but simply endangers public order, such as possession of a drug or a forbidden weapon, only a public prosecutor will be able to initiate the prosecution, as there will be no right to bring a civil action.

Should death occur, the victim's heirs can act in their personal capacity or as the victim's legal successor. If the victim dies without having started proceedings, the victim's heirs can bring the action in their capacity as heirs for both the material and psychological harm suffered (*Cass. crim.* 30 April 1976).

There is always the option of bringing the civil action before the civil courts (article 4 CPP), though once the civil court has been chosen, the case cannot be withdrawn and presented to a criminal court (article 5 CPP). The advantages of bringing the civil action before a criminal court are that this can be cheaper, simpler and quicker; the civil party can benefit from the evidence gathered by the public prosecutor's office or by the investigating judge; and it avoids the risk of conflicting judgments from the civil and criminal courts, as an award of damages will only normally be made if the defendant is found guilty. Unlike the public prosecution, which can only be brought against the person who has committed the crime and their accomplices, the civil action can also be brought against their heirs and third parties civilly responsible for the offender, such as their parents. A disadvantage is that the civil party, being a party in the criminal proceedings, cannot be heard as a witness. As the victim would frequently be the principal prosecution witness, this can considerably weaken the prosecution case, leading to acquittals which could otherwise have been avoided.

Though the civil party may have started the prosecution by bringing the action for damages, once commenced it is the public prosecutor's office that is responsible for continuing the prosecution, and the civil party has very little influence over it. They can ask the investigating judge to carry out certain investigations or demand the annulment of acts which breached the law (article 89.1 CPP). They are notified of any important decisions that have been made in relation to the case (article 183 CPP). The civil party has a right to appeal some decisions (article 186 CPP). Recent legislation has tried to strengthen the rights of the victim, so that the preliminary article to the Code of Criminal Procedure now states that the judge is responsible for guaranteeing the victim's rights during the criminal procedure.

If the public prosecutor's office decides that the prosecution is ill-founded, it can call for a ruling of no case to answer by the investigating judge or for an acquittal by the trial court. Should the exercise of the independent action for damages be found to have been abusive or time wasting, its author can be ordered to pay a fine (articles 91 and 392.1 CPP).

PART III: THE PROSECUTION

The public prosecutor's office

Once the police investigation is completed, a prosecution can be brought by a civil servant, who is normally the public prosecutor. The prosecutor competent to bring a prosecution is the one who has jurisdiction in the area where the crime was committed, where the suspect lives, where they were arrested (article 43 CPP), or occasionally where they are being detained (article 664 CPP).

Alternatives to a prosecution

Before deciding whether or not to prosecute, public prosecutors often in practice seek to apply intermediary solutions. Thus they can issue warnings which will only be followed by a prosecution if the person re-offends;

or they can temporarily classify the case for no further action, with an order for the suspect to put the situation right by, for example, paying their road tax.

In recent years efforts have been made towards encouraging mediation (article 41-1 CPP). Under the mediation procedures, the victim and the defendant agree to meet, frequently in a *Maison de justice et du droit*, and, if the mediation is successful, the public prosecutor's office can decide not to pursue the prosecution. When it is unsuccessful, the prosecution will be commenced. The defendant has a right to the assistance of a lawyer during these procedures. As part of the mediation package, the prosecutor has the power to impose a fine, order the return of property, confiscate a driving or hunting permit for up to four months or order the carrying out of up to 60 hours of work in the community. Any such order has to be ratified by the President of the relevant court.

Legislation has also been passed to encourage out of court settlements in criminal matters (*la composition pénale*, articles 41-2 and 41-3 CPP). An out of court settlement can be proposed to a person who admits that they have committed one or several major or minor offences punishable with a fine or with a sentence of imprisonment not exceeding five years. This procedure is not available for minor or major offences committed by the media or politicians, or involuntary homicide. Under an out of court settlement the offender can be ordered to carry out one of thirteen possible sentences. These include a fine not exceeding the maximum for the offence, up to one year's imprisonment or half the maximum sentence, handing over anything used to commit the offence or gained by its commission, handing over their car, driving licence or hunting licence for 6 months and undertaking work experience for up to 3 months, undertaking 60 hours' work in the community, being banned from entering a certain geographical area or providing a remedy to the victim. The defendant has 10 days to consider whether to agree to the proposed punishment and has the right to consult a lawyer. If the defendant agrees to the sentence, the Prosecutor refers the matter to the President of the *Tribunal de Grande Instance* for the settlement to be ratified. If the defendant rejects the proposed punishment, or the President refuses to ratify the settlement, the case will be sent for trial. Following ratification, should the offender fail to complete their sentence, the case will be sent to trial with the trial court being informed of any part of the sentence that has been carried out.

▶ The prosecution

The public prosecutor's office can use a number of different methods to institute criminal proceedings according to the gravity of the offence, as follows:

- a request for the setting up of a judicial investigation into the case (article 80 CPP);
- a summons to appear before the trial court, served by the court bailiff (article 394 CPP). This is the normal procedure for bringing a person before the *tribunal de police*, and it cannot be used for serious crimes as a prior judicial investigation is required;
- a notice to attend a court voluntarily (article 388 CPP). This is not available for hearings before the *Cour d'assises*;
- a formal order to attend the *tribunal correctionnel* in relation to a major offence;
- an immediate court attendance (which will take place the same day) before the *tribunal correctionnel* in relation to either a major offence with a maximum sentence of one to seven years which has been subjected to an expedited investigation; or a straightforward case where the maximum sentence is between two and seven years, if it appears that the evidence is sufficient and the case is ready to be judged (article 395 CPP).

The Act of 9 March 2004 has given statutory authority to the Minister for Justice to lay down policy guidance on the decision whether or not to prosecute. Article 30 now states that the Minister defines the prosecuting policy to be followed by the prosecutors, and monitors how this policy is applied in practice to try to achieve consistency. The prosecution policy seeks to fix priorities taking into account the contemporary problems facing society.

This still leaves the individual prosecutors discretion on whether to prosecute in a particular case, but the exercise of this discretion should be informed by this national policy. A matter that has caused public concern in the past is that because prosecutors have a discretion whether or not to bring a prosecution, they are perfectly entitled to decide that, although an offence has been committed, no further action should be taken. Prosecutors may, for example, decide that though a crime has been committed, it is not in the public interest to bring a prosecution as it was a minor offence which posed no real threat to society. A decision to take no further action has no legal effect, in that it does not extinguish the right to bring a prosecution in the future. As a result, if new evidence should come to light or the prosecutor simply realises that their earlier decision was wrong, he or she can subsequently decide to commence a prosecution. The decision not to prosecute is not a judicial decision, but a purely administrative decision. Against it, there exists no judicial appeal, but only a hierarchical appeal to a more senior prosecutor, who can order the junior prosecutor to bring a prosecution (article 40-3 CPP).

There are three main justifications for allowing prosecutors to have a discretion to decide whether or not to prosecute. First, more and more cases are coming to their attention, due to an increased crime rate, legislation creating more offences, and the development of legal aid which facilitates access to justice. By selecting which cases to prosecute, prosecutors reduce delays and are able to regulate the flow of cases according to the resources available. Secondly, there are other solutions available beyond a criminal prosecution to deal with wrongful conduct, such as disciplinary proceedings and mediation. Finally, a decision to prosecute could aggravate problems of public disorder, for example where there has been rioting in a neighbourhood.

However, the use of the discretion and some decisions to take no further action have caused considerable controversy. Public prosecutors are unusual in that they are both judges and civil servants – they belong to the professional body of the judiciary and are also subordinated to the Minister of Justice. In the past the Minister of Justice could instruct public prosecutors to prosecute a particular case, though orders not to prosecute were technically excluded. Following the Act of 24 August 1993, such instructions had to be written and placed in the file of the case. The Truche Report nevertheless made the comment that in practice less formal communications took place coming from the top to those lower down the hierarchy, which often resemble instructions or are regarded as such. The Truche Report recommended that article 36 should be repealed. Article 36 has now been amended so that Ministers can no longer issue these instructions.

There has been a general feeling that prosecutors have ordered no further action to be taken in too many cases. In 1995, of 5.2 million crimes formally referred to the prosecutors of the TGI, 4.2 million (that is to say, 80%) were classified for no further action. This may be acceptable where it has not been possible to trace the alleged offender, but 50% of cases were classified for no further action where there was a named suspect.

In addition, there have been strong suspicions that in ordering no further action in cases that risked causing political embarrassment, prosecutors have been directly influenced by politicians. Secret interventions have been made by the Ministry of Justice in favour of political friends. Revelations of such practices have seriously discredited both the political class and the judiciary. The subordination of public prosecutors to the politicians was highlighted in research carried out by Alain Bancaud and presented at a conference on François Mitterrand in January 1999. This revealed how frequent and routine Mitterrand's interventions were in matters of justice between 1981 and 1984. He did not hesitate to intervene directly in sensitive cases. A confidential note of a senior member of staff of the President of June 1981 indicated that 'it seems desirable that the President conserves – as he has always done – a minimum of control over what happens in judicial matters'.

Public concern increased when certain highly remunerative, corrupt practices by politicians and heads of business, involving the siphoning off of public funds, eventually came to the attention of the prosecution service. As case after case was classified for no further action, suspicions of political interference were apparently confirmed. For example, in the Urba scandal, the public prosecutor for the court of appeal of Aix-en-Provence contacted the Ministry of Justice on 8 May 1989 to let it know that it was proposing to open an investigation that would look into the financing of the socialist party in the south of France. The socialist Minister of Justice of the time, Henri Nallet, wrote a book, *Tempête sur la Justice*, discussing this matter. In it, he states that the Ministry of Justice understood that this investigation would have 'unfortunate and unforeseen consequences for a number of political representatives'. He wrote to the public prosecutor instructing him to classify the case for no further action to block the investigation. Nallet's justification for this decision is that it was necessary to protect the state. An amnesty law was subsequently passed to avoid a large number of elected people of all political persuasions from being incriminated.

The Longuet scandal concerned the funding of a project organised by Gérard Longuet, minister in the government of Edouard Balladur. The then Minister of Justice, Pierre Méhaignerie, is reported to have said that he would ask the opinion of the Prime Minister to see what course of conduct he would prefer in relation to that criminal investigation (*Le Monde*, 12 July 1997). He then delayed the opening of the judicial investigation by one month, prolonging unnecessarily a preliminary police investigation which had already been completed. This allowed M. Longuet to resign discreetly from office before being charged. He subsequently benefited from a decision that there was no case to answer in this matter.

The Tiberi scandal occurred in 1996 when Jacques Toubon, the then Minister of Justice, learnt that the public prosecutor for Evry was getting ready to open a judicial investigation on allegations concerning the salary of 200,000 FF received by Xavière Tiberi, the wife of a leading politician, for a report she was supposed to have written. A helicopter was sent to Kathmandu, in Nepal, where the senior public prosecutor was on holiday, in order to give him a document to sign that would have ordered the inquiry to be limited to an initial police investigation. In fact, the helicopter's mission was unsuccessful as the senior public prosecutor had already left when it arrived.

As suspicions mounted with regard to possible abuses of power by politicians to stop sensitive prosecutions, the situation was seen to be undermining the country's respect for the whole legal system. The independence of judges was itself seen as compromised due to the fact that judges are members of the same professional body as public prosecutors, and are also partly dependent on the Ministry of Justice for progress in their careers. Therefore when the Truche Commission was set up, its terms of reference included consideration of the relationship between the office of public prosecutor and politicians.

The Act of 9 March 2004 provides that prosecutors should systematically inform complainants and victims of any decision to take no further action, including the legal or practical reasons for this decision (article 40-2 CPP). This was a recommendation made in the Truche report and this reform will be brought into force on 31 December 2007.

Michel Jéol, a leading lawyer before the *Cour de cassation*, commented in 1994, 'Like the administrative courts and the Eiffel Tower, the Public Prosecutor is one of those monstrosities which doubtless one would no longer build today, but which no one can seriously envisage demolishing' (*Le Monde*, 4 June 1998). While no government is prepared to abolish the office of public prosecutor altogether, there have been suggestions that it should be reformed. Some have argued that the prosecutor's discretion should be removed so that a prosecution would have to be brought if an offence appeared to have been committed. This is the approach that gives the greatest satisfaction to the rule of law and is the practice in Italy and Germany. However, it does not allow for regulating the flow of cases to take into account the availability of resources.

PART IV: THE JUDICIAL INVESTIGATION

The investigating judge is the central figure responsible for a judicial investigation. The key practical difference between the police investigation and the judicial investigation is that the investigators under a judicial investigation are given greater coercive powers, such as placing a person on remand in custody or tapping telephones. A judicial investigation can only take place once a prosecution has been commenced. There are only two ways that a judicial investigation can be opened: following a request from the public prosecutor's office (article 80 CPP); or alternatively, and less frequently, through an application by the victim or their representative for damages to be determined by the criminal courts (article 51 CPP). The investigating judge can refuse to open a judicial investigation and issue a decision to this effect where it is evident from the documentation that no offence has been committed or that the prosecution is inadmissible (article 87 CPP).

The judicial investigation seeks to build on the work undertaken during the police investigation, in an effort to discover the truth and determine whether the case should be referred for trial. It is compulsory in relation to serious offences (article 79 CPP) and discretionary for all other offences. In practice it is only used in about 10% of all cases, and only very exceptionally for minor offences. For a major offence, a public prosecutor will tend to request a judicial investigation where particular measures only open to the investigating judge need to be carried out. This will be the case where expert reports are required, investigations have to be undertaken abroad, or a warrant for arrest needs to be issued for a fugitive suspect. In 1995, only 7.3% of cases submitted to the *tribunaux correctionnels* were preceded by a judicial investigation. While statistically such cases are in the minority, these are actually the most important ones due to their gravity, complexity, international nature or threat to social order.

▶ The investigating judge

Investigating judges are members of the bench and are nominated to their position for three years (article 50 CPP). They are competent to deal with a case when the crime, the suspect's residence, the arrest or the detention takes place within their jurisdiction (articles 52 and 663 CPP), and such cases are allocated to them by the President of the TGI. Usually an investigating judge works alone, but where a case is particularly serious or complex, additional investigating judges can be attached to the case (article 83 CPP). For example, four additional investigating judges were attached to the inquiry into the collapse of Crédit Lyonnais. Some of these investigating judges have become extremely well known by the public due to the high-profile cases they have been responsible for. This is particularly true of the 11 judges in the specialist financial section of the public prosecutor's office in Paris, including Judge Eva Joly who was in charge of the investigations into Crédit Lyonnais and Elf Aquitaine.

The role of the investigating judges is primarily to watch over the regularity of investigations carried out in their name, to prevent abuse of the broad coercive powers available at this stage. In addition to their role of investigator, the investigating judge also technically acts as a court of first instance when taking judicial decisions, such as whether to send a case for trial. These judicial decisions are then controlled by the Judicial Investigation Division of the court of appeal.

The original *Code d'instruction criminelle* of 1808 had conceived the procedure of judicial investigation as an inquisitorial process, being written (all the acts of the judicial investigation and all the decisions which it gives rise to are collected in the file) and taking place out of the public's view and without automatically allowing the parties to present their case. But in recent years elements of the adversarial procedure have been introduced. For example, the person charged and the victim who has commenced a civil action before the criminal courts can be kept informed of the procedure by their lawyer, who is informed of the contents of the file at all times.

The request to investigate may either refer to a suspect by name, or where the police investigation has not found a clear suspect, it will be left to the investigating judge to identify the offender. A judicial investigation is necessary in practice if the author of the crime is unknown.

▶ Powers to investigate

Investigating judges aim to discover the objective truth, rather than the guilt of the particular suspect. They have wide powers, though these have been curtailed in recent years by removing their power to place a suspect in custody on remand (see p. 212). According to article 81 of the Code of Criminal Procedure:

> The investigating judge carries out, in accordance with the law, all acts of investigation that he considers useful to establish the truth.

They can visit the scene of the crime (article 92 CPP), carry out a reconstruction of the offence (when the accused and their lawyer will normally be present), hear witnesses, search and seize property, arrest the person charged and place someone on conditional bail (article 138 CPP). The main bail conditions applied aim to prevent the suspect from becoming a fugitive, for example by imposing a condition that they must not go outside a fixed geographical area.

The investigating judge can interrogate the parties and the judge cannot end the investigation without having questioned the suspect, unless they conclude there is no case to answer. To avoid abuse of the right to interrogate, this process is now regulated by articles 114 onwards of the Code of Criminal Procedure.

The Act of March 9 2004 allows bugging devices to be used as part of a judicial investigation. If such a device is to be placed in a home, the permission of the judge of freedom and detention is required. Biological samples can be taken to determine a person's genetic make-up as part of the investigation of a serious offence (article 706-56 CPP).

A social investigation destined to shed light on the personality of the offender is compulsory for serious offences, and discretionary for major offences (article 81 paragraph 6 CPP). This involves looking at the suspect's personality (sometimes through a psychologist's examination) and at the environment in which they live. The judge can also investigate the impact of the crime on the victim and gather information about the personality of the victim (article 81-1 CPP).

Investigating judges can only investigate the criminal conduct referred to in the request or complaint. They cannot extend their investigation to other criminal acts. If they discover such acts during the investigation, they must inform the prosecutor. If the latter considers it appropriate, the investigating judge can be instructed by the prosecutor to widen the field of investigation. By contrast, investigating judges are not bound to limit their inquiries to the people referred to in the order or complaint; they can extend the charge to all those who appear to them to have participated in the criminal conduct under investigation.

Following the Act of 24 August 1993, article 114 of the Criminal Procedure Code provides that the suspect and the civil party have access to the file four days before any questioning. After the first interrogation, the file is always available to their lawyer, provided it does not cause too much disruption to the judicial investigator's office, and the lawyer can provide a copy to their client.

The investigating judge is not the only person who can initiate investigative acts during the judicial investigation. At any stage of the judicial investigation, the public prosecutor's office can demand to see the file on the case and request an investigating judge to carry out any acts which it considers would be useful to find out the truth and to take all necessary security measures (article 82-1 CPP). The suspect and the civil party can also ask the investigating judge to carry out 'any act that they consider necessary to find out the truth'. Any refusal by the investigating judge must contain reasons and can be the subject of an appeal.

One difficulty facing investigating judges is that it is impossible for them to carry out most of the investigative procedures themselves. Instead, they have to delegate this activity to police officers, over whom they have no direct control. While investigating judges can fix the time limits for the execution of their orders by the police (article 151 CPP), the Truche Report pointed out that they cannot ensure that such orders are fully complied with. Given that the police are answerable to either the Minister of the Interior or the Minister of Justice, the Truche Report was of the view that this position feeds the suspicion that the judiciary is dependent on politicians. There is also a danger that the police will communicate information about an investigation in breach of the principle of secrecy.

The conflicts that can result from the dependency of the investigating judge on the police were highlighted by the case of Olivier Foll, who was at the head of the criminal investigation police in Paris. Eric Halphen was an investigating judge who was carrying out a judicial investigation into corrupt practices involving council flats in Paris. As part of this investigation he decided to carry out a search of the home of Jean Tiberi who was both a Member of Parliament and the mayor of Paris. Jean Tiberi was suspected of having given his son a council flat at a low rent and then arranging for it to be renovated at vast expense to the state. Eric Halphen asked for the assistance of three police officers to carry out the search without specifying the nature of the operation. Once they arrived at the building, the judge informed the police what he wanted them to do. The police officers telephoned Olivier Foll, who ordered them not to participate in the search. Olivier Foll was subsequently condemned by the *chambre d'accusation* for failing to carry out his duties as a senior police officer and, thereby, obstructing the course of justice. It imposed the penalty of forbidding him to carry out the functions of a senior police officer for the next six months. His appeal was dismissed by the *Cour de cassation* on 26 February 1997. Though he was temporarily prevented from exercising the functions of a senior police officer, he was not removed from his position as director of the investigating police in Paris, so to members of the public his punishment seemed something of a sham.

One solution would be to place a certain number of investigators directly under investigating judges for particularly sensitive cases. This has been done in Italy for the investigation of Mafia-related offences. The Truche Report favoured experimenting with improvements to the current system, and considered that only if these failed should more radical solutions such as these be resorted to. It proposed that within the Ministry of Defence and the Ministry of Home Affairs a judge should work alongside the chief police administrator, in order to ensure the political independence of the police when carrying out investigations. The office of chief police administrator would also be open to a judge. The Report recommended that there should be judges among the teaching personnel for police training to encourage tighter links between the two. On being accepted into the profession, the police should be made to take an oath promising to respect human rights and the secrecy of investigations and to carry out investigations according to the Code of Criminal Procedure. Where there is an incident that gives rise to an inquiry, it should be headed by a judge and judges should form part of the team of inspectors.

Assisted witness

The Act of 15 June 2000, in accordance with recommendations made in the Truche Report, has extended the role of the assisted witness. Before 2000, the concept of an assisted witness was rarely used in practice and it will be interesting to see how far the change in legislation will lead to a change in the field. At the start of a judicial investigation, the investigating judge should only charge a suspect if the status of assisted witness is not appropriate (article 80-1 CPP). The status of assisted witness has been developed both to prevent suspects being treated as ordinary witnesses who benefit from no rights to a defence lawyer and are obliged to give evidence on oath (article 113-7 CPP), and also to prevent suspects being charged prematurely for an offence before adequate evidence has been gathered against them. This status of assisted witness automatically applies to every person named as a suspect by a victim or witness, or by the prosecution (articles 113-1 and 113-2 CPP). In addition, the investigating judge and police must treat as an assisted witness any person against whom there exists evidence of participation in the crime but who has not yet been charged (article 105 CPP).

Assisted witnesses benefit from rights and guarantees comparable to those which are given to the suspect charged, in particular the right to the assistance of a lawyer who has access to the file on the case, and the right to be informed in advance of any hearings. They can request a hearing with their accusers (article 82-1 CPP) and the termination of the judicial investigation (article 175-1 CPP). At their first hearing with the investigating judge they must be informed of their rights. The assisted witness cannot be placed on bail or placed in custody on remand (article 113-5 CPP).

Under the English criminal system, a person in a similar position to the assisted witness would frequently be described by the media as 'helping the police with their inquiries'.

Charging the suspect

During the course of the judicial investigation, serious evidence may come to light against suspects rendering it probable that they committed the offence, at which point suspects will lose the status of assisted witness and be charged. Investigating judges must inform suspects (usually through a letter sent by recorded delivery) that they intend to charge them with specific offences, inform them of their rights and allow them an opportunity to put forward any arguments on the proposed charge (article 113-8 CPP). At any stage during the procedures, assisted witnesses can themselves request charges be brought against them to benefit from the full rights of a defendant. There is no appeal available against a decision to charge, and the Truche Report did not recommend that one should be introduced.

Surveillance operations

During a judicial investigation an order can be issued for telephones to be tapped, something that cannot be carried out during a police investigation. A distinction must be drawn between telephone tapping during a judicial investigation for the detection and investigation of crime, and telephone tapping by the administration for reasons of security – national security, the prevention of terrorism and the prevention of organised crime. The latter are authorised by the Prime Minister and controlled by a national Commission for security interceptions. These have been the subject of some controversy, especially when it became known that Mitterrand had ordered the telephones of his political rivals to be intercepted.

As regards telephone tapping carried out during a judicial investigation, until recently there was no statutory control, but the Act of 10 July 1991 amended the Code of Criminal Procedure in order to regulate this important infringement of a person's right to privacy. The provisions are contained in article 100 onwards of the Code of Criminal Procedure.

Two conditions have to be satisfied to be able to tap a telephone:

1 the maximum sentence of the offence investigated must be at least two years;
2 the measure is necessary, in other words traditional means of investigation are insufficient.

To tap the line of an *avocat* the investigating judge must inform the President of the local bar; to tap the line of a judge the President of the court of appeal must be informed; and to tap the phone of a Member of Parliament or a senator, the President of their House of Parliament must be informed (article 100-7 CPP).

The decision to allow a telephone to be tapped is valid for four months and is renewable. It is not considered to be of a judicial nature, and therefore there is no right of appeal. Any recordings of conversations must be placed under seal and communications which are useful to the investigation will be transcribed onto affidavits.

The Act of 9 March 2004 has extended the powers of the police to carry out surveillance operations in relation to the investigation of organised crime (article 706-80 CPP). The police can infiltrate an organised gang by pretending to be a criminal (article 706-81 CPP). To facilitate this process, a police officer can take on a false identity and handle stolen goods and the products of crime without personally incurring criminal liability.

Remand and the judge of freedom and detention

A person is remanded in custody when they are placed in prison prior to a conviction during the course of a judicial investigation. Reform of the remand procedure has been a recurrent feature of the political agenda since 1789, and there has been considerable legislation on the subject under the Fifth Republic. Since the two important statutes of 1970 and 1975 establishing conditional bail and obliging judges to give reasons for their decisions to place on remand, Parliament has regularly reconsidered the question: the rules on remand have therefore been changed in 1984, 1985, 1987, 1989, 1993, 1996, 2000 and 2004. Two of these laws, the Act of Badinter of 1985 and the Act of Chalandon of 1987, were repealed before they were even brought into force.

Despite this intense legislative effort, detention on remand remains an unresolved problem in France. The use of remand in custody is controversial, primarily because it is felt that too many people are placed on remand. Unfortunately, France has one of the highest levels of litigation before the European Court of Human Rights, and 30% of this litigation concerns the excessive length of the criminal procedure or of a detention on remand (*Le Monde*, 16 April 1998). While the Code of Criminal Procedure states that custody on remand should only be used exceptionally (article 137 CPP), this does not appear to be the case in practice, as three out of four people held in prison are being held on remand. In 1995, 23,979 people were placed on remand, while 18,042 were given bail by investigating judges. For 30 years the average duration of remand has increased: between 1970 and 1995 it went from 2.1 months to more than 4 months, and in 1996, 33 people were being held on remand for every 100,000 inhabitants. Today, France holds more people on remand than most of its European neighbours, despite the fact that it has a comparable rate of criminal activity. Statistics of the Council of Europe in Strasbourg show that in 1996, the only countries of Western Europe which had higher levels than those of France were Moldavia, Poland, Portugal and Turkey. These figures are all the more worrying as remand in custody goes against the presumption of innocence and increases the likelihood of a conviction.

There has been concern that investigating judges who traditionally decided whether to place a person in custody on remand had too much power. They were accused of abusing their powers, by placing suspects on remand in custody to put pressure on them to provide a confession, despite the fact that this was not included within the grounds legally permitted for making such an order. A case in point is that of M. Miara, who was a suspect placed on remand in custody during the investigation of the high-profile Elf Aquitaine affair, involving the misuse of large amounts of public funds (see *Le Monde*, 29 December 1997). The research carried out for the Royal Commission for Criminal Justice in the United Kingdom in 1993 also considered that the legislative terms were too widely drafted, pointing in particular to the broad interpretation that was possible that there was a risk to 'public disorder' which justified placing a person on remand.

To try to reduce the use of detention on remand, two Acts were passed in the 1980s so that the decision would be taken by three judges rather than a single judge, but these Acts were both repealed for lack of resources before being brought into force. The Act of 4 January 1993 had conferred for several months the decision to place someone on remand in custody on a judge belonging to the bench (*le juge délégué*), but this Act was repealed on 24 August 1993.

The Truche Commission proposed that the powers of the investigating judge should be restricted, emphasising that the presumption of innocence needs to be respected first and foremost by the judiciary. It recommended that the power to place on remand in custody should be conferred to a collegial body of three judges which would not include the investigating judge and which would hear cases in public. This body would also consider applications contesting the regularity of a procedural act, the duration of the criminal process and a refusal to carry out certain acts of investigation. We have seen above that the creation of a collegial body of three judges had been accepted by Parliament in the past, but then abandoned for lack of resources. The Commission also favoured restricting the use of the public order criteria for allowing remand in custody, to where the maximum sentence for the relevant offence was more than three years' imprisonment.

The judge of freedom and detention was created by the Act of 15 June 2000. These judges, instead of the investigating judges, now decide whether a person should be placed on remand in custody (article 122 CPP). They also intervene whenever the freedom of an individual is threatened during a police or judicial investigation. In practice this reform has not caused any drop in the number of people being held on remand.

The investigating judge refers cases to the judge of freedom and detention to decide whether to place that person on remand (article 145 CPP). Both the investigating judge and the judge of freedom and detention have the right to decide that a person being held on remand should be released (article 147 CPP). Following the Act of 9 March 2004, in certain circumstances where the investigating judge does not consider that detention in custody is justified and has therefore not referred the matter to the judge of freedom and detention, the prosecutor can refer the matter directly to the judge of freedom and detention (article 137-4 paragraph 2 CPP).

The basic principle is that a suspect must remain free until they have been convicted, and an order to place them in custody must only be made in exceptional circumstances (article 137 CPP). A person can only be placed on remand in custody if it is the only way:

- to preserve the evidence, to stop pressure being placed on a victim or witness, or to avoid communications taking place between suspects and their accomplices; or
- to protect suspects, to guarantee their availability to the courts, to put an end to the crime or to prevent its repetition; or
- to put a stop to an exceptional and persistent breach of public order provoked by the gravity of the offence, the circumstances of its commission or the gravity of the harm it has caused.

Suspects can also be placed in custody where they have breached their bail conditions.

While one of these conditions may be satisfied when a person is first placed on remand, with time this may cease to be the case, and the investigating judge will order their immediate release with or without bail conditions. This decision can be taken after consultation with the prosecution or following a request of the prosecutor or the person being detained. Release can also be decided by the judge of freedom and detention if the investigating judge has refused to accept the prosecutor's request. The person released has to undertake to respond to the requirements of the investigative procedure. In addition, the detained person who has not appeared before an investigating judge for more than four months can demand immediate release before the Judicial Investigation Division. The rejection of an application to be released must contain specific reasons for the continuation of the judicial investigation and state its probable duration (article 145-3 CPP).

The detention cannot exceed a reasonable length of time, taking into account the gravity and complexity of the case (article 144-1CPP). As regards serious crimes, a person can be detained on remand for one year. Any subsequent extension of the detention period can only be ordered for six months and after all the parties have been heard on the issue. A reasoned order must specify the expected time for the end of custody on remand (article 145-2 CPP).

As regards major offences, the maximum length of detention on remand cannot exceed four months. Extensions of four months at a time can be given by a reasoned order and preceded by all the parties being heard on the issue.

Whatever the offence, when the relevant time limits have expired, the judge of freedom and detention can request a four-month extension from the Judicial Investigation Division. Two conditions must be satisfied: the investigation must be in process and the release would cause a particularly serious risk for the security of people and property. The prosecutor is immediately informed when an order to release a person being held on remand is issued. If, after four hours, no appeal against release is made, the person is released. If the prosecutor submits an appeal within four hours the person will be detained until the appeal has been decided by the president of the Judicial Investigation Division (article 148-1-1 CPP).

If at the end of six months from the start of being placed in custody, the person has not been the subject of a prosecution, he can ask the prosecution what is going to be the outcome of the procedure.

A person can be refused a right to communicate with people outside the prison for a maximum of 20 days. After a month, the detainee can only be refused the right to a visit from a member of their family if this refusal is necessary for the judicial investigation and the investigating judge issues a written decision to this effect (article 145-4 CPP).

If the case against the suspect proves to be ill-founded, and they are acquitted or no prosecution is brought following a decision that there is no case to answer, they can claim compensation for their wrongful detention. The Act of 30 December 1996 repealed the requirement of a loss 'manifestly abnormal and of a particular gravity', leaving simply a requirement to prove harm. The application is considered by the court of appeal and an award is almost automatic in these circumstances.

The creation of a judge of freedom and detention has been seen by some as a cynical move to punish investigating judges for having revealed, in recent public scandals, the failings of a section of the ruling class. It has been argued that there is no reason why this new judge should be any more effective at protecting liberties than an investigating judge, and that in fact the best person to decide the question of remand is the one who knows the case best – who will inevitably be the investigating judge. Indeed, faced with the complexity of certain files, delegated judges, who were appointed for a short-lived period in 1993, were sometimes content simply to accept the advice of the investigating judge of the case (*Le Monde*, 30 October 1997). In Marseilles, during this brief experiment, only 7% of requests to place on remand in custody were refused, though often the investigating judge exercised a form of self-censure, hesitating to submit cases which would have been contested.

Ending the judicial investigation

The judicial investigation should not exceed a reasonable length of time, taking into account the gravity of the facts, the complexity of the investigation and the rights of the defence (article 175-2 CPP).

An investigating judge must indicate to the interested parties how long they expect the investigation to take (articles 116 paragraph 8 and 89-1 paragraph 2 CPP). At the end of this period, or after one year in relation to major offences and 18 months in relation to serious crimes, or when no investigatory act has been carried out for four months, the suspect and the civil party can apply for the investigation to end (article 175-1 CPP). If the investigating judge fails to decide the application within one month, the applicant can refer the case to the president of the Division for Judicial Investigation. A new request can be made six months later.

Once the investigating judge has completed the investigation, a closing order is issued which brings the investigation to an end (article 175 CPP). This order states either that the case should be transferred for trial or that there is no case to answer when the judge feels that it is inappropriate to proceed with the prosecution (article 177 CPP). Of the 63,942 people who had been subjected to a judicial investigation and whose cases came to an end in 1995, 7,801 (12.2%) benefited from a ruling that there was insufficient evidence to proceed.

In the past, if the case concerned a serious criminal offence it was not automatically transferred to the *Cour d'assises*. Instead, the file was sent to the public prosecutor who asked the former *chambre d'accusation* (now known as the *Chambre de l'instruction*) to examine it, to decide whether to go ahead with the transfer or not. The *chambre d'accusation* exercised judicial control over the work carried out by the investigating judge. It would refer the case to the *Cour d'assises* if it found that there was sufficient evidence to support the charges and that the earlier procedure was complete and lawful. Now the investigating judge unilaterally decides whether a case involving a serious crime should be referred to the *Cour d'assises* (article 181 CPP). The automatic control over this decision is no longer thought to be necessary as a further appeal against a decision of the *Cour d'assises* is now available before another *Cour d'assises.*

The judicial investigation tends to be slow. On average the procedure will take 15 months to complete and some investigations take over three years. Certain investigating judges have complained that they suffer from a lack of resources, particularly in relation to financial crime (*Le Monde,* 15 November 1997). Until the 1980s, financial corruption with regard to state funds was rarely prosecuted. From 1984 to 1994 the number of convictions for corruption and abuse of power increased from 44 to 104. In relation to abuse of public funds, the number increased by over 50%, from 198 in 1990 to 310 in 1994. The rise in large cases, such as that of Crédit Lyonnais, requires an increase in funding for the investigators to confront the challenge and more specialist training should be provided for investigating judges working in this field, due to the particular complexity of their work.

PART V: THE TRIAL

The rules which govern first instance trial proceedings are generally the same for all criminal courts, except the *Cour d'assises* whose peculiarities were studied at p. 108.

Trials of criminal cases are fairly short. As a general rule, cases are heard by a minimum of three judges, which has the advantage of reducing the risk of judicial error, bias and corruption. For reasons of economy, there are an increasing number of exceptions to this general principle. Minor offences are tried by a single judge in the neighbourhood court and the *tribunal de police.* While three judges may sit in the *tribunal correctionnel,* in practice only one judge may have been allocated the file and will have studied it in detail. The law also provides for certain major offences to be tried by a single judge. Originally, the President had a discretion to refer such cases to three judges where this was felt to be appropriate, but the *Conseil constitutionnel* considered that such an approach violated the principle of equality before the law, as defendants of the same type could be tried by different court formations. To avoid this problem, the Act of 8 February 1995 renders the competence of the single judge obligatory for a range of major offences listed at article 398-1 of the Code of Criminal Procedure. This list includes road traffic offences, theft and certain non-fatal offences against the person. Such offences are all tried by a single judge unless the defendant has been refused bail, or has been brought directly before the court after the commission of the offence.

A judge can be challenged where there is a suspicion of bias (article 668 CPP) and transferred from their post where there is a legitimate suspicion that the judge will not be impartial (article 662 CPP). Where there has been an accusation of bias, the court has a duty to verify this accusation, and a failure to do so will be a breach of article 6 of the European Convention on Human Rights protecting the right to a fair trial. This was found to be the case in *Rémilly v France* (1986) where the *Cour d'assises* refused to act upon a suggestion of racism.

The intention of the drafting of the 1958 Code of Criminal Procedure, as with that of the 1808 Code, was to organise the hearing in accordance with the adversarial model (while still retaining some elements of the inquisitorial model). It therefore has the three fundamental characteristics of the adversarial system: public, oral and with a due hearing of the parties. Thus, the judges cannot give judgment after simply reading the file, but must have gained a personal experience of the human reality of the parties and witnesses at the trial. Though the hearing is primarily oral (article 427 CPP), it focuses around the written file, and written affidavits recording the occurrence of certain major offences are sufficient to convict unless there is proof to the contrary or proof of forgery. As a general rule, the trial takes place in public. If a public hearing might give rise to public disorder or be harmful to public morals, the court can order that the matter be heard *in camera* (article 306 CPP). In cases concerning rape or sexual attacks involving torture and barbaric acts, the civil party can request for the case to be heard *in camera*. In other cases the public can be excluded if the civil party does not object. If the trial is of a minor, there are restrictions on the members of the public who are allowed to attend: even the minor can be excluded and simply represented by his or her lawyer. The proceedings cannot be filmed or recorded (article 308 CPP), though this will be allowed, for example, to keep archives of important judicial cases. Thus, recordings were made of the trial of Maurice Papon who was convicted in 1998 for crimes against humanity. These crimes had been committed against Jewish people in France during the Second World War.

The parties have a right to be represented by a lawyer in accordance with article 6(3) of the European Convention on Human Rights, and the *Cour de cassation* has acknowledged the constitutional nature of this right (decision of 30 June 1995). Such representation is compulsory before the *Cour d'assises*, for minors and for those suffering from an infirmity preventing them from defending themselves (articles 114 and 274 CPP).

The defendant is presumed to be innocent. The presumption of innocence only comes to an end when a person is declared guilty by a court. Because of the presumption of innocence, the prosecution has the burden of proving that the accused committed the offence, though the defendant has to prove the existence of a defence. In a few circumstances, presumptions of law exist where suspects are presumed to have committed the offence unless they prove the contrary. For example, if children habitually commit offences against property, their parents will be presumed liable for handling (article 321.6 Criminal Code). This provision was introduced as a result of public concern that gangs of children were being encouraged by their parents to commit street robberies. Where a person is habitually keeping the company of drug traffickers there is a presumption that they are handling the proceeds of drugs; and if a person is living with a prostitute there is a presumption that they are living off immoral earnings (articles 222.39.1 and 225.6 of the Criminal Code). The European Court of Human Rights considers that such presumptions do not breach the presumption of innocence, provided a defendant has the opportunity of proving that the opposite is true.

In principle, all evidence legally obtained is admissible. The European Court of Human Rights has ruled that where people claim that they suffered physical abuse during police custody, the burden of proof is on the state to show that this is untrue (*Tomasie v France* (1992)). The court is provided with details of the defendant's criminal record not just to decide questions of sentencing, but also in determining guilt. This approach has been justified by the Truche Commission as allowing the court to understand fully the person before them, but would normally be excluded by a UK court when determining guilt as being dangerously prejudicial to the defendant. For serious offences and some major offences, the court will also have available information on the personality of the person charged, their material situation, and family or social situation (article 81 CPP).

Due to the inquisitorial system that underlies the criminal process, the judiciary plays an active role throughout the hearing, with the President of the court being responsible for directing proceedings. The hearing can be divided into two parts. The first is the final investigation which mainly serves to recall elements already featured in the file, while adding the human aspect resulting from the oral hearing of witnesses and providing a final opportunity to fill in any gaps in the previous investigations. The second concerns the closing speeches where the parties draw their conclusions from this evidence.

A guilty plea

Historically, in France, there was no system for a guilty plea to be entered. The full investigation and trial automatically took place, regardless of whether the accused had confessed. The Truche Report considered whether the guilty plea procedure, with the promise of a reduced sentence where the defendant pleads guilty, should be imported from countries with common law systems in the hope of reducing delays. Such a proposal was rejected as undermining the principle that the prosecution must prove guilt, and on the basis of the inconvenience caused by a suspect later retracting a confession, having already prevented a full investigation from taking place.

The Act of 9 March 2004 has now, however, introduced into France a system for accepting guilty pleas (article 495-7 to 495-16 CPP). For major offences punished on the basis of a fine or of imprisonment not exceeding five years, prosecutors can, on their own initiative or on the request of the interested party (or his or her lawyer) have recourse to this procedure following an acknowledgement of guilt. This procedure does not apply to minors, major offences committed by the media or politicians or involuntary homicide (article 495-16 CPP). The prosecutor can propose one or several punishments. Imprisonment cannot exceed one year or half the maximum for the relevant offence. Suspects have seven days to decide whether or not to accept the proposed sentence, and can consult their lawyers.

The absence of the defendant

Defendants should normally be present at their trial. If, however, they fail to attend the case without a valid excuse, the trial can proceed, but the defendants' lawyer must be allowed to put their case in their absence (article 379-3 and article 410 para 3 CPP). This procedure is known as *le défaut criminel*. In the past the lawyer would not have been heard but this was held to be in breach of the European Convention in the cases of *Voisine* (2000) and *Kromback* (2001). The *Cour d'assises* can either adjourn or hear the trial without a jury. Following conviction and sentence, a warrant for the person's arrest is issued. If the defendant is convicted, they cannot later appeal against their conviction. However, if the convicted person hands themselves over to the prison authorities, or if they are arrested before the time limits for their sentence have run out, the preceding decision is disregarded and the *Cour d'assises* commences its ordinary procedures.

Ordinary proceedings

When the defendant is present, the normal order of the hearing is to start with the cross-examination of the defendant. The evidence is presented, which may involve the reading of the statements and the hearing of witnesses and experts. All suspects have the right to question, or to have questioned, the prosecution witnesses and to demand the summoning and questioning of the defence witnesses in accordance with the same conditions as the prosecution witnesses (European Convention on Human Rights, article 6(3)(d)). The witnesses must swear on oath to say 'the truth, nothing but the truth'; in addition, before the *Cour d'assises* they swear to 'speak without hate and without fear'. The court can order new measures of investigation to be carried out, for example, by summoning a witness for a later hearing, or ordering the production of certain documents.

Where there is a civil action brought by the victim or their representatives, their claim will be heard, and this will specify the amount of damages sought. The prosecution will make its closing speech which includes arguments as to the appropriate punishment, followed by the defence lawyer and, if wished, the defendant.

At the end of the hearing, the President of a trial of major and minor offences will inform the parties present of the day when the judgment will be given (article 462 CPP). The judge or judges deliberate in private and verdicts are reached according to their personal conviction (articles 353 and 427 CPP). In the past, judges were obliged to convict in the presence of particular evidence, but this approach was abolished with the Revolution for fear that it could cause injustice, as it ignored the individual circumstances of a case. The court can order an acquittal or a conviction, which can be imprisonment for life, and the execution of the sentence is supervised and monitored by the *juge de l'application des peines*. The death penalty was abolished in 1981. According to the *Cour de cassation*, a criminal court cannot discharge a defendant for lack of evidence and the judgment can only be based on the evidence before the court. The judgment, although given orally by the President of the court, will nevertheless be written (often after the event). The judge must justify the verdict by the evidence which was provided in the file and at the hearing (article 353 CPP).

Where a person is convicted, the civil party will be awarded damages if the court is satisfied that the harm suffered by the victim was the direct consequence of the acts entering within the definition of the offence. If the court acquits it cannot normally award damages in the civil action, though exceptionally the *Cour d'assises* can make such an award.

BIBLIOGRAPHY FOR CHAPTER 10

Code de procédure pénale (2005), Paris: Dalloz
Elliott, C. (2001), *French Criminal Law*, Devon: Willan Publishing
Garé, T. and Ginestet, C. (2004), *Droit pénal – procédure pénale*. Paris: Dalloz
Larguier, J. (2004), *Procédure pénale*, Paris: Dalloz
Leigh, L. and Zedner, L. (1993), A Report on the Administration of Criminal Justice in France and Germany, London: HMSO.
Pradel, J. (1997), *Le juge d'instruction*, Paris: Dalloz
Regards sur l'actualité – Réformes de la justice pénale, (2004) Paris: La documentation française
Soyez, J.-C. (2004), *Droit pénal et procédure pénal*, Paris: LGDJ
Stefani, G., Levasseur, G. and Bouloc, B. (2004), *Procédure pénale*, Paris: Dalloz

11 Administrative procedure

PART I: THE GENERAL CHARACTERISTICS OF ADMINISTRATIVE PROCEDURE

▶ Legal sources

The rules on administrative procedures are contained in the Code of Administrative Justice (*Code de justice administrative*, CJA) which came into force on 1 January 2001. In addition, certain legal principles have been developed by the judges, as administrative law is one of the few areas of French law where it is accepted that case law plays an important role. Most of these principles have been developed by the *Conseil d'Etat* (C.E.), for example, the obligation to give reasons for a judgment and the duty to keep judicial deliberations secret. Some have constitutional status, having been recognised by the *Conseil constitutionnel*, such as the principle of equality before the law, based on article 2 of the Declaration of Human and Civil Rights 1789; or the respect of the rights of the defence.

The European Convention on Human Rights has also had a significant effect on its development in recent years. Article 6(1) of the Convention, protecting the right to a fair trial, has been particularly influential.

The rules of administrative procedure before the different courts but are very similar and therefore can be treated together. They have been heavily influenced by the rules of civil procedure, and the similarities have been heightened by the 1953 and 1987 legislative reforms (see Chapter 6, p. 115).

▶ Inquisitorial system

Administrative procedure is characterised by its inquisitorial nature, with the parties addressing themselves to the judge rather than to each other as would be the case in a civil action. Pleadings are sent to the judge and then copies transferred to the opposite side. And it is the judge who is responsible for organising the pre-trial investigation. Thus the parties are never in direct contact, as the whole preliminary phase takes place via the administrative court, and in particular the reporting judge.

The litigation process is essentially a written process, with the oral presentations at the hearing playing only a very minor role. The pre-trial investigation is based on the parties' written statements of their case, and the written documents such as the experts' reports. It comes to an end with the writing of a written report.

The procedure has been traditionally secret in nature, though there has been a move in recent years towards greater openness. The preliminary investigation has remained fairly secretive, but article L.6 CJA lays down that the hearings of the ordinary administrative courts are in public; thus a hearing in private is the exception. Due to article 6(1) of the European Convention on Human Rights, there is now a right to have the case heard in public. The Litigation Division of the *Conseil d'Etat* was initially reluctant to apply this article to disciplinary hearings (C.E. Sect. 27 October 1978, *Debout*) but in the light of the European Court of Human Rights case law in this field, the *Conseil d'Etat*, in a full hearing of the court, was forced to change its position (C.E. Ass., 14 February 1996, *Maubleu*).

Because of the *principe contradictoire* (L.5 CJA), the parties have a full opportunity to put forward their case, and to respond to the arguments of the other side. All relevant documentation has to be made available to the other side to make this a reality. Following a decision of the *Conseil d'Etat* on 6 December 2002, a judge cannot see a document when one of the parties is not able to see it. Instead the judge will simply be given a summary that is adequate for the purposes of hearing the case. As a general rule, claimants cannot represent themselves, but must employ a lawyer to put forward their case. There are, however, numerous exceptions to this general principle, in particular with respect to the *recours pour excès de pouvoir* (see below). Legal aid is available to help those with limited financial means pay their lawyers' fees.

▶ The government commissioner

Government commissioners (*commissaires du gouvernement*) play a central role in an administrative case. They are not a party to the action and they do not, despite their title, represent the interests of the government. In the leading case of *Gervaise* (C.E. Sect. 10 July 1957), the *Conseil d'Etat* made it clear that the government commissioners' role is to give an independent and impartial opinion on the case, looking at both the facts and the law, principles which can now be found in article 18 of the Act of 6 January 1986. Thus, they are not required to state the view of the government, but to provide an opinion based on a personal assessment of the case.

▶ **Types of litigation**

In administrative law the nature of the application will depend on the type of remedy sought, which in turn has procedural implications. There are four possible remedies that can be granted. A judge can be requested to annul an administrative decision; this is known as the *contentieux d'annulation* of which the *recours pour excès de pouvoir* attacking the legality of an administrative decision is the best known. Secondly, an applicant can ask the court to use all its powers, not purely its power to annul, and in particular its power to award damages. This is known as the *contentieux de pleine juridiction* and includes litigation arising from a contract and tortious wrongs. Thirdly, the court can be asked to interpret or decide the legality of an administrative act, known as the *contentieux d'interprétation*. Finally and exceptionally, the administrative judge has a penal role as it can criminally sanction people who have committed certain minor offences against public property. It is the first two scenarios which represent the greatest part of administrative litigation.

▶ **A preliminary decision**

Before an action can be brought before an administrative court, there must be a preliminary administrative decision which forms the subject of the action (article R 421 CJA). This is true even where the litigation arises from a tort, so where a tort has been committed, the victim would also have to contact the administration for a preliminary decision on the claim. It is the administration's complete or partial refusal to accept a claim, which constitutes the decision for these purposes. If the administration fails to respond, it will be treated as having impliedly rejected the request after two months have passed. The time limit prevents the administration from blocking an action by simply keeping silent. The requirement of a preliminary decision does not apply to applications concerning public works, emergency procedures or where the administration is bringing an action against a private individual.

PART II: THE INVESTIGATION AND THE HEARING

▶ **Commencing an action**

Administrative proceedings are commenced by filling in a form that can be obtained from a local newsagents, laying out the statement of claim. This must contain the facts and the grounds for the complaint, and any omissions can only be amended within the time limits for the bringing of a fresh action. A small court fee must be paid, an innovation which was introduced to try and discourage futile litigation, but which has been criticised as being both too small a sum to be effective and in breach of the principle of free access to justice. Those entitled to legal aid are exempt from making this payment.

The application needs to be accompanied by a copy of the administrative decision that is the subject of the complaint, or proof that a request was made where the decision under attack is an implied rejection. In addition, all the documentation in support of the case must be attached. Multiple copies of the application and supporting documentation must be deposited with the court office.

The application must usually be submitted within two months from the date of notification of the attacked decision or, where the object of the litigation is a regulation, its publication. This is an extremely short timescale, which means that the applicant must act swiftly. Where the administration has failed to respond to a request, the time limit is two months after the implied decision of rejection was made. Therefore an applicant has to be particularly careful when bringing an action in such circumstances, as if they bring the action before two months have passed from the date of their request, it will be inadmissible due to the absence of an implied decision to reject; if they bring the action more than six months after this date, it will be out of time.

There are, in addition, special time limits for certain types of litigation. For example, complaints arising from certain local elections must be brought within five days, those arising from regional and European elections within ten days, and a person only has 24 hours to make an application against a town hall's decision to order their repatriation. The administrative courts in France, unlike their counterparts in the United Kingdom, have no discretion to allow actions to proceed that have been submitted outside the time limits.

The admissibility of the application

This is dependent on two factors: the nature of the applicant and the nature of the application.

The applicant

The rules of standing that are applied to applicants are generally more lenient than the equivalent rules in English law. Applicants must satisfy two conditions: they must have the capacity to bring the action and an interest in the case.

Capacity

Applicants must have the capacity to bring an action. This can exist for both physical and moral persons. For physical persons in being, this question is governed by civil law provisions; thus, for example, a minor lacks legal capacity. If a physical person lacks legal capacity, their legal representative can bring an action on their behalf; so a parent can bring an action on behalf of his or her child. The administrative judge has accepted that those who lack capacity can bring an action for judicial review against decisions affecting their personal freedom (C.E. 10 June 1959, *Dame Poujol*). For moral persons, such as a company, capacity is dependent upon having legal personality. The person bringing the application on behalf of the moral person must show that they have been mandated to act as the agent of that moral person.

Interest

The applicant must have an interest in the case, a question that has given rise to considerable case law. Where the case concerns a *recours de plein contentieux*, such as a breach of contract, the action is personal by nature so that this interest will be easy to identify. Actions for judicial review against regulations are more impersonal, but the courts have been prepared to apply a broad interpretation of the concept of an 'interest' in this context.

The applicant must have a personal interest, which can be either material or emotional, individual or collective (such as a charity or trade union). The existence of this interest is interpreted very leniently. Thus a civil servant has been found to have an interest when a person was nominated to a position to which he could have applied (C.E. 11 March 1903, *Lot*); and a camping enthusiast had an interest when a local byelaw banned camping even though he had never camped in that area (C.E. Sect. 14 February 1958, *Abisset*).

The interest must be legitimate, thus a person occupying public land without permission has no right to bring an action against a building permit relating to it: C.E. Sect. February 1985, *SA Grand Travaux et Constructions Immobilières.*

The person's interest must be directly affected by the decision under attack, though this has been given a broad interpretation. The *Conseil d'Etat* has ruled that the interest of a national association against alcoholism had been affected by decisions favouring home distillers: C.E. 25 April 1934, *Ligue nationale v alcoholisme*; and the interest of the National Federation of Catholic Family Associations was found to have been directly affected by the decision to recommence the sale of an abortion pill: C.E. Ass. 25 January 1991, *Confédération nationale des associations famili-ales catholiques et autres.*

The interest must be fairly specific to the person rather than result from a general characteristic. For example, the fact of being a taxpayer does not give rise to an interest sufficient to found an action against provisions increasing the national expenditure (C.E. 25 June 1920, *Le Doussal et Métour*). However, local taxpayers can bring actions against decisions increasing council spending (C.E. 29 mars 1901, *Casanova*).

Occasionally the law imposes an interest to act, for example, a Prefect automatically has a right to refer an administrative act to an administrative court.

The rules on admissibility are of a public nature and therefore can be raised at any stage in the proceedings, and on the judge's own initiative. On detection, certain irregularities can be put right, rather than the case being thrown out; for example, during the course of the proceedings applicants can produce the necessary proof that they have been mandated to act as the agent of the person with the legal interest in the case.

The application

Three conditions must be satisfied in order for the application to be admissible. It must be submitted within the relevant time limit, it must be accompanied by the decision of the administration which is the subject of the action, and the court fee must have been paid. Those entitled to legal aid are exempt from making this payment. If a Prefect submits an application, the state has to pay the fee, which amounts to a pointless payment to itself.

The application must specify both the factual and legal grounds for the action. As regards the legal grounds, a distinction is drawn between the legal grounds founded on 'external legality' (for example, incompetence or a procedural error) and 'internal legality' (for example, the reasons for the decision or the abuse of power). This distinction is important, because during the proceedings applicants will only be allowed to rely on the category of illegality that they invoked in their statement of claim; any other arguments will be treated as new and inadmissible. This problem is easily avoided in practice by pleading legal grounds from both categories.

Those grounds that are of a public as opposed to a private nature can be invoked at any stage of the legal process, even on appeal and even on the judge's own initiative. Where the judge does consider taking this path, the parties should be warned so that they have an opportunity to present their views. Matters which are considered to be of a public nature include the argument that the person who made the decision under attack lacked the authority to do so, and failure to consult the *Conseil d'Etat*.

▶ Interlocutory procedures

Normally an administrative decision continues to have effect even after a legal action has been brought against it. This can be problematic as the carrying out of the decision which is the subject of the litigation may have irreversible consequences, rendering any legal action meaningless. If, for example, the administrative decision is to demolish a house, once that house has been demolished, any subsequent ruling by the courts that the decision was illegal will not be able to provide a satisfactory remedy for the home owner. As the instigation of court proceedings does not suspend the legal effect of an administrative decision and there are often significant delays before a case comes to trial, temporary emergency provisions are essential in the interim before the hearing of the substantive case, in order to render judicial control in the field effective.

Because of concern for the smooth running of the administration, interlocutory orders were only introduced into the administrative system in 1955, and were rarely issued in practice. As administrative decisions were executory, this reluctance always benefited the administration. The result was to reduce the credibility of the administrative courts due to the fact that in many cases an injustice cannot be undone once an administrative decision has been executed. While in a high-profile case an application made on Saturday at 11 am on 18 January 1997 was successful and resulted in the cancellation of a football match due to take place that afternoon, this is the exception rather than the rule.

This problem led some individuals to start proceedings in the civil courts despite the fact that the matter strictly fell outside their jurisdiction, because the civil courts were regarded as more willing to allow interlocutory applications and had been sympathetic to claimants seeking redress from administrative decisions. While an application can then be made to the Jurisdiction Disputes Court to have the case heard in an administrative court, there is a time delay before this court will make a ruling. This occurred in the case known as the *Stowaways of Honfleur* of May 1997. Two stowaways from Morocco were on a foreign boat which had docked at Honfleur. The police had ordered them to remain on the boat, when they should have put them in a detention centre. The ship owner issued an application to the civil courts on the basis that they had a right of action due to a serious illegal act by the administration that violated rights of freedom of the person. The civil judge then ordered the administration to allow the two men to disembark. However, the Prefect did not agree with this decision and applied to the Jurisdiction Disputes Court for an order that the civil courts did not have jurisdiction in the case. The Jurisdiction Disputes Court ruled in favour of the Prefect, which meant that there would be a long wait before the administrative court ruled on the matter. This left the Moroccans in an awkward situation, especially when in an earlier case stowaways on a ship called *The McRuby* had been thrown into the sea by its crew.

To avoid such difficulties in the future, interlocutory procedures have been the subject of a major reform introduced by the Act of 30 June 2000, which sought to make sure that French administrative law conformed with the European Convention on Human Rights. The legislation was carefully prepared by a working party of the *Conseil d'Etat* presided over by the president of the litigation division, M. Labetoulle. The Act does not seek to abolish the executory character of administrative decisions, but instead seeks to strengthen the possibility of suspending the impact of such a decision until a case has been decided by the administrative courts. This Act created two new interlocutory procedures: the interlocutory injunction (*le référé-suspension*) and the interlocutory application to safeguard a fundamental freedom (*le référé-liberté*). These two new procedures replace temporary orders to suspend execution, which had been very restrictively applied by the courts and so were only of limited practical use. It is expected that the two new procedures will be more widely available. Alongside these two new procedures, Parliament has left in place the old emergency measures which will continue to be available where appropriate (L.521-3 and R.531-3 CJA). The cases are heard by an interlocutory judge (*le juge des référés*) who usually sits alone. All parties must be able to put their case, though the hearing can either be oral or on paper. The government commissioner does not provide his or her opinion on the case at this stage. Each of these interlocutory procedures will be considered in turn.

The interlocutory injunction

The legislative provisions for interlocutory injunctions (*le référé-suspension*) can be found in article L.521-I CJA. This provides that an administrative decision, including a rejection, which is the subject of litigation, can be suspended when this is justified by an urgent situation and where there is serious doubt as to the legality of the decision. In the past a rejection could not be suspended. The requirement of an urgent situation is intended to be wider than the old requirement that the consequences of executing the decision would be difficult to repair. Under the old case law, a claim for damages could not give rise to a suspension because money could be paid at any stage, whereas now such a claim could satisfy the requirements for an injunction. In one of the first cases on the point, the *Conseil d'Etat* ruled that 'the condition of emergency to which is subordinated the issuing of a measure of suspension must be regarded as satisfied when the contested administrative decision prejudices in a sufficiently serious and immediate way a public interest, the situation of the applicant or the interests which he is seeking to defend' (CE, S., 19 January 2001).

Whilst previously an administrative decision was only suspended if it was almost certain to be rendered void by the final court hearing, now a judge will be able to order a suspension as a precautionary measure.

Interlocutory application to safeguard a fundamental freedom

Article L.521-2 CJA provides that in urgent situations an interlocutory judge can order any measures necessary to safeguard a fundamental freedom which is illegally threatened. A judgment on the matter has to be handed down within 48 hours. This application can be made even before proceedings have been commenced. 'Fundamental freedoms' is a wide concept, as most freedoms are fundamental. Such freedoms include freedom of movement (C.E. 9 January 2001, *Deperthes*), the right to request refugee status (C.E, 2 May 2001, *Ministry of the Interior v Dziri*) and the right to vote (C.E. 7 February 2001, *Cne de Pointe-à-Pitre*). However, the right to practise a sport is not a fundamental freedom (C.E. 22 October 2001, *Caillat and others*).

The emergency report

The emergency report (*le constat d'urgence*) is a well-established practice, having been given legislative recognition back in 1889. Under this procedure, a judge designates an expert to ascertain the facts of a case without delay, and before the main investigation has even commenced, where there is a risk that the evidence may disappear. The expert is only concerned with the facts of the case and not with the law. In order to obtain such an order, the applicant must show the urgent need for such an expert in the circumstances; this might be because the site is on the point of being transformed by the commencement of some building works. Few formalities need be followed in order to obtain such an order; there is no requirement for any preliminary administrative decision, nor do any lawyers need to be present. It can be made *ex parte* if the judge so chooses and, where this is the case, the defendant has no right of appeal. This power can prove particularly useful in the context of public works. In a 1985 case, a report was ordered into the obstruction of a postal sorting office affected by a strike involving a sit-in: C.E. 9 January 1985, *Min. chargé des PTT. v Société Manufacture du Val de Vienne*.

The interlocutory investigation

The interlocutory investigation (*le référé-instruction*) enables a judge to order the appointment of an expert to undertake certain investigatory procedures to clarify the facts of a case. There is no requirement for there to be an emergency; it must simply be shown that the investigation would be useful. A decree of 29 May 1997 states that when public works are being carried out, the President of a court can order an expert to advise on the state of the buildings likely to be damaged by the development.

The interim payment

A creditor can seek payment of a sum of money before a final award has been made. This order, known as *le référé provision*, will only be made if the creditor has at the same time commenced legal proceedings for the money and it is clear the debtor has no serious defence. This was an important innovation, and went some way to remedying the problems that arise from the delays in hearing administrative cases.

The preservation order

Through a preservation order (*le référé conservatoire*) the judge can order any measures necessary to preserve a situation in the general interest before the trial judge hears the case. In this context, the judge can, for example, issue injunctions against private individuals to carry out work to prevent the collapse of a building. The judge can also order public bodies to send a document to a private individual.

The pre-contractual application

Any person having an interest in the conclusion of a contract who has been wrongly excluded from the contractual arrangements, can refer the matter to the interlocutory judge. This application is known as *le référé précontractuel* and it is not available once the contract has been made if this occurs before the proceedings are commenced.

▶ The investigation

On receipt of an application, an investigation into the case is normally undertaken to prepare the case for trial, though exceptionally an investigation can be dispensed with where it is clear that the case is going to be rejected. To this end a reporting judge is allocated to the case by the President of the court, or in relation to the *Conseil d'Etat*, the President of the division. A copy of the application is sent to the other party who in turn submits their defence. Where the application is a *recours pour excès de pouvoir* seeking to annul a decree, it is also sent to the Prime Minister, who may draw it to the attention of the Cabinet. The reporting judge fixes time limits for both parties to exchange more detailed pleadings presenting their case in full. In fixing these dates the judge aims to achieve a balance between the interests of justice and efficiency.

While it is up to the parties to provide the proof to support their claims, the judge has the power to order certain investigations so that all the necessary information is available to reach a just decision. Thus the parties can be ordered to provide particular documents or to explain certain matters, places of interest can be visited by the judge, witnesses can be questioned and experts consulted.

The reporting judge then prepares a written report ready for the hearing of the case, outlining the arguments of the parties, the legal issues and the relevant law applicable. The investigation is terminated by an official order to this effect granted by the President of the court that is going to hear the case. The end of the investigation is communicated by registered post at least two weeks before the termination is to take effect, and is not open to appeal. In practice, delivery of the notification often leads to the late submission of documents. If no such order of termination is made, the investigation automatically comes to an end when the government commissioner stands up to make his or her representations at the main hearing.

▶ The trial

Where there is to be a hearing, the parties are informed, usually by registered post, at least seven days in advance (four days for the *Conseil d'Etat*) and reduced to two days if there is an emergency. Cases are normally heard by several judges, but certain minor matters can be tried by a single judge. The hearing is usually held in public (L.6 CJA). In the past, professional disciplinary bodies tended to hold their hearings in private but, in the light of rulings from the European Court of Human Rights, this is no longer the case (C.E. Ass. 14 February 1996, *Maubleu*).

At the trial, the reporting judge reads out his or her report, which gives an objective summary of the case. The parties or their lawyers can make oral representations to emphasise certain issues, but the oral representations must only raise matters mentioned in the written statements of their case. Only the lawyers and not the parties can make representations before the *Conseil d'Etat*. In practice, administrative courts never summon ordinary witnesses and rarely hear expert witnesses.

Finally, the government commissioner presents to the court the legal issues raised by the case, and puts forward a proposed solution. The views thereby expressed must be given with complete independence and impartiality, a point that was emphasised by the *Conseil d'Etat* in its decision of 10 July 1957, *Gervaise*. The views of the government commissioner are highly respected and are often followed by the court. Their most important submissions are published and can be helpful to understand the court's judgment.

At the end of the hearing the judges usually withdraw to consider their verdict (article L.8 CJA), accompanied by the government commissioner. This is highly anomalous, as government commissioners are not judges and while their presence is merely on an advisory basis, it can be compared with the role of the clerk to the magistrates' court in England and Wales, where the clerk is strictly forbidden from taking part in the magistrates' decision. The role of the government commissioner was considered in a very important decision of the European Court of Human Rights on 7 June 2001, *Kress v France*. The European Court held that the fact that the parties did not see the government commissioner's report in advance and had no opportunity to respond to it did not breach the principle of impartiality contained in Article 6 of the Convention. However, it held that the commissioner's presence in the subsequent deliberations of the judges did breach the Convention as the parties might have the impression that the commissioner influenced the deliberations. Following this decision, the *Conseil d'Etat* made it known that from now on the commissioner would no longer be allowed to speak during these deliberations. In the administrative courts, consideration of the verdict takes place strictly in private and the discussion is kept secret. The judgment is then read out at a later hearing (usually two weeks after the original hearing). The judges provide reasons for their decision (article L.9 CJA). No mention is made of whether it was a majority verdict, or of any dissenting judgment.

▶ The decision of the court

If the application is successful, the judge will normally order that the administrative decision be nullified and/or the payment of damages. The people who need to be informed of the decision of the court are listed at the end of the judgment. Notification to the parties of the court's verdict renders it enforceable and failure to execute the judgment within a reasonable time is itself a civil wrong.

Administrative judges have traditionally refused to order any injunctions against the administration. The justification that has tended to be given by the *Conseil d'Etat* for this is the principle of the separation of powers, on the basis that in ordering an injunction a court would in effect be stepping into the role of the administrator. Many academics consider this argument to be artificial and the refusal to order injunctions has been the subject of considerable criticism over the years. It has been suggested that the real reason for this self-imposed limitation on the court's powers is an ill-placed deference to the administration and a fear of confronting the administration head-on in case of failure. Such caution is seen as undermining the role of the administrative judge, which is all the more unfortunate as it sometimes weakens the control exercised by the courts and prevents their decisions from having any real impact. In such situations the administrative courts are failing to protect the rights of private individuals. By contrast, the civil court judges do not hesitate to order injunctions where appropriate.

The legislature, in an effort to strengthen the authority of the administrative courts, passed the Act of 8 February 1995. This provides that the trial judge can, when ordering a decision to be annulled, specify the measures that must be taken in order to give effect to this annulment (article L.911-1-2 onwards CJA). For example, where an employee has been wrongly dismissed, it can specify not only that he or she must be re-appointed but that an employee who was promoted in his or her place must be demoted. The administrative court can now, therefore, order an injunction as an accessory and in support of its main order, but does not have the power to order an injunction as its principal remedy. While this reform is important in theory, in practice its impact has been limited since, as a general rule, the administrative courts have only made limited use of this power.

▶ Execution of the judgment

While a judgment of the court is immediately enforceable, there are unfortunately no means of forcing the administration to carry out a judgment made against it, and the administration has occasionally shown a marked reluctance to bring a judgment into effect. This is particularly the case where the judgment orders an administrative decision to be annulled and the administration refuses to put the situation back to what it would have been if the decision had never been made. Where this occurs, the applicant can only go back to the judge and seek damages for the harm caused by the administration's failure to execute the original judgment. The administration is usually willing to pay damages, but succeeds thereby in buying its way out of applying the judgment.

The legislature has felt forced to intervene on several occasions to reduce this problem where there was a risk it would compromise the efficiency of the judicial system. Following a reform of 1963, if a decision of the *Conseil d'Etat* has not been executed after three months, the applicant can draw this to the attention of the Report and Research Division of the court. Its President can appoint a member of the *Conseil d'Etat* to study the case, along with a member of the relevant section of the administration and a reporting judge. This still does not give the *Conseil d'Etat* the power to force the administration to carry out the judgment, but it means that the applicant is not without further recourse and the *Conseil d'Etat* can exert its moral influence over the administration, reinforced by the fact that a failure to implement can be mentioned in the *Conseil d'Etat*'s annual report. These powers were extended to the administrative courts in 1969. Under a decree of 15 May 1990, the President of the Report and Research Division of the *Conseil d'Etat* can delegate the power to seek the execution of the judgment to the administrative court of appeal within whose jurisdiction the judgment was given, as this court will be geographically closer to the relevant section of the administration.

An Act of 16 July 1980 was an important step towards effective enforcement of administrative court judgments. It introduced several important innovations. First, when a judgment orders a public body to pay damages, this sum must be paid within four months. If payment has not been received by this date, the creditor can proceed to obtain payment directly. Secondly, the 1980 Act gave the *Conseil d'Etat* the power to order penalty fines to be paid for each day that the judgment is not carried out, which may be imposed against public institutions failing to enforce a judgment of an administrative court. The Act of 8 February 1995 extended this power to administrative courts and administrative courts of appeal, specifying that the judges could lay down the measures that needed to be taken within a fixed time limit to carry out the judgment, and where appropriate attach to the injunction a penalty fine. This order can be sought when six months have passed from the pronouncement of the judgment, or in an emergency, immediately. It is a temporary measure and, if it does not induce performance, will be ended by ordering the payment of a fixed sum, separate from any award of damages. In practice, such orders remain rare: it took five years before the first order was made under this Act and of the 800 applications made between 1981 and 1992 only five were successful. There has been some improvement in recent years.

To impose a certain level of personal liability on the individual administrator who is failing to fulfil his administrative duties, he or she can be fined up to a year's salary by the Budget and Finance Disciplinary Court.

▶ Rights of appeal

Where there is a right of appeal, this can be made by any party to the action within two months from receipt of notification of the judgment. The time limit is reduced to two weeks where an order has been made to suspend execution, or where emergency procedures have been followed. Unlike the rules for civil procedure, the fact that an appeal has been submitted does not suspend the judgment, though there are limited exceptions to this principle. There are two main types of appeal available, appeals on the facts and the law (*un appel*), and appeals on points of law only (*un pourvoi en cassation*).

Appeals on the facts and the law

Most appeals on both the facts and the law are now heard by the administrative courts of appeal, though the *Conseil d'Etat* has reserved a limited jurisdiction in this domain. Not all first instance cases can be subject to such an appeal, for example where the case was heard by the *Conseil d'Etat* itself. The appeal judge has the same powers when hearing the case as the first instance judge.

Appeals on points of law only

Appeals on points of law are heard by the *Conseil d'Etat* where the parties must be represented by a lawyer, known as an *avocat aux Conseils*. A preliminary admissions procedure was introduced by the Act of 31 December 1987. An appeal committee (*Commission d'admission des pourvois en cassation*, CAPC) was also created by the Act of 31 December 1987, providing an initial filter of cases. No equivalent body exists for the *Cour de cassation* in the civil and criminal justice system. There is currently a 12-month waiting period before this hearing takes place. Three judges hear the application and decide, after a public hearing during which lawyers can make representations on behalf of their clients, whether to allow the case to proceed. The application will be rejected if the case is inadmissible or there are no serious grounds for the appeal. The filter is highly effective, with only two cases in every five being allowed to proceed to a full hearing. The refusal to admit such appeals is particularly marked for litigation relating to applications for refugee status, where 95% of applications were rejected at this stage between 1989 and 1996, mainly on the ground that the applicant's case had not been presented by a lawyer.

If, at the full hearing, the judges find that there has been an error of law, the decision is quashed and is usually sent back to another court to consider the facts and law of the case.

▶ Delay

Delay has been a major problem before the administrative courts due to the rapid increase in administrative litigation. The problem has been exacerbated in recent years by legislation encouraging a more open government (Act of 17 July 1978) and the legislative requirement that reasons be given for an unfavourable decision by the administration (Act of 11 July 1979). The delays within the administrative judicial system have been sanctioned by the European Court of Human Rights. In one case, it ruled that a four-year delay for an administrative trial at first instance was excessive and breached article 6(1) of the Convention since the case was not complex. This ruling was made despite the fact that the claimant's own lawyer was partly to blame for the delay. On the other hand, three years for an appeal to be heard was held not to be in breach of the Convention (see C.E.D.H. 24 October 1989, *H v France*). The length of delay that will be acceptable will depend on the facts of the case. France was condemned by the Strasbourg Court for a delay of 19 months where the claimant was a haemophiliac who had been contaminated by the AIDS virus. The specific circumstances of the case, particularly his terminal illness and reduced life expectancy, rendered this shorter delay period unacceptable (C.E.D.H. 31 March 1992, *X v France*).

Various legislative reforms have attempted to tackle the problem of delay, and some progress has been made. In 1987 the administrative courts of appeal were created to reduce the number of cases being referred up to the *Conseil d'Etat*. The Act of 6 January 1995, laying down a five-year plan to be applied from 1995–99, sought to limit the average wait for a hearing before an administrative court to one year, by recruiting 75 additional judges and 200 court officers and by creating two new administrative courts and two new administrative courts of appeal. These reforms have had some success.

The *Conseil d'Etat* also succeeds in hearing urgent cases with considerable speed. For example, the actions against the decrees dated 12 August 1992 organising the referendum on the Maastricht Treaty to be held on 20 September were heard by the court on 10 September. Equally, the application by Greenpeace against the announcement of the French President to carry out nuclear tests was heard within two months.

BIBLIOGRAPHY FOR CHAPTER 11

Brown, L. N. and Bell, J. (1998), *French Administrative Law*, Oxford: Oxford University Press

Chapus, R. (2004), *Droit du contentieux administratif*, Paris: Montchrestien

Code de justice administrative (2004), Paris: Litcc

Maurin, A. (2001), *Droit administratif*, Paris: Sirey

12

The legal profession

PART I: JUDGES AND THE *MINISTÈRE PUBLIC*

▶ Introduction

This chapter looks at both the judiciary in the civil and criminal court system and judges in the administrative system. In the civil and criminal system, each court has at its disposal, in addition to the ordinary judges who decide cases, a number of civil servants known as *magistrats du parquet* and collectively as the *ministère public*. Their function is, for civil cases, similar to that of advocates general in the European Court of Justice and, for criminal cases, to that of the Crown Prosecution Service in England and Wales. They receive the same training as judges and are considered to form part of the same profession. People can switch from practising as a member of the *ministère public* to sitting as a judge on the bench deciding cases.

▶ Ordinary judges in the civil and criminal courts

The judicial hierarchy

In France, judges are regarded as civil servants providing a service to the public. Appointments to judicial office are made by the President of the Republic, on a proposal of the Minister of Justice (*ordonnance* of 22 December 1958). This recommendation is in practice made by an independent body known as the *Conseil supérieur de la magistrature* (CSM). The composition of this body is regulated by article 65 of the Constitution. It consists of the President of the Republic, who is its President, the Minister of Justice, who is its Vice President, five judges of the civil justice system and five judges of the criminal justice system, one judge of the administrative system, one member of the *ministère public*, and three independent members, who may not be either Members of Parliament or judges and are nominated by the President of the Republic, the President of the National Assembly and the President of the Senate. Thus it consists of 12 judges and a small minority who are not judges.

The most senior appointments, namely to the posts of judge of the *Cour de cassation*, First President of the courts of appeal and Presidents of the *Tribunaux de Grande Instance* (TGI), are chosen by the CSM. The CSM forwards their nomination to the Minister of Justice and the President of the Republic, who will normally appoint that person. Other senior appointments, such as judges to the courts of appeal, are made on the advice of the CSM, which again is customarily followed by the Minister of Justice and the President. More junior appointments are recommended by a separate commission which proposes names to the CSM, to be formally appointed by the Minister of Justice and the President of the Republic. The most junior judges are trainee judges on posting during their studies at the *Ecole nationale de la magistrature*.

Termination of appointment and disciplinary action

Article 64 of the 1958 Constitution provides that judges enjoy security of tenure (*inamovibles*). This means that judges cannot be removed or assigned to another position, even to be promoted, without their consent. The *ordonnance* of 22 December 1958, as amended by the constitutional statute of 25 June 2001, includes a number of exceptions to this principle, such as the limitation to seven years' service as a First President or public prosecutor in the same court of appeal or to ten years for a *juge d'instruction* or a *juge aux affaires familiales* in the same TGI.

Any decision to dismiss a judge is taken by the CSM, sitting as a court and presided over by the President of the *Cour de cassation*. The President of the Republic and the Minister of Justice do not take part in the decisions made in these circumstances, to emphasise that dismissal does not take place on political grounds. The same body may also consider cases where the judgment may include less serious consequences, such as a reprimand or demotion to a less important post. Even though article 57 of the *ordonnance* of 22 December 1958 states that there is no right of appeal from its decisions, the *Conseil d'Etat* decided on several occasions that a right to appeal could be granted as the CSM could be viewed as an administrative court.

Judges cannot be required to take premature retirement, but may be removed on grounds of infirmity. They may also choose to resign.

The question of miscarriages of justice made the headlines in the French media at the end of 2005. The conduct of the judiciary in the recent scandal known as *l'affaire d'Outreau* led to the prosecution of 13 innocent people for paedophile offences. The *Cour d'assises d'appel* pronounced their acquittal on 1 December 2005. The investigating judge, in particular, was criticised for having pressurised defendants into confessions and having ignored parts of the evidence. This has caused a debate in France regarding the apparent lack of accountability of the judges who had held these innocent individuals in custody for two years without trial. See this book's website for further information on the subject.

Independence of the judiciary

It is a fundamental principle of the Constitution that judicial power should be exercised by a judiciary independent of the bodies exercising legislative and executive power, namely Parliament and the government. The 1958 Constitution specifically states in article 64 that this independence is guaranteed by the President of the Republic. However, to achieve independence it is essential that appointments are made by an independent body. To achieve this goal the composition of the CSM was reformed in 1993 to include a larger number of judges, but there is still a significant political membership and further reforms may be introduced in the future. To increase the independence of judges further, they may never be obliged to accept a new post, even one involving promotion.

In addition, to ensure that judges are seen to be independent, the *ordonnance* of 22 December 1958 bars them from practising another profession or carrying on business. Only a limited number of occupations are permitted, such as university teaching (with permission) or carrying out artistic activities. They are also forbidden to express political opinions in public. There are, however, many judges whose political opinions are well known, and this does indeed lead the public (rightly or wrongly) to consider that their decisions are influenced by their political views. They can, in particular, legitimately express their views as members of unions protecting judges' interests.

In June 2005, the French Home Secretary, Nicolas Sarkozy, expressed his outrage when he found out that the suspected murderer of a woman called Nelly Cremel was a convicted murderer, Patrick Gateau sentenced for life, who had been released on licence after 13 years in prison. He declared that the judge who had taken the fateful decision would have to pay for his mistake of having released somebody who still represented a danger to society. Judges currently escape any liability in case of error in their decision-making. M. Sarkozy was subsequently criticised for these remarks by the judges' trade unions, who were keen to remind the minister that the judiciary should remain independent and not subject to the influence of the executive. The President of the Republic, guarantor of the judiciary's independence according to the Constitution (see Chapter 2), declared a few days later that the separation of powers and the judiciary's independence were essential principles and that he would not allow anything to put that into question. Though judges do not have the right to strike, they can express their discontent through other forms of protest, such as street demonstrations. In January and March 2001, large demonstrations took place in protest, some judges symbolically throwing their Criminal codes in front of the Ministry of Justice complaining about the lack of funding and support. Their main concern at the time was the introduction of an Act of 15 June 2000 on the presumption of innocence (see chapter 10) which, they claimed, would increase their workload even more when judges frequently already dealt with 100 to 150 cases at any one time.

Impartiality of judges

It is important that the judges are both impartial and seen to be impartial in order to keep the public's trust in the legal system. For instance, judges are unable to hear cases in which they have a personal link. An important obligation imposed on a judge, in and out of the court, is to behave in a dignified and loyal manner. A number of cases have arisen, in the past few years, when judges have behaved in an unacceptable way while wearing the robe. A family court judge in Papeete (Tahiti) was disciplined when he developed a habit of seducing the mothers of the children placed in his care. Since 2002, the Court Presidents are entitled to refer to the CSM directly if disciplinary sanctions have to be imposed on judges.

▶ The *ministère public*

In Chapter 10 the role of the public prosecutor's office was discussed, together with the proposed reforms in relation to the profession of public prosecutor in the context of criminal litigation. In France the public prosecutor's office is part of a wider body of civil servants that also has a role to play in civil cases. It is known as the *ministère public* or the *magistrature du parquet*. In criminal cases, public prosecutors are parties to the cases. In civil matters, members of the *ministère public* are not usually parties to the litigation, but in important cases they make representations to the court on behalf of the public. Their aim is to ensure thereby that in reaching its decisions the court has the benefit of independent expertise, though it is not bound to follow their advice.

Hierarchy of the *ministère public*

Appointments to the *ministère public* are made, as for members of the judiciary, by the President of the Republic, on a proposal by the Minister of Justice. The CSM, which for this purpose is composed of the President of the Republic, the Minister of Justice, five members of the *ministère public*, one judge of the civil and criminal justice system, and three independent members, also plays a part. However, its recommendations are not considered as authoritative as those for appointments to the bench. It would be more accurate to describe its role as merely consultative. The most important members of the *ministère public* are appointed by the government, and the CSM is not even consulted (article 65 paragraph 7 of the 1958 Constitution).

The services of members of the *ministère public* are available to all courts in the civil and criminal system. Members posted to the *tribunal de grande instance* (TGI) are known as *procureurs de la République*. Those operating in the courts of appeal and the *Cour de cassation* have the title of *procureur général* or *avocat général*, according to rank. None are allocated to the specialised courts but members may be lent, when required, by the local TGI.

Termination of appointment and disciplinary action

Members of the *ministère public*, unlike the ordinary judiciary, do not benefit from security of tenure. However, before being removed from office they are entitled to a hearing, and the CSM, headed by the public prosecutor of the *Cour de cassation*, is required to give its advice on the matter (article 65 paragraph 8 of the 1958 Constitution). The final decision is pronounced by the Minister of Justice who will listen to, but need not follow, the CSM's advice.

Independence of the *ministère public*

The independence of the public prosecutor's office in criminal cases is the subject of much discussion (see pp. 201–206 above). This is not such an issue in civil cases where the role of the *ministère public* is, in effect, advisory only.

Judges in the administrative courts

There is no *ministère public* as such in the administrative courts. The judges are civil servants who are employed by the Home Office rather than the Ministry of Justice. They have a reputation for acting independently, despite the fact that they are not directly protected by the 1958 Constitution. In a landmark decision of 22 July 1980 the *Conseil constitutionnel* declared that the independence of administrative judges was a fundamental principle of the Republic. Since then, Acts of 6 January 1986 and 31 December 1987 have confirmed that judges of Administrative Courts and Administrative Courts of Appeal enjoy security of tenure. Rather surprisingly, the most important administrative judges, the judges of the *Conseil d'Etat*, cannot rely on any statutory protection. According to French academics, the main reason for this is that the members of the *Conseil d'Etat* act as governmental advisors in addition to their judicial role. They also have the benefit of a number of different laws regulating their profession, which differ according to the court and position of the judge.

An Act of 9 September 2002 created assistants to the administrative judges (articles L.227-1 onwards and R.227-1 onwards of the Code of Administrative Justice). Their role is to provide assistance, including legal research, to the administrative judges. There are currently 200 of these assistants. The qualifications required are four years' successful completion of university level studies in law. Appointments are made to this position on two-year contracts for part-time employment.

▶ Magistrats de liaison

The desire to improve international judicial cooperation led France to set up in 1993 a scheme for the posting or exchange of magistrates (liaison magistrates) with a number of other States, on the basis of bilateral or multilateral arrangements. The arrangement aims to facilitate the understanding of other legal systems and increase the speed of judicial cooperation.

PART II: AVOCATS

The *avocats* are the oldest legal profession in France, with origins dating back to Roman times. They are independent and have the privilege of self-regulation by their local *Barreau*, which fulfils a similar function to the English and Welsh Bar, and will for convenience be translated in this text as the 'Bar'. The closest English and Welsh equivalent to *avocats* are barristers. The best have, in common with their English and Welsh counterparts, a public image of performing feats of brilliant oratory in court. French *avocats* did indeed, for the years preceding the latest reforms in 1971 and 1990, concentrate largely on pleading at court hearings. They had ceased, since the fifteenth century, to deal with the drafting of pleadings and other written parts of legal procedure and in practice did not give much legal advice which was unconnected with litigation. Others had taken on this discarded work. Those responsible for drafting pleadings and the written part of procedures had developed into the independent profession of *avoués*, and those specialising in giving legal advice were subsumed separately into the profession of *conseils juridiques* (which will be referred to as 'legal advisers'). The Act of 31 December 1971, in effect, merged the professions of *avoués* and that of *avocats* (with the exception of *avoués* at the Court of Appeal which form a separate profession we will look at later). The Act of 31 December 1990 merged the profession of legal adviser with that of *avocat*. There are currently more than 44,000 *avocats* in France.

The current role of *avocats* and the organisation of their profession is set out below.

> ## Role of the *avocat*

The *avocat* has four main roles: acting as an advocate at pre-trial and trial court hearings (known as *assistance*), drafting written submissions on behalf of the client (known as *représentation*), giving legal advice and drafting documents.

Advocacy

Acting as an advocate before the courts is the traditional role of the *avocat*. A great deal of work is done by the judge during the pre-trial phase, including interviewing witnesses, the suspect and, if necessary, experts. The *avocats* are present at these proceedings where they involve their client and make oral representations on their behalf where necessary. They have a monopoly on the right to make oral pleading in the ordinary courts in criminal cases except where the parties are allowed to plead for themselves. *Avocats* have rights of audience throughout the country, though they are not allowed to act before the two highest courts in the land, the *Cour de cassation* and the *Conseil d'Etat*. A specialist body of senior *avocats*, known as *avocats aux conseils*, carries out that function (see p. 249).

Drafting court documents

The *avocat* drafts pleadings and other written papers required during the pre-hearing stage of proceedings. Since the reform of 1971, they carry out this role for litigation before all courts except the courts of appeal, the *Cour de cassation* and the *Conseil d'Etat*, which have specialist lawyers (*avoués*) to fulfil this function. They can only draft pleadings for litigation in their own regional Bar, and for all other litigation they must instruct an *avocat* from the relevant regional Bar. Thus, while judges will accept oral representations made by a lawyer they do not know, they insist on all written documentation being made by a member of their own Bar, who will be familiar with the requirements of the particular court. *Avocats* have an implied mandate to act as agents for their client, and it is not necessary for them to be expressly granted this status.

Legal advice

*Avocat*s have no monopoly on giving legal advice, and other legal professionals, such as *notaires* and people with no professional qualification other than a law degree, also give advice in a number of circumstances. *Avocats* traditionally only gave advice to clients connected to litigation, but since the 1990 merger with the profession of legal adviser, they give advice on many matters, such as tax and company law.

Non-litigious drafting

Avocats also now draft documents other than pleadings and documents required in the course of litigation. Again, they have no monopoly of such functions but could, for instance, be instructed to draft a commercial contract, an employment contract, the constitution of a company, or a document effecting the transfer of a patent.

▶ Organisation of the profession

Avocats belong to the Bar (*Barreau*) attached to their local TGI. Each Bar is administered by its own council, elected by its *avocats* (decree of 27 November 1991). Members sit for a period of three years, and a third of the members stand for election every year. The President of the Bar Council, known as the *bâtonnier*, is elected by senior *avocats* for a term of two years (Act of 31 December 1971).

The Bar Council (*Conseil de l'ordre*) exercises a number of functions of which the most important are the calling of new *avocats* to the Bar, and ensuring efficient self-regulation of the Bar. Following a decree of 25 May 2005, new regional disciplinary bodies were established, *les Conseils de discipline*. Responsibility for discipline had formerly been carried out by the Bar Council. However, this arrangement was potentially in breach of the right to a fair trial under article 6 of the European Convention on Human Rights, as the Bar Council was not a sufficiently impartial judge in such cases. The Paris Bar Council was allowed to retain its disciplinary function.

Avocats may appeal to the court of appeal against decisions made by the Bar Council. In a recent example, the Bar Council of Bergerac held that an *avocate* had been in breach of her oath to exercise her profession with dignity by having played music in the streets of villages of the South of France during her weekends and holidays. Leaving a violin case open for people to put coins in, while playing, amounted to begging and was incompatible with an *avocat*'s obligation to behave with dignity at all times so as not to damage the profession's reputation. On appeal, the Bordeaux court of appeal on 3 June 2003 overturned the decision of the Bar Council as it held that an artistic activity by itself could not be contrary to the obligation to behave with dignity, and that the few coins donated by passers-by in order to show their appreciation could not amount to begging. Furthermore, the court of appeal considered that no damage to the profession was established as the *avocate* did not wear any sign which would indicate her profession to the public.

Since 31 December 1990, individual *avocats* and their local Bars are also represented by a National Bar Council. This is composed of a number of *avocats* elected according to complex rules which are designed to ensure both individual representation and representation of the interests of the various regional Bars.

▶ EU recognition

The past few years have seen a continuing expansion of British city law firms with offices in France, mostly in Paris, with the number of British lawyers working in France increasing as a result. Seen as pure business machines by their French counterparts, their popularity has not been enhanced by the opportunistic and aggressive headhunting of many top French commercial lawyers. In order to practise in French courts on a regular basis, a British lawyer has to join a French Bar. Until recently, a European Directive of 21 December 1988 allowed lawyers from the European Union to practise in another Member State subject to their passing an aptitude exam or gaining additional work experience in the relevant country. A Directive of 16 February 1998 simplified the procedure by allowing an already practising lawyer who is a member of a Bar in a Member State, to join the Bar of another Member State in order to practise there permanently. The Directive removes the requirement to sit an aptitude exam or gain further work experience. It was brought into force in France in 2004, three years later than Europe intended.

▶ The *avocat* profession in turmoil

Through a range of different forms of protest in 2005 (demonstrations, strikes, refusal to plead), *avocats* expressed their anger at seeing two of their colleagues remanded in custody for, apparently, merely doing their job of defending their clients. The *avocate* Catherine Maizière was charged for having divulged elements of an ongoing criminal investigation to third parties, in breach of an Act of 2 March 2004 (commonly known as the *Perben 2* Act, see chapter 10) incorporated into the Criminal Code under article 434-7-2. Catherine Maizière was defending a client accused of rape. The client claimed he was innocent on the basis that he had been ill on the day of the rape and had been to see his GP. She telephoned her client's family asking them to come up with evidence of his visit to the doctor. The police overheard the conversation, having tapped the family's telephone, and the *avocate* was charged by the investigating judge. Another *avocate*, France Moulin, was remanded in custody for 23 days on the same charges. The *avocats* demanded that this provision be amended as it prevented them from properly defending their clients. Seven eminent criminal lawyers wrote a letter to the Minister of Justice asking to be charged just like their two colleagues, explaining that every day they breached article 434-7-2 of the Criminal Code. They highlighted that the mere fact of telling a client's family the reason why a person might be detained in custody would be in contravention of the above-mentioned legislation. Future developments in this subject will be included on this book's website.

• •

PART III: *OFFICIERS MINISTÉRIELS*

Important legal functions are carried out by *notaires, avoués, avocats aux conseils,* and *huissiers* who are all officers of the court (*officiers ministériels*). This title refers to legal professionals who are formally appointed by the Minister of Justice after they have acquired a practice. A practice is usually acquired either by purchasing it from an existing practitioner, or by receiving it under a legacy or a gift. Occasionally the Ministry of Justice will open new practices for which qualified entrants may compete. These will usually be in the suburbs of large towns or other areas where existing practitioners do not meet the legal needs of the local population. Most commonly the new professional acquires the practice of a person who is retiring and proposes the new applicant to the Ministry of Justice. The Minister will then usually grant a certificate of practice to the person proposed by the retiring professional and accept the contract made between the parties for the sale of the existing practice. Conditions may however be imposed if, for instance, it is considered that the agreed provisions ask the new practitioner for too high a payment.

Once candidates have acquired both a practice and the required certificate, they become officers of the court in their chosen profession. The various professions are governed by professional bodies, which perform similar functions to those of the Bar Council in relation to *avocats*. These include responsibility for the training of new applicants and the self-regulation of the profession by enforcing a disciplinary code. The societies are centralised and hierarchical, unlike the various Bar Councils which are locally based. Furthermore, while the societies may themselves enforce minor sanctions such as a reprimand, more serious sanctions, such as requiring a practitioner to resign, must be imposed by the judgment of a court, after an application to the Minister of Justice.

Notaires

There are currently 8,143 notaires in France. As well as being *officiers ministériels, notaires* are public legal officers (*officiers publics*). As such they are entitled to draw up authenticated and enforceable legal instruments. Officials other than *officiers ministériels* may also be public legal officers, for example mayors who register births, marriages and deaths.

The role of the *notaire*

Notaires have three functions:

• Drawing up authenticated and enforceable documents

This is a role for which there is no equivalent in the English legal system. By tradition many documents, such as sale contracts, are drawn up by *notaires*. In general, there is no legal requirement for such formalities but it is traditional, for instance, for documents involving the transfer of property rights to be executed in this way. The advantage is that there is a presumption that the document is authentic (articles 1317 and 1319 of the Civil Code). It is only possible to challenge this, in the case of suspected fraud, by following a complex procedure, and very few cases are brought. In addition, unlike ordinary legal documents, they can be enforced without the need for a separate judgment confirming that the contract is enforceable. Certain documents are by law required to be drawn up by *notaires*, such as donations (article 931 of the Civil Code), marriage contracts (article 1394 of the Civil Code) and mortgages (article 2127 of the Civil Code). Thus, *notaires* are used at salient points in many people's lives, for example, marriage, property purchase and death, in the latter case to ensure a smooth handling of the succession to the deceased's estate. The original documents are kept at the *notaire*'s office, and parties may only obtain certified copies. These can be endorsed by the *notaire* to allow them to be enforced by the court as if they were originals. While authenticated documents are not generally used in England and Wales, the family solicitor who drafts the documentation at similar stages in a person's life is fulfilling a similar role. In England and Wales, if authenticated documents are required, which will usually be in matters containing an international element, these can be drawn up by a member of the very small profession of notary public.

• Giving legal advice

Notaires give legal advice in connection with the types of transaction mentioned above and other matters such as business and commerce.

• Acting as officers of the court

Notaires are occasionally required by the court to draft documentation in connection with a divorce settlement or the liquidation of a company.

Organisation of the profession

Like other *officiers ministériels*, *notaires* belong to their own professional body. They are also required to take out insurance cover for liability for negligence claims.

Avoués

The law relating to *avoués* is contained in an Act of 2 November 1945 modified by the decrees of 21 December 1990 and 22 May 1998. This profession used to have a monopoly over the drafting of all court pleadings. In 1971, this role in relation to litigation before courts of first instance was passed to the *avocats*, while the separate profession of *avoués* was kept for the court of appeal. No doubt the profession was initially retained at this level as a first step to full abolition, but the *avoués* at the court of appeal, now a very small profession of 437, have proved useful enough to be retained. The main reason for this is the purely practical one that it is convenient for the courts of appeal to be able to rely on a body of lawyers who are well known to them, available at all times, within close proximity of the court and with an expert knowledge of intricate procedural rules. They have accordingly kept their monopoly of this work. The one exception is that parties in cases which do not require such documentation (for example, employment cases) may choose to do the work themselves. The *avoués* have an implied mandate to act as their client's agent in the preparation of all pleadings and it is not necessary for them to be expressly given this status.

Avocats aux conseil

Avocats at the *Conseil d'Etat* and *Cour de cassation*, known as *avocats au conseil*, have the right both to act as an advocate and draft court pleadings for the two highest courts. They are thereby exercising the equivalent role to the *avocats* before the courts of first instance and the *avoué* and *avocat* jointly before the court of appeal. In doing so they enjoy a monopoly, except that in a limited number of cases parties are allowed to represent themselves.

This profession is governed by an Act of 10 September 1817, as amended by the decrees of 28 October 1991 and 20 December 1999, which gives them a unique status. They are *officiers ministériels*, and are required both to purchase a practice and be appointed by the Minister of Justice. The profession is very small, with only 91 members. Most are experienced *avocats*, and in addition they will have passed a special examination and completed a three-year practical course organised by the *avocats* at the *Conseil d'Etat* and *Cour de cassation*. Like the *avocats* and the *avoués*, they have an implied mandate to act as agents for the parties in respect of the particular case and it is not necessary for the parties to appoint them specifically to this status.

Huissiers de justice

Huissiers de justice have a monopoly on serving court documents and on taking measures necessary for the enforcement of judgments, for example by seizing and selling a debtor's goods. As such, they do work which would be done by a bailiff in England and Wales. Others work as court officers, assisting at court hearings and generally ensuring the smooth running of the court. This type of work is similar to that carried out by court ushers in England and Wales. They may also prepare sworn statements to be used in evidence in court, for instance a statement as to defective work carried out by a builder, where the defects are obvious on inspection. They share this work with, for example, experts, but are frequently called on for matters requiring no particular technical expertise. The profession is at present governed by an Act of 2 November 1945. *Huissiers* operate in the jurisdiction of their local TGI, which supervises their work.

Clerks of the court (*greffiers*)

Only the clerks of the commercial courts are *officiers ministériels*; the others are civil servants. Those of the administrative courts have always had this status, but those of the civil and criminal courts were *officiers ministériels* until an Act of 30 November 1965. Existing clerks were compensated for the loss of their practice and continued their work as civil servants.

Chief clerks, assisted by ordinary clerks, are responsible for the administration of the court. Their functions include keeping an accurate transcript of the hearings, arranging for the judgment to be typed, maintaining the court records. No hearing is valid unless a clerk is present. Clerks also exercise a number of other functions: they maintain the commercial and companies register (*registre du commerce et des sociétés*, (RCS)), and draw up a range of formal declarations by private individuals such as a declaration renouncing an inheritance. The chief clerk also has additional administrative functions, including preparing the court's budget. In practice, the clerk's role extended to a number of functions ordinarily expected from a judge. The legislators acknowledged this, when an Act of 8 February 1995 officially transferred a number of functions to the clerks, such as issuing documents certifying a person's nationality. The clerk is often the first court official that the parties meet; in small matters before the *tribunal d'instance* where parties appear in person, the clerk is responsible for ensuring that they complete the correct forms before passing the forms to the judge.

BIBLIOGRAPHY FOR CHAPTER 12

Canivet, G. and Joly-Hurard, J. (2004), *La déontologie des magistrats*, Paris: Dalloz
Crignon, A. (2000), *Les métiers du droit*, Paris: L'Etudiant
Martin, R. (2004), *Déontologie de l'avocat*, Paris: LexisNexis – Litec
Martin, R. (2004), 'Les modifications au statut de l'avocat par la loi No 2004–130 du 11 février 2004', *JCP* 2004, 373

Web resources

Website: www.conseil-superieur-magistrature.fr: The *Conseil supérieur de la magistrature.* Includes some text in English

Website: www.ena.fr: The *Ecole Nationale d'Administration.* Includes some text in English

Website: www.enm.justice.fr: The *Ecole Nationale de la Magistrature*

Website: www.justice.gouv.fr: The Ministry of Justice

Website: www.justice.gouv.fr/metiers/metiers.htm: The legal profession explained by the French Ministry of Justice

Website: www.syndicat-magistrature.org: *Syndicat de la magistrature*

Website: www.conseil-etat.fr/ce/organi/index_or_me01.shtml: Recruitment to the *Conseil d'Etat*

13 Academic and professional legal studies

PART I: ACADEMIC STUDIES

French universities have been awarding law degrees since their creation, and law is a popular subject taken not just by future lawyers, but also by those seeking a good foundation for a career in business or the public sector. A recent study published in the *Figaro* newspaper shows that out of a total of 1 400 000 students, 176 000 will be studying law in 2005–6. The aim accordingly is not just to train lawyers but to provide a general education, and students are required to study general topics such as economics, modern history, accounting, sociology and a foreign language as well as law. While the government still has a substantial say in the syllabus taught, universities are much freer than they were in the past to design their courses. However, there is less variety than in the United Kingdom, and no clear hierarchy between universities, even if some of the Parisian universities like *la Sorbonne* have traditionally had the best reputation, especially internationally. Therefore, students can expect a reasonably similar experience regardless of the university chosen.

Throughout their studies, students attend lectures and seminars. Lectures are delivered in large lecture halls. A thousand students in one lecture hall is not unusual in the first year, with considerably lower numbers in subsequent years owing to the high drop-out and failure rates. Because of recurrent rooming difficulties, some lectures might start at 8.00 a.m. whereas others might end at 9.00 p.m. Photocopies of lectures are often available, but attendance is high even though it is not compulsory. Students have to arrive early to lectures to make sure they get a seat. Seminars, on average two per week, and known as *travaux dirigés (TD)*, are compulsory in the first two years, and marks for work done in them and class participation count for up to 50 per cent of the module mark for the first year.

The remaining marks are usually obtained by taking a variety of assessments, such as written and oral examinations and multiple choice questionnaires. The latter, a novelty in Law, serve mainly as a first-year assessment. During these examinations, students rely heavily on learning off by heart the courses delivered. Universities have different methods of

Table 13.1 Legal Studies before and after the 2002 education reforms

Title before 2002	Total of years studied	Current title
	1	
DEUG	2	
Licence	3	*Licence*
Maîtrise	4	
DEA / DESS	5	*Master*
	6	
	7	
Doctorat	8	*Doctorat*

marking assessments but an average of 10 out of 20 is usually required to achieve a pass. Of the many students who fail, a substantial number choose to retake the year.

The French university system was recently further reformed (Table 13.1). The Government decided to follow recommendations made in a report commissioned by the Ministry for Education in 1997. The report highlighted the problems encountered by the dramatic rise in student numbers, as it had almost doubled since 1980 (from 1.2 million to 2.1). Worryingly, less than a third of university students obtained a two-year qualification called the *diplôme d'études universitaires générales* (DEUG) within a two-year period. Unsurprisingly, the report advocated more tuition in smaller sized groups and proposed the creation of a harmonised European higher education system. The report's proposals were followed up a year later by a common declaration between France, Italy, Germany and the UK to go ahead with the unification idea. In 1999, a meeting in Bologna declared the intention of 29 European governments to increase European integration by introducing a unified higher educational system. A declaration in 2001 in Prague explained that the best way to achieve this would be by introducing a common first cycle of university studies lasting three years, creating a system for recognising foreign degrees, establishing a process of European credit accreditation, promoting student and staff mobility and adding a European dimension to university studies. France was one of the first countries to introduce measures to implement the Bologna and Prague declarations, with a series of ministerial decrees in 2002. A transitional phase will take place, the gradual implementation of measures to be complete in all French universities by 2010.

The study for an undergraduate degree used to be divided into three stages, each leading to a recognised qualification. A diploma of general university studies (DEUG) was awarded for successful completion of the first two years, a *licence* for successful completion of the third year and a *maîtrise* for successful completion of the fourth year. Having obtained their first degree, students could pursue advanced legal studies. Those with an academic bent would study for a diploma of advanced legal studies, a *diplôme d'études approfondies* (DEA). Those with a more practical bent would study for a specialist diploma in legal practice, known as a *diplôme d'études supérieures spécialisées* (DESS), which would include university classes and practical training with a lawyer's firm or in business. The new system aims to simplify the entire process by enabling students to gain an undergraduate degree at the end of the third year of study by delivering a qualification called *une licence* and a postgraduate degree after five years of studies, called *un Master*. Just like the previous division between *DEA* and *DESS*, students will be entitled to choose between a research Master, which will have a more academic bent, and a professional Master, which will include practical experience. The students wishing to remain in academia will go on to study a further three years to write their doctoral thesis. While the structure of the educational system has changed, universities appear intent on continuing to teach the same types of courses.

Reforms introduced in 1997 divided the academic year into two semesters. Students in their first year have to enrol on a foundation programme. This includes classes on study skills (such as the effective use of learning resources, note taking in lectures and group work) and on law and non-law subjects. Students at the end of the first semester may either confirm their choice to enrol for a degree in law or choose related subjects such as economics or management studies. The aim of this initial semester is to cut down on the very high drop-out rate of students. Currently, out of approximately 25 000 students enrolling in the first year in law, half of them will fail and will have to retake the first year. The high failure rate in France is partly due to the large number of students enrolled in the first year of law. It is not uncommon to have in excess of 2000 students enrolled in the first year of a law degree of a university in larger cities (Paris, Lyon, Marseilles, Lille, Toulouse). Unlike in the United Kingdom or the USA, French universities cannot choose their students, or limit the intake, as no selection takes place except for the requirement of having passed the equivalent of A-Levels. Furthermore, the principle of free education signifies that students only have to pay a nominal amount for administrative costs.

During the first two years, apart from the foundation course mentioned above, students study an introduction to subjects equivalent to the English core law subjects: constitutional law, public law, administrative law, criminal law, law based on the Civil Code (including contract, tort, family, succession and property law), and the institutions of the European Union. They also study background and general subjects such as the history of law and of the legal institutions, economics, politics and a foreign language.

In the third year students deepen their study of the subjects based on the Civil Code, administrative law and European law, and also study a number of other subjects including civil liberties, business law, tax law, employment law, public international law, and a foreign language. Students can choose certain combinations of subjects and most will already have decided whether they want to specialise in private or public law. Private law concerns the rights between private individuals, while public law is concerned with the relationship between the State and the individual or the organisation of the State. The choice of whether to go down the public or private law route is important. Public law options, such as social law, are chosen by those considering a career in the public sector; while private law options, such as business law, will be chosen by those wanting to become lawyers in private practice, or to pursue other careers in the private sector.

Students in their fourth year continue to specialise in either private or public law. Those wishing to become practising lawyers will pursue further studies (discussed below). They may indeed do so as soon as they have obtained their Masters, though because of the competition for places, many will obtain one or two higher qualifications before pursuing their professional studies.

PART II: QUALIFYING FOR PRACTICE IN A LEGAL PROFESSION

A student who wants to pursue a career as a lawyer in private practice or in the public sector will need to obtain the appropriate qualifications, after graduation with a law degree. This will usually involve studying on specified courses, passing examinations and complying with practical training requirements. A feature of the French system is that many professional examinations are competitive. Only a set number of students will pass, so that students not only need to reach the required standard, but must usually perform better than fellow students to be chosen, as it is likely that more than the required number will reach that standard.

▶ Avocats

Academic stage

Candidates for the profession of *avocat* are required to have successfully completed four years of university study in law. A small number of degrees with a high judicial content listed in a decree of 7 August 1995 are recognised as equivalent, but the vast majority of candidates will have at least the standard four-year law degree discussed above. Many will also obtain a postgraduate degree. There are special provisions for European Union and foreign lawyers, and for senior French lawyers (see below).

Obtaining professional qualifications

The current provisions are contained in an Act dated 31 December 1971 as amended by an Act of 31 December 1990, and by an Act of 11 February 2004. There are now two stages.

First stage – Entrance Examination

Students must pass the entrance examination for the school which will prepare them for the examination of aptitude for the profession of *avocat* (*certificat d'aptitude à la profession d'avocat*, CAPA). Courses leading to the entrance examination are run by institutes of legal study (*Institut d'études juridiques*, IEJ). Most are attached to universities but there are also a number of private institutes. Candidates with a four-year law degree may study the course at any time, and students often do so concurrently with their final year at university. The examinations are set either by the university or the IEJ. They are academically based, and are partly oral and partly written. Examinations are set in two stages: the first is the written stage (*épreuves d'admissibilité*) and covers assessments on the law of obligations, procedural law and a choice of options including family law, criminal law, commercial law, administrative law, employment law and European law. Candidates must reach an overall average of 10/20 to be allowed to the second stage, the oral examinations (*épreuves d'admission*). These include a series of five different oral assessments, including a foreign language. An average of 10/20 will entitle the candidate to move on to stage two.

Second stage – Study for the CAPA

Students who have passed the entrance examination can now study for the CAPA at one of the centres for professional study (*Centre régional de formation professionnelle des avocats*, CRFPA). These are attached to the courts of appeal and are also responsible for providing continuing professional education after qualification. The courses include skills based on practical study, on the same lines as the English courses preparing for qualification as a barrister or solicitor. This second stage has been the subject of major reforms by the Act of 11 February 2004 and a decree of 21 December 2004. Before, students studied for 12 months, passed the CAPA and were then required to find a lawyer's practice which would take them on as trainees for a set period of two years. Now, students prepare for the CAPA for a period of 18 months and qualify directly as *avocat*.

The study period is divided into three six-month periods. The first six months cover rules of professional conduct and procedure. The exercises include learning to draft pleadings, advocacy skills and the study of a foreign language. For the second six months students are given a more personalised timetable, and study a range of subjects from criminal law to competition law, family law or company law, depending on their career direction. During their final six months, students are required to complete a training period with a French *avocat*. At the end of the 18 months candidates must pass the CAPA, where their ability to carry out various practical exercises is tested. The examination includes a five-hour written assessment in the shape of a client advice and four oral assessments. These include assessments on substantive law, professional conduct and a discussion with the examination panel on a report written about the training period. The examination panel consists of academic law teachers, judges and *avocats*. About 90% of students pass the examination. Once successful, students will directly qualify as *avocats* as the requirement of training first for an additional two years before qualifying has been abolished.

The newly qualified *avocats* must choose the Bar they want to practise in. Following the Act of 11 February 2004, *avocats* are now required to undertake a programme of continuing education. There is approximately one Bar for each appeal court. Their name must be inscribed on the roll of trainees for their chosen Bar. They must be approved by the Council of the local Bar and they must swear to 'carry out their duties with dignity, conscience, independence, probity and humanity' (Act of 31 December 1971).

Other routes to qualification

The Act of 11 February 2004 has fundamentally amended the rules for lawyers from European Union countries. Previously, they had to pass a qualifying lawyers' transfer test, including oral and written examinations in one to four subjects according to the profile of the particular applicant. The 2004 Act, which incorporates into French law a European Directive of 15 February 1998, enables lawyers from the European Union, exercising similar functions in their own countries as *avocats* in France,to practise freely in France if they so request it. They will retain their own title, but are entitled to use the title of *avocat* if they have practised in France on a regular basis for at least three years.

Lawyers from outside the European Union must pass a qualifying lawyers' transfer examination.

There are a number of other exemptions from the standard route described above. These include an exemption from any admission tests to the Centres for Professional Study (*Les centres régionaux de formation professionnelle* (CRFPA)) for law professors at French universities. They are, however, not exempt any more from the training requirements or from the CAPA exams.

▶ *Avoués* at the court of appeal

The current provisions are contained in a decree of 19 December 1945, as amended by a decree of 22 May 1998.

Academic stage

Candidates must have successfully undertaken four years of law studies at University.

Obtaining professional qualifications

Candidates must complete a two-year traineeship, at the end of which they are required to pass a specialised professional examination.

▶ *Notaires*

Academic stage

The requirements are the same as for candidates who want to qualify as *avocats*. They must therefore pass the equivalent of four years' university study.

Obtaining professional qualifications

Candidates may qualify by studying for the specialised postgraduate degree in law for *notaires*, and undertaking a further two-year sandwich course preparing for the Diploma in Notarial Studies. Alternatively, they may choose to complete a one-year course at a regional training centre followed by a two-year training contract with a notary. The postgraduate degree is increasingly becoming the preferred route, as it gives candidates a useful qualification even if they do not decide to become *notaires*. Practising *notaires* have themselves also come to appreciate the course. The non-university course is open to the more practically inclined, and might well be chosen by a candidate who had some expectation of inheriting a relative's practice. Brief details of both routes to qualification are given below.

Academic route
A number of universities prepare students for the postgraduate degree in law for *notaires*. The course is taught by *notaires* and other practising lawyers as well as academic law teachers. It covers the subjects which a *notaire* is likely to practise on qualification, such as civil law, commercial law, property law and tax law. Students are also required to do one

month's practical training in a *notaire*'s office. Examinations are sat on completion of the course.

The successful candidates go on to do a two-year practical course based at one of the regional training centres for the profession, and concurrently complete a two-year training contract with a *notaire*'s practice. The course is divided into four semesters. Students concentrate on contract law in the first semester, property law in the second, insolvency law, the law of succession and administration of estates in the third, and company law and social law in the final semester. Students' work is tested by continuous assessment. At the end of the two-year period they must submit a report on their traineeship or a dissertation. Successful candidates obtain the Diploma in Notarial Studies and can work as an assistant notary at an established practice. They may in due course either buy or inherit a *notaire*'s practice.

Professional route

Students must pass an entrance examination to a course run by a regional centre. The course lasts 12 months and includes practical and theoretical training in the relevant law, as well as rules of professional conduct and management of a *notaire*'s practice. At the end of the course the student sits an examination for the certificate of aptitude for the profession of *notaire*. The student then completes a two-year training contract with a firm of *notaires*, and is not required to take any more courses or examinations.

▶ Huissiers de justice

Academic stage

Candidates must have successfully completed four years of university study in law.

Professional qualifications

The decree of 14 August 1975 specifies that candidates must complete a two-year traineeship, of which at least half is undertaken in the practice of a *huissier*. The candidate also follows professional courses by distance learning. After completing the traineeship, candidates must pass a professional examination.

▶ Court clerks

Academic stage

The head clerk in a court is required to have a law degree. Others only need the school leaving examination, the Baccalaureate, though most will have studied for the first two years of a law degree at university.

Obtaining professional qualifications

The *Code de l'organisation judiciaire* indicates that ordinary clerks (*les greffiers*) need to pass a specialist competitive examination. They then learn through the hands-on experience of a work placement. To become head clerk, candidates must pass a tough competitive examination and then take a year's course at the national school for court clerks at Dijon. This consists of a mixture of courses and practical training at various courts and tribunals.

▶ Civil and criminal court judges and members of the *ministère public*

The general provisions are contained in two *ordonnances* dated 22 December 1958 and 22 December 1970 as amended by an Act of 22 December 1992. As we saw in Chapter 12, judges and members of the *ministère public* are all civil servants. While most people will pursue a career, either as a judge or a member of the *ministère public*, some move laterally from one branch to the other. This is possible partly because, though the work done is very different, most have received a thorough training in the same school, the *Ecole Nationale de la Magistrature* (ENM) in Bordeaux. A small number of members of both branches of the judiciary are also recruited directly from other professions. We will look at this method briefly later on, but will first discuss education at the ENM, which is the way most judges have started their careers.

Academic stage

Candidates for the ENM must usually be under 27 years old and have studied for four years at university, but it need not be in law. In practice, successful candidates are likely to have studied a law degree and many will also have a postgraduate qualification. Candidates may take courses at the local *Institut d'études juridiques* concurrently with their academic studies, in the same way as aspiring *avocats* take the appropriate courses. The entrance examination includes written papers in civil law, public law or criminal law and various oral examinations in such subjects as commercial or administrative law. The successful applicants will go through to the second stage, *l'admission,* which will assess applicants in various oral examinations in such subjects as commercial, administrative law, languages and sports. It is seen as a very selective assessment, with less than 10% of applicants successful (228 out of 2888 in 2003, for instance). Since the late 1980s, the ever-increasing presence of women has become a striking feature of the French judiciary. Successful female applicants in the entrance examination currently outnumber men by more than three to one, and the gap is increasing steadily!

Obtaining professional qualifications

All students at the ENM are civil servants and receive a salary, currently of approximately €1600 per month. The course lasts 31 months and is divided into periods of study and practical training. The first 11 months are a mixture of secondments to suitable placements, either with a company, in the public sector or in a foreign court, and study at the ENM at Bordeaux. The classes are practical and designed to introduce students to the work they might do as judges, and to train them to think and act as judges. Then follows a period of 14 months where students assist judges in various tasks. They might also spend some time with a firm of *avocats,* so as to obtain first-hand experience of the work of the people who will appear before them later. At the end of this period, students take an examination. They are then classified in order of merit (based on the results of the examination and reports on the work they have done in their various placements) and allocated specialities. They spend the last six months of their training working in their designated field. This may be helping a judge in the smallest court, the *Tribunal d'instance,* or working with a judge for young people or with a member of the *ministère public* at a local court. Successful candidates will normally start their first post as a full judge in the area they have worked in during the last six months of the course. As full judges they will take continuing education courses from time to time at the ENM. As their career progresses, the Minister of Justice will appoint them to more senior posts.

Other routes to appointment

While most candidates apply to the ENM shortly after finishing their studies at university, a number of mature students are entitled to take a modified type of examination, even without having studied at university, if they have a certain level of professional experience. Others, including candidates with a law degree who have practised in another branch of the law for at least four years, are exempted from the examination altogether and will be directly admitted at the ENM.

More controversially, some people are immediately admitted as judges without the required training at the ENM. This kind of recruitment has increased in recent years but still only affects a very small number of people. It is limited to persons listed in the *ordonnance* of 22 December 1958, and includes *avoués* and *avocats* who have been in practice for at least seven years. Accordingly a small minority of judges have a background similar to English and Welsh judges in that they trained as *avocats*, who do similar work to barristers and solicitors, before joining the judicial profession. Judges are sometimes also appointed for temporary periods to provide expertise or simply to effect an immediate increase in the number of judges until enough people have qualified using the longer route.

▶ Administrative court judges

Judges of the administrative courts are not members of the ordinary judiciary (see Chapter 12 above). They are civil servants who happen to work in the administrative court system. Recruitment is by the same methods as that for other civil servants, with judges needing to be of suitable calibre for a career leading to high-ranking posts in government administration.

Academic stage

It is a requirement to have studied for four years at university and to have obtained a *licence* or an equivalent qualification as listed in the regulations. A high level of general education is also necessary and a favoured way of obtaining this is through study at a school of political science, particularly the one in Paris, known as *Sciences-Po*. Students can also take courses specifically preparing them for the competitive entrance examination to the civil service college known as the *Ecole Nationale d'Administration* (ENA). ENA produces students who play a highly influential role in French society and has been subject in recent years to increasing criticism, mainly in relation to the insufficient democratisation of the top civil servant positions, an outdated syllabus, and failing to admit a greater diversity of students by putting an end to the near monopoly of students from *Sciences-Po* – who make up almost 90% of the students. The government reacted in 2003 by deciding to increase the international focus of the ENA and amending its syllabus.

Qualifying as an administrative judge

The entrance examination to ENA is composed of two stages. The written tests include assessments in public law, economics, general knowledge, the European Union and optional subjects which can include a foreign language or other legal topics. The oral tests include assessments in public finance, the European Union or social questions, and a foreign language (other than the one chosen during the written tests). The entrance examination has been open to citizens of the European Union since a decree of 31 March 2004. There are indications that the language barrier may prove too difficult for non-francophone students to pass the same tests as their French counterparts. ENA has decided to set up special courses, in Strasbourg and Paris, to prepare these students for the entrance examination. ENA's director, however, fears that this might not be sufficient and believes that a different entrance examination should be set up specifically for foreign students. Successful candidates are assured of a post in the civil service but not necessarily in the administrative courts. The course lasts for 27 months and includes a number of placements, conventional teaching and high-level seminars, and has been subject to a number of changes. The course was previously divided up into two 12 month periods involving work placements and a 15-month period of lectures. The new curriculum model, first implemented in 2006, will have four successive modules which will include internships sandwiched in between lectures. The modules will focus on Europe, the territories, management and a series of options including Economics, Law, Financial and International issues. Internships are available in European institutions, regional and central administration and private companies. Students then sit a final examination which tests the work done during the course. All students pass this examination but they compete against each other for classification in order of marks achieved. Students who obtain the highest marks can choose the branch of government in which they would like to work. The *Conseil d'Etat* and the *Cour des comptes* are very popular choices, only available to the highest ranking. Other students who want to pursue a career as an administrative judge could still obtain a post in one of the lower administrative courts outside Paris. Appointment is at the lowest rank of assistant judge, helping to prepare reports on cases. However, those appointed to the *Conseil d'Etat* can expect, in due course, to attain the exalted rank of full judge in the *Conseil d'Etat*, where they will give judgments with the help of the work done by their assistant judges.

Administrative judges are also recruited from the ranks of the civil service. At a junior level, candidates must pass a separate competitive entrance examination for ENA, and at more senior levels they can be appointed as either assistant or full judges at the *Conseil d'Etat*. As administrative judges work closely with other civil servants, a fairly high proportion of judges will have made their career initially in other branches of the civil service. They then bring the experience they have earned to the service of the *Conseil d'Etat*. A further way of qualifying for this profession is by competitive examination open to holders of a *licence* in law. As the examination is very competitive, successful candidates are likely to have obtained further postgraduate qualifications. Successful candidates then spend a six-month training period at the *Conseil d'Etat* and can expect to be appointed as administrative judges outside Paris.

In addition, mature candidates with relevant work experience will be considered for a place at ENA. Such candidates have to be under the age of 40 and have at least eight years' experience in one of a range of professions or as an elected member of one of a number of elected bodies.

BIBLIOGRAPHY FOR CHAPTER 13

Bronner, L. (2005), 'Un rapport préconise la sélection des étudiants étrangers', *Le Monde*, 29 January 2005

Chagnollaud, D. (1997), *Je m'inscris en droit*, Paris: Dalloz

Crignon, A. (2004), *Les métiers du droit*, Paris: L'Etudiant

Grynbaum, L. (2005), 'Et la recherche?', *D.* 2005, 4

La 'lutte pour le droit' (2004), *Recueil Dalloz* du 14 octobre 2004, Paris: Dalloz

Navarro, S., Person, L. and Yala, A. (2005), *Que faire avec des études de droit?*, Levallois-Peret: Studyrama

Web resources

Website: www.ena.fr: The *Ecole Nationale d'Administration*. Includes some text in English

Website: www.enm.justice.fr: The *Ecole Nationale de la Magistrature*

Website: www.univ-lyon3.fr: The University Jean Moulin Lyon 3

14 Practical guidance on studying law

When students from the United Kingdom or the USA go to study in France, they should be aware that French academic study has developed certain traditions which differ from those in their home countries. In this chapter, we look at two issues that are of practical importance to students: how to write a French legal essay and how to write a commentary about a French judgment.

PART I: LEGAL ESSAYS

In France, legal essays traditionally follow a very rigid plan which is articulated around two main sections (Fig. 14.1). While students of the arts are generally required to write essays with three divisions (*Thèse, synthèse, antithèse*), this structure is discouraged for legal essays.

The two main sections of a legal essay provide its backbone around which the rest of the text is constructed. They are each divided into two, or occasionally three, subsections, which can occasionally be divided into sub-subsections (together these will be described as the 'parts' of the essay). Each section and subsection starts with a letter or number and a subheading, though these are not necessary for the sub-subsections.

If no headings and numbers are given to the sub-subsections, then the writer simply starts a new paragraph for each sub-subsection. Each section must be approximately the same length. The transitions between each part of the essay are considered to be very important, and the end of each one must contain a few lines introducing the next, to prevent the essay from being disjointed, but instead making it flow smoothly from one idea to the next.

The introduction

The essay must start with an introduction which aims both to gain the attention of the reader and delimit its subject. It will normally take

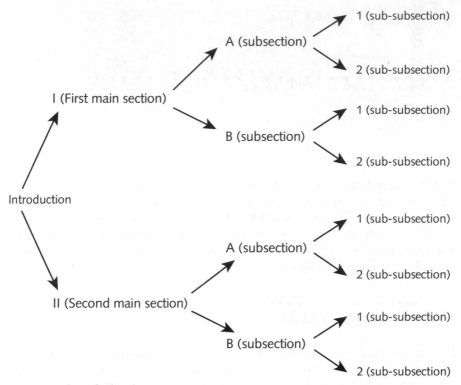

Fig. 14.1 Plan of a legal essay

the form of a funnel, starting off with very general ideas and then gradually narrowing down to more precise details. The first five to ten lines will seek to gain the attention of the reader by showing the intrinsic interest of the subject. This may be achieved in a variety of ways, such as through a brief historical analysis, a discussion of relevant comparative law, or by showing that the issue is very topical through references to recent legislative reform, case law developments or its repercussions in everyday life. The introduction will then lay down the boundaries to the subject, which may require certain technical terms to be defined. If you are proposing not to cover certain topics which might have been considered relevant, you must justify your stance. You can make passing comments on topics you consider to be of only secondary importance and which will not be discussed further in the essay, in order to avoid criticism of there being gaps in the coverage of the subject. Finally, the plan is presented by stating the two main parts to the essay (without entering into detail as this could lead to repetition). This provides a very natural end to the introduction while at the same time assuring the link with the main part of the essay. In all, the introduction will be about one quarter of the length of the essay.

▶ The body of the essay

After the heading of the first main section, several lines introduce what will be considered in the following part of the essay (*le chapeau*). In the same way, after the heading of each subsection, there should be a short summary of what will be discussed in the sub-subsections (also called *le chapeau*). The sub-subsections constitute the detailed discussion of the essay and, as a result, tend to be longer than the other parts of the essay. The second main section follows an identical structure.

The two main sections are independent of each other. Each part only treats one idea. The first idea must be different from the second and you must never repeat what has already been stated. They follow a logical sequence, with the reasoning of the first section serving to introduce the point to be tackled in the second section.

▶ Conclusion

The essay will normally have a conclusion, though this should be brief. There are different views as to what should be actually written at this stage. There is agreement, however, that important new ideas should not be introduced, which should have been discussed in the body of the essay. The conclusion to the essay could simply summarise the key arguments, but where it is felt to be wrong to repeat what has already been stated, the conclusion may instead consist of looking at how the subject may evolve in the future, drawing attention to possible reforms.

▶ The title

The title of an essay in France tends to be much shorter and more general than those which students are used to from their studies in the United Kingdom. Titles rarely consist of a full sentence or question; instead they often consist of a single word, such as 'Parliament' or 'Divorce' or of two concepts linked together such as 'Democracy and elections'. Such titles often require the student to take a broad critical approach to a topic, and work will be criticised if the main relevant issues are not covered. The plan must therefore be chosen to allow the relevant topic to be covered fully and in a logical, structured order.

▶ Choice of essay plan

While the basic structure of the essay is fixed, the contents of the plan are not, and considerable emphasis is placed during a university course in writing good essay plans. For any particular topic there is never a single, right plan; instead students should choose one that best fits their knowledge in the field and reflects their personal ideas. The aim is to fit all the legal points into a basic structure. Sometimes the classic structure of the relevant material in a textbook can provide the basis for an essay plan: for example, if the title of the essay was 'The effect of divorce' the plan could be: 'I – The effect of divorce on the spouses, and II – The effect of divorce on third parties'.

Certain 'ready-made' plans do exist, but these should be used with care and will always need to be adapted to fit the particular subject. The danger with such plans is that they can sometimes lead to rather dull essays which lack originality. Examples of such plans are:

I	Before	II	After
I	The present	II	The future
I	Theory	II	Practice
I	Myth	II	Reality
I	Similarities	II	Differences
I	Things as they are	II	Things as they should be
I	In the short term	II	In the long term
I	Conditions	II	Consequences
I	Principle	II	Exceptions
I	For	II	Against
I	Formation	II	Execution

If given the title 'Fraud and contracts', for example, you could take the plan 'I Formation, II Execution' and adapt it to this subject to become 'I Fraud and the formation of contracts, II Fraud and the execution of contracts'.

Once the idea behind each of the main sections has been chosen, it is then easier to find appropriate sections and subsections, which can themselves draw on the divisions suggested by the ready-made plans. A good plan must fit the title given, and no other.

If you are asked to compare two institutions, you must never treat one in each main section of the essay. Instead you should seek to extract particular traits which can be compared, and build the plan around these. In the same way, where the title links two concepts, for example 'The President and the Referendum', you must not consider the President in the first section and the referendum in the second, as you are being asked to consider these two simultaneously throughout your essay.

▶ Subheadings

The subheadings must be short and simple. They should normally share a certain symmetry, in length and in content, for example, I Valid marriages, II Void marriages. The headings should not be in the form of questions and nor should they contain exclamation marks or conjugated verbs.

●
PART II: COMMENTARY ON A JUDGMENT AND CASE SUMMARIES

▶ Commentary on a judgment

Writing a case commentary consists in both providing a clear factual explanation of the judgment and also a critical analysis. This exercise is often the subject of a law examination and the focus of discussions in tutorials, mainly in French civil and criminal law. It is at the same time the most challenging type of assessment and the most foreign to common law students. In general students are asked to comment on a recent case of a senior court which lays down a legal principle that is still in force. The whole commentary must be closely linked to the judgment itself, rather than being a theoretical summary of the relevant area of law: while theoretical knowledge is required, its discussion must be applied to the judgment in hand. To highlight this link between the commentary and the judgment, key parts of the decision can be quoted at appropriate points. In a three-hour examination, approximately one hour should be spent analysing the judgment, 20 minutes writing a plan and one and a half hours writing the commentary itself, leaving 10 minutes to read over the commentary at the end. Somewhat surprisingly, the notes that follow judgments in legal journals and law reports do not generally follow the structure and approach required of a student writing a commentary on a judgment. The latter essentially applies the same structure as a legal essay, though there are certain minor differences which will be considered here.

The introduction

As with legal essays, the introduction to a commentary on a judgment should normally start with a few lines highlighting the interesting aspects of the subject to be tackled. This can be done by, for example, drawing the reader's attention to the contemporary importance of the case or by placing it in its historical context. It is important to determine which court gave the decision and to specify its date if known. To find which court gave the decision you can first look at the start of the judgment where this may be specified. If it simply states '*La Cour*' this could be a reference to either the *Cour de cassation* or a *Cour d'appel*, in which case you need to look at the end of the judgment where the verdict will make it clear whether this was an ordinary appeal on points of law and/or fact (*un appel*) or an appeal on points of law only (*un pourvoi en cassation*).

The introduction tends to be about a quarter of the length of the whole commentary and also contains a number of other pieces of information related to the judgment that students are being asked to comment on: a summary of the facts, the procedure, the legal problem and the solution provided by the court.

Summary of the facts

After the general introductory sentence, the introduction should summarise in chronological order the facts of the case that gave rise to the litigation – knowledge of which is judged necessary to understand the legal problem posed by the case. For the lower court decisions, there will be more scope for the student to select the salient facts, since the court has had to respond to all the issues that the parties raised, even though many of these have proved to be of little significance. By the time the case reaches the *Cour de cassation* the important facts have been established and the court simply reiterates these without having to enter into any further debate in their regard. Thus, where the commentary is of a decision of this court, all the facts contained in the judgment will usually need to be repeated. The role of the student will then simply be to tidy up the presentation of the facts by removing the stylistic terms such as *attendu que* and presenting the events in a flowing narrative that will be more accessible to the reader. This summary must make it clear what the claim is that was considered by the court which gave the judgment being analysed. Students are expected to use their own vocabulary, and not merely to repeat the words used in the judgment, so as to show that the facts have been properly understood. The parties should be referred to by their names, rather than simply as the plaintiff or the appellant, as their status will vary during the course of the proceedings.

The procedure

Having considered the facts, you must then outline the procedures that have been followed, again putting each procedure in chronological order. The decision that has to be analysed is rarely the first given in the course of the litigation, and you need to outline the different procedural stages that have been completed. For each court that has heard the case you are essentially asking: Which court heard the case? When? Why? What was decided? For example, if you are looking at a decision of the *Cour de cassation*, you will usually need to answer the following questions:

- Who brought the case before the first instance court? Why? When was the case heard? What was its ruling?
- Who appealed to the court of appeal? Why? When was the case heard? What was its ruling?
- Who brought the action before the *Cour de cassation*? Why? When was the case heard? What was its ruling?

The legal problem

The legal problem is the legal question that the court has had to answer. To find this you need to look at the main legal reason (*attendu*) given by the court for its judgment. The legal problem then has to be formulated as a question in an abstract and theoretical way.

The solution

This provides the answer to the legal question posed above. It will be found in the main legal reason and if this is not too long, this can be quoted in full, otherwise it can be summarised in your own words. You should also specify the legal text which was relied upon to reach this conclusion, which may be, for example, an article of the Civil Code. Where the *Cour de cassation* has allowed the appeal, this will be referred to at the beginning of its judgment in the section known as the *visa*.

The presentation of the plan

Again, the introduction will end with the presentation of the plan that will be followed, by mentioning the headings given to the main sections of the commentary.

The body of the commentary

As with legal essays, the commentary is usually divided into two main sections, though it is a little more acceptable for it to be divided into three, and there is less emphasis on the parts being of equal length. The easiest and often the best way of finding a plan for a commentary is to look for the principal reason adduced for a judgment (found in the main *attendu*) which was given as the solution to the case in the introduction. You then need to divide this into two, with each half forming the basis for one of the main sections. Where this approach proves impossible you may need to have recourse to the ready-made plans discussed at p. 268 above.

You need to compare and contrast the reasoning adopted in the judgment with that preferred by academics and other court judgments. The judgment should be located within the current law, by stating whether it is a judgment of principle and whether it changed the law or merely illustrates the established law.

The conclusion

There are different views as to what should actually be written at this stage. It is not usually appropriate to write a long conclusion. It is important that new ideas should not be introduced, as they should have been discussed in the body of the essay. For some academics, the conclusion to the essay should summarise the key arguments, but for others this is viewed as an unnecessary repetition, and it should simply consist of looking at how the subject may evolve in the future, drawing attention to possible reforms.

▎ Case summary

A case summary is called in French *une fiche d'arrêt* or *une analyse objective d'arrêt*. This consists of writing a short and concise analysis of a judgment, which will often be required for the preparation of a tutorial, or as the first step towards writing a full commentary. Students are expected to extract as much information as possible from the judgment. This summary will consist of a list of:

- the undisputed facts that have given rise to the litigation in chronological order;
- the procedure (as discussed for a case commentary above);
- the claims of the parties before the court which gave the decision being analysed;
- a statement of the legal problem or problems;
- the solution.

For practical examples of these exercises please look at the companion website.

BIBLIOGRAPHY FOR CHAPTER 14

Ancel, P. (1994), *Travaux dirigés d'introduction au droit et droit civil*, Paris: Litec
Bocquillon, J.-F. and Mariage, M. (2001), *Droit*, Paris: Dunod
Bronner, L. (2005), 'Un rapport préconise la sélection des étudiants étrangers', *Le Monde*, 29 January 2005
Bros, S. (1999), *Méthodes d'exercices juridiques*, Paris: Francis Lefebvre
Chagnollaud, D. (1997), *Je m'inscris en droit*, Paris: Dalloz
Cohendet, M-A. (1994), *Méthodes de travail, droit public*, Paris: Montchrestien
Defrénois-Souleau, I. (2004), *Je veux réussir mon droit. Méthodes de travail et clés du succès*, Paris: Colin
Frison-Roche, Marie-A. (1994), I*ntroduction générale au droit*, Paris: Dalloz
Frison-Roche, M-A. (1995), *Droit des contrats*, Paris: Dalloz
Goubeau, G. and Bihr, P. (1993), *Les épreuves écrites du droit civil*, Paris: LGDJ,
Grynbaum, L. (2005), 'Et la recherche?' D. 2005, 4
Lobry, C. (1995), *Droit: BTS. Tome 1.* Paris: Techniplus

Mazeaud, H. and Mazeaud, D. (2001), *Méthodes de travail. DEUG Droit*, Paris: Montchrestien

Mendegris, R. and Vermelle, G. (2004), *Le commentaire d'arrêt en droit privé. Méthode et exemples*, Paris: Dalloz

Pansier, F.-J. (2005), *Méthodologie du droit*, Paris: LexisNexis / Litec

INTRODUCTION

At a time when the English legal system is seeking to remove one foreign influence from legal language – Latin – and the French continue to worry about the 'invasion' of English words in the French language, it seems highly apt to be considering the influence of French on English legal language. In the field of law, the impact of English over the French language is insignificant compared to the impact that the latter has had over the former. As a result of this Continental influence, the English language was considerably enriched with technical legal vocabulary that served to protect the English culture rather than endanger it, and it is hoped that this would also be true of the current influence of the English language on French.

HISTORICAL BACKGROUND

There are three languages that have all affected the development of English legal language: Latin, Norman French and later Parisian French. Norman French and Parisian French were themselves influenced by Latin, so Latin affected legal English from two perspectives: directly through the heritage of the Roman Empire and indirectly through the French language.

The influence of the French language really started with the Norman Conquest in 1066, though the impact of this conquest on legal language was not immediate. This delay was partly because there were only a small number of conquerors, and partly because William the Conqueror did not try to impose Norman law in England, decreeing instead that the law of King Edward applied, with a few amendments such as the introduction of the general theory of tenure under which 'all land is held of the king'. Indeed, William was particularly keen to preserve those areas of English law that gave him royal rights, and thus the English legal terminology that encapsulated these rights also remained. But as the new king successfully established his authority over England, it became inevitable that the language of his courtiers would become the language of business and the law.

French started to be used in the law courts in the middle of the thirteenth century, and slowly supplanted Latin as the literary language of lawyers. The form of French used at this time is sometimes called Anglo–Norman, and the quality of the French was reasonably high because it was taught in the schools and spoken by some of the English gentry and business people as well as by lawyers. After the wars with France under Edward III, however, French slowly ceased to be the language of the ruling classes and was no longer taught in the English classroom. Its continued use by the courts was considered by some as anachronistic and a symbol of Norman tyranny. Thus in 1362 Parliament attempted to restrict the use of French in the law courts, as being '*trop desconue*' (though, ironically, the statute itself was in French) but the measure was only of limited success. French continued to be used for many written documents; thus the old law reports, known as the *Year Books*, were written in law French (discussed below) until the seventeenth century and most legal literature before the seventeenth century was written either in French or Latin. By contrast, the oral use of French in the courts became limited to the reading out of formal pleadings, a practice that continued until the eighteenth century.

The legal profession was eventually forced to abandon law French by a statute of 22 November 1650. This stated:

> That all the Report-Books of the Resolutions of Judges, and other
> Books of the Law of England, shall be Translated into the English
> Tongue: And that from and after the First day of January 1650 all
> Report-Books of the Resolutions of Judges, and all the books of
> the Law of England, which shall be Printed, shall be in the English
> Tongue only.

With the Restoration, the Act was treated as void and many lawyers briefly reverted to law French, but the language had deteriorated to such an extent that it gradually died a natural death, a state of affairs which was rendered final by an Act of Parliament of 1731 forbidding the use of Latin and French in legal proceedings.

While the quality of the French used by the lawyers was initially quite good, it was in steady decline after 1300. This deterioration meant that it became a separate professional dialect known as 'law French'. Though grammatically and stylistically this language might be frowned upon by a linguist, legal historians J.H. Baker and F.W. Maitland both argue that law French allowed lawyers to create new legal vocabulary to express new laws. Ordinary French words were given special meanings which could become terms of art. This facilitated change, because the existing legal terminology had fixed meanings which could not have been adapted to the new rules. These technical concepts were then protected from the corruption of vernacular usage.

• • • • • • • • • • • • • •
LAW FRENCH

An excellent book on this dialect is the *Manual of Law French* by J.H. Baker. The grammar of law French was weak, the range of vocabulary became increasingly limited, the pronunciation was idiosyncratic and the spelling was erratic. Looking first at the grammatical rules, these were gradually assimilated to those of the English language. Thus, law French took little notice of declension. Even in the earlier *Year Books*, nouns had no cases, with the accusative being used throughout. It was only later that this approach was adopted by the French language, which led Maitland to comment that '[I]n matters of language the careless, the slovenly, the vulgar, are often the pioneers and ultimately the victors.' (F.W. Maitland, *Year Books of Edward II*). Declension for plurals was assimilated to the English system, so that they usually simply required the addition of an *s* or *z*. Initially, words ending in *al* or *el* became *aux* or *eux*, but after the mid-fifteenth century this rule was often forgotten. The lawyers were careless about putting the final 'e' for feminine agreements, though usually recognised gender when using distinct words such as *le, la, mon, ma, son* and *sa*.

Looking, secondly, at the law French vocabulary, by mid-Tudor times the active vocabulary of law French had diminished to fewer than a thousand words. English terms were increasingly used in the *Year Books* for everyday objects, such as 'shoe', 'plough', 'deer', 'fowl', 'keeper', 'hunting' and 'fox' because the lawyers no longer knew the French terms. This did not worry the English lawyer as these were not technical terms so nothing turned on the language used.

When law French was spoken, the pronunciation was rather peculiar, with the lawyers pronouncing the French terms as if they were English.

The spelling of law French was very unsystematic. For example, Maitland found eight versions of the modern English word 'suit' in three reports of one short case: *siwte, siwete, sywte, suwite, suwte, sute, swte, seute*. Some of these difficulties arose from the habit of the clerks to use abbreviations to save precious parchment. Thus, instead of writing words in full they often put a dash, known as a tittle. This then led to confusion for the transcribers in determining what the appropriate ending for the word actually was.

Difficulties were added to by the fact that England had originally imported Norman French, when subsequently Parisian French became recognised as 'standard French'. It has been observed that:

> *La langue transportée sur le sol anglais par les conquérants normands subissait sur bien des points un développement particulier. L'analogie engendrait sans cesse des formes nouvelles que le français de France ne connaissait pas. A ces formes, les écrivains nés en Angleterre en ajoutaient*

d'autres qu'ils puisaient dans la lecture des livres venus de France. De là résultaient des variétés et des inconséquences qui affectent en des proportions diverses la langue de chaque écrivain, et qui s'opposent à ce qu'on puisse traiter l'anglo-normand comme un dialecte régulier. (Paul Meyer, Romania, xii. 201)

THE IMPACT OF LAW FRENCH ON MODERN ENGLISH

Even when law French finally disappeared, some of the grammatical formations of the language and the technical words lived on to become part of the legal language of modern English. Looking first at the grammatical formations, Maitland observed that old French allowed a free conversion of infinitives into substantives and that many English legal terms have originated in this way. Illustrations are 'disclaimer', 'merger', 'remainder' and 'ouster'. Modern English has also preserved verbal substantives formed from the past participle, the double 'ee' in modern English playing the role of the 'é' in modern French. Illustrations are employee, mortgagee, donee and lessee. This has proved to be particularly useful for forming pairs of words denoting passive and active aspects of the same transaction: for example, the lessor and lessee of a lease, or the contractor and the contractee of a contract. While this usage is grammatically slightly inaccurate as the 'lessee' was not him or herself leased, lawyers have not worried about these finer grammatical points. The device was applied even after law French fell into disuse, for example with the English word 'trust' in the seventeenth century creating the word trustee, which was less clumsy than the earlier phrase *cestuy que trust*.

Looking, secondly, at the technical vocabulary, Maitland commented:

> We enter a court of justice: court, justices, judges, jurors, counsel, attorneys, clerks, parties, plaintiff, defendant, action, suit, claim, demand, indictment, count, declaration, pleadings, evidence, verdict, conviction, judgment, sentence, appeal, reprieve, pardon, execution, every one and every thing, save the witnesses, writs and oaths, have French names. (F. Pollock and F. W. Maitland, *History of English Law before the Time of Edward I*)

French even affected the pronunciation of some of the existing English words. For example, before the Norman Conquest both the 'k' and the 'g' in the Anglo-Saxon word 'knight' would have been pronounced. While clearly modern English legal vocabulary is heavily indebted to law French, as Maitland pointed out, some of the Anglo-Saxon terms do survive. Thus, in the twelfth century old English had some technical terms with regard to crime and punishment, which remain today. The word 'outlaw' survived despite the French term *forbannir* and, while *faire les amendes* led to the English phrase 'to make amends', the English language never adopted the word *amende* to mean 'a fine', its main meaning in modern French. English lawyers also fall back on Anglo-Saxon terms if they wish to find a new term of art. A recent instance is the replacement of 'larceny' by 'theft' in the Theft Act 1968.

A COMPARISON BETWEEN MODERN ENGLISH AND MODERN FRENCH LEGAL TERMINOLOGY

The French language clearly made a significant impact on the development of English legal vocabulary, while, by contrast, the impact of the English language on French legal terminology has not been so significant. But the French terms were not directly incorporated into the English legal language, instead they were often adapted to fit English grammatical rules and the English tongue. For example, the English language is not keen on the 're' ending so such words when preserved in English were altered to end in 'er', so *chartre* became 'charter' and *outre* became 'ouster'. The term 'ouster' also illustrates the English tendency to add an extra 's' when it was not required in French.

Over time French terms used in England frequently developed their own technical meanings which could often differ significantly from their original sense. A word might develop separately in England and in France and, although still the same word, could finish being spelt in a different way, with a different pronunciation and a different (though often similar) meaning. The result for a student studying the legal terminology of the two systems can be a large number of 'false friends'. In the legal context, the fine nuances between different terms can be of particular importance and mistakes can have dire consequences. The legal systems of the two countries developed in very different ways so that terms applied to one system are often not translatable into the country's language. For example, there is no direct equivalent in England to the *Conseil constitutionnel*.

This situation has led J.H. Baker to observe that though most of the terminology of the common law is of law French origin, 'yet very few of the terms have any close equivalent in the French of France'. Examples are provided by terms 'to try', 'to indict', 'to lie' and 'to impeach' and their derivatives, which will be considered in turn. First, the term 'trial' is of French origin, deriving from the verb *trier*. In modern French this verb retained its basic meaning of 'to separate' or 'to sort'. We can originally see this verb being used in the context of selecting the jury, itself a characteristic of the English legal system, and it evolved through this context to its current modern meaning. However, no similar development took place in France, so modern French has no equivalent term.

Secondly, the Old French word *enditer*, along with its Latin parent word *indictare*, gave rise to the modern English words 'indict' and 'indictment', but not to equivalent concepts in modern French. Again, this could be because of the jury system as the writing down of the jury's statement would in Old French have been an *enditement*, linking in to the modern English word.

Thirdly, in French the verb *lier* preserved the meaning that it had borne in Latin from its parent verb *ligare*, but in English its usage was developed by the courts and it was the source for words such as 'liability', and phrases such as 'the case was laid before the court', while *relier sur* gave rise to 'to rely on'. It also led to the English word 'lien' in the context of contracts, but this is rarely used today.

Lastly, the French term that would become *empêcher* is the source of the term 'impeachment' in English but not to any equivalent term in French, where the concept is translated as simply '*la mise en accusation*'.

In the eleventh century French lacked negative forms, limited primarily to *ne*, and the use of the additional *pas* had not yet been developed. The use of negation is fundamental to legal language, with issues relating to rejection, contradiction and denial being central to court proceedings. English lawyers therefore borrowed from Latin the use of negative prefixes. For example, they applied the prefix *non* to create such words as non-payment, non-attendance, non-compliance and nonsuit. Another negative prefix that was used was *des*, and the English lawyers used this more frequently than their French counterparts, leading to words such as 'disability' and 'disallow' which have no French equivalent.

• • • • • • • • • • • • • • •

CONCLUSION

As the isolated sovereignty of the legal systems of individual states is gradually being whittled away, the influence of the English and French languages on their mutual development in the legal context is likely to continue and, indeed, gain fresh momentum. The European Court of Justice and the International Court of Justice work in both English and French, cases involving France and the United Kingdom are heard by the European Court of Human Rights, and the case law deriving from these courts has an impact on the law in both these countries. Soon there should be a permanent International Criminal Court whose jurisdiction could potentially extend to all members of the United Nations. Languages are in a permanent state of transition, adapting and developing according to the climate in which they are used. As the legal context becomes increasingly international, it is inevitable that the legal languages of both England and France will repeatedly come into contact and affect each other's future evolution.

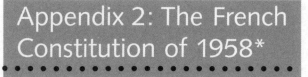

Appendix 2: The French Constitution of 1958*

PREAMBLE

The French people solemnly proclaim their commitment to human rights and to the principles of national sovereignty defined in the Declaration of 1789 and confirmed and completed by the Preamble to the 1946 Constitution, as well as the rights and obligations defined in the Charter for the Environment of 2004.

By virtue of these principles and that of self determination of peoples, the Republic gives to overseas territories which express an interest in joining them, new institutions based on the shared ideals of liberty, fraternity and equality and designed to develop democracy.

▶ Article 1

France is an indivisible, secular democratic and social Republic. It guarantees the equality before the law of all its citizens, irrespective of their origin, race or religion. It respects all faiths. Its administration is decentralised.

TITLE I – SOVEREIGNTY

▶ Article 2

The language of the Republic is French.
The emblem of the Republic is the tricolour, a blue, white and red flag.
The national anthem is '*La Marseillaise*'.
The maxim of the Republic is 'Liberty, Equality, Fraternity'.

---

*Translation by the authors, including all amendments up to 1 January 2006. See www.elysee.fr/instit/txt58.co.htm to check on latest updating. The official French text of the Constitution is published by *La Documentation Française*, 29 Quai Voltaire, 75007 Paris.

It is ruled by the principle of government of the people, by the people and for the people.

▶ Article 3

National sovereignty belongs to the people. They exercise it through their representatives and by means of referenda.

It cannot be appropriated by any section of the public or by any individual.

The right to vote may be exercised directly or indirectly under the conditions laid down in the Constitution. It shall always be universal, equal and secret.

All adult citizens, of either sex, who have not been deprived of their civil or political rights, are entitled to vote under the conditions determined by legislation.

French law favours equal access for women and men to electoral mandates and elected posts.

▶ Article 4

The right to vote is exercised through the participation of political parties and associations. They shall be freely formed and may exercise their activity with freedom. They must respect the principles of national sovereignty and democracy. They contribute to the implementation of the principle set out in the last paragraph of article 3 according to the requirements laid down in legislation.

TITLE II – THE PRESIDENT OF THE REPUBLIC

▶ Article 5

The President of the Republic is the guardian of the Constitution. By arbitration, the President ensures the proper operation of public authorities and the continuity of the State.

The President guarantees national independence, territorial integrity, and respect for treaties.

▶ Article 6

The President of the Republic is elected for five years by direct universal suffrage. A constitutional statute shall determine the procedure for implementing this article.

▶ Article 7

The President of the Republic is elected by an absolute majority of the votes cast. If no one achieves this at the first ballot, a second ballot shall be held fourteen days later. The only candidates who may present themselves for election at this ballot are the two who have obtained the most votes at the first ballot, discounting candidates who have withdrawn, some of whom may have obtained more votes.

The ballot is held on formal orders from the government.

The election of the new President shall take place not less than twenty and not more than thirty-five days before the end of the mandate of the incumbent President.

Should the post of President fall vacant for any reason whatsoever, or should the *Conseil constitutionnel*, by an absolute majority of its members on reference from the government, decide that the President is incapable of carrying out presidential duties, such duties, save for those laid down in articles 11 and 12 below, shall be temporarily carried out by the President of the Senate, and if he is unable to do so, by the government.

In the case of a vacancy or where the incapacity is declared to be permanent by the *Conseil constitutionnel*, the ballot for the election of the new President shall take place not less than twenty and not more than thirty-five days from the date of the vacancy, or the declaration of that incapacity, unless the *Conseil constitutionnel* certifies that an insuperable obstacle prevents this.

If within the seven days preceding the last date set for the lodging of nominations, one of those persons who at least thirty days before that date publicly announced their candidature dies or becomes incapable of carrying out their duties, the *Conseil constitutionnel* may decide to postpone the election.

If, before the first ballot, one of the candidates dies or becomes incapable of carrying out presidential duties, the *Conseil constitutionnel* shall declare the election postponed.

If one of the two candidates who received the most votes in the first ballot before any withdrawals dies or becomes unable to stand for election, the *Conseil constitutionnel* shall call fresh elections. It shall also do so if one of the two candidates eligible to stand for the second ballot dies or becomes unable to stand for election.

All these cases shall be referred to the *Conseil constitutionnel* according to the conditions laid down by the second paragraph of article 61 below, or according to those for the presentation of candidates laid down in the constitutional statute mentioned in article 6 above.

The *Conseil constitutionnel* may extend the time limits prescribed in the third and fifth paragraphs above, provided that the ballot takes place within thirty-five days of the decision of the *Conseil constitutionnel*.

If the application of the powers granted by this paragraph results in the postponement of the election until after the expiry of the mandate of the old President, the latter shall remain in office until a successor is announced.

While the post of President of the Republic is vacant or between the declaration of incapacity of the old President and the election of a successor, articles 49, 50 and 89 of the Constitution may not be applied.

▶ Article 8

The President of the Republic appoints the Prime Minister. He shall terminate the appointment if the Prime Minister tenders the resignation of the government. He appoints and dismisses other members of the government on the recommendation of the Prime Minister.

▶ Article 9

The President of the Republic presides over the Cabinet.

▶ Article 10

The President of the Republic shall promulgate an Act of Parliament within a period of fifteen days after the final version of the text has been transmitted to the government.
The President may, before the expiry of this period, ask Parliament to debate further on the Act or certain parts of it. The request cannot be refused.

▶ Article 11

When Parliament is in session, the President of the Republic may on the recommendation of the government submit to a referendum any Bill which deals with the organisation of public authorities, or reforms relating to national economic or social policy and the institutions which administer it, or calls for authorisation to ratify a treaty and which, while not being contrary to the Constitution, would affect the operation of its institutions. Recommendations for a referendum may also be made on the joint motion of the two Houses of Parliament, published in the Official Journal.

If the referendum is called on the government's recommendation, it will make a declaration in the two Houses of Parliament, followed by a debate.

If the Bill is approved by referendum, the President of the Republic shall promulgate it, within fifteen days from the date when the result is announced.

▶ Article 12

The President of the Republic may, after consultation with the Prime Minister and the Presidents of the two Houses of Parliament, pronounce the dissolution of the National Assembly.

General elections shall take place not less than twenty days and not more than forty days after the dissolution.

The National Assembly shall convene as of right on the second Sunday following its election. If this takes place outside the periods provided for ordinary sessions, a special session shall be held as of right for a period of fifteen days.

There may be no further dissolution in the year following these elections.

▶ Article 13

The President of the Republic signs the *ordonnances* and decrees approved by the Cabinet.

He makes appointments to civil and military state offices.

The members of the *Conseil d'Etat*, the Grand Chancellor of the Legion of Honour, the ambassadors and special envoys, the judges of the Audit Court, the senior local administrative officers, the state representatives in the overseas territories to which article 74 applies and in New Caledonia, the general army officers, the chief education officers, the heads of central governmental services are appointed by the Cabinet.

A constitutional statute determines the other positions which are appointed by the Cabinet as well as the conditions in which the president may delegate his power to appoint on his behalf.

▶ Article 14

The President of the Republic accredits ambassadors and special envoys to foreign powers; it is to him that foreign ambassadors and special envoys are accredited.

▶ Article 15

The President of the Republic is the head of the armed forces. He presides over the councils and higher committees for national defence.

Article 16

When the institutions of the Republic, the Nation's independence, the integrity of its territory, or the implementation of international agreements are under serious and immediate threat, and the orderly operation of public authorities established by the Constitution is suspended, the President of the Republic shall take such measures as are required under the circumstances, after formal consultations with the Prime Minister, the Presidents of the two Houses of Parliament and the *Conseil constitutionnel.*

The President shall inform the nation of this by message.

The measures must be inspired by the desire to ensure for the public authorities established by the Constitution, in the shortest possible time, the means of fulfilling their obligations. The *Conseil constitutionnel* shall be consulted.

Parliament shall convene as of right.

The National Assembly may not be dissolved during the exercise of the emergency powers.

Article 17

The President of the Republic has the right to grant pardons.

Article 18

The President of the Republic may address written messages to the two Houses of Parliament which shall be read, and which shall not be open to debate.

Article 19

Decisions of the President of the Republic, other than those provided for under article 8 (first paragraph), 11, 12, 16, 18, 54, 56 and 61 shall be approved and countersigned by the Prime Minister and where appropriate by the relevant minister.

• •

TITLE III – THE GOVERNMENT

▶ Article 20

The government shall determine and conduct national policy.

It shall have the administration and the armed forces at its disposal.

It shall be responsible to Parliament under the conditions and following the procedures laid down in articles 49 and 50.

▶ Article 21

The Prime Minister leads the government. He is responsible for national defence and ensures the implementation of legislation. He exercises the power to make regulations, and makes appointments to civil and military posts.

He may delegate certain powers to ministers.

If appropriate, the Prime Minister may act as deputy for the President of the Republic and chair the councils and committees mentioned in article 15.

In exceptional circumstances, the Prime Minister may be expressly authorised to preside over the Cabinet to stand in for the President of the Republic for a specified agenda.

▶ Article 22

Where appropriate the decisions of the Prime Minister shall be countersigned by the ministers responsible for implementing them.

▶ Article 23

The duties of a member of the government are incompatible with any parliamentary mandate, any position involving representing a profession at national level, and with any post in the public sector or professional activity.

A constitutional statute shall determine the conditions under which the holders of such mandates, positions or posts are replaced.

• •

TITLE IV – PARLIAMENT

▶ **Article 24**

There are two Houses of Parliament; the National Assembly and the Senate.

Members of the National Assembly are elected by direct suffrage. The Senate is elected by indirect suffrage. It ensures the representation of the local authorities of the Republic. French citizens living outside France are represented in the Senate.

▶ **Article 25**

A constitutional statute shall determine the terms for which each House is to sit, the number of its members, their remuneration, the conditions for eligibility and the system for exclusions and declarations of incompatibility.

It shall also lay down conditions under which persons shall be elected to replace members of the National Assembly or senators whose seats fall vacant, until the next partial or general election to the House in which the vacancy occurred.

▶ **Article 26**

Members of Parliament may not be prosecuted, investigated, arrested, detained or tried as a result of opinions expressed or votes cast while carrying out their duties.

Members of Parliament may not be arrested or be subjected to any other measure restricting their freedom in connection with criminal matters without the permission of the relevant House. This permission is not required where the member has been caught in the act of committing a serious crime or a major offence or has been convicted.

Detention, measures restricting a member's freedom, or prosecution shall be suspended for the duration of the parliamentary session if the House to which the member belongs so requests.

The relevant House shall convene as of right for additional sessions in order to enable the provisions in the above paragraphs to be applied.

▶ Article 27

All orders purporting to be binding on Members of Parliament are null and void.

A member's right to vote is personal.

A constitutional statute may authorise delegation of a vote in exceptional circumstances. In that case, no member may cast more than one proxy vote.

▶ Article 28

Parliament shall convene as of right in one ordinary session which starts on the first working day of October and ends on the last working day of June.

The number of days for which each Assembly may sit during the ordinary session shall not exceed one hundred and twenty. Each Assembly fixes the weeks when they sit.

The Prime Minister, after consulting the President of the Assembly concerned, or the majority of the members of each Assembly can decide to hold additional sittings.

The days and times of the sittings shall be determined by the rules of each Assembly.

▶ Article 29

At the request of the Prime Minister or the majority of the members of the National Assembly, Parliament shall convene in an extraordinary session to consider a specific agenda.

When an extraordinary session is held at the request of members of the National Assembly, the session shall be closed by decree at the latest twelve days after it was convened, or if earlier as soon as Parliament has completed the agenda.

Only the Prime Minister may request a new session before the expiry of a period of one month from the date of closure.

▶ Article 30

Save when Parliament convenes as of right, extraordinary sessions shall be opened and closed by decree of the President of the Republic.

▶ **Article 31**

Members of the government shall have access to the two Houses. They shall be heard on request.

They may be assisted by government advisers.

▶ **Article 32**

The President of the National Assembly shall be elected for the duration of the term for which the National Assembly was elected. The President of the Senate shall be elected after each partial renewal of its membership.

▶ **Article 33**

The sittings of the two Houses of Parliament shall be open to the public. The full minutes of the debate shall be published in the Official Journal.

Each House may sit behind closed doors at the request of the Prime Minister or of one tenth of its members.

TITLE V – RELATIONS BETWEEN PARLIAMENT AND GOVERNMENT

▶ **Article 34**

Legislation is enacted by Parliament.

Legislation shall determine the rules concerning:

- civic rights and the fundamental freedoms granted to citizens for the exercise of their civil rights; the obligations imposed upon citizens with respect to person or property as required for the purpose of national defence;
- nationality, status and legal capacity of persons, the law relating to matrimonial property, inheritance and gifts;
- the determination of what constitutes a serious crime or a major offence, and the prescribed sentence; criminal procedure; amnesty; the creation of new types of court and the status of the judiciary;
- the basis of assessment, the rate and methods of collection of taxes of all kinds; the conditions and terms for the issue of currency.

Legislation shall also determine the rules concerning:

- the election of Parliament and local councils;

- the creation of new categories of state enterprise;
- the fundamental guarantees afforded to civil servants and members of the armed forces;
- the nationalisation and privatisation of companies.

Legislation shall determine the basic principles of:
- the general organisation of national defence;
- the self-government of territorial units, the scope of their power and their budget;
- education;
- the protection of the environment;
- the right of ownership, law of property, and civil and commercial obligations;
- employment, trade union and social security law.

Acts on the financing of the social security system shall determine the general conditions for its budget and, depending on revenue forecasts, fix their expenditure targets as laid down in a constitutional statute.

Acts laying down plans set the aims of the economic and social action of the State.

The provisions of this article may be clarified and complemented by a constitutional statute.

Article 35

A declaration of war shall be authorised by Parliament.

Article 36

A state of emergency shall be declared by decree in the Cabinet. Only Parliament can authorise a prolongation beyond a period of twelve days.

Article 37

Subjects other than those which are in the legislative domain have a regulatory character. Existing Acts of Parliament concerning such subjects can be amended by decree, issued after consultation with the *Conseil d'Etat*. Such Acts of Parliament as are enacted after this Constitution has come into effect can only be amended by decree if the *Conseil constitutionnel* has confirmed that, in accordance with the preceding paragraph, they have a regulatory character.

Article 37-1

Acts and regulations may contain, for a specific purpose and for a limited period, provisions to enable pilot projects to be tested.

▶ Article 38

In order to carry out its programme, the government may ask Parliament to authorise it for a limited period to take measures which are normally within the legislative domain by means of *ordonnances* instead of the usual procedure.

They shall be adopted by the Cabinet after consultation with the *Conseil d'Etat*. They shall come into force on publication, but shall lapse if the government Bill calling for ratification is not laid before Parliament by the date specified in the enabling Act.

At the expiry of the time limit referred to in the first paragraph of this article, *ordonnances* on subjects within the legislative domain may be modified only by parliamentary legislation.

▶ Article 39

The right to propose legislation is exercised both by the Prime Minister and Members of Parliament. Government Bills are discussed at the Cabinet after consultation with the *Conseil d'Etat* and filed with the secretariat of one of the Houses of Parliament. Finance Bills and Bills relating to the funding of the social security system shall be introduced in the National Assembly. Without prejudice to the first paragraph of article 44, Bills having as a primary purpose the organisation of territorial units, and Bills relating to the representation of French nationals settled outside France are first presented to the Senate.

▶ Article 40

Bills and amendments to legislation proposed by Members of Parliament shall not be allocated time if their adoption would result in either a reduction in public revenues, in the creation of new public expenditure or increase of existing expenditure.

▶ Article 41

Should it appear in the course of parliamentary proceedings that a Bill or proposed amendment is not within the legislative domain or is counter to a delegation of authority under article 38, the government may declare that it is out of order. If the government and the President of the House concerned fail to reach agreement, either may request the *Conseil constitutionnel* to rule on the matter within eight days.

▶ Article 42

The House which first receives a government Bill shall debate the text submitted by the government.

The House which receives a text on which the other House has already voted, shall debate the text as transmitted to it.

▶ Article 43

All Bills may be referred at the request of the government or the House concerned for consideration by a committee established for the purpose.

If no such request is made, Bills shall be sent to one of the standing committees, the number of which shall be limited to six in each House.

▶ Article 44

Amendments may be proposed by both Members of Parliament and the government.

After the debate has begun, the government may refuse to consider any amendment which has not been previously submitted to the relevant committee.

If the government so requests, the House concerned shall decide by a single vote on the whole or a specified part of a text under debate, including only those amendments proposed or accepted by the government.

▶ Article 45

The Houses of Parliament shall debate Bills in turn with a view to each adopting the same wording.

When the two Houses fail to reach agreement after two readings in each House, and as a result fail to adopt the Bill, (or where the government has declared the matter urgent), where the Houses have failed to reach agreement after the first reading, the Prime Minister is entitled to call a meeting of a special joint committee, composed by an equal number of members from each House, and to instruct it to propose a text on the provisions still under discussion.

The government may submit the text drafted by the special joint committee, for approval by the two Houses. No amendment can be accepted without the government's agreement.

If the special joint committee fails to reach agreement on a common text or if its text is not adopted under the preceding paragraph, there shall be a further reading in the National Assembly and the Senate after which the government may ask the National Assembly to make a final decision. If so, the National Assembly may adopt again either the text drafted by the special joint committee or the text which it originally adopted, modified, if it so wishes, by one or more of the amendments made by the Senate.

▶ Article 46

Legislation which the Constitution defines as a constitutional statute shall be passed and amended in the following ways:

The Bill must be laid before the first House to which it is passed for fifteen days before the formal debate can take place and before any vote can be taken.

The procedure of article 45 shall apply. However, in the absence of agreement between the two Houses, the National Assembly can pass the statute on its final reading only if it is voted with an absolute majority of its members.

Constitutional statutes concerning the Senate must be voted in identical terms before both Houses.

Before being promulgated constitutional statutes must be submitted to the *Conseil constitutionnel* which must confirm that the statute does not conflict with the Constitution.

▶ Article 47

Parliament shall pass Finance Bills under the conditions set out in a constitutional statute.

If the National Assembly has not voted on the first reading, within forty days of the tabling of the Bill, the government shall refer it to the Senate which must reach a decision within fifteen days. Thereafter, the procedure of article 45 shall be followed.

If Parliament fails to vote on the Bill within seventy days, the provisions of the Bill may be implemented by means of an *ordonnance*.

If a Finance Bill determining the revenue and expenditure for a fiscal year is not tabled in time to be promulgated before the start of that year, the government shall request as a matter of urgency the authorisation of Parliament to the collection of taxes and shall make available by decree funds needed to meet the commitments already made.

The time limits laid down in this article are suspended while Parliament is not in session.

The Audit Court assists Parliament and the government in monitoring the implementation of Finance Acts.

Article 47-1

Parliament passes Bills to finance the social security system as laid down by a constitutional statute.

If the National Assembly has not pronounced on the first reading within twenty days after the laying of a Bill, the Government refers the Bill to the Senate which must decide within fifteen days. The procedures laid down in article 45 are then followed.

If Parliament has not decided within fifty days, the provisions of the Bill can be brought into force by an *ordonnance*.

The time periods laid down in the present article are suspended when Parliament is not in session and, for each Assembly, during the weeks when it has decided not to hold a sitting, in accordance with the second paragraph of article 28.

The Audit Court assists Parliament and Government in controlling the application of the Acts to finance the social security system.

Article 48

Without prejudice to the implementation of the last three paragraphs of article 28, the agenda of the Houses of Parliament shall give priority, in the order determined by the government, to Bills tabled by the government, and members' Bills which have been approved by the government.

At one sitting a week at least, priority shall be given to questions from Members of Parliament and the government's answers.

At no less than one sitting a month priority shall be given to the Agenda established by each House of Parliament.

Article 49

The Prime Minister shall, after consultation with the Cabinet, pledge the responsibility of the government before the National Assembly to the government's programme or alternatively to a statement of its general policy.

By means of a censure motion the National Assembly may call into question the confidence in the government. Such a motion is only admissible if it is signed by at least one tenth of the members of the National

Assembly. A vote may not be taken until forty-eight hours after the motion was tabled. Only votes in favour of the censure motion are counted, and it will only be passed if a majority of the members of the National Assembly voted to adopt it. Save as provided by the following paragraph, a deputy may sign a maximum of three motions of censure during an ordinary session of Parliament, and may only sign one during an extraordinary session.

After conferring with the Cabinet the Prime Minister may make the vote of the National Assembly on the passing of a single legislative provision a matter of confidence in the government. In that case, the provision is deemed to be adopted unless a motion of censure tabled within the next twenty-four hours is passed following the procedure described in the preceding paragraph.

The Prime Minister shall be entitled to request the Senate's approval of a general policy statement.

▶ Article 50

When the National Assembly passes a motion of censure, or when it rejects the programme or general policy statement of the government, the Prime Minister must tender the resignation of the government to the President of the Republic.

▶ Article 51

The closure of ordinary or extraordinary sittings of Parliament shall be postponed as of right when appropriate to allow for the implementation of the procedures set out in article 49. Additional sittings shall take place as of right if required.

TITLE VI – TREATIES AND INTERNATIONAL AGREEMENTS

▶ Article 52

The President of the Republic shall negotiate and ratify treaties.
He shall be informed of all negotiations on the conclusion of an international agreement not requiring ratification.

▶ Article 53

Peace treaties, commercial treaties, treaties or agreements relating to international organisations, those which commit national resources, which modify legislation, which affect the status of people, which involve the transfer, exchange or annexation of territory, may only be ratified or approved by legislation.

They only take effect after ratification or approval.

No transfer, no exchange, no annexation of territory is valid without the approval of the population concerned.

Article 53-1

France may enter into agreements with European countries, which are bound by the same undertakings relating to the granting of asylum, protection of human rights, and fundamental freedoms to determine their respective competence for the examination of asylum requests.

However, even if France is not competent to grant the request under these agreements, the Republic always has the right to grant asylum to any foreigner persecuted because of action taken to further freedom or who asks for the protection of France for another reason.

Article 53-2

France may recognise the jurisdiction of the International Criminal Court in the circumstances envisaged by the Treaty signed on 18 July 1998.

▶ Article 54

If on reference by the President of the Republic, the Prime Minister, the President of the National Assembly, the President of the Senate or sixty members of one of the Houses of Parliament, the *Conseil constitutionnel* rules that an international agreement contains a clause contrary to the Constitution, its ratification or approval may be authorised only after the Constitution has been amended.

▶ Article 55

Treaties or agreements duly ratified or approved shall from the date of publication prevail over legislation, subject, for each agreement or treaty, to its implementation by the other party.

TITLE VII – THE *CONSEIL CONSTITUTIONNEL*

▶ Article 56

The *Conseil constitutionnel* is composed of nine members whose term of office shall last nine years and shall not be renewable. One third of its membership shall be renewed every three years. Three of its members are appointed by the President of the Republic, three by the President of the National Assembly and three by the President of the Senate.

In addition, former Presidents of the Republic shall be members of the *Conseil constitutionnel* for life as of right.

The President of the *Conseil constitutionnel* shall be appointed by the President of the Republic and shall have a casting vote in the case of a tie.

▶ Article 57

The office of member of the *Conseil constitutionnel* is incompatible with that of Minister or with the exercise of any parliamentary mandate. Other incompatibilities shall be defined by a constitutional statute.

▶ Article 58

The *Conseil constitutionnel* shall ensure the regularity of the election of the President of the Republic.

It shall investigate complaints and announce the result of the vote.

▶ Article 59

The *Conseil constitutionnel* shall give rulings in disputed cases on the regularity of the election of members of both Houses of Parliament.

▶ Article 60

The *Conseil constitutionnel* shall ensure the regularity of referendum procedures, laid down in articles 11 and 89 and in title XV. It announces the results thereof.

▶ Article 61

The *Conseil constitutionnel* shall examine all constitutional statutes before they are promulgated and all standing orders of the Houses of Parliament before they come into force, to check that they are in conformity with the Constitution.

The President of the Republic, the Prime Minister, the President of the National Assembly, the President of the Senate, or sixty members of one of the Houses of Parliament, may refer Acts of Parliament to the *Conseil constitutionnel*, for the same purposes.

In cases provided for by the two preceding paragraphs, the *Conseil constitutionnel* must make a ruling within a month. Nonetheless, in an emergency, the government may request that this period be reduced to eight days.

In the above cases, the reference to the *Conseil constitutionnel* shall suspend the time limit for promulgation.

▶ Article 62

A provision which has been declared unconstitutional may not be promulgated or put into effect.

The decisions of the *Conseil constitutionnel* shall not be subject to review. They are binding on public bodies and all administrative or judicial authorities.

▶ Article 63

A constitutional statute lays down the rules concerning the organisation and functioning of the *Conseil constitutionnel*, the procedure that is followed before it and particularly the time limits for the submission of applications.

TITLE VIII – THE JUDICIARY

▶ Article 64

The President of the Republic is the guardian of the independence of the judiciary.

He is assisted by the *Conseil supérieur de la magistrature*. A constitutional statute shall regulate the status of judges.

Judges cannot be removed from office.

▶ **Article 65**

The *Conseil supérieur de la magistrature* is presided over by the President of the Republic. The Minister of Justice is ex-officio Vice President. He may act as deputy for the President of the Republic.

The *Conseil supérieur de la magistrature* sits in two divisions, one for judges and one for members of the *ministère public.*

The division relating to judges shall include, in addition to the President of the Republic and the Minister of Justice, five judges of the civil and criminal justice system, one judge of the administrative system, one member of the *ministère public* and three independent members, who may not be either Members of Parliament or judges. They are nominated respectively by the President of the Republic, the President of the National Assembly and the President of the Senate.

The division relating to the *ministère public* shall include, in addition to the President of the Republic, and the Minister of Justice, five members of the *ministère public,* one judge of the civil and criminal justice system, and three independent members.

The division relating to judges puts forward proposals for appointments to the post of judge to the *Cour de cassation,* First Presidents of the courts of appeal and Presidents of the *tribunaux de grande instance.* The other judges are appointed in accordance with its advice.

It acts as a disciplinary court for judges, when it is presided over by the President of the *Cour de cassation.*

The division of the *Conseil supérieur de la magistrature* relating to members of the *ministère public* advises on appointments to the *ministère public* save for those made by the Cabinet.

It advises on disciplinary sanctions on members of the *ministère public* when it is presided over by the public prosecutor of the *Cour de cassation.*

A constitutional statute shall settle the conditions of application of this article.

▶ **Article 66**

No one may be arbitrarily detained.
The judiciary, guardian of individual freedom, shall ensure the respect of this principle in accordance with the conditions laid down by legislation.

• •

TITLE IX – THE HIGH COURT OF JUSTICE

▶ Article 67

The High Court of Justice shall be established.

It shall be composed of Members of Parliament elected by their peers, in equal numbers, by the National Assembly and the Senate after each general or partial renewal of each House. Its President is elected by its members.

A constitutional statute shall lay down the composition of the court, its regulations and procedure.

▶ Article 68

The President of the Republic is only responsible for acts committed in the course of his office if these amount to high treason. He may be impeached only by both Houses, if an absolute majority of members of both Houses vote for identical decisions in an open ballot. He shall be tried by the High Court of Justice.

• •

TITLE X – CRIMINAL LIABILITY OF MEMBERS OF THE GOVERNMENT

Article 68-1

Members of the government are criminally liable for serious crimes and major offences committed by them while carrying out their duties.

They shall be tried by the Court of Justice of the Republic.

The Court of Justice of the Republic must follow the definition of what constitutes a serious crime or a major offence as laid down in enacted legislation and must also pronounce sentence as provided for by such legislation.

Article 68-2

The Court of Justice of the Republic is composed of fifteen judges: twelve Members of Parliament elected by their peers, in equal numbers by the National Assembly and the Senate after each general or partial renewal of each House, and three judges of the *Cour de cassation*. It shall be presided over by one of the judges of the *Cour de cassation*.

Any person who considers they have been the victim of a serious crime or a major offence committed by members of the government while carrying out their duties may bring a case before an applications committee.

The committee may either strike out the action or refer it to the public prosecutor of the *Cour de cassation* to arrange for the case to be heard by the Court of Justice of the Republic.

The public prosecutor of the *Cour de cassation* may also ex-officio refer a case to the Court of Justice of the Republic on the recommendation of the applications committee.

A constitutional statute shall lay down the conditions of application of this article.

Article 68-3

The provisions of this article shall apply retrospectively to matters which took place before its enactment.

TITLE XI – THE ECONOMIC AND SOCIAL COUNCIL

Articles 69-71 ...

TITLE XII – TERRITORIAL UNITS

Articles 72-75 ...

TITLE XIII – TRANSITIONAL DISPOSITIONS RELATING TO NEW CALEDONIA

Articles 76-77 ...

TITLE XIV – ASSOCIATION AGREEMENTS

...

. . . .

TITLE XV – THE EUROPEAN COMMUNITY AND THE EUROPEAN UNION

▶ Article 88

The Republic may enter into agreements with States that wish to associate themselves with it in order to develop their civilisations.

Article 88-1

The Republic is a member of the European Community and the European Union, whose Member States have chosen freely by means of treaties which established these organisations to exercise some of their powers in common.

It may be a member of the European Union under the conditions laid down by the Treaty establishing a Constitution for Europe signed on 29 October 2004.

Article 88-2

Subject to reciprocity and according to the terms laid down by the Treaty on European Union signed on 7 February 1992, France agrees to the transfer of powers required for the creation of the European Economic and Monetary Union.

Subject to the provisions mentioned above, and according to the terms laid down by the Treaty which established the European Community, as amended by the treaty signed on 2 October 1997, France agrees to the transfer of powers required to set up rules relating to the free movement of persons and related matters.

Statutes fix the rules relating to the European arrest warrant pursuant to instruments passed under the Treaty of the European Union.

Article 88-3

Subject to the principle of reciprocity, and according to the terms laid down in the Treaty on European Union signed on 7 February 1992, citizens of the European Union residing in France may be granted the right to vote and to stand as candidates for local elections. These citizens may not hold the office of mayor or deputy mayor, nor may they participate either in the nomination of those who elect senators nor directly in the election of senators.

A constitutional statute passed in the same terms by both Houses of Parliament shall lay down the conditions of application of this article.

Article 88-4

The Government shall lay before the National Assembly and the Senate, as soon as they are sent to the Council of the European Union, proposals and projects relating to the action of the European Community if these include elements of a legislative nature. It may also lay down in the same manner any other proposals or projects and any other document received from an institution of the European Union.

Resolutions may be voted as required outside the sessions of Parliament on the proposals, projects and documents mentioned in the preceding paragraph, on the terms laid down by the Standing Orders of each House.

Article 88-5

Every Bill authorising the ratification of a treaty relating to a state joining the European Union and the European Communities is submitted to a referendum by the President of the Republic.

TITLE XVI – AMENDMENTS

▶ Article 89

Amendments to the Constitution may be proposed both by the President of the Republic on the proposal of the Prime Minister and by Members of Parliament. The Bill proposing the amendment must be voted by both Houses of Parliament in identical terms. The amendment shall come fully into force after approval by referendum.

However, the Bill proposing revision shall not be put to referendum, if the President of the Republic decides to lay it before the two Houses of Parliament meeting together. In this case the amendment shall be approved only if it is adopted by three fifths of the votes cast. The secretariat of the National Assembly shall serve as secretariat for this joint meeting of the Houses of Parliament.

The Constitution may not be amended in any way when territorial integrity is in jeopardy. The Republican form of government may not be subjected to any amendment.

Select bibliography

Books published in English

Baker, J. H. (1990), *Manual of Law French*, Aldershot: Scolar Press.
Bell, J. (1995), *French Constitutional Law*, Oxford: Clarendon Press.
Bell, J., Boyron, S. and Whittaker, S. (1998), *Principles of French Law*, Oxford: Oxford University Press.
Brown, L. N. and Bell, J. (1998), *French Administrative Law*, Oxford: Oxford University Press.
Cairns, W. and McKeon, R. (1995), *Introduction to French Law*, London: Cavendish.
David, R. (1972), *French Law: Its Structure, Sources and Methodology*, Baton Rouge: Louisiana State University Press.
David, R. and Brierley, J. (1985), *Major Legal Systems in the World Today*, London: Stevens.
Dickson, B. (1994), *Introduction to French Law*, London: Pitman.
Elliott, C. (2001), *French Criminal Law*, Devon: Willan Publishing.
Elliott, C, Geirnaert, C. and Houssais, F. (1998), *French Legal System and Legal Language*, London: Longman.
Faran, S. and Dadomo, C. (1996), *French Legal System*, London: Sweet & Maxwell.
Jackson, V. and Tushnet, M. (1999), *Comparative Constitutional Law*, St. Paul, MN: Foundation Press
Kahn-Freund, O., Lévy, C. and Rudden, B. (1998), *A Source-Book on French Law*, Oxford: Clarendon.
Maitland, F. W. (1950), *Year Books of Edward II* (1903), London, Selden Society.
Merryman, J. H. (1970), *The Civil Law Tradition: An Introduction to the Legal Systems of Western Europe*, Stanford, CA: Stanford University Press.
Pollard, D. (1998), *Sourcebook on French Law*, Oxford: Cavendish.
Pollock, F., and Maitland, F. W. (1996), *History of English Law before the Time of Edward I, Vol 1,* London: Lawbook Exchange Ltd.
West, A. (1998), *The French Legal System: An Introduction*, London: Butterworths.
Weston, M. (1991), *An English Reader's Guide to the French Legal System*, Oxford: Berg.
Zweigert, K. and Kötz, H. (1998), *Introduction to Comparative Law*, Oxford: Clarendon Press.

BOOKS PUBLISHED IN FRENCH

Aubert, J.-L. (2004), *Introduction au droit*, Paris: Armand Colin.
Bastien, F. (2000), *Quinquennat – Conséquences politiques*, Paris: Economica.
Beauvalet, C. and Cirendini, O. (2004), *Cour d'Assises*, Paris: Jalan.

Le bicentenaire du Code civil, Numéro spécial, (2004), Paris: Recueil Dalloz

Brachet, B. (2000), *Droit constitutionnel et administratif: capacité en droit, DEUG droit,* Paris: A.E.S.

Bros, S. (1996), *Méthodes d'exercices juridiques,* Paris: Francis Lefebvre.

Burdeau, G., Hamon, F. and Troper, M. (2001), *Droit constitutionnel,* Paris: Librairie générale de droit et de jurisprudence.

Canivet, G. and Joly-Hurard, J. (2004), *La déontologie des magistrats,* 2004, Paris: Dalloz.

Carbonnier, J. (2002), *Droit civil – Introduction,* Paris: Thémis.

Chagnollaud, D., (1997) *Je m'inscris en droit,* Paris: Dalloz.

Chagnollaud, D. (2004)**,** *Droit constitutionnel contemporain, tome 2 (Histoire constitutionnelle – La Vème République),* Paris: Dalloz – Armand Colin.

Chantebout, B. (2005), *Droit consitutionnel et science politique,* Paris: Armand Colin.

Chapus, R. (2004), *Droit du contentieux administratif,* Paris: Montchrestien.

La Vème République, permanence et mutations, janvier–février 2001, Paris: La documentation française.

Code civil (2005), Paris: Dalloz.

Le Code civil 1804–2004 – Livre du Bicentenaire (2004), Paris: Dalloz and Lexis/Nexis Litec.

Code de procédure pénale (2005), Paris: Dalloz.

Cohendet, M.-A. (2002), *Le président de la République,* Paris: Dalloz.

Le conseil de prud'hommes (2002), Ministère des affaires sociales, du travail et de la solidarité, Paris: La documentation française.

Constitution de la République française (2005), texte présenté par Ferdinand Mélin-Soucramanien, Paris: Armand Colin.

Cornu, G. (2002), *Vocabulaire juridique,* Paris: Quadrige / PUF.

Couchez, G. (2004), *Procédure civile,* Armand Colin.

Crignon, A. (2000), *Les métiers du droit,* Paris: L'Etudiant.

Croze, H. (2004), *Le procès civil,* Paris: Dalloz.

Croze, H. and Morel, C., (2001), *Procédure civile,* Paris: PUF.

David, R. (1970), *Le droit français. Tome 1: les données fondamentales du droit français,* Paris: Librairie générale de droit et de jurisprudence.

Debbasch, Charles (2004), *Constitution – Vème République,* Paris: Dalloz.

Defrénois-Souleau, I. (2004), *Je veux réussir mon droit. Méthodes de travail et clés du succès,* Paris: Colin.

Dekeuwer-Défossez, F. (2004), *Droit commercial,* Paris: Montchrestien.

De La Gorce, P.-M. and Moschetto, B. (2005), *La Vème République, Que Sais-je?,* Paris: PUF.

Documents d'études, Le Gouvernement de la Cinquième République (2002), La documentation française.

Dreyfus, F. and d'Arcy, F. (1997), *Les institutions politiques et administratives de la France,* Paris: Economica.

Dubourg-Lavroff, P. A. (1994), *Les décisions essentielles du Conseil constitutionnel: des origines à nos jours,* Paris: L'Harmattan.

Favoreu, L. et Philip, L. (2003), *Les grandes décisions du Conseil constitutionnel,* Paris: Dalloz.

Favoreu, L. and Philip, L. (2005), *Le Conseil constitutionnel, Que sais-je?,* Paris: PUF.

Foillard, P. (2005), *Droit constitutionnel,* Orléans: Paradigmes – CPU.

Formery, S.-L. (1996), *La Constitution commentée – article par article,* Paris: Hachette Supérieur.

Frison-Roche, M.-A. (1997), *Introduction générale au droit,* Paris: Dalloz.

Garé, T. and Ginestet, C. (2004), *Droit pénal – procédure pénale,* Paris: Dalloz.

Ghestin, J. and Goubeaux, G. (2000), *Traité de droit civil. Tome 1. Introduction générale,* Paris: Librairie générale de droit et de jurisprudence.

Gondouin, G. and Rouxel, S. (2004), *Les institutions juridictionnelles*, Presses Universitaires de Grenoble.

Gouaud-Tandeau de Marsac, C. (2005), *Droit constitutionnel – la Vème République*, Paris : Ellipses.

Guillien, R. (2005), *Lexique de termes juridiques*, Paris: Dalloz.

Héraud, A. and Maurin, A. (2002), *Institutions judiciaires*, Paris: Sirey.

Jestaz, P. (2005), *Les sources du droit*, Paris: Dalloz.

Kernaleguen, F. (2003), *Institutions judiciaires*, Paris: LexisNexis / Litec.

Larguier, J. (2004), *Procédure pénale*, Paris: Dalloz.

Larguier, J. (2005), *Procédure civile: droit judiciaire privé*, Paris: Dalloz.

Lavroff, D. G., (1999), *Le droit constitutionnel de la Vème République*, Paris: Dalloz.

Leclerq, C. (2002), *Travaux dirigés de droit constitutionnel: documents, dissertations, commentaires*, Paris: Litec.

Lobry, C. (1995), *Droit: BTS. Tome 1*. Paris: Techniplus.

Martin, R. (2004), *Déontologie de l'avocat*, 8th edn, Paris: LexisNexis – Litec.

Maurin, A. (2001), *Droit administratif*, Paris: Sirey.

Maus, D., (1998), *Les grands textes de la pratique institutionelle de la Cinquième République*, Paris: La documentation française.

Mazeaud, H. and Mazeaud, D. (2001), *Méthodes de travail. DEUG Droit*, Paris: Montchrestien.

Mendegris, R. and Vermelle, G. (1975), *Le commentaire d'arrêt en droit privé. Méthode et exemples*, Paris: Dalloz.

Les notices – Justice et Institutions Judiciaires, (2001), Paris: La documentation française.

Nouveau code de procédure civile, (2005), Paris: Dalloz.

Pactet, P. (1995), *Exercices de droit constitutionnel*, Paris: Masson.

Pactet, P. (1998), *Textes de droit constitutionnel*, Paris: Librairie générale de droit et de jurisprudence.

Pactet, P. and Mélin-Soucramanien, F. (2004), *Droit constitutionnel*, Paris: Dalloz-Armand Colin.

Pansier, F.-J. (2005), *Méthodologie du droit*, Paris: LexisNexis / Litec.

Perrot, R. (2004), *Institutions judiciaires*, Paris: Montchrestien.

Portelli, H. (2005), *Droit constitutionnel*, Paris: Dalloz.

Pradel, J., (1997), *Le juge d'instruction*, Paris: Dalloz.

Regards sur l'actualité – Réformes de la justice pénale (2004), Paris: La documentation française.

Rousseau, D. (2004), *Le Conseil constitutionnel en questions*, Paris : L'Harmattan.

Roussillon, H. (2001), *Le Conseil constitutionnel*, Paris: Dalloz.

Scarano, J.-P. (2005), *Institutions juridictionnelles*, Paris: Ellipses.

Soyez, J.-C. (2004), *Droit pénal et procédure pénal*, Paris: LGDJ.

Stefani, G. (2004), *Droit pénal général*, Paris: Dalloz.

Stefani, G., Levasseur, G. and Bouloc, B. (2004), *Procédure pénale*, Paris: Dalloz.

Stolowy, N. (2002), *Organisation judiciaire*, Paris: Vuibert.

Terré, F. (2003), *Introduction générale au droit*, Paris: Dalloz.

Terré, F., Lequette, Y. and Capitant, H. (2000), *Les grands arrêts de la jurisprudence civile, Tome 2*, Paris: Dalloz.

Turpin, D. (1995), *Le Conseil constitutionnel – Son rôle, sa jurisprudence*, Paris: Hachette Supérieur.

Vincent, J., Guinchard, S., Montagnier, G. and Varinard, A. (2005), *Institutions judiciaires*, Paris: Dalloz.

Waline, M. (1969), *Précis de droit administratif*, Paris: Montchrestien.

Legal Journal Articles

Abbreviations:

RTDCiv:	Revue trimestrielle de droit civil
Gaz. Pal:	La Gazette du Palais
D.:	Recueil Dalloz
JCP:	Le Juris-classeur périodique – La semaine juridique

Aubert, J.-L. (2005), 'La distinction du fait et du droit dans le pourvoi en cassation en matière civile', *D.* 2005, 1115

Bailleul, D. (2004), 'Quand le juge ressemble au constituant', *D.* 2004, 3089

Beaud, O. and Lauvaux, P. (2003), 'Sur le soi-disant *"impeachment* à la française"', *D.* 2003, 2646

Béguin, J. (2004), 'Entretien avec M. Jean Foyer – "Le Code civil est vivant. Il doit le demeurer!"', *JCP* 2004, 543

Beignier, B. and Mouton, S. (2001), 'La Constitution et la Convention européenne des droits de l'homme, rang et fonction', *D.* 2001, 1636

Bell, J. (2000), 'Celebrating 200 years of the *Conseil d'Etat*', *International and Comparative Law Quarterly* 2000, at 660

Bénabent, A. (2005), 'Doctrine ou Dallas?', *D.* 2005, 852

Boré, L. and De Salve de Bruneton, J. (2005), 'Quelques idées sur le pourvoi en cassation', *D.* 2005, 180

Cachard, O. (2004), 'Aux grands arrêts, les juristes reconnaissants ...', *D.* 2004, 429

Canivet, G. (2002), 'La procédure d'admission des pourvois en cassation: bilan d'un semestre d'application de l'article L 131–6 du COJ', *D.* 2002, 2195

Cornu, G. (2002), 'Un Code civil n'est pas un instrument communautaire', *D.* 2002, 351

Cottin, M. (2002), 'La Cour de cassation se dote d'une procédure d'admission des pourvois en cassation', *D.* 2002, 748

Croze, H. (2004), 'Qu'est-ce qu'enseigner le droit?', *D.* 2004, 1315

Dubois, L. (1999), 'Les trois logiques de la jurisprudence Sarran', *Revue Française de droit administrative* 1999, 57

Favoreu, L. (2001), 'L'application de l'article 62, al. 2, de la Constitution par la Cour de cassation', *D.* 2001, 2683

Favoreu, L. (2003), 'Le statut pénal du chef de l'Etat', *D.* 2003, 430

Feldman, J.-P. (2004), 'Le projet de loi constitutionnelle relative à la Charte de l'environnement', *D.* 2004, 970

François, B. and Montebourg, A. (2005), 'Une nouvelle Constitution: la fin de l'exception française', *D.* 2005, 2473

Grynbaum, L. (2005), 'Et la recherche?' *D.* 2005, 4

Idriss, M. (2005), 'Laïcité and the banning of the 'hijab' in France', *Legal Studies* vol. 25, 260

Lequette, Y. (2002), 'Quelques remarques à propos du projet de code civil européen de M. von Bar', *D.* 2002, 2202

Martin, R. (2004), 'Vous avez dit proximité?', *D.* 2004, 507

Martin, R. (2004), 'Les cheminements des pouvoirs judiciaires depuis 1789', *RTD civ.* 2004, 251

Martin, R. (2004), 'Les modifications au statut de l'avocat par la loi No 2004-130 du 11 février 2004', *JCP* 2004, 373

Mathieu, B. (2003), 'Les propositions de la "commission Avril" relatives au statut juridictionnel du Président de la République', *JCP* 2003, 53

Mathieu, B. (2004), 'Le Conseil constitutionnel conforte la construction européenne en s'appuyant sur les exigences constitutionnelles nationales', *D.* 2004, at 1739

Mathieu, B. (2004), 'La "Constitution" européenne ne menace pas la République', *D.* 2004, 3075

Mathieu, B. (2005), 'Le respect de la Constitution: risque ou exigence?', *D.* 2005, 2401

Morvan, P. (2004), '"Partisane" mais paritaire donc impartiale: la juridiction prud'homale', Aperçu rapide, Actualité, *JCP* 2004, 269

Morvan, P. (2005), 'Le revirement de jurisprudence pour l'avenir: humble adresse aux magistrats ayant franchi le Rubicon', *D.* 2005, 247

Moutouh, H. (2003), 'Le contrôle de constitutionnalité des lois constitutionnelles: suite et fin', *D.* 2003, 1099

Perdriau, A. (2001), 'Le pragmatisme de la Cour de cassation', *JCP* 2001, 2141

Piastra, R. (2004), 'Quelques propos sur l'article 49-3 de la Constitution', *D.* 2004, 2659

Piastra, R. (2004), 'Les 46 ans de la Ve République', *D.* 2004, 3147

Piastra, R. (2005), 'Du devoir de réserve des conseillers constitutionnels ...', *D.* 2005, 233

Pontier, J.-M. (2000), 'A quoi servent les lois?', *D.* 2000, 57

Puig, P. (2001), 'Hiérarchie des normes: du système au principe', *RTD civ.* 2001, at 749

Rancé, P. (2001), 'Interview de Christophe Pettiti, La Cour nationale de l'incapacité et de la tarification', *D.* 2001, 789

Rancé, P. (2002) 'La réforme des tribunaux de commerce', *D.* 2002, 1050

Rousseau, D. (1998), 'Les transformations du droit constitutionnel sous la Vème République', *Revue du droit public* 1998, 1780

Ruel, F. (2005), 'La juridiction de proximité: retouchée mais pas encore coulée', *JCP* 2005, 417

Tricot, D. (2004), 'L'élaboration d'un arrêt de la Cour de cassation', Doctrine, *JCP* 2004, 225

Verpeaux, M. (2004), 'Les Principes fondamentaux reconnus par les lois de la République ont-ils encore un avenir?', *D.* 2004, 1537

Verpeaux, M. (2005), 'La loi constitutionnelle du 1er mars 2005 modifiant le titre XV de la Constitution, ou la révision', *D.* 2005, 2485

Zarka, J.-C. (2003), 'La réforme du Sénat', *JCP* 2003, 1341

Zarka, J.-C. (2005), 'A propos de l'inflation législative', *D.* 2005, 660

Zenati, F. (1992), 'La saisine pour avis de la Cour de cassation', *D.* 1992, 247

Newspaper articles

Bréhier, T. (1997), 'Une lecture stricte de la Constitution', *Le Monde*, 3 June 1997

Bréhier, T. (1999), 'Roland Dumas est isolé à la présidence du Conseil constitutionnel', *Le Monde*, 23 March 1999

Bremner, C. (2002), 'Poll victory gives Chirac complete control', *The Times*, 18 June 2002

Bronner, L. (2005), 'Un rapport préconise la sélection des étudiants étrangers', *Le Monde*, 29 January 2005

Chemin, A. (2002), 'Jacques Chirac est réélu à l'Elysée grâce à la gauche mobilisée', *Le Monde*, 7 May 2002

Colombani, J.-M. (2000), 'La réduction du mandat présidentiel est approuvée à une majorité des deux tiers', *Le Monde*, 25 September 2000

Courtois, G. (1999), 'Son président par intérim assure que le Conseil constitutionnel fonctionne "normalement"', *Le Monde*, 14 May 1999

Courtois, G. (2000), 'Le Conseil constitutionnel est invité à trancher la situation de M. Dumas', *Le Monde*, 21 February 2000

Courtois, G. (2000), 'Roland Dumas annonce sa démission du Conseil constitutionnel', *Le Monde*, 11 March 2000

De Virieu, H. (1998), 'Les élections sénatoriales, une affaire de "professionnels"', *Le Monde*, 13 August 1998

Duhamel, O. (2002), 'Osons la VIème République', *Le Monde*, 5/6 May 2002 'French universities – Elite syncopations', *The Economist*, 29 November 2003

Gattegno, H. (2002), 'Sur le statut pénal du président, dires d'experts', 7–8 July 2002

Gattegno, H. and Ridet, P. (2002), ' Le duel Chirac–Le Pen provoque un séisme politique', *Le Monde*, 23 April 2002

Prevost, J.-F. (1987), 'L'éclipse partielle du chef de l'Etat en cas de cohabitation', *Le Monde*, 3 February 1987

Robert-Diard, P. (2005), 'Jacques Chirac, l'absent de son procès', *Le Monde*, 7 July 2005

Rousseau, D. and Spitz, E. (2001), 'Le crépuscule du Conseil constitutionnel', *Le Monde*, 7 December 2001

The Internet

www.assemblee-nat.fr: The National Assembly. Includes some text in English.

www.caa-paris.juradm.fr/caa/paris/index.shtml: Paris Administrative Court of Appeal

www.ca-paris.justice.fr: Paris Court of Appeal

www.ccomptes.fr: The audit court

www.conseil-constitutionnel.fr: The *Conseil constitutionnel*

www.conseil-etat.fr: The *Conseil d'Etat*

www.conseil-superieur-magistrature.fr: The *Conseil supérieur de la magistrature*. Includes some text in English.

www.courdecassation.fr: The *Cour de cassation*. Includes some text in English.

www.elysee.fr: The President of the Republic. Includes some text in English.

www.ena.fr: The *Ecole Nationale d'Administration*. Includes some text in English.

www.enm.justice.fr: The *Ecole Nationale de la Magistrature*

www.gip-recherche-justice.fr: French Ministry of justice website on law and justice.

www.journal-officiel.gouv.fr: Internet version of the Official Journal.

www.justice.gouv.fr: The Ministry of justice. Includes some text in English.

www.ladocfrancaise.gouv.fr: La documentation française.

www.legifrance.gouv.fr: Légifrance. Includes legislation in English.

www.premier-ministre.gouv.fr: The Prime Minister. Includes some text in English.

www.senat.fr: The Senate.

www.syndicat-magistrature.org: *Syndicat de la magistrature*

www.tgi-angouleme.justice.fr: The TGI in Angoulême

www.tgi-macon.justice.fr: The TGI in Macon

www.vie-publique.fr: An official government website providing general information on the Constitution and administration of France.

www.ucl.ac.uk/laws/global_law: Institute of Global Law. Includes French cases and statutes translated into English.

www.univ-lyon3.fr: The University Jean Moulin Lyon 3

Glossary

A

à charge d'appel	open to appeal
à huis clos	in camera
à perpétuité	life, for life
à temps	fixed term
à titre exceptionnel	in exceptional cases
aborder	to discuss, tackle
abus (m) d'autorité	abuse of authority
abus (m) de confiance	abuse of confidence
abus (m) de pouvoir	abuse of power
accomplir les diligences normales	to exercise normal care
accord (m)	agreement
accru (infinitive: accroître)	increased, enhanced
accusatoire	adversarial
accusé(e)	accused, defendant
acte d'huissier (m)	document served by the court bailiff
actes (m) d'information	means of investigation
acte (m) de barbarie	inhumane act
acte (m) de commerce	commercial transaction
acte (m) de procédure	procedural documentation, pleadings
acte (m) exécutoire	enforceable instrument/deed
acte (m) instrumentaire	instrument
acte (m) signifié par huissier	official document served by the court bailiff
action (f) civile	civil action
action (f) en divorce	divorce proceedings
action (f) en justice	*right to bring and defend an action*
action (f) publique	public prosecution
actuel	immediate
administration (f) des preuves	presentation of evidence
administration (f) pénitentiaire	prison service
affaire (f)	case

affichage (f)	publication
agent (m) de police judiciaire	police officer
agir sous l'empire de	to act under the influence of
agissements (m) incriminés	criminal conduct
alinéa (m)	paragraph
aménagement (m)	arrangements (for)
amende (f)	fine
amende (f) honorable	public confession, apology
amphithéâtre (m)	lecture theatre
ancien droit (m)	*pre-revolutionary law*
animer	to lead (a team)
appel (m)	appeal (on facts and/or law)
appel (m) des causes	n.t. (nearest English equivalent: pre-trial hearing)
appel (m) téléphonique malveillant	malicious telephone call
appelant (m)	appellant
arbitrage (m) juridique	judicial arbitration
arme (f)	weapon
arrestation (f)	arrest
arrêt (m)	judgment (of higher court)
arrêt (m) de cassation	n.t. (*decision to quash a judgment of the lower courts*)
arrêt (m) de principe	*case stating a legal principle*
arrêt (m) de rejet	*final decision rejecting an appeal on points of law*
arrêt (m) définitif	*decision open to appeal on law rather than fact*
arrêté (m)	order, decision
assassinat (m)	assassination
Assemblée (f) nationale	National Assembly, *lower chamber of Parliament*
assemblée (f) parlementaire	parliamentary assembly
assemblée (f) plénière	*full sitting of the Cour de cassation*
assignation (f)	writ, summons
assigné	summoned
assigner	to sue, to summon
association (f) de malfaiteurs	conspiracy
atteinte (f)	attack
attendu (m)	*reason adduced for a judgment*
attendu que	whereas, given that
attribution (f) administrative	administrative power, competence
attributions (f)	powers
au premier tour	at the first ballot
au sein de	within
au suffrage indirect	by indirect suffrage

au suffrage universel direct	by direct universal suffrage
audience (f) des plaidoiries	hearing the action, hearing the case
audience (f)	court hearing, hearing
audition (f)	questioning
audition (f) des témoins	hearing of witnesses
auteur (m)	principal offender, defendant, author
auteur (m) intellectuel	a person who is treated as the principal offender, though he/she did not personally carry out the *actus reus* of the offence; also known as *l'auteur moral*
auteur (m) matériel	principal offender
auteur (m) moral	a person who is treated as the principal offender, though he/she did not personally carry out the *actus reus* of the offence; also known as *l'auteur intellectuel*
autorité (f) judiciaire	judiciary, judicial power
autorité (f) légitime	legitimate authority
aux pouvoirs renforcés	with increased powers
aux torts de	against
auxiliaire (m) de justice	officer of the court
avant .. ans révolus	before turning ..
avènement (m)	advent
avertir les autorités judiciaires	to alert the legal authorities
avertissement (m)	notice to attend
avis (m)	opinion, formal opinion
avocat(e)	n.t. (nearest English equivalent: barrister)
avocat(e) stagiaire	trainee lawyer
avoir force authentique	to have been authenticated
avoir force exécutoire	to be enforceable
avoir force de précédent	to constitute a precedent
avoir intérêt pour agir	to have sufficient interest to bring an action
avoir qualité pour agir	to have authority to bring an action
avoir un caractère réglementaire	to have a regulatory character
avoué (m) près de la cour d'appel	n.t.

B

baïonnettes (f) intelligentes	principle according to which subordinates are expected to ensure the legality of an order before executing it

bande (f) organisée	organised gang
barre (f)	court (referring to the bar at the front of the court)
barreau (m)	n.t. (fulfils a similar role to the English 'Bar')
bâtonnier (m)	n.t. (fulfils a similar role to the 'President of the Bar')
bicaméral	bicameral
bien (m)	property
bien fondé (m)	validity
bien immobilier (m)	immovable property, real property
bien (m) incorporel	intangible property
bien ou mal fondé	well or ill-founded
blanchiment (m)	money laundering
blesser	to injure
bloc (m) de constitutionnalité	*ensemble of constitutional rules,* constitutional block
bon père de famille	reasonable person
bourreau (m)	state executioner
branche (f)	limb, branch
bureau de dépot des usages professionnels	registry of professional practices

C

Cabinet d'avocats (m)	law practice, chambers
caduc, caduque	null, void, obsolete
carcan (m)	iron collar
le cas échéant	if needed, if considered necessary, where necessary
casser	to quash (a judgment)
cause (f) de non-imputabilité	defence which is directly linked to the defendant; subjective defence; excuse
céder	to supply
cession (f) de brevet	transfer of a patent
cession (f) de stupéfiants	supply of drugs
chambre (f) correctionnelle	Criminal Division (of the *tribunal correctionnel, tribunal de grande instance* or *Cour d'assises*)
chambre (f) criminelle	the Criminal Division (of the *Cour de cassation*)
chambre d'accusation	division of the appeal court concerned with controlling

	the judicial investigation, now known as the *chambre de l'instruction*
chambre (f) de l'instruction	Judicial Investigation Division. The name given to the old *chambre d'accusation* following the Act of 15 June 2000
chambre (f) des appels	appeal division
chambre (f) mixte	joint bench of the *Cour de cassation*
chambre (f) sociale	Social Division
charge (f)	practice
charges (f)	proof
Charte de l'environnement	Charter for the Environment
chef (m) de l'Etat	(French) Head of State
chef (m) du gouvernement	Head of Government
circuit (m) long	*long procedure* (civil courts)
circuit (m) court	*short procedure* (civil courts)
citation (f) directe	summons
citer	to quote, cite
citer à comparaître	to summon
classement	see '*décision de classement*'
classer une affaire	to close a case
clôture (f) des débats	closing of oral submissions
coauteur (m)	joint principal
Code (m) civil	Civil Code
Code (m) de commerce	Commercial Code
Code (m) de la construction et de l'habitation	Construction and Housing Code
Code (m) de la consummation	Consumer Code
Code (m) de l'action sociale	Social Action Code
Code (m) de l'éducation	Education Code
Code (m) de l'environnement	Code for the Environment
Code (m) des douanes	Customs Code
Code (m) de justice administrative	Code of Administrative Justice
Code (m) de justice militaire	Code of Military Justice
Code (m) d'instruction criminelle	Code of Criminal Procedure/ Criminal Investigation Code
Code (m) général des impost	General Tax Code
Code (m) monétaire et financier	Monetary and Financial Code
Code de l'organisation judiciaire	Main legislative provisions regulating the civil courts
Code (m) pénal	Criminal Code
Code (m) de procédure civile	Code of Civil Procedure

Code (m) de la route	Highway Code
Code (m) rural	Countryside Code
Code (m) de la santé publique	Public Health Code
Code (m) du travail	Employment Code
coercitif	coercive
cohabitation (f)	situation occurring when President of the Republic does not retain parliamentary majority
Comité (m) constitutionnel	Predecessor to the Conseil constitutionnel
commentaire (m) d'arrêt	commentary of a judgment
commerçant (m)	tradesman
commettre	to commit
commissaire (m) du gouvernement	n.t. (sometimes translated as: Government Commissioner)
Commission (f) d'indemnisation des victimes d'infraction	Commission for the Victims of Crime, the equivalent to the English Criminal Injuries Compensation Board
commission (f) d'instruction	n.t. (*Committee responsible for opening a judicial investigation*)
commission (f) des requêtes	n.t.
comparution (f)	court attendance
comparution (f) immédiate	immediate court attendance
comparution (f) volontaire	voluntary court attendance
compétence (f) d'attribution	prescribed powers, designated jurisdiction, designated competence
compétence (f) juridictionnelle	judicial powers
complice (m)	accomplice
complicité (f) corespective	analysis according to which the joint principal is also automatically an accomplice
complot (m)	conspiracy
composition (f) pénale	formal plea bargain, *an out of court settlement in criminal matters*
comptable (m) public	n.t. (*state accountant responsible for recovery and payments of debts owed by public authorities and for administering the public purse*)
conciliation (f)	conciliation phase
conclusions (f)	submissions, findings
concours (m)	competitive examination
concubin(e)	live-in partner

condamnation (f)	conviction
condamné(e)	convicted person
confier à	to entrust with
confirmer le jugement	to uphold the judgment
confiscation (f) d'un objet	confiscation of assets
conflit (m) de compétence	jurisdictional dispute
conflit (m) négatif	n.t.
conflit (m) positif	n.t.
Congrès (m)	both Houses of Parliament sitting together
conseil (m)	advice
Conseil (m) constitutionnel	n.t. (sometimes translated as: Constitutional Court)
Conseil (m) de discipline	disciplinary body for the *avocats*
Conseil (m) d'Etat	n.t.
Conseil (m) de l'Ordre	n.t. (nearest English equivalent: Bar Council)
conseil (m) de prud'hommes	*industrial conciliation tribunal*
Conseil (m) des ministres	n.t. (nearest equivalent: French cabinet)
conseil (m) juridique	legal adviser
Conseil (m) Supérieur de la Magistrature	n.t.
conseiller (m)	appeal judge, senior judge
conseiller (m) général	departmental councillor
conseiller (m) régional	regional councillor
conserver les moyens de preuve	to safeguard the evidence
considérant que	considering that, in view of
consommation (f)	commission, perpetration
constituant (m)	constitutional legislator
constitution (f) de partie civile	*independent action for damages*
consultatif	advisory
contentieux (m) d'annulation	action for annulment
contentieux (m) de pleine juridiction	action for damages
contentieux (m) électoral	*litigation arising from the electoral process*
contestation (f)	dispute, objection
contradiction (f)	debate
contradictoire	*giving due hearing to the parties*
contrainte (f)	constraint
contravention (f)	minor offence
contreseing (m)	counter-signature
contrôle (m) judiciaire	bail
contrôle (m) juridictionnel	judicial control

contumace	see *la procédure en contumace*
convocation (f)	summons
convocation (f) par procès-verbal	*formal order to attend*
corps (m) du devoir	main body of an essay
Corps (m) législatif	post-revolutionary assembly
correctionnel	Criminal Division
coupable	guilty
coupable (m)	guilty person
coups et blessures volontaires	crime of intentionally injuring another
Cour (f) administrative d'appel	Administrative Court of Appeal
Cour (f) d'appel	court of appeal
Cour (f) d'assises	n.t.
Cour (f) d'assises des mineurs	n.t.
Cour (f) de cassation	n.t.
Cour (f) des comptes	Audit Court
Cour (f) de justice de la République	Court of Justice of the Republic
Cour (f) de Justice des Communautés Européennes	European Court of Justice
cour (f) nationale de l'incapacité et de la tarification de l'assurance des accidents du travail	the national disability disputes appeal court
Cour (f) pénale internationale	International Criminal Court
cour (f) régionale des comptes	regional audit court
cours (m) magistral	lecture
coutumes (f) germaniques	Germanic customs
crime (m)	serious crime
crime (m) contre l'humanité	crime against humanity
crime (m) de guerre	war crime
culpabilité (f)	guilt
cumul (m) des mandats	plurality

D

d'office	automatically
d'usage	usual
dans un temps très voisin	within a very short space of time
de droit	as of right
de fond	fundamental
de portée limitée	of limited scope
de tout fait	of any act
débats (m)	arguments
débouter	to dismiss
décerner un mandat	to issue a warrant
déchéance (f)	disqualification
décision (f)	judgment, decision, presidential edict

décision (f) de classement	decision not to bring a prosecution
décision (f) d'espèce	decision on the facts
décision (f) de condamnation	conviction and sentencing
décision (f) de mise en vigueur	decision to put into effect
décision (f) de non-lieu	*decision that there is no case to answer; to dismiss a case*
décision (f) de relaxe	acquittal
décision (f) de renvoi	*decision to send the defendant for trial*
Déclaration (f) des droits de l'homme et du citoyen	Declaration of the Rights of Man (modern translation: Declaration of Human and Civil Rights)
déclencher	to set in motion
déclencher l'action publique	to institute criminal proceedings
décolation (f)	decapitation
se décomposer en	to split into
décret (m)	decree
défaut (m) criminal	trial in the absence of the defendant
se défendre	to defend oneself
défense (f) au fond	*defence based on the merits of the case*
défendeur (m)	defendant
déférer une affaire à la justice	to refer a case to a court
déférer un accusé devant un tribunal	to bring a defendant before a court
défit (m)	wrongful conduct
défunt(e)	deceased (n)
dégager	to extract
délai-butoir (m)	time limit
délai (m) de prescription	limitation period
délibérer	to deliberate, to debate
délit (m)	major offence
délit (m) matériel	major offence which only required as a *mens rea* that the defendant's conduct be voluntary
demande (f)	claim
demande (f) additionnelle	further claim
demande (f) de la partie civile	*application by the victim or his or her representative*
demande (f) en intervention	third party notice (of a claim made by or against a third party)
demande (f) incidente	annexed claim
demande (f) introductive d'instance	statement of claim

demande (f) reconventionnelle	counterclaim
demande (f) en réparation du préjudice	claim for damages
demandeur (m)/demanderesse (f)	plaintiff, appellant, applicant
demandeur (m)/demanderesse (f) en indemnisation	claimant for damages
démission (f)	resignation
déni (m) de justice	miscarriage of justice
dénonciation (f) de	informing on, denunciation of
se dépêcher sur les lieux	to hasten to the scene of a crime
déportation (f)	deportation
déposer en justice	to give evidence in court
dépôt (m) de plainte	(formal) registering of a complaint
député (m)	deputy, *member of the National Assembly*
déroulement (m) du scrutin	conduct of the election
déroulement (m) du procès	trial proceedings
dès	upon, from the moment of
désormais	henceforth, from now on
détention (f)	detention
détention (f) provisoire	remand in custody
détournement (m) de fonds	embezzlement, misappropriation of funds
détourner	to misappropriate
diligences (f)	care
discernement (m)	ability to reason
discours (m)	speech
disposer d'une compétence normative de droit commun	*to have general powers to make regulations*
disposer de pouvoirs réglementaires	to have regulatory powers
dispositif (m)	court's finding (stated at the end of the decision)
disposition (f)	provision
disposition (f) législative	legislative provision
dissolution (f)	dissolution
doctorat (m)	PHD
doctrine (f)	legal writing (*the body of opinion on legal matters expressed in books and articles*)
dol (m)	fault
dol (m) aggravé	additional *mens rea* beyond general or special intention
dol (m) éventuel	oblique intention, indirect intention

dol (m) dépassé	the result caused goes beyond the intention and foresight of the defendant
dol (m) général	general intention
dol (m) imprécis	where a person does an act seeking a result without being able to foresee what exactly the result will be. Also known as *dol indéterminé*
dol (m) indéterminé	where a person does an act seeking a result without being able to foresee what exactly the result will be. Also known as *dol imprécis*
dol (m) spécial	special intention
dommage (m)	damage
dommages-intérêts (m)	damages
domaine (m) de la loi	legislative domain, *field of parliamentary legislation*
domaine (m) du règlement	regulatory domain, *field of government regulations*
domaine (m) législatif	legislative domain, *field of parliamentary legislation*
domaine (m) réglementaire	regulatory domain, *field of government regulations*
donner un avis consultatif	to give an advisory opinion
donner volontairement la mort à autrui	to kill voluntarily another person
dossier (m) de plaidoiries	written submissions
dresser un acte authentique/ un acte notarié	to draw up an authenticated and enforceable instrument/deed
dresser un constat	to draw up an affidavit
droit (m) civil	civil law
droit (m) commercial	commercial law
droit (m) constitutionnel	constitutional law
droit (m) d'agir	right to bring an action
droit (m) d'aînesse	primogeniture (*law whereby an estate passes to the eldest male*)
droit (m) d'association	right of association
droit (m) de faire grève	right to strike
droit (m) de saisine	right to make an application
droit (m) des contrats	contract law
droit (m) des obligations	law of obligations
droit (m) des sociétés	company law
droit (m) du travail	employment law

droit (m) communautaire	community law
droit (m) fiscal	tax law
droit (m) intermédiaire	intermediate law
droit (m) international	international law
droit international privé	conflict of laws
droit international public	public international law
droit (m) interne	domestic law
droit (m) pénal	criminal law
droit (m) privé	private law (is concerned with the rights between private individuals)
droit (m) public	public law (is concerned with the relationship between the State and the individual or the organisation of the State)
droit (m) romain	Roman law

E

ébaucher	to outline, to sketch
écartèlement	quartering
échevinage (m)	term used to describe the courts composed simultaneously of career judges and lay judges
édicté	drawn up
s'efforcer de	to endeavour to
élaboration (f) de la loi	law-making
élection (f) partielle	by-election
élément (m) intellectuel	*mens rea*
élément (m) matériel	*actus reus*
élément (m) moral	*mens rea*
élément (m) psychologique	*mens rea*
éléments (m) de preuve	pieces of evidence
élu (infinitive: élire)	elected
élus par leurs pairs	elected by their peers
empiètement (m) du parlement	parliamentary infringement
empoisonnement (m)	poisoning
emprisonnement (m)	imprisonment
encombrement (m) de la voie publique	obstructing the highway
encourir une peine	to incur a punishment
enfeindre les prohibitions légales	to break the law
en fonction de	according to
engager une action	to bring an action
enlèvement (m)	abduction
en matière contraventionnelle	for minor offences, *in cases involving minor offences*

en matière correctionnelle	for major offences, *in cases involving major offences*
en premier et dernier ressort	*not open to appeal*
en revanche	on the other hand
en tout état de cause	at any point, in any case
en vertu de	by virtue of
en vigueur	in force
encourir de poursuites judiciaires	to be exposed to legal proceedings
engendrer	to engender, to generate
énoncer	to state
enquête (f)	investigation
enquête (f) de flagrance	expedited investigation (with extended powers)
enquête (f) préliminaire	ordinary investigation (without special powers)
enrôler	to list (a case)
entamer	to initiate
entraver	to impede
entrée (f) par effraction	entrance by force
entrer dans la compétence de	to fall within the remit of
s'entretenir avec l'avocat	to consult with one's lawyer
erreur (f) sur le droit	error of law
escroquerie (f)	fraud
étatique	derived from the state
être assigné à comparaître	to be summoned
être assigné en divorce	to be sued for divorce
être assimilé à une arme	to be classed as a weapon
être astreinte aux obligations du contrôle judiciaire	to be subjected to conditional bail
être atteinte de	to be affected by, to suffer from
être débouté de sa demande	to have one's case rejected
être défendu	to be forbidden
être poursuivi	to be prosecuted
être puni de	to be punished with
être reconnu coupable	to be found guilty
être responsable pénalement	to be criminally responsible
être saisi d'un pourvoi (en cassation)	*to have an appeal referred on points of law only*
être tenu	to be legally obliged
étude (f)	office (of a *notaire*)
éventuel	hypothetical
examen (m) de classement	*examination ranking the student according to the mark awarded*

exception (f) d'inconstitutionnalité — *plea that an Act breaches the Constitution*

exception (f) de procédure — *plea based on procedural irregularity*

exécutif (m) — executive

exécution (f) forcée — compulsory execution

exécutoire — enforceable

exercer l'action publique — to bring a prosecution

exercer une profession libérale — to practise a profession (in private practice)

exercer un droit de garde — to act as legal guardians

exercer un ascendant — to exert (undue) influence

F

faire droit à — to accept

faire grâce — *to grant a presidential pardon*

faire grief à — to attack

faire l'objet de mesures — to be the subject of measures

faire une reconstitution de l'infraction — to carry out a reconstruction of the crime

fait (m) incriminé — criminal conduct

fait (m) justificatif — a defence that provides a justification for the criminal conduct which ceases to be viewed as antisocial; justification; objective defence

faute (f) caractérisée — established fault

faute (f) contraventionnelle — the *mens rea* of minor offences

faute (f) d'imprudence — carelessness

fiche (f) d'arrêt — case summary

fin (f) de non-recevoir — striking out of a case

force (f) — force

formation (f) collégiale — *sitting of at least three judges*

fouet (m) — flogging

frapper quelqu'un d'une peine — to impose a punishment on someone

frauduleux — with guilty intent

fuite (f) — escape

G

garant (m) — guarantor, guardian

garde à vue (f) — police custody

Garde (m) des Sceaux — Minister of Justice

Gaule (f) — Gaul

génocide (m) — genocide

Gouvernement (m) Général — Government House

grande partie (f)	main section
greffe (m)	court office
greffier (m)	clerk of the court
grosse (f)	formal copy of the judgment

H

Haute cour (f) de justice	High Court of Justice
hiérarchie (f) des normes juridiques	hierarchy of legal rules
homicide (m)	homicide
homicide (m) volontaire	voluntary homicide
homicide (m) involontaire	involuntary homicide, involuntary manslaughter
homologuer	to approve, to ratify, to confirm, to authorise
honorifique	honorary
huissier (m) de justice	n.t. (sometimes translated as: court bailiff, usher)

I

idée (f) directrice	main theme
s'immiscer dans	to interfere with
immixtion (f)	interference
immobilisation (f) d'un objet	freezing of assets
immunité (f)	immunity
s'implanter	to become established
impliquer	to imply
impossibilité (f) matérielle	physical impossibility
imprudence (f)	imprudence
impunité (f)	impunity
imputation (f)	existence
incapacité (f)	incapacity
incapacité (f) totale de travail	total incapacity to work
in concreto	subjective
inculpation (f)	charge
indemnisation (f)	compensation
indemniser	to compensate
indices (m) graves	serious incriminating evidence
infirmer le jugement	to reject the decision
infraction (f)	offence
infraction (f) contre la personne	offence against the person
infraction (f) contre un bien	offence against property
infraction (f) flagrante	*offence giving rise to expedited investigation*
infraction (f) formelle	complete offence that does not require a result

infraction (f) matérielle	offence which only requires as a *mens rea* that the defendant's conduct be voluntary. The nearest English equivalent is a strict liability offence
infraction (f) pénale	criminal offence
injonction (f)	injunction
injustifié	unjustified
inquisitoire	inquisitorial
inscription (f) de faux	plea of forgery
instance (f) juridictionnelle	court
instruction (f)	*judicial investigation*
intention (f)	intention
intention (f) frauduleuse	guilty intent
interdiction (f)	banning
interjeter appel	to lodge an appeal
interrogatoire (f)	cross-examination
intervention (f) forcée	n.t. (*joining of a third party to the proceedings*)
intervention (f) volontaire	n.t. (*a third party joining the proceedings*)
intime conviction (f)	personal conviction
intimé (m)	defendant in a court of appeal
intitulé	heading
irresponsable	non-accountable

J

jeu (m) démocratique	democratic process
jour (m) amende	daily fine
jour (m) ouvrable	a working day
Journal officiel	n.t. (sometimes translated as: Official Journal)
juge (m)	judge
juge (m) arbitre	*judge acting as an arbitrator*
juge (m) consulaire	*lay judge in the commercial court*
juge (m) des libertés et de la détention	judge of freedom and detention, judge responsible for deciding whether to grant bail or to place on remand
juge (m) de proximité	neighbourhood court judge
juge (m) d'instruction	n.t. (*judge in charge of the judicial investigation*; sometimes translated as: examining magistrate or investigating judge)
juge (m) de la mise en état	n.t. (sometimes translated as: preparatory judge)

juge (m) de première instance	court of first instance
juge (m) des référés	judge in chambers
juge (m) du droit	*judge who considers only points of law*
juge (m) du fond	*judge who considers both the facts and the law*
juge (m) électoral	judge of election disputes
juge (m) rapporteur	n.t. (sometimes translated as: reporting judge)
jugement (m)	judgment, decision (generally in lower courts)
jugement (m) avant dire droit	interim, provisional decision
jugement (m) définitif	definitive judgment
jugement (m) sur le fond	*a decision on the facts and the law*
juré(e)	juror
juridiction (f) à juge unique	*court presided over by a single judge*
juridiction (f) collégiale	*court presided over by a minimum of three judges who deliver a single judgment*
juridiction (f) d'exception	specialised court
juridiction (f) de droit commun	court of general jurisdiction
juridiction (f) de jugement	trial court
juridiction (f) de première instance	court of first instance
juridiction (f) de proximité	neighbourhood court
juridiction (f) de renvoi	*court to which a case is referred after a successful appeal on the law*
juridiction (f) non rattachée	*court outside the ordinary and administrative court system*
juridiction (f) pénale	criminal court
juridiction (f) répressive	criminal court
juridiction (f) spécialisée	specialised court
juridictions (f) d'instruction	*courts overseeing the investigation*
juridictionnel	judicial
jurisprudence (f)	case law
jurisprudence (f) constante	when case law is settled on a point of law
jurisprudence (f) controversée	conflicting case law
juriste	lawyer
jury (m)	jury
justiciable (m)	litigant

L

laïcité (f)	secularity
lecture (f)	reading
législateur (m)	Parliament, legislator
légitimement	legally

lésé	prejudiced
lettre (f) de rémission	pardon
liberté (f) contractuelle	freedom to enter into a contract
licence (f)	three-year degree
licenciement (m) abusif	unfair dismissal
lié par	bound by
lien (m) de causalité	causal link
lien (m) de droit	legal relationship
litige (m)	legal dispute, litigation
loi (f)	Act, Act of Parliament, statute, legislation
loi (f) d'habilitation	enabling Act of Parliament
loi impérative	compulsory law
loi (f) ordinaire	Act, statute of Parliament
loi (f) organique	n.t.
loi (f) parlementaire	Act, statute of Parliament
loi (f) référendaire	*statute passed by means of a referendum*
loi (f) supplétive	law which parties can choose not to follow
lors des scrutins	at the time of the elections

M

machination (f)	scheming
magistrat (m)	judge
magistrat (m) de carrière	professional judge
magistrature (f)	n.t. (can sometimes be translated as: judiciary)
magistrature (f) assise	judiciary, bench
magistrature (f) debout	n.t. (sometimes translated as: public prosecutor's office or the prosecution)
magistrature (f) du parquet	n.t. (sometimes translated as: public prosecutor's office or the prosecution)
magistrature (f) du siège	judiciary, bench
maire (m)	mayor
majorité (f) absolue	absolute majority
majorité (f) relative	relative majority
maladresse (f)	ineptitude
mandant (m)	mandator
mandat (m)	mandate, warrant
mandat (m) *ad litem*	automatic mandate
mandat (m) de dépôt:	warrant to detain, committal order

mandat (m) de recherché	warrant to arrest and detain
mandat (m) parlementaire	parliamentary mandate
maniement (m) juridique	legal transfer
manifestation (f) de la vérité	establishing the truth
manifestement	obviously
manoeuvre (f) frauduleuse	fraudulent tactic
manquement (m) à une obligation de prudence ou de sécurité	failure to fulfil an obligation of care or of security
marque (m) au fer rouge	branding with a red hot iron
massacre (m)	massacre
master (m)	two-year degree obtained after the *licence*
mémoire (m)	dissertation, statement of case
mémoire (m) en duplique	*applicant's statement in reply*
mémoire (m) en réplique	*respondent's statement in reply*
menace (f)	threat
menacer	to threaten
mention (f)	mark, grade, specialisation in
mesures (f) provisoires	interim measures
mettre au point	to finalise
meutre (m)	murder
mineur (m)	minor
ministère (m) d'avocat	legal representation in court
ministère (m) public	n.t. (can sometimes be translated as: public prosecutor's office or the prosecution)
ministre (m) d'Etat	*senior minister*
ministre (m) délégué	n.t. (equivalent to British Minister of State)
ministre (m) à portefeuille	minister with portfolio (equivalent to British Secretary of State)
minute (f)	original of deed or judgment
mis en délibéré	discussed (by trial judges)
mise au rôle (f)	listing of a case
mise (f) en cause	placed under suspicion
mise (f) en danger délibérée de la personne d'autrui	deliberately putting another in danger
mise en accusation (f)	bringing charges
mise en état (f)	*preparatory phase (of case)*
mise en examen (f)	*charging of the suspect*
mise (f) en scène	scheming
motif (m)	ground, reason
motivation (f)	legal reasoning

moyens (m)	legal reasons
moyens (m) de défense	grounds for the defence
moyens (m) de droit	points of law
moyens (m) de fait	issues of fact

N

navette (f)	n.t.
né	in existence, born
nécessité (f)	necessity
ne disposer que d'une compétence d'attribution	to have limited powers
négligence (f)	negligence
nomination (f)	appointment
nommé	nominated, proposed, appointed
non-lieu (m)	see *'décision de non-lieu'*, and *'rendre une decision de non-lieu'*
norme (f) communautaire	community law
normes (f) juridiques	legal rules
notaire (m)	n.t.
notamment	in particular
nul n'est censé ignorer la loi	*ignorance of the law is no defence*

O

octroyer	to grant
office (m)	practice
officier (m) ministériel	n.t.
officier (m) de police judiciaire	senior police officer
opportunité (f)	appropriateness
oralité (f)	oral character
ordonnance (f)	type of delegated legislation
ordonnance (f) de clôture	closing order
ordonnancement (m) juridique	legal hierarchy
ordre (m)	n.t. (fulfils a similar role to the English "Bar")
ordre (m) administratif	administrative system
ordre (m) judiciaire	*civil and criminal system*
organe (m) juridictionnel	judicial body

P

pacte civil de solidarité	civil partnership between two individuals
par ces motifs	for these reasons
par la voie de	by means of
par voie d'action	by means of legal action
par voie d'exception d'inconstitutionnalité	by means of raising a defence of unconstitutionality

parquet (m)	n.t. (sometimes translated as: public prosecutor's office or the prosecution)
partie (f) civile	civil party, private claimant
partiel (m)	mid-sessional examination
passer outre	to ignore
patrimoine (m) immobilier	inherited real property, inheritance
pays (m) de *common law*	common law country
pays (m) de coutumes	land of customary law
pays (m) de droit écrit	land of written law
peine (f)	sentencing
peine (f) complémentaire	complementary punishment
peine de mort (f)	death penalty
peine (f) de sûreté	minimum period to be spent in prison
peine (f) privative de liberté	sentence of imprisonment
pénal	criminal
période (f) de sûreté	minimum period to be spent in prison
permis (m)	licence
permis (m) de chasse	hunting licence
perpétration (f)	commission
perquisition (f)	search of property
personne (f) physique	natural person
personne (f) mise en examen	accused (n)
personnalité (f) de premier plan	key figures
pièce (f)	document
pillage (m)	looting
plaider	to plead
plaideur (m)	litigant
plaidoirie (f)	oral submission, plea, defence speech
plan (m)	plan (of legal essay)
plan (m) concerté	concerted plan
pleins pouvoirs (m)	full (emergency) powers
police (f) administrative	crime prevention police
police (f) judiciaire	criminal investigation police
porter à	to increase to
porter atteint à l'integrité d'autrui	to attack another
porter plainte	to report an offence
porter une arme	to carry a weapon
possibilité (f) d'auto-saisine	self-empowerment
postérieur à	after
postulation (f)	*acting on behalf of a client*

potence (f)	gallows
pour se faire contrepoids	to counterbalance one another
poursuite (f)	prosecution, *decision to bring charges*
poursuite (f) pénale	criminal prosecution
poursuivre	to bring charges
poursuivre au pénal	to prosecute
pourvoi (m)	appeal
pourvoi (m) en cassation	*appeal on point of law only*
pourvoir (m) exécutif	executive, executive power
pourvoir (m) judiciaire	judicial power
pourvoir (m) partagé	shared power
pourvoir (m) propre	sole power
pouvoirs (m) publics	authorities
préambule (m)	Preamble
précédent (m) obligatoire	binding precedent
préfet (m)	Prefect, *chief administrative officer of a French 'département'*, senior local administrative officer
préjudice (m)	loss, harm, damage
préméditation (f)	premeditation
prendre d'assaut	to storm
prescrire	to order
se prescrire	to be subject to a limitation period
présenter un caractère délictueux	to constitute a major offence
présomption (f) d'innocence	presumption of innocence
prétention (f)	claim
prêter serment	to take an oath
preuves (f)	evidence
prévenu(e)	defendant
prévoir	to provide, to lay down
primauté (f)	supremacy
primordial	of paramount importance
principe (m) de la séparation des pouvoirs	principle of the separation of powers
principe (m) général du droit	general principle of law
principes (m) fondamentaux reconnus par les lois de la République	fundamental principles recognised by the laws of the Republic
prise (f) de connaissance	awareness
procéder à la rectification	to correct
procédés (m)	procedures

procédure (f) de contumace	Proceedings held in the absence of the accused. These proceedings have now been abolished.
procédure (f) d'irrecevabilité	*procedure opposing legislation outside the remit of Parliament*
procédure (f) pénale	criminal procedure
procès (m)	trial
procès-verbal (m)	statement
procureur (m) de la République	senior public prosecutor
procureur (m) général	public prosecutor
profane	lay (adj)
professeur (m) agrégé	n.t. (title awarded following successful completion of the *agrégation*, a national selection process for senior academics)
project (m) de loi	government Bill
projet (m) d'élaboration	drafting
projet (m) de décision	draft decision
promulgation (f)	promulgation (*publication that brings into force*)
promulguer	to promulgate, to pass
prononcé (m)	declaration
se prononcer	to pass judgment, decide
prononcer une peine à l'encontre de	to impose a punishment on
prononcer la réclusion criminelle à perpétuité	hand down a life sentence
proposition (f) de loi	private members' Bill
provoquer	to provoke
puni de	punishable by
punir	to punish
punissable	punishable

Q
quinquennat (m)	a five-year term

R
se rallier à	to be in agreement
rapport (m) de stage	report on a work placement
ratifié	ratified
recenser	to summarise
recevable	admissible
recherche (f) de paternité naturelle	establishing paternity
réclamation (f)	complaint
réclusion (f) criminelle	imprisonment
réclusion (f) criminelle à perpétuité	life imprisonment

reconnaître le bien fondé de la demande	to accept the grounds of the application
recours (m)	action (administrative), appeal
recours (m) pour excès de pouvoir	application for judicial review
recrutement (m) latéral	internal system of recruitment
recueil (m)	law report
récusation (f) de juré	challenging a juror, objecting to a juror
rédacteur (m)	drafter, writer
rééligible	eligible to stand again
réexaminer en fait et en droit	*to rehear the case on its facts and points of law*
régime (m) parlementaire	parliamentary democracy
régime (m) présidentiel	presidential democracy
régir	to govern
règle (f)	rule
règle (f) de droit	legal rule
règle (f) impérative	mandatory rule
règle (f) du précédent	rule of precedent
règle (f) supplétive	non-mandatory rule
règlement (m)	regulation
règlement (m) autonome	autonomous regulation
règlement (m) d'application	implementing regulation
relevés (m) signalétiques	identification data
remise (f)	handing over
rendre un arrêt	to hand down a decision, to give a decision
rendre une décision	to hand down a decision, to give a judgment
rendre une décision de non-lieu	to dismiss a case; to rule that there is no case to answer
renvoi (m)	dismissal, adjournment
répartition (f)	separation
représentation (f)	representation, *acting as client's agent*
réprimer	to incriminate
requérant(e)	applicant
requête (f) introductive d'instance	application (commencing the action)
réquisitoire (m)	submission (by the prosecution)
réquisitoire (m) introductif	*application for judicial investigation*
résolution (f) de mise en accusation	decision to bring charges
responsabilité (f) délictuelle	tort law
responsabilité (f) pénale	criminal liability
responsable devant	answerable to

retenir	to acknowledge
revirement (m)	overturning, reversal, overruling
revirement (m) de jurisprudence	n.t. (situation occurs when a court takes a different view from its previous case law)
ruse (f)	fraud

S

sages (m)	wisemen
saisie (f)	seizure
saisine (f)	*submission of a case to a court*
saisir	to refer, submit a case
sanction (f)	sanction
sciemment	knowingly
scrutin (m) majoritaire à deux tours	*election, in up to two ballots, requiring a majority vote*
secrétaire d'Etat (m)	n.t. (equivalent to British junior minister, Parliamentary Under-Secretary)
secrétariat-greffe (m)	court office
section (f) du rapport et des études	Report and Research Division
section (f) du contentieux	Litigation Division
section (f) administrative	Administrative Division
sénateur (m)	senator
septennat (m)	seven-year term, mandate
siéger	to sit
signalétique	identifying, identification
signifier	to serve notice of
signifier à	to serve on
sous-partie (f)	subsection
sous-section (f)	section
sous-sous-partie (f)	sub-subsection
sous peine de forfaiture	with the sanction of criminal liability
soustraction (f)	appropriation
soutenance (f) d'une thèse	viva
souveraineté (f) nationale	national sovereignty
stage (m) en entreprise	work placement
statuer sur	to rule on
stupéfiant (m)	drug
subordonné à	subject to
suffrages (m) exprimés	votes cast
suite (f)	sequence
suites (f) à donner	action to be taken
suivre une scolarité	to attend a course of study

supplice (m) de la roue	torture on the wheel
sur le fond	on the substance
sur le fondement de	under
sur proposition de	on the advice of
surgi	arising from
surprise (f)	abuse
surveillance (f)	supervision
survenir	to take place, to occur
susceptible d'appel	open to appeal
susvisé	aforementioned
système (m) de la personnalité des lois	personal law, *system of law based on racial origin*
système (m) moniste	monist system
système (m) de la territorialité	*system of law based on place of residence*
système (m) dualiste	dualist system

T

le talion	law or retaliation
témoin (m)	witness
témoin (m) assisté	represented witness
temps (m)	stage, phase
tentative (f)	attempt
tentative (f) achevée	failed attempt
tentative (f) stérile	failed attempt
tenter	to attempt
tiers (m)	third party
Tiers Etat (m)	the Third Estate
tirage (m) au sort	random selection
titre (m)	certificate of practice
torture (f)	torture
traité (m)	treaty
trancher	to adjudicate, to resolve
se transporter sur les lieux	to go to the scene of the crime
travail (m) d'intérêt général	work in the community
travaux (m) dirigés	tutorial
tribunal (m) administratif	administrative court
tribunal (m) correctionnel	n.t.
Tribunal (m) de cassation	n.t. (predecessor to the *Cour de cassation*)
tribunal (m) d'instance	n.t.
tribunal (m) de commerce	commercial court, commercial tribunal
tribunal (m) de grande instance	n.t.
tribunal (m) de police	n.t.

tribunal (m) des affaires de Sécurité Sociale	social security tribunal
Tribunal (m) des conflits	Jurisdiction Disputes Court
Tribunal (m) du contentieux de l'incapacité	disability disputes tribunal
tribunal (m) paritaire des baux ruraux	agricultural tenancy tribunals
tribunal (m) pour enfants	juvenile court, youth court
tribunal (m) répressif	criminal court
Tribunat (m)	post-revolutionary assembly
tromper	to trick, to deceive
trouble (m) neuropsychique	neuro-psychological illness
trouble (m) psychique	psychological illness
troubler la tranquillité d'autrui	to disturb someone's peace of mind
tuer	to kill

V

valeur (f) constitutionnelle	constitutional status, constitutional value
veiller au respect de	to oversee compliance with
victime (f)	victim
viol (m)	rape
violation (f)	breach
violence (f)	violence, force
violer	to breach
visa (m)	*reference to legal text*
visite (f) domiciliaire	house search
voie (m) de fait	offence of violence
voie (f) de recours ordinaire	*ordinary means of appeal*
se voir décerner	to be awarded
vol (m)	theft
vol (m) d'usage	theft by temporarily using property
volontairement	intentionally
volonté (f)	will
vu	given, having seen

Index